The International Theological Library.

PLANNED AND FOR YEARS EDITED BY

The late Professor CHARLES A. BRIGGS, D.D., D.Litt.,

AND

The late Principal STEWART D. F. SALMOND, D.D.

THE CHRISTIAN PREACHER.

By A. E. GARVIE, D.D.

THE
CHRISTIAN PREACHER

BY

ALFRED ERNEST GARVIE

M.A.(Oxon.), D.D.(Glas.)

PRINCIPAL OF NEW COLLEGE, LONDON

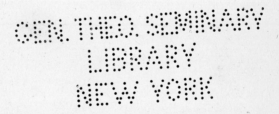

NEW YORK
CHARLES SCRIBNER'S SONS
1921

TO THE SACRED MEMORY
AND BLESSED PRESENCE
OF
A WIFE BELOVED

PREFACE.

AGGRIEVED artists have said that art critics are artists who have themselves failed. Preachers may cherish a similar suspicion when there comes to them a book on preaching from a theological college, as it is commonly assumed that, whatever may be known and taught within its walls, the science and art of preaching is not. Thirty-five years ago the call came to the writer to abandon the work on which he was then engaged to give himself to the preaching of the Gospel. The sense of that call has never failed; and although God's Providence has led him to his present work as a teacher of preachers, it is the same holy task in which he knows himself engaged. Preaching, as much as when he was in the pastorate, is still the work which is his life's aim and joy. The writer has found enough acceptance and appreciation in his manifold labours throughout the length and breadth of Great Britain to encourage him in the hope that he may be able to expound the doctrine as one who has not altogether failed in the practice. The favourable reception accorded to his previous book, *A Guide to Preachers,* which was intended for lay preachers, but which has been found helpful by ministers also, further emboldens him to essay the perilous task. This he can at least claim, that none could be more interested in, and devoted to, the work of preaching than he knows himself to be. It is not improbable that some who have a genius for preaching might be less successful in dealing with the science and art than others who, lacking that supreme gift,

have given more attention to the theory and method. The
writer trusts that his volume will at least show that he has
not spared his labours to discharge faithfully the task
undertaken.

In deciding on the plan of the book, the writer first
asked himself the question, For whom should he write, for
the scholar delighting in the minutiæ of the history and
the literature of the subject, or for the minister desiring to
be helped to make the best of his calling as a preacher ?
While some of his interests drew him to the first, the
dominating purpose of his life has driven him to the
second. He believes that in this way he can be most
useful to the largest number. If scholars do not find as
formidable an array of footnotes, references, and lists of
books as has been offered in other volumes of the series, it
is hoped that the omission will not be put down to ignorance or incompetence on the part of the writer, but to his
deliberate intention to write a book that would be read
from cover to cover by preachers, who might be alarmed by
any display of learning.

It is this purpose which explains the treatment in the
first division of the history of preaching, and the adoption
of the third division. Instead of attempting an exhaustive
account of the life and work of the great preachers, such as
histories of preaching offer, he has thought it more in
accord with his purpose to throw into prominence the
different types of preaching in the past, in order to show
the large place filled, and the great part played, by preaching in the Progress of the Kingdom of God, for he believes
with Paul that it has ever been " God's good pleasure
through the foolishness of the preaching to save them that
believe," [1] and to accomplish His purpose in the world.
The fact that the Masters in other religions were all

[1] 1 Co 1²¹.

preachers, shows how indispensable to moral and religious life preaching is. This historical survey will, it is hoped, give every Christian preacher a higher sense of the dignity, blessedness, and responsibility of his vocation.

To some readers the third division may seem unnecessary, but the writer found, when the minister of a church, that he had to face and answer for himself just such questions as he endeavours to deal with. He desires to hand over to others some of the results of his own experience. In training men for preaching, he has further discovered how needful just such simple, practical counsels are, especially for men at the beginning of their ministry. The present situation for the Christian pulpit presents so many perplexities and difficulties, that an attempt to face it frankly and fully may prove helpful to many. As the preacher may invoke God's blessing in his preaching of the Gospel, with a like confidence would the writer ask for God's blessing on his endeavour to help and encourage preachers to preach better.

The illustrations of the history in quotations from sermons are purposely taken from popular collections, as likely to be more accessible to those for whom the book is written than if taken from volumes difficult to obtain; and for permission to make these extracts the writer is much indebted to the editors and publishers:

The International University Society: *Crowned Masterpieces of Eloquence.*

Funk & Wagnalls Company: *The World's Great Sermons.*

Messrs. Cassell & Co.: *The Library of English Literature* (" Illustrations of English Religion ").

Messrs Sands & Co.: *Great French Sermons.*

In dealing with the history of preaching, the writer gratefully acknowledges his great indebtedness to the works

of Hering, Dargan, Van Oosterzee, and Ker. Without
their assistance the book could not have been written, and
to their works he would refer all who desire to become
familiar with the records of preachers in greater detail than
the scope and purpose of the present volume allowed. His
own independent contribution to Homiletics he has ventured
to offer in the second and third divisions. If in any degree
he can communicate to preachers his own enthusiasm for
his calling, he will thankfully acknowledge that he has not
laboured in vain.

The volume was nearly completed when the great
world-war came to shake so many things that can be shaken
only that the things which cannot be shaken may remain,
and its publication has been delayed on that account. It
has not been found necessary to alter much that had been
written, as the Gospel to be preached remains; and little
had been written about the purpose and the method of
preaching that Gospel which appeared to need revision in
the light of the new day dawning upon the world with the
conclusion of peace. The necessity and the urgency of the
preacher's task has been only emphasised by the tragedy of
human sin and suffering which is now drawing to a close;
and no discovery has been made in human thought and life
which need alter the conviction that the Gospel is the
power and the wisdom of God unto the salvation of all that
believe, and that accordingly there is no worthier calling
for any man than to be a Christian preacher.

ALFRED E. GARVIE.

TABLE OF CONTENTS.

INTRODUCTION.

PART I.

THE HISTORY OF PREACHING.

INTRODUCTORY.

CHAPTER I.

JESUS CHRIST THE LORD.

CHAPTER II.

APOSTLES, PROPHETS, TEACHERS.

CHAPTER IV.

PRIEST, MONK, AND FRIAR : SCHOLASTIC AND MYSTIC.

CHAPTER VII.

ORATORS AND COURTIERS.

b

CHAPTER IX.

EVANGELISTS AND MISSIONARIES.

CHAPTER X.

The Repairers of the Breach.

PART II.

THE CREDENTIALS, QUALIFICATIONS AND FUNCTIONS OF THE PREACHER.

INTRODUCTORY—THE HISTORY OF PREACHING AND THE PREACHER TO-DAY.

CHAPTER I.

THE PREACHER AS APOSTLE, PROPHET, AND SCRIBE.

CHAPTER III.

THE PREACHER AS PRIEST, TEACHER, PASTOR AND EVANGELIST.

PART III.

THE PREPARATION AND THE PRODUCTION OF THE SERMON.

INTRODUCTORY.

CHAPTER I.

THE CHARACTER OF THE SERMON.

CHAPTER II.

The Choice of Subjects and Texts.

CHAPTER III.

The Contents of the Sermon.

CHAPTER IV.

The Arrangement of the Sermon.

PAGE

ABBREVIATIONS.

As very frequent reference will be made to certain works, the following abbreviations will be used:

Crowned Masterpieces of Eloquence . . .	CME
The World's Great Sermons . . .	WGS
Library of English Literature: Religion . .	LELR
Ker's *History of Preaching* . . .	KHP
Dargan's *History of Preaching* . . .	DHP
Hering's *Lehrbuch der Homiletik* . .	HLH
Van Oosterzee's *Practical Theology* . .	OPT

THE CHRISTIAN PREACHER.

INTRODUCTION.

I.

1. WHERE Christ is, there is His Church, for His own promise is that " where two or three are gathered together in my name, there am I in the midst of them." [1] To this Church, in virtue of His authority and in reliance on His presence, He entrusted a mission to the world. " All authority hath been given unto me in heaven and on earth. Go ye therefore, and make disciples of all the nations, baptizing them into the name of the Father, and of the Son, and of the Holy Ghost : teaching them to observe all things whatsoever I commanded you ; and, lo, I am with you alway, even unto the end of the world." [2] Paul, the chief of the apostles, did not misunderstand his commission when he subordinated the symbolic ordinance to the evangelical proclamation and boldly declared, " Christ sent me not to baptize, but to preach the Gospel." [3] At the Reformation the Protestant Churches, in opposition to the Roman Catholic, carefully defined the nature and the functions of the Church.   John Knox in the *Scots Confession* in 1560 declares, " The notes of the true Kirk of God, we believe, confess, and avow to be—First, the true preaching of the Word of God, in the which God has revealed Himself to us.   Secondly, the right administration of the

[1] Mt 18[20].
[2] Mt 28[18-20].   Even if the commission is not the very words of Jesus, it presses the Church's sense of its calling.
[3] 1 Co 1[17]

Sacraments, which must be annexed to the word and promise of God, to seal and confirm the same in our hearts. Lastly, ecclesiastical discipline uprightly ministered as God's Word prescribed, whereby vice is repressed and virtue nourished." In the *Augsburg Confession* in 1530, Luther and the Saxon Reformers defined the Church to be "the congregation of saints (or general assembly of the faithful) wherein the Gospel is rightly taught and the Sacraments are rightly administered." Article XIX. in the *Thirty-nine Articles* of the Church of England runs thus: "The visible Church of Christ is a congregation of faithful men, in the which the pure Word of God is preached, and the Sacraments be duly ministered according to Christ's appointment in all those things that of necessity are requisite to the same." Coming nearer our own time, Ritschl's account of the Church is "that it is recognised as the community of saints by the proclamation of the Gospel, and the administration of the Sacraments in accordance with their institution, as these are the channels of the distinctively sanctifying activity of God."[1] In all these statements the preaching of the Gospel is not only put first in order, but also in importance; for the Sacraments are significant and valuable only as the symbols and the channels of the truth and grace offered in the Gospel. The discipline of which Knox speaks, is also dependent on, expressed in, and enforced by the preaching of the Word of God.

2. This appreciation of preaching as the first duty of the Church of Christ is widely challenged to-day. On the one hand the worship is exalted over the sermon, and on the other practice is said to be more important than doctrine. In this connection the text, "the Kingdom of God is not in word, but in power,"[2] is sometimes quoted, as if for Paul the preaching of Christ crucified were not the power and wisdom of God.[3] If a sermon is merely a literary essay or an elocutionary display, in which grace or

---

[1] Garvie's *The Ritschlian Theology*, 2nd ed., pp. 422-423.
[2] 1 Co 4[20].   [3] 1 Co 1[24].

finish of style or charm and force of delivery is the primary consideration, in which the verbal mode is more important than the spiritual matter, then preaching must yield first place to worship or to work. If the preacher is not consciously or voluntarily God's ambassador, if he is not freely giving unto men what he is freely receiving from God by the enlightenment of His Spirit, if he cannot claim humbly and yet confidently to stand in the succession of the prophets and the apostles; but if he has taken his office unto himself for hire, if he is merely delivering his own opinions and sentiments, then the pulpit is one of those shows and shams of which the Church cannot rid itself too soon, and which it tolerates only at the peril of the souls entrusted to its care. With such shepherds, what Milton says about the clergy of his own day must prove true in any age :

> "The hungry sheep look up, and are not fed,
> But, swoln with wind and the rank mist they draw,
> Rot inwardly, and foul contagion spread :
> Besides what the grim wolf with privy paw
> Daily devours apace, and nothing sed." [1]

However far short the Christian ministry may often have fallen in this holy calling, yet the note of the true Church remains the preaching of the Word of God. As the history to be unfolded in the following pages will clearly and fully show, the periods of decadence have been marked by the loss of the power of the pulpit; and the eras of revival and reform have been heralded by a renewal of the preacher's influence. The preaching of the Word of God does not mean merely that the text is taken from the Bible, that the phraseology is scriptural, that the doctrine is orthodox according to the generally received standards, and the sentiments pious according to the conventional pattern ; but it means nothing less and else than this—that the preacher is an inspired man because he is experiencing the presence and power of God's Spirit in his reason, conscience, affections, and purposes, that his own "life is hid with

[1] Lycidas, ll. 125–129.

Christ in God,"[1] that he is in all meekness and lowliness, because of his unworthiness, yet with all boldness and trustfulness, because of God's call and endowment, fulfilling a Divine mission in delivering a Divine message.

3. If this be the ideal of Christian preaching, then it is as essential and necessary even as worship: for God's approach to man in grace through His Gospel must come before man's appeal to God in faith through prayer and praise.   "We can speak of an intercourse with God only when we are sure of this, that God speaks to us intelligibly, but also understands our speech and has regard to it in His operations on us."[2]   God's revelation must precede and evoke our religion.   It is at least as important that we should know God's will as that we should make our wishes known to God.   God is worshipped in the humble and obedient acceptance of His preached Word as in the offering of prayer and praise.   Preaching is decried and worship magnified for this among other reasons, that intellectual difficulties have so obscured the glory of the Divine revelation in Jesus Christ, that the preaching of the Gospel is not felt to be the Word of God.   But in such a case the question is justified : how long can worship be sustained sincerely and fervently without some assurance of God's grace?   Where devotion is divorced from truth, it is to be observed that the external aids—"the dim, religious light" of the pictured window, the symbolism of the sculptured stone or the carved wood, the suggestion of human costume, picture, and gesture, the stimulus of music and song—become and must become more prominent. Can it be doubted that the appeal to the conscience, reason, and affections through the declaration of the truth and grace of God will be more effectual in inspiring true devotion than the excitement of devout feelings through fair sights and sweet sounds?   It would be beyond the province of this volume to discuss the true nature and the proper methods of Christian worship ; but the writer feels justified in vindicating the claim of preaching to the fore-

[1] Col 3³.   [2] Herrmann, *Verkehr des Christen mit Gott*, p. 44.

most place in the Christian Church, in insisting that
worship cannot supplant preaching, which is, rightly understood, itself worship, without danger and loss to Christian
life. It is noteworthy that the Churches which have
exalted preaching have generally been indifferent to ritual;
and that where ritual has been elaborated, preaching has
declined.[1] Without straying out of bounds to discuss the
larger question [2] thus suggested, the writer may venture to
express his own personal preference in Browning's
confession :

> "I then in ignorance and weakness,
> Taking God's help, have attained to think
> My heart does best to receive in meekness
> That mode of worship, as most to his mind,
> Where earthly aids being cast behind,
> His All in All appears serene
> With the thinnest human veil between."[3]

4. This age is more practical than devout; and it is
for the sake of action rather than emotion that doctrine is
neglected. The mistake is just as great. We cannot do
rightly unless we know truly. God's will must be under-

---

[1] Attention may be called to the most significant and valuable *Report
of the Archbishops' First Committee of Inquiry* on *The Teaching Office of the
Church.* The candid and courageous confession of failure should not be
taken up as a reproach by the other churches against the Church of England
solely, as much that is thus said is *mutatis mutandis* true of all the churches ;
but although express mention is not made of the attention to ritual as one
of the causes of this failure, the writer is persuaded that it is one of the
factors in the problem generally to be taken into account. The other
churches have much reason for heart-searching as regards the effectiveness of
their preaching, despite their greater interest in it, in the abundant evidence
which has been gathered among the soldiers at the front and in the camps
of the prevalent ignorance of, and indifference to the Gospel of the vast
majority of the manhood of the nation. The volume, giving the results of a
searching inquiry, entitled *The Army and Religion,* is a solemn summons to
all the churches to self-scrutiny in regard to all their methods of work, and
especially the spirit in which that work is being done. The content and
the character of the preaching especially calls for examination, and in this
examination it is hoped that this volume, although not written with this
specific object in view, may be of some worth and use.

[2] See the subsequent chapter on the Preacher as Priest.

[3] Christmas Eve, XXII. ll. 64-70.

stood to be done. Pious efforts and charitable schemes there may be without the guidance and control of the wisdom of God; but genuinely Christian work there cannot be without the instruction and direction which the preaching of the Word of God alone can give. To the Church are committed "the keys of the kingdom of heaven";[1] but the Church's foundation is the confession of Jesus the Christ. It is not by an instinct or impulse that the practical man can tell the methods and the organs by which the kingdom of God can be most speedily and surely brought on earth. As the Hebrew people of old before entering on any enterprise for God sought His counsel, so the Church of Christ in these days more than ever needs in all its efforts to inquire what He would have it do.[2] The sense of our need of guidance as regards personal duty in social relations is very widely spread; and if the Church fails to lead along the new paths of service, it will lose its influence and fail in its vocation. It is only the faith which is nourished by the grace of God presented in the Gospel which can have the confidence and the courage to enter on the heroic and strenuous labours by which alone the cause of Christ in the world can be advanced. It is only the love of Christ presented in the Cross which can constrain the loyalty and obedience which the service in the world demands. It is only the wisdom which a study of this revelation inspires which can afford the insight and the foresight to apply wisely and rightly the Church's resources to the necessities of modern society. What should we think of a commander who set out on a campaign without any knowledge of the forces at his command, the nature of the country to be subdued, the purpose of the conflict, or the method of its prosecution? Yet not more foolish would his conduct be than is the action of those advisers of the Church who bid it work and not talk, when the talk is counsel, motive, and encouragement in

[1] Mt 16[19].
[2] The war has brought home to many consciences as never before the need of applying Christian principles to all human relations.

the work. If the Scriptures warn those who are hearers and not doers,[1] they have no beatitude for the man who wants to be a doer of God's Work but is unwilling to be a hearer of God's Word, in which His Will is made known.

5. No good reason can be shown for subordinating the preaching of the Gospel either to worship or to work; but it can be conclusively proved that the devout emotions and the practical activities of the Church must be stimulated and sustained, guided and guarded by the faithful and sincere proclamation of Christian truth. These three elements in the Church's mission—witness, worship, work—must be kept in their proper relation and due proportion. Doctrine which does not inspire devotion is not the living truth of God, for God's approach to man will evoke man's appeal to God. Preaching which is not followed by practice is not God's command to the soul, for that will constrain obedience. But, on the other hand, devotion which is not the soul's response to God's revelation will prove an aspiration which finds no satisfaction. Practice which is not informed and directed by the known and acknowledged will of God, will express only human prudence and policy, and not Divine wisdom and righteousness. So, too, the devotion which goes not hand in hand with practice will be hollow, and the practice which is not linked to devotion will be hard. The entire human personality must be addressed and exercised by the Church in its varied functions; but from this law of the soul's life there is no escape, that it is through the enlightening of the mind that the quickening of the heart and the energising of the will must come. Man's worship of and work for God must wait on God's witness in the Gospel of His grace through Jesus Christ our Lord. For the fulfilment of its mission, what is of primary importance for the Church is its *message*, the truth which it receives from God and communicates to man. While "every Scripture inspired of God is profitable for teaching, for reproof, for correction, for instruction which is in righteousness,"[2] while "the faith was once for all delivered

---

[1] Mt 7²⁴⁻²⁷, Jas 1²²⁻²⁵.　　　[2] 2 Ti 3¹⁶.

unto the saints," [1] while "Jesus Christ is the same yesterday, and to-day, yea, and for ever," [2] the apprehension and application of the revelation, as imperfect and partial, must be progressive; and so the Church must serve each generation by adapting its message to each age.

II.

1. Before passing to the Message of the Church we must look a little more closely at what we mean by *preaching*, which we have tried to show is the Church's first charge   The writer knows no definition with which he finds himself in closer agreement than that of the great preacher and writer on preaching, the late Bishop Phillips Brooks. Not only the definition, but the justification of that definition must be quoted in full: " Preaching is the communication of truth by man to men.   It has in it two essential elements, truth and personality.   Neither of these can it spare and still be preaching.   The truest truth, the most authoritative statement of God's will communicated in any other way than through the personality of brother man to men is not preached truth.   Suppose it is written on the sky, suppose it is embodied in a book which has been so long held in reverence as the direct utterance of God that the vivid personality of the men who wrote its pages has well-nigh faded out of it; in neither of these cases is there any preaching.   And on the other hand, if men speak to other men that which they do not claim for truth, if they use their powers of persuasion or of entertainment to make other men listen to their speculations, or do their will, or applaud their cleverness, that is not preaching either. The first lacks personality.   The second lacks truth.   And preaching is the bringing of truth through personality. It must have both elements.   It is in the different proportions in which the two are mingled that the difference between two great classes of sermons and preaching lies. It is in the defect of one or the other element that every

sermon and preacher falls short of the perfect standard.
It is in the absence of one or the other element that
a discourse ceases to be a sermon, and a man ceases to be a
preacher altogether." [1] This definition, excellent as it is,
lacks one thing. It does not state the end of preaching.
If one may borrow Aristotle's distinctions, it gives the
formal and the efficient, but not the final cause. It may
be completed thus—" truth through personality for faith,
duty, and hope," or perhaps the words " eternal life " might
be used to cover the three terms. To make the definition
more precise we may thus expand it, " divine truth through
human personality for eternal life." Each of the three
terms in the definition demands closer scrutiny.

2. What do we mean by *truth*? It is obvious that
when we regard it as the content of preaching we give it a
narrower extension and a fuller intention than the term
often bears. In history truth is fact; in science truth is
cause, law, order; in philosophy it is the interpretation
of the Universe which to the thinker makes it appear an
intelligible unity, with meaning, worth, and aim throughout.
In morality truth is the ideal which as the categorical
imperative claims recognition and realisation. In religion
man has a twofold interest, he is concerned about ultimate
reality and final destiny. This twofold object is expressed

---

[1] *Lectures on Preaching*, pp. 5–6. Compare Hooker's *Laws of Ecclesiastical Polity*, Books v. XVIII. " Because, therefore, want of the knowledge of
God is the cause of all iniquity amongst men, as contrariwise the very ground
of all our happiness, and the seed of whatsoever perfect virtue groweth from
us, is a right opinion touching things divine ; this kind of knowledge we may
justly set down for the first and chiefest thing which God imparteth unto
His people, and our duty of receiving this at His merciful hands for the first
of those religious offices wherewith we publicly honour Him on earth. For
the instruction, therefore, of all sorts of men to eternal life, it is necessary
that the sacred and saving truth of God be openly published unto them.
Which open publication of *heavenly mysteries* is by an excellency termed
Preaching. For otherwise there is not anything *publicly notified* but we
may in that respect, rightly and properly, say it is preached. So that
when the school of God doth use it as *a word of art*, we are accordingly to
understand it with restraint to such special matter as that school is accustomed to publish." It is to be observed that in the second sentence in the
words, "the instruction of all sorts of men to eternal life," Hooker notes
what Phillips Brooks omits, the end of preaching.

in the definition of faith in the words, " Faith is the giving substance to things hoped for, the test of things not seen." [1] Religion deals with the invisible as giving meaning to the visible, and with the future as offering an aim to the present. The savage even believes in gods and ghosts. Although morality and religion may be distinguished, yet they cannot be separated; even at a low stage of social development the tribal custom is under the guardianship of the tribal deity. At certain periods of degeneration ritual and righteousness may be divorced; but the higher the development the closer the alliance, nay, the more complete the identity of goodness and godliness. The unity of religion and morality is affirmed by the prophet in the words—" He hath showed thee, O man, what is good; and what doth the Lord require of thee, but to do justly, and to love mercy, and to walk humbly with thy God ? " [2] Ritual cannot take the place of righteousness. " I desire mercy and not sacrifice, and the knowledge of God more than burnt offerings." [3] In the Christian religion, holiness of life is the fruit of fellowship with God; morality and religion can be only abstractly distinguished; concretely they are inseparable. Kant's three postulates of the practical reason (God, freedom, immortality) are the reality, the knowledge of which is the truth disclosed in preaching.

3. While this is the range of truth ideally, it must be recognised that actually preaching may have a much narrower scope. Although preaching is most at home in the realm of religion, yet there may be a declaration of moral principle to secure moral obedience, which cannot be denied the name. The Positivist may preach Humanity as the object of worship and service; the Buddhist may preach a plan of salvation by man's own effort, without divine assistance; the Ethicist to-day may preach morality without any theological sanctions; and we must acknowledge them all as preachers. Nevertheless, preaching is generally concerned with God and immortality, as well as freedom and duty. Philosophy is also concerned about

---

[1] He 11[1] R.V. *marg.*　　　[2] Mic 6[8].　　　[3] Hos 6[6].

ultimate reality and final destiny; but its interest is speculative and not practical. When philosophy, as in Stoicism,
prescribes a moral end, or, as in Neo-Platonism, offers a
religious good, it can be preached. Where the communication of knowledge, whether in history, science, or philosophy,
is, however, the sole object of speech, we have not got
preaching in the proper sense. A lecture is given, and not
a sermon delivered. A speech on a political platform may
appear to approach a sermon more closely than a lecture
does in having a practical purpose; for the opinion or the
action commended may be represented as desirable, ex-
pedient, wise, and good, but the speaker does not claim to
be dealing with truth about ultimate reality, absolute ideal,
or final destiny: and so, whatever his manner may be, he is
not preaching, in the proper sense of the word.

4. The channel through which the truth is conveyed
is *personality*. The whole man must preach in a twofold
sense. Not only must the proclamation of the truth exercise the whole personality, as mind, heart, and will;
but the truth itself must possess and command all the
thoughts, feelings, and wishes. Without the one there
cannot be full effectiveness, without the other there cannot
be thorough sincerity. When both are conjoined we have
the highest type of preaching, where the lips confess con-
vincingly what the heart believes absolutely. When the
whole manhood of the preacher is consecrated unto God, it
is his duty to bring that whole man to bear upon the
hearers of the Word. The story of Elisha's recovery to life
of the son of the Shunammite suggests what the preacher's
method should be. " And he went up, and lay upon the
child, and put his mouth upon his mouth, and his eyes
upon his eyes, and his hands upon his hands; and he
stretched himself upon him; and the flesh of the
child waxed warm." [1] There may be, and ought to
be, a modest reserve regarding personal experience
and character; there may be a dignified restraint in
tone and gesture; and yet the entire personality may

[1] 2 K 4³⁴.

be in its fullest exercise, so as to transfer as completely as possible from speaker to hearer the whole content of the message, emotional and volitional as well as intellectual. The failure of a great deal of preaching to be fully effective is due to its being too intellectualist. The preacher is conveying only ideas and ideals from his own to another's reason and conscience, but he is not communicating the passion or enthusiasm he may himself feel. If the truth does not stimulate his own convictions, he must not pretend feelings, for then his preaching is rhetoric, which is " sounding brass, or a clanging cymbal," [1] and not the eloquence which passes from heart to heart. It is probable, however, that many preachers fail to express the feelings they experience. Without weak sentimentalism and violent emotionalism, effective preaching does demand that there shall be warmth as well as light. That truth, known and owned as truth, does not move the heart as might be expected, is probably due to lack of imagination, or, as the word might suggest unreality, vision, the faculty of realising the spiritual, the ideal, the divine, the inward sense of the supersensible. Truth is often apprehended in the abstractions of the intellect, instead of being presented as concrete reality for the spiritual discernment. This is the difference between the scholar or the sage and the seer who sees Him who is invisible.[2] And the preacher must be, to grow to his full stature, seer as well as scholar and sage. Volition must not be excluded from preaching. The sermon must be a deed as well as a word. The preacher must will with the full force of his soul the salvation, in the full New Testament sense, of the hearers. The human will must at its utmost stretch commit itself in prayer to the divine will that God may work the good pleasure of His will.

5. Preaching is not merely a communication of knowledge. As it exercises the whole personality of the preacher, so it is addressed to the whole personality of the hearer as a moral and religious subject. As the truth with which

[1] 1 Co 13¹.   [2] He 11²⁷.

it deals concerns God, freedom, and immortality, so its aim
is to evoke faith, stimulate to duty, and sustain hope.   There
must be an enlightening of the mind, a quickening of
the heart, and a strengthening of the will in goodness
and godliness.   It is not necessary that any sermon should
produce this total effect.   A preacher may sometimes aim
at instruction ; at another, work for decision : even to bring
God's peace to the soul in emotional distress may be his
purpose.   But, whatever may be the immediate result, the
ultimate intention must always be to bring the whole personality more fully under the influence of the truth.   It is
sometimes said that every sermon should be practical, in
the narrow sense that it should give the hearer something
to do.   But a sermon does not fail if it teaches the
distressed spirit to " rest in the Lord, and wait patiently
for him," [1] if it induces the too self-sufficient to " be still,
and know that *God* is God," [2] if it persuades the man
who wants to rush the kingdom of God that " he that
believeth shall not make haste." [3]   A deeper confidence
in God, a fuller committal to Him, even if no task is
assigned, is a worthy object of the preacher's endeavour.
While one may agree with Canon Simpson that
" preaching is something more than the art of oratory
applied to religious themes," yet he does limit its appeal
too narrowly when he declares that this " is made neither
to the intellect, nor to the emotions, nor to the æsthetic
sense, but to what, however we may account for its existence, we are accustomed to call the conscience.   The power
of its appeal to conscience may at once be set down as the
supreme and ultimate test of preaching, for it is this which
differentiates the pulpit." [4]   If by conscience be meant the
moral sense, or the practical reason of Kant, the writer
may be charged, although this is far from his intention,
with repeating Kant's mistake in regarding religion as the
apprehension of our moral duties as divine commands.   The
pulpit does not merely summon to duty ; it may awaken

[1] Ps 37⁷.   [2] Ps 46¹⁰.
[3] Is 28¹⁶.   [4] *Preachers and Teachers*, pp. 2, 3.

faith by the assurance of grace. If, as Luther taught, sin is even more distrust of God than disobedience to Him, the appeal of the pulpit may be addressed to the religious disposition, and its end is not missed if a more thankful and trustful mood is inspired. A sermon which so sets forth God and His grace that all the hearers are awed with adoration and gratitude, is not vainly delivered. Worship may be, as well as work, the proper design of preaching. It is the whole moral and religious personality which preaching must strive to reach.

III.

1. So far we have been dealing with the definition of preaching generally; we must now attempt to describe the characteristics of *Christian preaching*. To the Christian Church is committed not only the task of preaching, but also the message to be thus delivered. The Christian preacher does not discover or invent the truth he imparts to others. Christian preaching is not merely one of the functions of a human religion, it is the continuation of the divine revelation, culminating in Christ, of which the Holy Scriptures are the record and interpretation. It is not a mere formality, although some preachers may so regard it, and chafe at being subject to the custom, that the text of a sermon is taken from the Bible, for it is the confession that the preacher is perpetuating and diffusing a gift which God has bestowed. The common assumption in the Christian Church is that preaching will not be the power and the wisdom of God unto the salvation of sinners and the perfecting of saints unless the preacher is himself convinced, and can convince his hearers, that he has a message from God to deliver, that his words are not of his own invention and imagination, but are by the inspiration of the Almighty, who hath given him the understanding clearly to discern and rightly to divide the Word of Life. He must be devout so as to maintain that communion with God by which alone the vision of God can be won. He

must be scholarly, not that he may make a parade of his learning, or that he may use it to impose his own authority on others, but that he may know how to gain all that the Scriptures are fitted to give the diligent and sincere student. The Christian preacher is not an explorer or adventurer, but a messenger.

2. This message, however, is not a stereotyped formula—it is a Gospel to be interpreted for the thought and applied to the need of every age. Men are so bound to one another by common needs and dangers, doubts and fears, wishes and aims, are so subject to the same mental, moral, and spiritual conditions that for the men of every age there is a common interpretation and application which has meaning and worth for all. In every age there are general tendencies as there are general necessities. There are individual men, however, who, as it were, incarnate the spirit of the age, and who are thus specially fitted to receive a message from God which has more than individual significance and value, and which, therefore, it will be for the advantage of others to receive from them. Every Christian preacher's aim must be to fulfil this demand to be the channel between the permanent and universal truth and the local and temporary thought. As the history of Christian preaching with which we shall be in the first part of this volume specially concerned will abundantly illustrate, while individual preachers have their own peculiarities, yet the preaching of each age has its common characteristics.[1]

[1] How necessary it is that the preaching of each age should be adapted to its needs is the theme of the latest series of the Yale Lectures on Preaching, entitled *In a Day of Social Rebuilding*, by Henry Sloane Coffin, in which he faces the demands of the Christian ministry, with constant and immediate reference to the situation which has arisen through the war, and its manifold results, mental, moral, and spiritual, as well as material. He confronts that situation undaunted, as every Christian preacher should. "Wherever in diplomacy, in industry, in family life, in the personal dealings of man with man, the spirit of Jesus has been dominant, there is no sign of damage. We can challenge the world to show us the instance where love like Christ's has been employed in social construction and has failed. True the instances are pathetically rare, but they are none the less

3. We may now address ourselves to the question how the message, permanent and universal, entrusted to the Church, may by the Christian preacher be adapted to-day. It is with the Gospel of the grace of God that the Church is charged, and it belongs, therefore, to the permanent and universal essence of the Christian message to be *evangelical*. The conditions of the age generally, and especially the results of the war, make a demand for, and can offer a special encouragement to, evangelical preaching. The easy and vain optimism of the earlier part of last century is becoming less common, and the note of pessimism is more often touched than it was. In spite of all mental advance and material progress, the social problem is more menacing, international relations are more perilous, the moral imperative is less commanding, the soul's aspirations fail of their satisfaction. Disappointment and discontent, not to say disgust and despair, are more common ; and the world now needs a message of comfort and courage, help and hope. That message the Christian Gospel offers. We must not use the term evangelical as the badge of any sect or the shibboleth of any school. What have been regarded as the distinctively evangelical doctrines cause intellectual difficulty to many minds ; and this is not the place to discuss them. Nevertheless it should be easier to-day to believe in salvation by sacrifice. All the writer insists on here is that the Christian preacher should be a bearer of good news of God's saving grace in Christ, bringing men assurance of divine comfort, succour, power, and promise. The Christian Gospel does offer answers to the questions the mind asks ; but the *speculative* tendency, which is concerned mainly about the solution of intellectual problems, must be a subordinate element in preaching. The *practical* tendency which thinks of Christianity as affording a supreme

significant. The Church's failure is not due to lack of means with which to build an enduring world-order, but to their non-employment. The disaster that has ensued upon the use of other means gives us the chance to come forward and ask to be accorded a fair trial, and to back up our plea with a reasonable number of cases where the Spirit of Christ has been applied socially and has splendidly succeeded " (pp. 17-18).

moral principle in the law of love, and a supreme moral
example in the character of its Founder, belongs necessarily, as we shall immediately show, to the Gospel; but
when detached from, or even opposed to the evangelical, it
fails adequately to realise that the sufficient moral motive
for the fulfilment of the law and the following of the
example is found only in the constraint of the love of
Christ and His Cross. The *mystical* tendency which finds
the highest good that Christianity offers in communion
with God, in devout meditation and emotion, represents an
essential element in the Christian life; yet when it ignores,
as it sometimes does, that it is only through the forgiveness offered in the Gospel that the sinful soul can enjoy
fellowship with God, and that distinctively Christian communion with God is with the Father through the Son in
the Spirit, then it does not represent the complete Christian
message. *Evangelical* preaching may and should recognise
and harmonise all these tendencies, but can never allow to
fall into the background the fact of redemption in Jesus
Christ. It is after God as Comforter, Helper, Saviour
that the religions of the world are seeking; and Christianity claims to be the universal religion, because in its Gospel
it offers the divine answer to the human cry.[1]

4. The Christian Gospel offers, not a doctrine to be
believed, but an experience to be shared. The faith that
saves is not an intellectual assent to a plan of salvation,
or a theory of atonement, but a personal confidence in,
dependence on, submission to God in Christ, which produces
an inward change of thought, feeling, will. The human
personality becomes "a new creation."[2] This does not
involve only one type of Christian life; but, however
manifold the types, common to them all is the work of God
within each man. There may be a secondary Christianity
of acceptance of doctrines, observance of rites, conformity to
customs in the Christian community; but the primary

[1] The writer has dealt more fully with this subject in his work, *The
Evangelical Type of Christianity.*
[2] 2 Co 5^{17}, Gal 6^{15}.

Christianity is always a personal experience of God's grace in Christ. Accordingly, Christian preaching must express and appeal to experience; if it is *evangelical*, it will also be *experimental*. In this emphasis on experience the Christian pulpit to-day will be in accord with, and not in antagonism to, the spirit of the age. Modern science is experimental in its method; history wants to get at the facts, outward or inward; philosophy aims at interpreting experience. The attention being given to religious psychology shows the importance attached to the effect of belief in life. Christian Apologetics is less and less appealing to the authority of the Bible or the Church, and relying more and more on the testimony of experience. In the present intellectual situation, we may confidently affirm that there is no preaching which will meet the needs of men as that which is born of, and begets, experience. The Christian preacher must have tested the value of his message in his own life, so that he can with full confidence subject it to its being tested in like manner by those who hear him. Is not this personal certainty, and so urgency, wanting in a good deal of preaching ? How can a man fully persuade others who is not himself fully persuaded ? How can he expect to convince others of the supreme importance to them of a message the value of which he has not in his own soul realised, and the authority of which does not dominate his whole personality ? Will not the range of a preacher's influence be measured by the depth of his experience ? For mighty preaching the Christian life of some men has been too easy. Born and bred, taught and trained, in a Christian home, they have gently and slowly grown in the knowledge of the grace of Christ, and have endured no terrible moral conflicts, nor passed through any severe spiritual crises; consequently there is a wide range of the Christian salvation beyond their own experience. Only by greater intensity in their Christian living, and wider sympathy with other lives more sternly tested, can they transcend this disadvantageous limitation. For surely only he who has himself realised that the only help and

hope of men perishing is in the Cross of Christ, can preach
with such force and fervour as to arouse others to their
danger and their need, and to call forth their faith in Him
who " is able to save them to the uttermost that come unto
God by Him." [1]

5. The new creation of the human personality by the
grace of Christ involves a holy character as well as a
blessed experience. The Christian message is *ethical* because
evangelical and experimental. We may be grateful to
God that this age does not want a Gospel which in the
slightest degree encourages men to " continue in sin, that
grace may abound "; [2] and that it will show respect to
a Gospel which can prove a greater power working for
righteousness than any other form of religious teaching.
The Moderates of a previous century in Scotland were
blamed for preaching morality. That need not have been
any reproach to them. And if the Evangelicals in any
degree neglected to preach morality, theirs was the shame.
What one could find fault with in the Moderates was that
the morality they preached was not large and lofty enough.
Had it been, they would have been compelled to preach, as
well as morality, the only adequate motive and sufficient
power for holy living, the grace of God in Jesus Christ.
The only salvation for man that is worth preaching is
a deliverance from the bondage of evil, and an endowment
of freedom to do right and be good. It is not in the
thoughts or feelings, but in the actions, that the religious
life shows most decisively its sickness or health, its weakness or strength. If the older evangelicalism was sometimes not so distinctly and intensely ethical as the very
nature of the Christian salvation should have made it, the
newer evangelicalism is not likely to repeat the mistake,
for all the tendencies and necessities of the age challenge it
to be passionately and consistently ethical. It is a stunted,
a mutilated Gospel which does not demand and stimulate a
morality larger and loftier than any that the mere moralist
has ever conceived. Calvary's ideal is greater and grander

[1] He 7²⁵.   [2] Ro 6¹.

than Sinai's law could be.   This inward impulse meets an
outward demand.   Modern society needs moral guidance,
enforced by a religious sanction, or, rather, inspired by a
religious motive.   Is not Comte's grotesque and yet
pathetic attempt to make a new religion, the Religion
of Humanity, a proof of the insufficiency of morality
without religion ?   In the Romanes Lecture, Huxley confessed that the cosmical process, as interpreted by science,
does not yield the regulative principles for man's ethical
progress.   In all European societies for more than a century,
and for a generation at least in China, Japan, India, moral
development has not been keeping step with mental and
material, and hence the social problem is likely to become
ever more acute.   Economic knowledge and political
prudence are needed, as well as moral judgment and
religious motive.   With the former conditions the Christian
preacher is not directly concerned ; but the latter are his
pressing charge.   If this problem, great as it is, cannot be
solved by the consistent and courageous application of
Christian principles, the Christian Church must abandon
its claim for its Christ as " the power and wisdom of God
unto salvation."   This modern challenge of the authority
and sufficiency of His message must be accepted by the
Christian preacher.

6. The world situation to-day calls for the realisation
of the Christian ideal, not only within each nation in the
solution of its social problem, but, if this attempt is to
have any chance of success, in the relation of nations to
one another.   Christianity offers a universal morality, from
the claims and duties of which no race, nation, or tribe can
be excluded ; for all these divisions of men, as limitations
of the range of obligation, have been abolished in the one
humanity, loved of the Father, redeemed by the grace of the
Son, and inhabited by the Spirit of God.   If the proposed
League of Nations is not to remain a mechanism with no
driving power, the Christian Church must preach a new
internationalism as the application in politics of the Christian universalism.   To the Christian preacher is given a

wider range of influence, if he has only the wisdom and courage to use to the full the opportunity that is offered by the age still under the shadow of the world-war, and eager to escape into the light of a world-peace. The angel song must ring from all Christian pulpits : " Peace on earth to men of good will." This indeed to-day will be " good tidings of great joy to all peoples." [1]

[1] Lk 2^{14}.

PART I.

THE HISTORY OF PREACHING.

INTRODUCTORY.

1. THE best approach to any subject is by its history; if it be a science, we must learn all we can about previous discoveries; if an art, about previous methods. The Christian preacher will be better equipped for his task to-day, if he has some knowledge of how men have preached in former days. He will also be inspired by the value of the vocation he has accepted in discovering how prominent a place has been filled, and how important a part has been played in human history for the furtherance of men's progress in morals and piety by the preacher. While in preaching even, as in human activities of less moment, there are fashions of the hour which it would be folly to reproduce when they have fallen out of date, yet there are abiding aims and rules of preaching, which must be taken account of in each age, and which can be learned by the study of the preaching of the past. Admiration of the great and the good, even without imitation, makes a man wiser and better; and the Christian preacher will enrich his own manhood by intimacy with those in whose worthy succession he stands. While all antiquated methods, "good customs which corrupt the world," must be laid aside, and the preacher to-day must adapt himself to his age, he will be least in bondage to the past, who is least ignorant of it, and he will be most master of the present whose knowledge is least confined to it. Accordingly of the science

and art of homiletics the history of preaching is an essential division.[1]

2. But the subject may be treated in two ways. The history of preaching may become little more than a series of biographies of preachers; and the reader may be overwhelmed by a multitude of dates, facts, and names. This is not the method which will be here pursued. The biographical interest will be subordinated to the typical. It is with preaching that we are concerned—the functions it has fulfilled, the phases through which it has passed, the forms which it has assumed, the purposes it has set before itself, and the methods it has adopted. Preachers will be dealt with, not according to their individual importance, but according to their relative significance in these respects, although often these points of view may coincide. In the titles of the chapters no exhaustive account of the character of the preaching of any period will be attempted, but rather the throwing into prominence of the distinctive type. When the first of the methods of treatment is adopted, it is often difficult to see the wood for the trees; in the second method, the reader may sometimes miss the sight of a favourite tree in all its stately proportions, but it is hoped he will carry away a wider view of the abundance, variety, and value of the timber in the forest as a whole.

3. Had limits of space permitted, the writer would have included a chapter on Hebrew prophecy, and another on preaching in other religions. He must, however, content himself with calling attention to the altogether unique importance of the Hebrew prophet, in his preaching, as an agent of divine revelation. The subject has been dealt with by a master-hand in the article on "Prophecy and Prophets" of the late Dr. A. B. Davidson, in Hastings' *Bible Dictionary*, iv. pp. 106–127. The founders of Confucianism, Buddhism, Zoroastrianism, and Islam all accomplished their task as teachers and preachers, varied as were the forms of their instruction. In this connection, mention should be made of Socrates, who, though he founded

[1] See Dale's *Nine Lectures on Preaching*, pp. 93–94.

no religion, did initiate a movement of human thought of profound significance for morals and religion.   His twofold method of feigning his own ignorance and leading others to discover theirs, on the one hand, and, on the other, of eliciting by his questions the thoughts of others so as to disclose the truth, is one deserving careful study by the Christian preacher.   The history of Christian preaching must begin with Him who is both the model and the message, Jesus Christ the Lord.

CHAPTER I.

JESUS CHRIST THE LORD.

I.

1. In no other religion is the position of the founder comparable with that of Jesus in Christianity. Confucius was the editor of the ancient classics, and the interpreter of the ancestral wisdom of his people. Gautama the Buddha had discovered the secret of salvation for himself, and he imparted it to others; but he did not offer himself as Saviour, as each man must follow the path of deliverance for himself. Mohammed was the prophet of Allah, in whose name and by whose authority he taught and ruled; but he claimed no more intimate relation to God. But Jesus is Himself the object of the Christian faith as the Divine Saviour and Lord. He not only reveals God's Fatherhood, but is Himself the Son alone knowing God, and known of God, as no other man can be; and so uniquely qualified by His nature for His function.[1] He does not discover and then impart to others a secret of salvation, a salvation resulting from man's own effort; but in His death and rising again He realises on behalf of man a salvation which men receive and possess by faith in Him. He does not present a law, a standard, an ideal above and beyond His own character, but in His own character. Here founder and religion are one as nowhere else.

2. In the Apostolic Witness, especially that of Paul, the significance and value for the Christian faith of Christ Himself is concentrated in the Cross and Resurrection.[2]

[1] Mt 11$^{25-27}$.　　　　[2] 1 Co 15$^{1-3}$.

If not ignorant of, or indifferent to, the earthly ministry of healing and teaching, the apostles in their writings do not give to it any prominence. Nevertheless, we must not dismiss the teaching of Jesus, with which we are here specially concerned, as an unimportant factor in the founding of the Christian Church. For, *firstly*, the existence of the Gospels shows that the apostolic speeches and letters do not give us a complete representation of the thought and life of the first community of believers, of all that was of interest to it, and of influence in it. The words of Jesus were cherished, prized, preserved, and diffused first in speech, then in writing. Probably there was a primitive piety which, as the *Epistle of James* shows, was more at home in these reports of Jesus than in the doctrines of the apostles.[1] *Secondly*, had the teaching of Jesus not gathered a company of disciples, there had been no united witness to His resurrection, and no common teaching of the meaning and worth of His death. The earthly Teacher had prepared for the heavenly Lord. *Thirdly*, the facts of the Crucifixion and of the Resurrection would be meaningless apart from the person of Jesus Himself, which has first to be apprehended in its historical reality before it can be conceived in its doctrinal significance. Could we properly construe the meaning of the Atonement in the Cross were we ignorant of the revelation of the Fatherhood of God Jesus had given, or the realisation of perfect manhood as divine sonship He had won ? *Fourthly*, that teaching itself about God, man, sin, forgiveness, duty, immortality could seem secondary in importance and influence to His Cross and Resurrection only to one whom a theological obsession had made insensitive to moral and religious values. But to contrast and oppose the one to the other is to rend the inner garment woven of one piece throughout. *Fifthly*, it can be confidently said that to-day the teaching of Jesus still holds with an irresistible influence many for whom the apostolic teaching has lost much of its

---

[1] *James* has more echoes of the Sermon on the Mount than any other apostolic writing.

authority. We may regret it as much as we will, but the fact remains as a reason why we should try to apprehend as accurately and appreciate as adequately as we can, Jesus as Teacher.

3. In dealing with the teaching of Jesus, we are confronted with a difficulty at the very outset. Just as we have in Xenophon's *Memorabilia* and in Plato's *Dialogues* complementary representations of the teaching of Socrates, so in the Synoptic and Johannine reports of the ministry of Jesus. Although each of the Synoptic Gospels has its own distinctive features, yet so much of the material is drawn from common sources, and the standpoints are so similar, that we are warranted, in a general treatment of the character of Jesus' teaching, in regarding the Synoptic representation as one in contrast with the Johannine. In a detailed study of the content of the teaching, we should need to take account of the editorial peculiarities of Matthew and Luke in dealing with their common sources ; but for the present purpose this is quite unnecessary. It is generally agreed among scholars that the Fourth Gospel is of later date than any of the Synoptics, and that, even if the authorship of an eye-witness be admitted, the original reminiscences have been to so great an extent affected by his subsequent reflections that it is a very difficult and delicate task to discover in these reports the teaching of Jesus just as He gave it.[1] We cannot, therefore, follow the lead of the Fourth Gospel as we can take the guidance of the Synoptics as regards the manner and the method of the teaching of Jesus. While we need not ignore nor refuse what the Fourth Gospel offers to us, yet, when we are seeking to determine with such accuracy and adequacy as is possible to us with the data at our disposal the characteristics of Jesus as Teacher, the Synoptics alone can give us our guiding principles, while the Fourth Gospel may offer supplementary and confirmatory illustration of these principles. This critical excursion has been as brief as possible.

[1] The writer has attempted this in *The Expositor*, 8th Series, vii. and viii.

4. Even although the present volume is on preaching, it is advisable to treat in this chapter Jesus as Teacher, as the greater part of His teaching cannot be properly described as preaching, and yet is full of instruction for the Christian preacher. It was seldom that He delivered a formal sermon. While probably in the Sermon on the Mount there is one discourse as the nucleus round which the evangelist, in accordance with his usual practice, has collected matter belonging to many different occasions, chaps. 5 and 6 may be taken, with some additions, as reporting that discourse, of which the parable in 7$^{24-27}$ was probably the closing warning. We have here more evidence of systematic treatment of a subject than anywhere else in the Gospels; the series of contrasts between the old law and the new, followed by the series of criticisms of Pharisaic piety, is not at all characteristic of Jesus' usual method. Much of His teaching was given in wayside or table-talk, in answer to questions, or in connection with His miracles. It consisted of single sayings, instances, illustrations, parables, rather than any sustained argument. Emphasis was gained by repetition of the same thought under different figures; complementary aspects of truth were presented by means of twin parables. Spontaneity, and not formality, is the distinctive feature; and one may ask if Christian preaching might not have gained much by being less rhetorical and more natural speech.

II.

In attempting to describe the characteristics of the teaching of Jesus, it would be easy to fill many pages with the tributes which have been freely offered to the supreme excellence of Jesus as Teacher. But when we have said, not that He is *above* all other teachers, for that would imply a possibility of comparison, but that there is *none like Him*, so that comparison seems irrelevant, not to say impertinent, need we multiply our words to gild the unalloyed gold of our gratitude, reverence, and devotion ?

Is He not too great for our praise ?   Instead of praising
Him who is beyond all praise, let us rather as simply,
clearly, and fully as we can describe His distinctive
features as a Teacher.   While the evangelists, as a rule,
present the ministry of Jesus to us without explanation or
commendation, leaving their record to make its own
impression, yet there are in the Gospels sayings about the
teaching which are of incalculable value in enabling us to
understand its manner and its method.   We are sometimes
allowed to become bystanders, and to witness directly the
impression the teaching made on those who first of all
heard the words of the eternal life.

1. Jesus' discourse in the synagogue of Capernaum on
the first Sabbath of His ministry, as recorded by the
Synoptists, astonished His hearers; " for He taught them
as having authority, and not as the scribes." [1]   Bruce thus
explains the statement :

" It is an ethical, not an artistic or æsthetical, contrast
that is intended.   The scribes spake *by* authority, resting
all they said on tradition of what had been said before.
Jesus spake *with* authority, out of His own soul, with direct
intuition of truth ; and, therefore, to the answering soul
of His hearers.   The people could not quite explain the
difference, but that was what they obscurely felt." [2]

The authority of Jesus was grounded in His personality ;
His moral discernment was due to His perfect moral
character, and His spiritual vision to His unbroken communion with God.   He Himself discloses the secret in the
confession regarding Himself, which is unique in the
Synoptic Gospels.[3]   As the Son alone knowing and known
of the Father, He alone can reveal Him unto men ; and
He graciously offers that revelation in His teaching and His
companionship, in lowliness and meekness of heart, as the
secret of rest to all to whom the moral task and the
religious trust present an unsolved problem.   The perfect
goodness and godliness for which men aspire is reality in

[1] Mk 1[22].   [2] *Expositor's Greek Testament*, i. p. 136.
[3] Mt 11[27-30].

His character and the consciousness. His word had absolute authority alike in criticism of the Old Testament
or censure of the scribes and Pharisees as in bringing
penitent and believing souls to God, because it expressed
moral and spiritual reality as ultimate as God Himself, to
whom He was related in constant dependence, and absolute
submission as well as immediate contact and intimate communion. God spake and wrought in Him, for He said and
did only what, and as God taught Him, and gave to Him.
It was the authority of humility, and not vanity.

2. The crowds which heard Jesus were no less impressed by the *novelty* of the doctrine than the *authority* of
the teacher. They testified that it was " a new teaching."[1]

(1) By gathering together similar sayings from various
sources, some scholars have attempted to challenge the
originality of Jesus. Indeed, the fashion of the hour is
to make Him as completely as possible only an echo of
His own age and surroundings. But even were the resem-
blances between what Jesus and other teachers have said
more numerous and exact, we need not reverse the judgment of His first hearers. Had He never said anything
which some one had said before, where would have been the
points of contact with the human reason or conscience on
which educationalists insist to-day as a primary condition
of intelligibility ? Had no gleams of the light from God
which shone so steadily in Him broken through man's
darkness, in the teaching of others, how could we have
maintained our belief that God has had His witness in all
lands and ages ? If, instead of comparing detached utterances of Jesus with sayings of others, we take His teaching
as a whole——and it should be always so taken, since a moral
and spiritual unity pervades it——it can be confidently
maintained that there is no other body of thought, Jewish
or pagan, which can come into comparison with it. Its
novelty must be judged relatively to the thought and life
around the teacher, the contemporary Judaism, for by that
alone could Jesus Himself be directly influenced. Would

[1] Mk 1[27].

He have provoked such misunderstanding, distrust, anger, and hate in so many of His hearers had He been simply repeating the familiar ideas? His conception of God as Father, His conjoining of absolute love to God and equal love to self and neighbour as the highest commandment fulfilling the whole law, the inwardness of the moral and religious life on which He insisted, the universality of God's goodness and consequently of man's duty He enjoined, the assurance of forgiveness of sin He offered, the faith in God's grace He required of man—all these are instances of the originality of His teaching.

(2) But this novelty was not innovation. There was continuity between His revelation of God and that contained in the Old Testament; He nourished His own life in God on these sacred Scriptures. He did not destroy, but fulfilled the law and the prophets; but this fulfilment was not repetition, but completion.[1] The contrasts in the Sermon on the Mount show how far the life to which He called men transcended the law; and His own life and work, how far He Himself transcended the prophecy which He thus fulfilled.

3. Luke, in carrying out the plan of his Gospel, begins the record of the public ministry with an account of the visit to the synagogue of Nazareth, which the other Synoptists place at a later date. The impression made by the discourse he describes in the words, " And all bare Him witness, and wondered at the words of grace which proceeded out of His mouth." [2] Bruce's comment here again deserves quotation :

" Most take χάρις here not in the Pauline sense, but as denoting attractiveness in speech. . . . In view of the text on which Jesus preached, and the fact that the Nazareth incident occupies the place of a frontispiece in the Gospel, the religious Pauline sense of χάρις is probably the right one, = words about the grace of God whereby the prophetic oracle read was fulfilled. . . . Words of grace about grace; such was Christ's speech, then and always—that is Luke's idea." [3]

---

[1] Mt 5[17-20].　　[2] 4[22].　　[3] *Expositor's Greek Testament*, vol. i. p. 490.

(1) The Fatherhood of God, the infinite worth of the human soul, God's sorrow in the loss and joy in the recovery of the sinner, the forgiveness of sin, the peace of God, the salvation from the power and love of sin, the assurance of a blessed and glorious immortality—all that is included in the grace Jesus taught so graciously. Reserving for further comment what is suggested about the manner of the teaching, we may fitly emphasise that *grace*, in as full a sense as Paul ever used the term, was ever the matter of the teaching of Jesus, and His own attitude to sinners confirmed His teaching. His tenderness, gentleness, kindness, and forbearance made Him the living commentary of what grace is, suffers, and does. But this grace was not amiability or good-nature merely; it was not tolerance for, or indifference to, sin, but compassion and solicitude for sinners, which went as far as the giving of Himself as a ransom for many. His Cross is the soul of all His teaching of grace.

(2) With His grace there was conjoined severity, a combination suggested by the varying estimates of Him as Jeremiah or Elijah. His condemnation of the scribes and Pharisees was scathing; and their offence was not only their hypocrisy, but still more the difficulty they put in the way of those who were looking to them for guidance in goodness and godliness. His severity to these teachers and leaders was the obverse of His solicitude for the common people. He did not join in the common cry against the fallen and outcast, but His judgment fell on those whom the world as well as their own conscience approved. The earthly ministry even gives meaning to so paradoxical a phrase as " the wrath of the Lamb."

4. The teaching of Jesus, because of the grace of its matter, was *attractive* to the multitudes. This the Gospels abundantly prove, even if Mark's comment, " the common people heard him gladly," [1] taken in its context does not refer directly to this common feature, but only to His skill in controversy, as Bruce maintains.

[1] 12³⁷.

"The masses enjoyed Christ's victory over the classes, who one after the other measured their wits against His. The remark is true to the life. The people gladly hear one who speaks felicitously, refutes easily, and escapes dexterously from the hands of designing men." [1]

(1) While this suggestion partly accounts for the popularity of Jesus, yet that was mainly due to the good news of grace He brought to those whom the authorised teachers treated with contempt, and on whom they sought to lay burdens grievous to be borne, to the gracious manner in which He ever bore Himself towards them, as well as to the wisdom and the skill of His method of teaching.

(2) While Jesus in the parable of the Sower gave an estimate of His own ministry, in which He recognised the only partial results of His efforts, yet His teaching was effective as well as attractive. He had not only *charm*, but what is sometimes lacking along with charm, *power*. Even if in Lk 4[32] we must render "His word was with authority" (R.V.), "not power" (A.V.), yet v.[14] tells us that "Jesus returned in the power of the Spirit into Galilee. . . . And He taught in their synagogues, being glorified of all."

"This power," says Dr. Stalker, "was the result of that unction of the Holy One, without which even the most solemn truths fall on the ear without effect. He was filled with the Spirit without measure. Therefore the truth possessed Him, It burned and swelled in His own bosom, and He spoke it forth from heart to heart. He had the Spirit not only in such degree as to fill Himself, but so as to be able to impart it to others. It overflowed with His words and seized the souls of His hearers, filling with enthusiasm the mind and the heart." [2]

If we consider the contrast between His truth and grace and the moral and religious life of His age and surroundings, we must recognise how great must have been both the charm and the power of the Teacher who could draw so many to Himself and lift them so far above themselves.

---

[1] *Expositor's Greek Testament*, vol. i. p. 426.
[2] *The Life of Jesus Christ*, pp. 67, 68.

5. Having indicated the fact of the attractiveness of the teaching of Jesus, we may now look more closely at the reason for it in the method of His teaching. (1) It was *occasional*, called forth by and adapted to the questions, needs, or dangers of the moment, the interests and capacities of His hearers; and yet it was not *ephemeral*, for it was eternal truth and grace which met the temporal occasion. The teaching was for the most part appropriate, but always elevated and never trivial conversation, leading men out of the common life of the world into the presence of God Himself. (2) The two excellences of this method have been stated by Wendt in words worth quoting:

"By this method of meeting the want of the occasion, Jesus has been able to impart two weighty qualities to His utterances and His instruction—viz., *popular intelligibility and impressive pregnancy*. The importance lies in the union of these two qualities. A mode of teaching which aims at popular intelligibility is exposed to the risk of degenerating into platitude and triviality; and one which aims at pregnant brevity easily becomes stilted and obscure. But Jesus perfectly combined the two qualities, and by this very means attained a peculiar and classic beauty of style. All the characteristic qualities and methods observable in His style can be classed under the head of means for obtaining those two special excellences."[1]

Holding over the discussion in detail of the method of Jesus, we may here lay emphasis on the fact that Jesus so taught that He could be readily apprehended by the multitude, but could not be fully comprehended even by the disciples. So apparently simple, His teaching was really profound. Men received from Him as much as at the time they could accept, but in such a form that, with the development of their capacity for, there would be increase of their possession of the truth He taught. There was not only open speech, but also reserve and suggestiveness of utterance. The parable of the Sower not only shows that there must be prepared soil as well as selected seed; but suggests, contrary to the natural analogy, which must

[1] *The Teaching of Jesus*, vol. i. p. 109.

always fall short of the spiritual reality, that the lodgment of the selected seed is a condition of the prepared soil. The truth imperfectly apprehended prepares for its own perfect comprehension. We may legitimately press the natural analogy in Wendt's term *pregnancy*, The multitude could not receive the entire truth taught in the parables, even as the disciples, when the parable was explained to them, could. "Therefore speak I to them in parables: because seeing they see not; and hearing they hear not, neither do they understand."[1] The parable did teach them something, if not all; it might even awaken a deeper interest, which would at last result, for some at least, in a fuller intelligence. This interest and intelligence Jesus took for granted in His disciples, favoured with His closer companionship. "Blessed are your eyes, for they see; and your ears, for they hear."[2] Yet, even the disciples often failed to understand; and with them also Jesus had to exercise a reserve. He did not declare His Messiahship till they were able to discover it by God's enlightening on His teaching and life; He did not speak openly about His passion till after His Messiahship had been confessed, and even then the disciples were not prepared for the disclosure.[3] Only after the Resurrection were some of His sayings understood. In considering Him as a Teacher we must remember His withholding as well as imparting. The scholar limits the teacher, and so defines the method. Does not this consideration suggest the possibility that Jesus in His earthly life was never able to complete His revelation, because not only the multitude, but even the disciples, were not able to receive it? Hence His teaching is continued and completed in the enlightening of the Spirit of truth.

III.

We are so impressed by the moral value and the religious significance of the teaching of Jesus that we are apt to ignore its intellectual ability. This was especially

[1] Mt 13¹³.   [2] V. ¹⁶.   [3] 16¹³⁻²³.

shown in His skill in controversy. We have already commented on the saying, "The common people heard Him gladly." A similar impression of knowledge and skill was made in the synagogue in Nazareth : "Many hearing Him were astonished, saying, 'Whence hath this man these things ?' and, 'What is the wisdom that is given unto this man ?'"[1] Jesus could use the Scriptures even better than the scribes could. While spiritual vision and moral discernment were the primary qualifications of Jesus as a Teacher, yet He would not have produced so great an impression as He did had not these excellences been conjoined with a capable mind, quickness and sureness of thought, readiness and resource in speech as well. This gave Him success in controversy; "No man after that durst ask Him any question."[2] And it was important that He should so triumph over His opponents. Yet this is not the side of His ministry on which we love to linger, but rather on the words in which truth and grace were expressed to draw and win men to Himself.

1. The teaching of Jesus was generally given in pithy, pointed, clear, and forceful sayings. It was with Him *multum in parvo*. Of these sayings Dr. Stalker has fittingly said :

"They are simple, felicitous, and easily remembered; yet every one of them is packed full of thought, and the longer you brood over it the more do you see in it. It is like a pool so clear and sunny that it seems quite shallow, till, thrusting in your stick to touch the pebbles so clearly visible at the bottom, you discover that its depth far exceeds what you are trying to measure it with."[3]

Many of the sayings have the characteristics of popular proverbs, easily remembered, and always suggesting more than they express. Antithesis, epigram, paradox abound. Only a few out of a multitude of illustrations may be given: "Many that are first shall be last; and the last first."[4] "For every one that exalteth himself shall be

---

[1] Mk 6².   [2] 12³⁴.
[3] *Imago Christi*, p. 253.   [4] Mk 10³¹.

humbled, and he that humbleth himself shall be exalted." [1]
" I came not to call the righteous, but sinners." [2]   " The
Sabbath was made for man, and not man for the Sabbath." [3]
" Whosoever would save his life shall lose it; and who-
soever shall lose his life for My sake and the gospel's shall
save it." [4]

2. In many of these brief sayings the truth is presented
in a picture; there are abundant *metaphors*, in which there
is no formal comparison, but an analogy of the natural and
the spiritual is assumed, and a figure from the realm of
nature suggests a truth of the realm of spirit. We may
recall, without quoting the sayings, how Jesus uses such
figurative forms of expression as leaven, cup, baptism,
ransom, trumpet, sheep's clothing, lost sheep, yoke, good
treasure, flock, fire. Each word should, to those familiar
with the Gospels, at once summon to remembrance the
whole saying. Sometimes the comparison is not merely
suggested in a word, but the *metaphor is allegorically
expanded*. Instances are the sayings about the narrow
gate, the plenteous harvest, the mote and the beam, the
hand to the plough, the fruits, the blind leaders. This
expanded metaphor is specially marked in the Fourth
Gospel. Let us remind ourselves of the use made of the
ideas of light, darkness, meat, bread, water, hunger, thirst,
way, etc.

" It is only to be remarked," says Wendt, " that, on the
one hand, the figurative phraseology used in the Johannine
discourses is less varied than that met with in the synoptical
discourses; and that, on the other hand, the figures used are
pretty often expanded in an allegorising way." [5]

Often the comparison is formally stated; there are *similes*
as well as metaphors. We may mention a few: " as a
little child," " as sheep among wolves," " wise as serpents,"
" harmless as doves," " as a hen gathereth her brood," " as
children in the market-place," " as a householder who brings

[1] Lk 14[11].   [2] Mk 2[17].   [3] 2[27].   [4] 8[35].
[5] *The Teaching of Jesus*, vol. i. pp. 146–147.

out of his treasure things new and old," " as a shepherd divideth the sheep from the goats." There are cases, however, in which the comparison is more than an illustration; it is a proof, an argument. A particular precept may be enforced by being brought under " a more general and otherwise valid rule." When this rule is presented in an independent narrative, we get a *parable*.

3. The parables of Jesus claim rather fuller notice. Wendt distinguishes two kinds of parables.

" The first class refers," he says, " to some natural event, or some fact of human intercourse or conduct, not as a separate concrete case, but as giving a rule in frequently recurring cases." [1]

One or two examples will suffice to show just what is meant. " The whole have no need of the physician, but the sick." [2] " No man seweth a piece of a new cloth on an old garment," etc.[3] " Do men gather grapes of thorns, or figs of thistles ? " [4] Some scholars would call these parabolic sayings, and reserve the distinctive term parable for the second kind, which, according to Wendt,

" has its distinctive mark in this, that it refers, not to some frequently recurring general fact, but to a single event which has occurred in quite definite circumstances."

In these parables the narrative as a whole is the work of the imagination, although the particulars are actual, or at least probable, in common life. Jesus tells what men do, or at least might do, in reality. In the Fourth Gospel there are no parables of this kind at all. There is a great difference between the present and the previous mode of interpreting the parables.

" In regard to all the parables of Jesus," says Wendt, " the principle holds good that they are not to be regarded as allegories in which, by way of illustration, an event is figuratively described, and in which, therefore, an ingenious meaning can be drawn out of every detail." [5]

---

[1] *Op. cit.*, p. 117. [2] Mk 2[17]. [3] 2[21].
[4] Mt 7[16]. [5] P. 120–121.

It is in one particular, and, as a rule, in one particular only, that the analogy between the natural and the spiritual, the earthly and the heavenly, holds, and the attempt to press an analogy into all the details is to reduce the whole to absurdity. In the parable of the Ten Virgins,[1] the point of comparison is the uncertainty of the coming of the bridegroom, and of Christ. Beyond that our interpretation need not go. There are parables in which the analogy does extend further. As the relation between father and son is the most fitting and worthy emblem of the relation of God and man, the details of the parable of the Prodigal[2] are invested with their own significance, of which it would be only pedantry to forbid the interpreter making the most. In some cases the pressing of the analogy further than the one point of comparison would lead us from truth to error. When the argument is *a minori ad majus*, or *a pejori ad melius*, we must be careful not to ascribe to God defects which attach to man. God is not an unjust judge,[3] even although importunity in prayer is commended; it is not from unwillingness He makes men wait. In general, we must remember that the kingdom of grace does and must transcend the kingdom of nature, and that consequently the analogy suggests, but cannot exhaust the truth. Accordingly, it is but seldom that the parable can present more than one aspect of the truth ; and for this reason Jesus often used twin parables which are complementary. The parables of the New Patch on the Old Garment, and of the New Wine in the Old Wine-skins, are necessary to show that both the old and the new order suffer from a forced alliance.[4] While the parable of the Mustard Seed presents the rapid expansion, the parable of the Leaven suggests the pervasive influence of the kingdom of God.[5] Although the Fourth Gospel gives the parable in partially allegorised form, yet the figures of Christ as the door and the shepherd are, in the same way, companion illustrations.[6] While laying stress on the point of com-

[1] Mt 25[1-13].   [2] Lk 15[11-32].   [3] 18[1-8].
[4] Mk 2[21-22].   [5] Mt 13[31-33].   [6] Jn 10[1-18].

parison in the parables, we must not dismiss all the other details as insignificant. They may not only be necessary to give completeness and interest to the story, but also be intended to throw into greater prominence what is the main feature of the parable, and so convey the lesson taught more emphatically. In revering the moral insight and spiritual discernment of Jesus, we cannot in His parables but admire His æsthetic sense and His artistic skill.

4. We should misunderstand the mind of Jesus, however, if we thought of His figurative language as only a rhetorical device. The analogy of the visible and the invisible, the natural and the spiritual, the human and the divine, had a meaning and worth for Himself. He was at home in both worlds, saw clearly and felt keenly in both ; and it was by a spontaneous impulse, an inevitable necessity of His own nature, that He presented the truth of the one world in symbols from the other. The wide range of the illustrations shows the keenness of His observation and the breadth of His sympathy. Nothing in nature or man was unnoticed by Him, or alien to Him.

" The Jewish life of Galilee," says Dr. Stalker, " in the days of Christ is thus lifted up out of the surrounding darkness into everlasting visibility; and, as on the screen of a magic lantern, we see, in scene after scene, the landscapes of the country, the domestic life of the people, and the larger life of the cities in all their details." [1]

But He saw all in the light of God, felt all in the love of God, and so all had for Him a deeper meaning and a higher worth. He brought out of His treasure things new and old ; [2] the familiar fact, simple, even homely, but never vulgar or commonplace, made plain the original truth. The thinker was also the poet, and could not but be ; for does not the imagination realise as the intellect cannot define the profoundest truth about God and man ?

5. Closely akin to Jesus' use of comparison is His practice of presenting truth and duty not in abstract terms,

[1] *Imago Christi*, p. 254.   [2] Mt 13⁵².

but in concrete instances. He states a general principle by giving a particular instance of its application. The contrast between the old law and the new life, to which He calls men, is in the Sermon on the Mount presented in a series of individual examples. He teaches humanity by the story of the Good Samaritan;[1] humility, by describing the prayer of the Pharisee and the publican;[2] generosity, by calling attention to the gift of the widow,[3] etc.

(1) In illustrating a principle, Jesus does not take the instances in which the *minimum*, but in which the *maximum* demand is made. Always return good for evil, He enjoins, even if it means turning the other cheek to the smiter, or giving up your cloak as well as your tunic, or going two miles instead of one.[4] Seek forgiveness of any wrong you have done a brother, even if you must interrupt your sacrifice to do it.[5] The severity of the demand enhanced the authority of the principle.

(2) But we must be careful to recognise that the same principle may demand varied application; and the concrete instances Jesus gives are not intended to be absolute rules, to be kept whether the situation demands such an application of the principle or not. What they do teach is the absoluteness of the demand; what is the utmost each case demands, conscience must always decide. As Wendt insists, Jesus always aimed at *the greatest clearness in the briefest compass*. Accordingly, He always gives the extreme instance of the application of any principle in which its import is most vividly presented.

"In dealing with the special cases selected for examples," says Wendt, "Jesus avoids all considerations and circumstances which, though neither nullifying nor limiting the general precept to be taught, would in any degree obscure it. In regard to many of His declarations and precepts, which strike us at first as hard and strange sayings, we find a satisfactory explanation in this method of dealing with

---

[1] Lk 10$^{25-37}$. [2] 18$^{9-14}$. [3] 21$^{1-4}$.
[4] Mt 5$^{39-41}$. [5] Vv.$^{23, 24}$.

examples. Otherwise we are speedily tempted to regard them as overstrained and unpractical, or to smooth away their edge on the ground of their being figurative."[1]

(3) This peculiarity is more than a means of effectiveness in teaching; it distinguishes morality from what casuistry has often become. Casuistry is very often so busy in discovering all the possible exceptions to, and all the legitimate qualifications of a general principle, that it makes the principle of none effect. This was just the accusation Jesus brought against the scribes; and His teaching was purposely directed against their casuistry.[2] Jesus was a moralist; He presented the moral ideal in its widest range, deepest reach, and highest claim, as in His teaching on divorce.[3] For Him, ever obedient to the Heavenly Vision, exceptions and qualifications would be meaningless and worthless; the absoluteness of His teaching expresses the perfection of His moral character and the certainty of His religious consciousness.

Conclusion.——While gratefully and reverently recognising the significance and the value of the teaching of Jesus, not only for His earthly ministry and as a preparation for His heavenly reign as Saviour, but also for the thought and life of mankind in all ages, while carefully and appreciatively studying His method not as an example to be slavishly imitated, but as an ideal to be freely realised, we must in closing, however, remind ourselves that His voice as the Christian preacher is not silent; but that He lives in, and so speaks through, the many witnesses of all the Christian generations who have declared His Gospel by His Spirit. However varied the forms of preaching in the Christian Church may have been, it has proved the power and wisdom of God unto salvation, as He has not only been the object, but even the subject of the preaching. Christ is preached, only as Christ by the enlightening, quickening, and renewing of the preacher by His Spirit Himself preaches. Accordingly, this chapter presents only a fragment of Christ the preacher: the volume itself cannot

---

[1] *Op. cit.*, p. 131.   [2] Mt 23[16-22].   [3] 19[3-9].

hope or attempt to exhaust the vast, wondrous, and glorious theme.[1]

[1] Besides Wendt's and Stalker's books already referred to, and the books of New Testament theology, there may be commended for further study, Sanday's *Outlines of the Life of Christ*, chap. iv. (see § 97 for other books); Selbie's *Life and Teaching of Jesus Christ*, chap. v. ; Robertson's *Our Lord's Teachings*, chaps. i. and ii. ; Seeley's *Ecce Homo* ; the writer ventures to add his own *Studies in the Inner Life of Jesus*, chap. x.

CHAPTER II.

APOSTLES, PROPHETS, TEACHERS.

I.

1. WHEN Jesus called His first disciples, according to the Synoptic tradition, His command was with promise, " Come ye after Me, and I will make you to become fishers of men." [1] It was to be their task to catch men for the kingdom of God. For their calling they were trained by His companionship, in following Him, learning of Him, and sharing His yoke.[2] Of the disciples He, according to Luke, chose " twelve whom also He named apostles." [3] " Moved with compassion for the multitudes, because they were distressed and scattered, as sheep not having a shepherd," He sent forth the few labourers He had so trained into the plenteous harvest, [4] giving them " authority over unclean spirits to cast them out, and to heal all manner of diseases and all manner of sickness," and charging them to preach, " saying, The kingdom of heaven is at hand." [5] The instructions He gave them respecting the method of their work were adapted to time and place, and need not be regarded as universal and permanent principles of the Christian ministry. According to Luke, Jesus at a later stage of His ministry " appointed seventy others, and sent them two and two before His face into every city and place, whither He Himself was about to come." [6] Similar instructions were given to the larger as to the smaller company of preachers. On both occasions the apostles were but heralds, preparing the way before Him.

[1] Mk 1[17]. [2] Mt 11[28-30]. [3] Lk 6[13].
[4] Mt 9[36-38]. [5] 10[1. 7]. [6] Lk 10[1].

There is no record of the effect of the preaching, but the Seventy rejoiced at the success of their exorcisms, and had to be warned against their self-satisfaction.[1]

2. In accordance with his method of arranging the sayings of Jesus in discourses having a unity of subjects, Matthew conjoins to the counsels given the disciples on their first mission, warnings about persecution, uttered at a later stage of the ministry, and relating to the circumstances of the Church after His departure. In one of these sayings the equipment for their work, which, however, is much more fully dealt with in the Johannine discourses, is mentioned. " When they deliver you up, be not anxious how or what ye shall speak ; for it shall be given you in that hour what ye shall speak. For it is not ye that speak, but the Spirit of your Father that speaketh in you." [2] When Peter, speaking for the disciples, confessed Jesus' Messiahship, he was pronounced blessed, because " flesh and blood *had* not revealed it unto *him*, but *the* Father which is in heaven." [3] The divine illumination promised is declared to be possessed.

3. Without entering into the question whether the two passages about the ἐκκλησία [4] are genuine sayings of Jesus, or express the consciousness of the early Christian Church, although the writer inclines to the former opinion, we may regard them as throwing some light on the apostolic functions. As the confession of the Messiahship (or the first confessor of the Messiah) is the foundation on which rests the Christian community, so the declaration of the Messiahship is the primary content of the apostolic preaching. To the apostles also is entrusted the stewardship of the kingdom of heaven,[5] the exercise of its authority in human affairs by the declaration of the obligations it may impose, or the liberties it may allow.[6] This function of declaring God's will is to find individual application in the discipline

---

[1] Lk 10[17-20].   [2] Mt 10[19, 20].   [3] 16[17].   [4] 16[18, 19] 18[15-20].

[5] This is the more probable interpretation (Weiss) than that given by Bruce (*The Expositor's Greek Testament*, vol. i. p. 225), *i.e.* that Peter would be the door-keeper, admitting to or excluding from the kingdom.

[6] The Christian ideal was a liberation from legal and ritual bondage.

of the community, the exclusion of any member refusing to be reconciled to another.   Not only is the Father's answer assured for united prayer, but also Christ's own presence in any gathering of His disciples in His name.   Although the same question arises as regards the great missionary commission,[1] we need not hesitate about using that passage for our present purpose.   A world-wide mission is entrusted to the disciples.   All nations are to be won for discipleship, and the new relation is to be confessed in, and signified by, baptism into the threefold name.[2]   So universal a task, with all difficulties it involves, is justified by the supreme authority of Christ, and its discharge is encouraged by the assurance of His constant presence.

4. When we turn from the Synoptic tradition to the Johannine, especially the farewell talk of Jesus with His disciples, these assurances of His constant presence and supreme authority, and of their equipment for their work by the Spirit, are emphasised and developed.   After His departure another Paraclete (Advocate, Helper, Companion) is promised to them in the Spirit of truth, the Holy Spirit, who will continue the revelation of Christ, both by recalling His teachings and by guiding them to an understanding of truths which they cannot now receive from His lips; but the Spirit's revelation will not supplant, but only make explicit what is already implied in the revelation of the Son.   The Spirit shall bear witness of Christ to the disciples, that they may become His witnesses to the world, doubly qualified by their knowledge of the entire course of His earthly ministry and by the enlightening of the Spirit.[3]   When Jesus appeared in the Upper Room after He had risen, the Fourth Gospel represents Him as conveying the Holy Spirit to the disciples by breathing upon them, and so giving them, in virtue of their possession of the Spirit, the authority to grant or withhold the forgiveness of sin.[4]   As regards the function, expressed in the

[1] Mt 28[18-20].
[2] The apostolic practice was baptism into Christ's name.
[3] Jn 14[6, 17, 26] 16[12-14] 15[26, 27].   [4] 20[22, 23].

words, "Whose soever sins ye forgive, they are forgiven
unto them ; whose soever sins ye retain, they are retained,"
it is similar to that assigned in the Synoptic tradition,[1] and
the three passages must be taken together as mutually
illuminative. The proclamation of the laws of the kingdom of God, the decision of the membership of the Christian
community, the granting or the withholding of the assurance of pardon, are all modes in which, through His chosen
channels, the Spirit of God continues and applies in the
Church the revelation of Christ. It need hardly be said
that we are here concerned not with official privileges, but
personal qualifications.

5. While the Synoptic tradition throws into prominence
the choice of twelve constant companions of Jesus, who
were with Him in His Galilæan ministry and in His last
days in Jerusalem, it would be a mistake to ignore the
larger company of disciples, one of whom, in the writer's
judgment, was the Fourth Evangelist,[2] who, as having a
knowledge of the ministry of Jesus, were also fit to be His
witnesses, and who could serve as His apostles or messengers. The choice of Matthias by lot to take the place
of Judas [3] had, as far as we can judge, no significance for
the subsequent history of the Church, and, with the exception of Peter, John, and James, the Twelve fall into the
background, and others come to the front in the witness
of the Gospel and the work of the kingdom. It is
significant that, when Paul refers to the ministries in the
Christian Church, he includes the apostleship among the
charisms ($\chi\alpha\rho\iota\sigma\mu\alpha\tau\alpha$), the gifts of the Spirit. "And God
hath set some in the church, first apostles, secondly
prophets, thirdly teachers, then miracles (R.V. marg. Gr.
powers), then gifts of healings, helps, governments (R.V.
marg., wise counsels), divers kinds of tongues."[4] This is no
exhaustive enumeration, for elsewhere he adds "evangelists
and pastors."[5] What Paul was concerned about was not
official status, but spiritual endowment; and the New

---

[1] Mt 16¹⁹ 18¹⁸.   [2] See articles in *The Expositor*, 1914–1915.
[3] Ac 1²⁶.   [4] 1 Co 12²⁸.   [5] Eph 4¹¹.

Testament as a whole does not warrant us in thinking of any rigid ecclesiastical organisation, but only of a religious community, the members of which were variously endowed, and so fitted for different functions. Keeping this general consideration before us, we may now look more closely at these different functions.

6. The term *apostle* is first used of the disciples when sent out on their mission [1] " to the lost sheep of the house of Israel," and is clearly used in the common sense of messenger. As we have already seen, before the Ascension Jesus declared the scope of this mission to be world-wide,[2] and their task to be witness.[3] The qualification for witness was that they had been with Him from the beginning, and had witnessed the Resurrection. The qualification is stated clearly and fully by Peter, in Ac 1[21. 22], in dealing with the appointment of an apostle to take the place of Judas. While probably the knowledge of the earthly ministry was not insisted on in an apostle, the ability to witness to the Resurrection was. For Paul, in claiming apostleship, does not claim any such personal companionship with Jesus,[4] but does claim to have seen Jesus as Risen.[5] James, the Lord's brother,[6] was not a disciple during the earthly ministry,[7] but he saw the Risen Lord [8] and believed.

" This mark of apostleship " (*i.e.* witness-bearing), says Hort, " is evidently founded on direct personal discipleship, and as evidently it is incommunicable. Its whole meaning rested on immediate and unique experience; as St. John says, ' that which we have heard, that which we have seen with our eyes, that which we beheld, and our hands handled,' (1 John i. 1). Without a true perceptive faith, such a faith as shewed itself in St. Peter, all this acquaintance through the bodily senses was in vain. But the truest faith of

---

[1] Mt 10[2], Lk 6[13]. The words "whom also He named apostles " in Mk 3[14] are of doubtful authenticity.

[2] Mt 28[18-20].   [3] Lk 24[48]; cf. Jn 15[27].

[4] 2 Co 5[16] makes no such claims.   [5] 1 Co 9[1]; cf. 15[8].

[6] Gal 1[19].   [7] Jn 7[3-5].   [8] 1 Co 15[7].

one who was a disciple only in the second degree, however precious in itself, could never qualify him for bearing the apostolic character."[1]

Since the inward revelation through the Spirit was consequent on, and subordinate to the outward revelation by the Son,[2] and Pentecost followed the Crucifixion and the Resurrection, we can understand how and why, even in a Spirit-filled community, the place of pre-eminence belonged to those who had seen and heard the Lord Himself, in His earthly life and in His appearance after His resurrection ; for surely their immediate contact and intimate communion with Him, when His truth and grace were received in faith, was the condition of the fulness of the Spirit's enlightening, renewing, and strengthening power, which enabled them not only to witness, but also to guide and guard the Christian community in the Way appointed and approved by the Lord Himself.

7. *Prophecy* was one of the gifts of the Spirit in the Christian Church, subordinate, however, to the apostolic function ;[3] esteemed more profitable than the gift of tongues,[4] yet pronounced transitory, and inferior to faith, hope, love.[5] The work of the prophets, as of the other ministers, is defined as " for the perfecting of the saints, unto the work of ministering, unto the building up of the body of Christ."[6] The prophetic movement in Israel as a religious revival in its earlier phases corresponded to the " sacred enthusiasm " which took possession of the Christian Church after Pentecost.[7] Its abnormal psychical accompaniments had a counterpart in some of the charisms, such as

---

[1] *The Christian Ecclesia*, p. 39.   [2] Jn 16[12, 15].

[3] 1 Co 12[28].   [4] 14[5].   [5] 13[8, 13].

[6] Eph 4[12] ; cf. Ac 13[3].   See Ac 11[28] 21[11] 13[1, 2] 15[3] 21[9], 1 Jn 4[1], Rev 2[20].

[7] " *Pneuma hagien* (without the article) denotes the sacred enthusiasm which marked certain elect souls before Christ's coming, such as Zacharias, Elizabeth, and their son John ; and after Pentecost, Christians generally, though also in various special degrees.   On the other hand, where the article is present, a further reference is usually intended, and it means ' the Holy Spirit,' or God as personally indwelling (immanent) and working in man " (*The Century Bible : Acts*, p. 386).

speaking with tongues.[1]   The revelation of God came both
to apostles and prophets in the Spirit,[2] but not necessarily
in a trance.[3]   As the Spirit works in prophecy, the prophet
is spiritual ; but the Spirit is under the prophet's control,[4]
so that his speech should be according to the proportion of
faith,[5] and, therefore, the neglect of self-control in exercising
the gift is censured.[6]

8. Both apostleship and prophecy were conceived as
χαρίσματα, gifts of God, not conferring an office, but
rather imposing a function.

" Much profitless labour," says Hort, " has been spent on
trying to force the various terms used into meaning so many
definite ecclesiastical offices.   Not only is the feat impossible,
but the attempt carries us away from St. Paul's purpose,
which is to show how the different functions are those which
God has assigned to the different members of a single body.
In both lists apostles and prophets come first, two forms of
altogether exceptional function, those who were able to
bear witness of Jesus and the Resurrection by the evidence
of their own sight—the Twelve and St. Paul—and those
whose monitions or outpourings were regarded as specially
inspired by the Holy Spirit.   Each of these held one kind
of function, and next to these in 1 Cor. come all who in any
capacity were ' teachers ' (διδάσκαλοι) without any of the
extraordinary gifts bestowed on apostles and prophets.   In
Ephesians this function is given in a less simple form.   First
there are ' evangelists,' doubtless men like Titus and Timothy
(2 Tim. iv. 5) and Tychicus and Epaphras, disciples of
St. Paul who went about from place to place preaching the
Gospel in multiplication and continuation of his labours
without possessing the peculiar title of apostleship.
Probably enough in St. Paul's long imprisonment this kind
of work had much increased.   Then come ' pastors and
teachers,' men who taught within their own community and
whose work was therefore as that of shepherds taking care
for a flock." [7]

---

[1] Ac 2[4].   The tongues are not foreign languages, but ecstatic utterances,
often unintelligible as prophecy was not.   See 1 Co 14[1-19].
[2] Eph 3[5], Rev 1[10].   [3] Ac 10[10] 22[17].   [4] 1 Co 12[10] 14[37] v.[32].
[5] Ro 12[6].   [6] 1 Co 14[29-31].
[7] The Christian Ecclesia, pp. 157–158.

We may recall in this connection Paul's solemn warning to the elders of Ephesus.[1]   The elders also are the
servants of the Spirit, if less richly endowed than apostles
and prophets.   While the elders or bishops and deacons
were the local settled ministry, the apostles, prophets, and
evangelists were the universal travelling ministry ; and
after the Apostolic Age, as the former gained authority, the
latter lost influence.   Impostors seem to have assumed the
functions of apostles and prophets, as the warnings in the
Didache, or *The Teaching of the Apostles*, show.[2]

II.

1. The *times* and *places* of apostolic preaching may be
very briefly referred to.

" As the Christian Church," says Schaff, " rests historically on the Jewish Church, so Christian worship and the
congregational organisation rest on that of the synagogue,
and cannot be well understood without it." [3]

Both Christ Himself and the apostles, wherever and
whenever practicable, used the synagogue as the scene of
their labours.   Even Paul, on his mission to the Gentiles,
first visited the Jewish synagogue, and there preached until
prevented by Jewish opposition.   In the synagogue " the
chief parts of the service were, according to the Mishna,
the recitation of the *Shema* (a confession of faith), *prayer,
the reading of the Thorah, the reading of the prophets,
the blessing of the priest*.   To these were added the
translation of the portions of Scripture read, which is
assumed in the Mishna, and the explanation of what had
been read by an edifying *discourse*, which in Philo figures
as the chief matter in the whole service." [4]   It is only
with the place of preaching in the synagogue that we are
concerned.

---

[1] Ac 20²⁸.   [2] See chaps. xi., xii.

[3] *Apostolic Christianity*, p. 456.

[4] Schürer's *The Jewish People in the Time of Jesus Christ*, Div. ii. vol. ii.
p. 76.

"The reading of the Scripture," says Schürer, "was
followed by an edifying lecture or sermon (דְּרָשָׁה), by which
the portion which had been read was explained and applied.
That such explanations were the general practice is evident
from the διδάσκειν ἐν ταῖς συναγωγαῖς,[1] so frequently mentioned in the New Testament from Luke iv. 20 sqq., and from
the express testimony of Philo. The preacher (דַּרְשָׁן) used
to *sit* (Luke iv. 20 : ἐκάθισεν) on an elevated place. Nor was
such preaching confined to appointed persons, but, as appears
especially from Philo, open to any competent member of the
congregation."[2]

The preaching, neither of Jesus nor of the apostles, was
confined to the synagogue. He preached in the fields,
roads, and streets of Galilee, and also in the temple at
Jerusalem; and so did they. When compelled to with-
draw from the synagogue at Corinth, Paul exercised his
ministry in a private house, that of Titus Justus, adjoining
the synagogue.[3] At Ephesus for two years he reasoned
daily in the school of Tyrannus.[4] Thus the Gospel was
transplanted from Jewish to Gentile soil, and the Christian
preacher ceased to be a Jewish scribe and became a Gentile
rhetor or sophist.[5]

[1] Mt 4²³, Mk 1²¹ 6², Lk 4¹⁵ 6⁶ 13¹⁰, Jn 6⁵⁹ 18²⁰.

[2] *Op. cit.*, p. 82. See Lk 4¹⁷⁻²⁰, Jn 6⁵⁹, Ac 6⁸⁻¹⁰ 9²⁰ 13¹⁵.

[3] Ac 18⁷.

[4] 19⁹, ¹⁰. Dr. Bartlet's comment may be quoted : "*i.e.* a lecture-room
such as *rhetors* or sophists (popularizers of philosophy) used for their
orations or 'displays.' This particular 'school' bore the name of Tyrannus,
perhaps from the *rhetor* who originally gave prestige to the spot. To the
general public Paul's 'reasoning' on the claims of the gospel would now
seem, more than ever, that of a specially piquant travelling sophist of
religious sympathies" (*The Century Bible: Acts*, pp. 314–315).

[5] This is a topic to which we shall return in the next chapter ; but attention may here be called to two articles by Dr. Maurice Jones on "The Style
of St. Paul's Preaching" (*The Expositor*, 8th Series, vol. xiv. p. 242 ff.),
in which he seeks to show the influence in Paul's method of preaching of
the Cynic-Stoic *Diatribe*. He recognises, however, that the strong personality of the apostle asserted itself. "If St. Paul wears the mantle of the
Greek preacher he wears it very loosely, putting it on and off at will."
How Paul thought of himself as a Christian preacher Dr. Robert Law
has sought to set forth in an article on "St. Paul on Preaching" (*The
Constructive Quarterly*, vol. v. p. 552 ff.), with special reference to the
passages in 1 Corinthians.

2. From the *times* and *places* we turn to the *contents* of apostolic preaching. We cannot claim the discourses in Acts as *verbatim* reports; but we must not dismiss them as free compositions of the author; for a careful study of them shows their appropriateness to the occasion, the purpose, the speaker, and the stage of theological development which had been reached. Peter's speech at Pentecost [1] is deserving of very close study; as it is the first statement of the apostolic message, it is the first endeavour made in the Christian Church to understand, and to make understood, the meaning of the Person of Christ, and especially of His death. We have in this speech five elements of the early Christian preaching—(1) testimony to fact, especially the Crucifixion and Resurrection; (2) interpretation of fact, in which throughout the book of Acts we can trace a development; (3) argument from prophecy, the most potent kind of reasoning for a Jewish audience, in which, however, Jewish modes of interpretation were employed, which our modern scholarship can no longer regard as valid; (4) appeal to conscience, to bring home to the Jewish nation the crime of Christ's death in order to awaken penitence; and (5) assurance of forgiveness and salvation through faith in Christ. Of the second address of Peter, in explanation of the first miracle,[2] the peculiar features are—(1) the milder tone adopted towards the Jewish people (v.[17]); (2) the advance in theology, as the death is now connected with the necessity of the fulfilment of prophecy (v.[18]); (3) the reference to the Second Advent, a subject which had not been mentioned in the previous address (v.[20]). In the defence of the apostolic preaching before the Jewish Sanhedrin, the characteristic feature noted is *boldness*.[3] Against all threats the imperative duty of obeying God rather than man, of testifying what they had seen

---

[1] Ac 2[14-40].   [2] 3[11-26].

[3] Ac 4[13]. παρρησίαν, a word on which Knowling's comment deserves quotation : "either boldness of speech, or of bearing; it was the feature which had characterised the teaching of Our Lord ; cf. Mark viii. 32, and nine times in St. John in connection with Christ's teaching or bearing ; and the disciples in this respect also were as their Master, iv. 29, 31 (ii. 29);

and heard, was asserted by the apostles. The experience of the truth and grace of Christ involved for them the obligation to proclaim Christ.

3. In Peter, the spokesman of the Twelve, we have the primitive apostolic preaching, beyond which we pass in Stephen [1] and Paul.

"The significance of Stephen," says Dr. Andrews, "can scarcely be over-estimated. His preaching marks the most decisive advance that had as yet been taken by the Church. Hitherto the Christian community had been bound up in the closest way with the Jews. In the era before Stephen, Christianity was practically a Jewish sect, like Pharisaism, for instance. The only point of separation was the distinctive belief that Jesus was the Messiah. It was Stephen who in the first instance saved the Church from remaining a mere branch of Judaism, and struck the first note of Universalism. He asserted that Christianity was independent of the Temple and of the Law, and must not be confined within the narrow channels of Jewish custom and belief."

This assertion he supported by an appeal to history.

"He shows (a) that long before either Temple or Law existed, God had made a covenant with Abraham; (b) that He had revealed Himself to Joseph and Moses in Egypt when they were far away from the sacred city of Jerusalem; (c) that He had been with Israel during their time of wandering in the wilderness, and had accepted their worship; (d) that even when the Temple was built by Solomon it was distinctly stated in the prayer of dedication that the presence of God was not restricted within its walls."

He also used the history of the past to prove

"that there had been men in every age who, like his accusers, persecuted the prophets and resisted the new revelation of truth which they brought to the world." [2]

4. Stephen was not, however, the only forerunner of

so, too, of St. Paul, xxviii. 31, and frequently used by St. Paul himself in his Epistles; also by St. John four times in his First Epistle, of confidence in approaching God; 'urbem et orbem hac parrhesia vicerunt' (Bengel)."— *The Expositor's Greek Testament*, vol. ii. p. 128.

[1] Ac 7.   [2] *Westminster New Testament: Acts*, pp. 93, 96.

Paul. In Peter's address to Cornelius [1] and his friends, the
opening statement shows how rapidly, under the Spirit's
guidance, the Church was moving; for the apostle not only
declares that Christ is Lord of all (v.[37]), but recognises that
God is no respecter of persons, but welcomes all godly and
good men (v.[35]). It was Paul, however, who became the
Apostle to the Gentiles. He, too, first appealed to the
Jews, and was driven by their unbelief to turn to the
Gentiles. Paul's sermon in the synagogue at Antioch in
Pisidia [2] is addressed mainly, but not solely, to the Jews
there, but also to the God-fearing Gentiles. The latter he
does not depreciate as an inferior class; but, " as the orator
proceeds and grows warm in his subject, his address becomes
still more complimentary to the God-fearing Gentiles and
actually raises them to the same level with the Jews as
' Brethren.' " Accordingly, the sermon " represented a new
step in his thought and method." [3] Nevertheless, the
sermon is typical of his mode of address to his countrymen. Like Peter in his speeches, Paul here makes the
appeal to history, and uses the argument from prophecy;
he lays stress on the fact of the Resurrection, and, while
mentioning the death of Christ as the fulfilment of what
was " written of him," he does not, as his letters might lead
us to expect, offer any doctrine of the Atonement. The
sermon falls into three parts. In the first part (vv.[17-25]) he
sketches the history of God's chosen people, to show how it
finds its divinely fixed goal in Jesus as Saviour; the second
part (vv.[26-37]) witnesses that, in spite of the prophetic
warnings, and yet in fulfilment of prophetic predictions, He
was rejected and crucified by men, but raised from the
dead by God, as had been also foretold; and the third part
(vv.[38-41]) makes the practical application in an offer of
forgiveness, and a warning against unbelief. While the
more fully developed Pauline theology is absent, yet its
outstanding doctrine is asserted in the words, " By him every
one that believeth is justified from all things, from which

---

[1] Ac 10[28-43].   [2] 13[16-41].
[3] Ramsay, *The Cities of St. Paul*, pp. 301, 303.

ye could not be justified by the law of Moses." [1] How
Paul, in his preaching, became all things to all men is
shown by the report given of two sermons addressed to
Gentiles. At Lystra,[2] in seeking to prevent the attempt to
worship Barnabas and himself as gods, he rebuked idolatry,
and appealed to the witness to God in nature, with its
supply for human needs. In Athens [3] he skilfully used
the inscription " to an unknown God," which he had seen
on an altar, to introduce the revelation of God, of which he
was the messenger, and enforced his own argument by an
appeal to the current Stoic philosophy, as expressed by a
widely known poet. Having thus secured a hearing, he
attacked idolatry, and insisted on the necessity of repentance in view of the final judgment. His intention to lead
his hearers to the Risen Lord was frustrated, however, by
their clamour. As the speech was never finished, there is
no warrant whatever for the assertion that Paul failed
because he substituted philosophy for Christ, and that he
confessed his own failure in the determination he expressed
in 1 Corinthians " not to know anything save Jesus Christ,
and Him crucified." [4] Had he begun with distinctively
Christian truth, would his audience have listened to him
as long as they did ? His failure on this occasion offers no
valid reason against the endeavour of a preacher to find
the points of contact with his hearers, and to follow the
lines of least resistance as long as he can. We admire and
do not censure Paul for trying to be the philosopher among
philosophers. This brief sketch of the speeches in Acts
has served, it is hoped, to indicate not only the message of
the Christian preachers in the Apostolic Age, but also the
manner and the method of its delivery.

" The preaching of the Gospel," says Schaff, " appears in
the first period mostly in the form of a missionary address to
the unconverted ; that is a simple, living presentation of the
main facts of the life of Jesus, with practical exhortation to
repentance and conversion. Christ crucified and risen was
the luminous centre, whence a sanctifying light was shed on

---

[1] Ac 13[39].   [2] 14[15-18].   [3] 17[22-31].   [1] 1 Co 2[2].

all the relations of life. Gushing forth from a full heart,
this preaching went to the heart; and springing from an
inward life, it kindled life—a new, divine life—in the
susceptible hearers. It was revival preaching in the purest
sense." [1]

5. The speeches recorded in Acts must be supplemented by the indications given, as in the Epistles.
(1) While it is certain that Paul in his ordinary preaching
did not discuss doctrinal and practical problems such as he
dealt with in his letters, yet his letters do supplement our
knowledge of the content of his preaching.   (2) The
space filled in our New Testament by the letters of
Paul should not be allowed to hide from us the fact that
the form in which he preached was not the only mode of
presenting the Gospel in the Apostolic Age.   Agreeing
with Paul as to the freedom of the believer from the Jewish
ceremonial law, many preachers did not accept his position
as to the abrogation of all external law for Christians, and
tended to regard the Gospel itself as a law of righteousness.[2]   In these circles the teaching of Jesus was presented
as the new law, and doubtless in preaching the words of
Jesus were much quoted, explained, and enforced.   The
Epistle of James has least of the distinctive Pauline teaching, and yet most of the teaching of Jesus.   This and other
writings in the New Testament have been treated by Dr.
Moffatt, in his *Introduction*, in a chapter entitled " Homilies
and Pastorals."   Of these writings he states :

" Even in form they vary.   Hebrews has no address, and
1 John has no definite address ; while neither James nor
1 John has any epistolary conclusion.   The more important
of them show how Paul had popularised the epistolary form
in primitive Christianity, but it is as homilies rather than as
epistles that they are to be ranked." [3]

The Epistle to the Hebrews, whether it was ever delivered
as a sermon or a series of sermons, may serve as an illus-

---

[1] *Apostolic Christianity*, pp. 461, 462.
[2] See McGiffert's *History of Christianity in the Apostolic Age*, p. 440 ff.
[3] *Introduction to the Literature of the New Testament*, p. 317.

tration of the blending of exposition and exhortation, which may be described by the term *homily*, the earliest form assumed by Christian preaching.[1]

[1] The subject of this chapter may be further studied in Hering's *Homiletik*, pp. 3–6 ; Schaff's *Apostolic Christianity*, p. 461 f. ; Bartlet's *The Apostolic Age*, p. 476 f. ; Ker's *History of Preaching*, Lecture III. ; Horne's *The Romance of Preaching*, Lecture III.

CHAPTER III.

APOLOGISTS AND FATHERS.

I.

1. WE can understand the development of the organism of Christian preaching only as we know the environment in which it was placed. In passing from the Jewish to the Gentile environment, Christianity did not abandon a world familiar with preaching for a world regardless of it. Probably there had never been in human history a period in which preaching had been so widely and keenly appreciated, as when the Christian Church went forth to conquer the world by "the foolishness of preaching."[1] An admirable account of the situation has been given by Dr. Angus:

"The ancient world resorted to preaching. Philosophy, which then covered the fields of morality and religion, led the way; Porphyry demands that the aim of philosophy should be 'the salvation of the soul.' Free speech was everywhere permitted. Oratory, of which antiquity was more appreciative than we, followed this practical trend. Philosophers avowed themselves to be physicians of the soul, ambassadors of God, whose functions were to cure diseased souls and produce conversions. These missionary philosophers revived the spiritual truths of religious teachers of the past, and condensed them into a popular form to suit the age. Some philosophers, like some theological professors nowadays, did not take the field themselves, but reduced their philosophy to a practical training for those who were to carry the message farther afield. Men went out from the lecture halls to preach self-examination and self-culture. They brought forth things new and old. In the burden of their preaching were many commonplaces—counsel to culti-

---

[1] 1 Co 1[21].

vate a good conscience, to act as if conscious that God sees
all; virtue is its own reward, and is attainable by all; sin is
its own punishment. They insisted on man's inherent dignity and his ability to save himself by his will. They knew
no original sin. Life should be a contemplation of death, so
that men may die without fear. This preaching was not
confined to the upper circles. One is more impressed by the
enormous amount of popular preaching. . . . Preachers, like
emperors, courted popularity with the masses. . . . The
street preaching was started by the Cynics, who were
exposed to as much ridicule as any street preachers have
ever been."

We need not reproduce the names mentioned by this
writer; and may pass to his last sentences on this topic:

"These, and such apostles, aimed at a moral and religious revival; they believed reformation of character possible,
and within the reach of all. They gave clear expression
to certain great truths. Who can say how many conversions they produced, or who can measure their influence for
righteousness? They claimed to be ambassadors of God,
and they executed their mission as well as they could. But
their truth was too abstract: they misplaced the seat of
authority; they failed to realize the true nature and extent
of human sin. Nevertheless they were voices crying in
the wilderness of Paganism, preparing the way of the
Lord."[1]

---

[1] *The Environment of Early Christianity*, pp. 74–78. An extract may
here be added, dealing with the same subject, from *Chantepie de la
Saussaye: Religionsgeschichte*, 2 Band, Dritte Auflage, p. 505: "The
philosophers in this period exercised the deepest influence as preachers to
the people. Actually only the cynics come into consideration in this
respect. Not only by their speeches, which one has often compared with
the sermons of the Capuchins, but also by their whole life, were these
'mendicant monks of antiquity' the teachers and trainers of their contemporaries. In this period cynicism attained a far greater significance
than it had ever possessed in ancient Greece. The cynic was a man who,
without property or family, free in life as in death, warned and exhorted all
men in free-spirited speech, a herald and messenger of the gods, a brother of
all men, whose soul-weal he bore upon his heart. Thus Epictetus (Arrian,
Diatrib, iii. 22) described him in ideal light as an overseer of other men
(the rest of mankind), who, following a divine vocation, shewed all by speech
and example the way of salvation. History offers several instances of the
great influence of the cynics. Thus in the first century in Rome one of the
best known personalities was the cynic Demetrius, who refused with scorn

2. This popular preaching of practical philosophy not only produced an interest in the discussion of questions of religion and morals, and so secured for the Christian preachers an audience ever ready to listen to the solution of these problems they could offer; but also the methods of composition and delivery did pass over into the Christian Church, and so determined the forms of Christian preaching. In ancient Greece young men were prepared for taking their part in public life by a course of instruction in rhetoric, the art of effective speech, of so presenting a political course or a legal case as to persuade and convince. The teacher of rhetoric illustrated the rules he gave by "model compositions of his own, in the first instance exercises in the pleading of actual causes, and accusations or defences of real persons," but afterwards they lost connection with the law-courts and became literary exercises ($\mu\epsilon\lambda\acute{\epsilon}\tau\alpha\iota$), arguments about topics or persons, sometimes fictitious, and sometimes taken from real history. *Rhetoric* thus became *sophistic*, when it lost touch with real life, and became an intellectual indulgence. It was again rescued from vain artificiality by an alliance with philosophy.

"It threw off altogether," says Hatch, "the fiction of a law-court or an assembly, and discussed in continuous speech the larger themes of morality or theology. Its utterances were not 'exercises,' but 'discourses' ($\delta\iota\alpha\lambda\acute{\epsilon}\xi\epsilon\iota\varsigma$). It preached sermons. It created not only a new literature but also a

---

large sums of money which Caligula offered to him, with whom Thrasea conversed in his last hour, who last of all opposed Vespasian; but he did not want to kill the 'barking dog.' Contempt of the emperors almost belonged to the office of the cynic; thus one of them even ventured publicly to scold Titus on account of Berenice. There were, however, besides good also some bad cynics, who, shameless and vain, selfish and dishonest, wore as a disguise the outer tokens of the cynic, long beard and staff, in order to swindle people and to enrich themselves. A specially hostile light falls on these popular preachers in Lucian, who makes an exception only for the Athenian Demonax. Most violently Lucian pursues Peregrinus Proteus, whose whole life he describes as a series of scandals, and whose suicide by fire in Olympia he mocks. . . . In any case, one can accord far less belief to the controversial writings of Lucian than to the idealising description of Epictetus."

new profession. The class of men against whom Plato had inveighed had become merged in the general class of educators : they were specialized partly as grammarians, partly as rhetoricians ; the word ' sophist,' to which the invectives had failed to attach a permanent stigma, remained partly as a generic name, and partly as a special name for the new class of public talkers. They differed from philosophers in that they did not mark themselves off from the rest of the world, and profess their devotion to a higher standard of living, by wearing a special dress." [1]

Some of them were settled in one place, others travelled about. They indulged in rhetorical contests with one another, especially at one of the great festivals, and were regarded as public entertainers, not much raised above jugglers and soothsayers. Dio Chrysostom carries us back through the centuries with his vivid picture of a scene in Corinth at the Isthmian games :

" You might hear many poor wretches of sophists shouting and abusing one another, and their disciples, as they call them, squabbling, and many writers of books reading their stupid compositions, and many poets singing their poems, and many jugglers exhibiting their marvels, and many soothsayers giving the meaning of prodigies, and ten thousand rhetoricians twisting law-suits, and no small number of traders driving their several trades." [2] They expected, and used their arts to secure applause ; but sometimes suffered the humiliation of signs of disapproval. They cared not for fame only, but gold also ; and some of them were very successful in securing both. The successful were puffed up with conceit, and often made themselves ridiculous by their pretensions. " The common epithet for them is ἀλαζών—a word with no precise English equivalent, denoting a cross between a braggart and a mountebank. But the real grounds on which the more earnest men objected to them were those upon which Plato had objected to their predecessors : their making a trade of knowledge, and their unreality." [3] " They preached, not because they were in

---

[1] Hatch's *Hibbert Lectures: The Influence of Greek Ideas and Usages upon the Christian Church*, p. 91.

[2] Quoted by Hatch, *op. cit.*, p. 94. [3] *Ibid.*, p. 99.

grim earnest about the reformation of the world, but because preaching was a respectable profession, and the listening to sermons a fashionable diversion." [1]

Against this movement there was a counter-movement, especially in the Stoic school; and we are justified in assuming that among the sophists there were serious and earnest men, who preached because they believed, and wished to share this good with others.

3. We must now try to estimate the influence of this sophistic on the Christian Church. (1) In the Apostolic Age there was an " inspired " ministry of apostles and prophets, who spoke as they were moved by the Holy Ghost. Their preaching was primarily by divine gift and not human art, although human talents were consecrated by the Spirit in His operations. Having undoubtedly in view the wisdom of the pagan sophist, Paul says of himself: " My speech and my preaching were not in persuasive words of wisdom, but in demonstration of the Spirit and of power ; that your faith should not stand in the wisdom of men, but in the power of God." [2] Prophecy was not studied, but spontaneous, utterance. As the high tide of " the holy enthusiasm " of the Apostolic Age ebbed (and the difference can be seen if we compare the Apostolic Fathers with the apostles), prophecy gave way to preaching. It was discredited by impostors, who pretended without possessing the charism ; and it was at last suppressed by ecclesiastical authority in the Montanist movement as a peril to the established order in doctrine, worship, and polity. It must be admitted that in its last phase it degenerated into fanaticism. The preaching, which now replaced " prophecy," became the regular function of the bishop ; and in it " were fused together, on the one hand, teaching,—that is, the tradition and exposition of the sacred books and of the received doctrine ; and, on the other hand, exhortation,—that is, the endeavour to raise men to a higher level of moral and spiritual life." Not depending as did prophecy on " inspiration," but on

[1] Pp. 100, 101.　　　　　[2] 1 Co 2[4. 5].

natural aptitude, developed by training and practice, it could be efficiently discharged by a permanent official, and came gradually to be limited to the official class. (2) The form of the *homily*, the term applied to this combination of instruction and exhortation, was taken from the sophists; and Christian preachers, in their methods, followed the example thus set them. The term itself,

"which was unknown in this sense in pre-Christian times, and which denoted the familiar intercourse and direct personal addresses of common life," was gradually superseded "by the technical terms of the schools—discourses, disputations, or speeches" ($\delta\iota\alpha\lambda\acute{e}\xi\epsilon\iota\varsigma$, disputations).[1] Even the external circumstances became similar. "The preacher sat in his official chair: it was an exceptional thing for him to ascend the reader's *ambo*, the modern 'pulpit'; the audience crowded in front of him, and frequently interrupted him with shouts of acclamation. The greater preachers tried to stem the tide of applause which surged round them: again and again Chrysostom begs his hearers to be silent; what he wants is, not their acclamations, but the fruits of his preaching in their lives."[2]

The quotation which Dr. Hatch gives from one of the sermons of Chrysostom, in illustration of this point, has so permanent an interest that it must be reproduced in full:

"There are many preachers who make long sermons: if they are well applauded, they are as glad as if they had obtained a kingdom; if they bring their sermon to an end in silence, their despondency is worse, I may almost say, than hell. It is this that ruins churches, that you do not seek to hear sermons that touch the heart, but sermons that will delight your ears with their intonation and the structure of their phrases, just as if you were listening to singers and lute-players. And we preachers humour your fancies, instead of trying to crush them. We act like a father who gives a sick child a cake or an ice, just because he asks for it, and takes no

---

[1] Hatch, *op. cit.*, pp. 108–109. We may recall Dr. Parker's definition of preaching as "dignified conversation."

[2] *Op. cit.*, p. 110. A modern parallel may be mentioned. The Rev. Dr. (now Sir) George Adam Smith rebuked an outburst of applause with the words, "We do not applaud, but obey, the Word of the Lord."

pains to give him what is good for him; and then when the doctors blame him, says, ' I could not bear to hear my child cry.' . . . That is what we do when we elaborate beautiful sentences, fine combinations and harmonies, to please and not to profit, to be admired and not to instruct, to delight and not to teach you, to go away with your applause in our ears, and not to better your conduct. Believe me, I am not speaking at random : when you applaud me as I speak, I feel at the moment as it is natural for a man to feel. I will make a clean breast of it. Why should I not ? I am delighted and overjoyed. And then when I go home and reflect that the people who have been applauding me have received no benefit, and indeed that whatever benefit they might have had has been killed by the applause and praises, I am sore at heart, and lament and fall to tears, and I feel as though I had spoken altogether in vain, and I say to myself, What is the good of all your labours, seeing that your hearers don't want to reap any fruits out of all that you say ? And I have often thought of laying down a rule absolutely prohibiting all applause, and urging you to listen in silence." [1]

Mutatis mutandis this passage exposes a constant peril of the Christian preacher, and shows that not only the forms, but even the spirit and purpose, of *pagan sophistic* had got into the Christian Church :

" Christian preachers, like the Sophists, were sometimes peripatetic; they went from place to place, delivering their orations and making money by delivering them." [2]

Thus was preaching prostituted to the base pursuit of fame and wealth. We must not exaggerate the evil, and suppose that all Christian preaching sank so low ; there were many good and godly men who, even in using the same forms of preaching, were seeking to serve the Lord alone.

II.

1. Preaching was a part of the public worship of the Christian Church, of which Justin Martyr, about 140 A.D., gives us an account :

" On Sunday, a meeting of all, who live in the cities and

---

[1] *Op cit.*, p. 111. [2] P. 112.

villages, is held, and a section from the Memoirs of the
Apostles (the Gospels) and the writings of the Prophets (the
Old Testament) is read, as long as the time permits. When
the reader has finished, the president, in a discourse, gives an
exhortation (τὴν νουθεσίαν καὶ παράκλησιν) to the imitation
of these noble things. After this we all rise in common
prayer. At the close of the prayer, as we have before
described (chapter 65), bread and wine with water are
brought. The president offers prayer and thanks for them,
according to the power given him, and the congregation
responds the Amen. Then the consecrated elements are
distributed to each one, and partaken, and are carried by the
deacons to the houses of the absent. The wealthy and the
willing then give contributions according to their free will,
and this collection is deposited with the president, who
therewith supplies orphans and widows, poor and needy,
prisoners and strangers, and takes care of all who are in
want. We assemble in common on Sunday, because this is
the first day, on which God created the world and the light,
and because Jesus Christ our Saviour on the same day rose
from the dead, and appeared to his disciples." [1]

This was the setting of the Christian preaching within the
Church.

2. Outside of the New Testament, the oldest Christian
homily which has come down to us is the so-called *Second
Epistle of Clement*,[2] which may be taken to represent the
transition from " prophesying " to " preaching."

"The work known as the Second Epistle of Clement,"
says Hatch, "is perhaps a representative of the form which
it (prophesying) took in the middle of the second century;
but though it is inspired by a genuine enthusiasm, it is
rather more artistic in its form than a purely prophetic
utterance is likely to have been." [3]

Its form is not borrowed from the rhetorical schools, but

---

[1] *Apol.* i. c. 67, quoted by Schaff, *Ante-Nicene Christianity*, pp. 223,
224. See Ante-Nicene Christian Library, vol. ii. 65-66.

[2] Lightfoot's *S. Clement of Rome*, Appendix, 378-390 ; or Ante-Nicene
Christian Library : *Recently Discovered MSS*, pp. 251-256; or *The Apostolic
Fathers*, pt. i., in *The Ancient and Modern Library of Theological Litera-
ture*, pp. 195-204.

[3] *Op. cit.*, p. 106.

appears to resemble the kind of speech in which Stoic teachers gave their practical instructions. Its pervading enthusiasm, of which Hatch speaks, rises to eloquence only in the opening passage, in which he states the motive of Christian living:

"that we ought to entertain a worthy opinion of our salvation, and to do the utmost that in us lies to express the value we put upon it, by a sincere obedience to our Saviour Christ and His Gospel."[1]

Ro 12[1] might have served as the text; but the Pauline tone in the beginning is not maintained throughout the sermon: the moralist, and even legalist, rather than the evangelical spirit prevails. The call to live well is enforced by prudential considerations, the reward or the punishment of the future life. The need of repentance is insisted on. A peculiar argument for sexual purity is advanced:

" If we say that the flesh is the Church, and the spirit is Christ, then verily he who hath dishonoured the flesh hath dishonoured the Church: such an one, therefore, shall not be a partaker of the spirit which is Christ."[2]

The teaching about fasting is so unevangelical in tone, that Bishop Lightfoot conjectures some corruption of the text. There is an evident reference to a similar statement in Tob 12[8, 9]; and it is possible that the preacher's words have been assimilated to that. Be that as it may, the passage runs as follows:

"Beautiful is almsgiving, even as repentance from sin. Better is Fasting than Prayer, but Almsgiving is better than both. *Love covereth a multitude of sins.* But prayer out of a good conscience delivereth from death. Blessed is every one that in these things is found full, for almsgiving removeth the burden of sin."[3]

The sermon rises again to a higher note in the closing ascription:

[1] The analysis of the sermon in *The Apostolic Fathers*, part i. p. 193.
[2] *The Apostolic Fathers*, part i. p. 202.
[3] Pp. 202–203.

"To the only God invisible, Father of truth, who sent forth to us the Saviour and Prince of incorruption, by whom also He made known to us the truth and the heavenly life, to Him be glory for ever and ever. Amen." [1]

3. A rapid development of the art of preaching is indicated by a sermon, " In Sanctam Theophaniam," which is ascribed to Hippolytus [2] (died 235), and which, if it is indeed his, justifies Eusebius' description of him as $\dot{a}v\dot{\eta}\rho$ $\lambda\delta\gamma\iota os$, and offers an interesting proof of the use of Greek in the worship of the Roman congregation in the earliest centuries. While it is very loosely attached to the passage which was read before it, Mt 3[13-17], it shows unity and progress in its structure; and is an excellent example of rhetorical art. While it does not, as the title indicates, refer to the feast of Epiphany, in its praise of and invitation to Baptism, it points to an approaching celebration of the rite, and so may be placed before Easter or Whitsuntide.[3] With many analogies, showing an appreciation of nature, it magnifies beyond measure the worth of water, to which so exalted a function is assigned. A brief passage to illustrate the rhetorical quality of this sermon may be quoted:

"Very good are all the works of our God and Saviour. . . . And what more requisite gift, again, is there than the element ($\phi\acute{v}\sigma\epsilon\omega s$) of water? For with water all things are washed and nourished, and cleansed and bedewed. Water bears the earth, water produces the dew, water exhilarates the vine, water matures the corn in the ear, water ripens the grape-cluster, water softens the olive, water sweetens the palm-date, water reddens the rose and decks the violet, water makes the lily bloom with its brilliant cups. . . . There is also that which is more honourable than all—the fact that Christ, the Maker of all, came down as the rain (Hos vi. 3) and was known as a spring (John iv. 14), and diffused Himself as a river (John vii. 38), and was baptized in the Jordan (Mat iii. 13). For you have just heard how Jesus came to John, and was baptized by him in

---

[1] P. 204.   [2] See Ante-Nicene Library, vol. ix. pp. 80–87.
[3] See HLH, p. 8.

the Jordan. Oh things strange beyond compare! How should the boundless River (Ps xlvi. 4) that makes glad the city of God have been dipped in a little water! The illimitable Spring that bears life to all men, and has no end, was covered by poor and temporary waters! He who is present everywhere, and absent nowhere—who is incomprehensible to angels and invisible to men—comes to the baptism according to His own good pleasure. When you hear these things, beloved, take them not as if spoken literally, but accept them as presented in a figure (œconomically)."[1]

Here we get a glimpse of the preacher's exegesis and theology as well.

4. Although not usually mentioned among preachers, *Justin Martyr*, who died about 166, deserves notice, not only for his own worth, but also because he is a proof, as is also Origen, that preaching was not as yet rigidly confined to the clergy, and is a conspicuous instance of the apologetic activity of the Church. He remained a layman, and yet none of his contemporaries rendered as great a service to the Christian cause as he did. His spirit is shown in his words:

" Every one who can preach the truth and does not preach it, incurs the judgment of God."

Having found in Christ what he had vainly sought in the philosophies of his age, he nevertheless after his conversion retained the philosopher's cloak, and so found easier access to the philosophical circles, in which he ever sought to witness for Christ. From his *First* and *Second Apologies* we may infer how in conversation and discourse he defended his fellow-Christians against heathen calumnies and persecutions, and sought justice for them. His *Dialogue* shows the line of argument from prophecy which he took against Jewish objections :

" In his *Apologies* he speaks like a philosopher to philosophers; in the *Dialogue* as a believer in the Old Testament, with a son of Abraham. The disputation lasted two days, in a gymnasium just before a voyage of Justin, and turned

---

[1] See Ante-Nicene Library, vol. ix. pp. 80, 81.

chiefly on two questions, how the Christians could profess to serve God, and yet break His law, and how they could believe in a human Saviour who suffered and died. Trypho, whom Eusebius calls 'the most distinguished among the Hebrews of his day,' was not a fanatical Pharisee, but a tolerant and courteous Jew, who evasively confessed at last to have been much instructed, and asked Justin to come again, and to remember him as a friend." [1]

Justin was unwearied in his labours for the Gospel, and travelled far and wide as an evangelist; and at last in Rome suffered martyrdom. He is a notable instance of one who not only sought to edify the Church, but also to convert the world.

5. In the North African Church a distinctive type of preaching is represented by *Tertullian* (born about 150, and died 220 or 240). Although no sermon of his has been preserved, yet his writings enable us to represent to ourselves the force and fire of his speech. He knew no compromise with the world and its wisdom in his passionate devotion to Christianity. If he was sometimes carried away in violence of speech against error or sin, he could also among his brethren strike the tender, humble note. In his *Apologeticus* he gives us a glimpse into the Christian assembly :

" We assemble to read our sacred writings, if any peculiarity of the times makes either fore-warning or reminiscence needful. However it be in that respect with the sacred words, we nourish our faith, we animate our hope, we make our confidence more stedfast; and no less by inculcations of God's precepts we confirm good habits." [2]

There can be little doubt that he was able in all these ways to edify his brethren. To North Africa also belonged *Cyprian* (born about 200, if not earlier; martyred Sept. 14, 258). So far as we are warranted in inferring his style of preaching from his writings, his language was more polished and accurate than Tertullian's; in both the Latin

---

[1] Schaff's *Ante-Nicene Christianity*, p. 718. See Ante-Nicene Library, vol. ii., *The Writings of Justin Martyr*, pp. 1–278.

[2] The Ante-Nicene Library, *Writings of Tertullian*, i. 118.

of North Africa shows a tendency to extravagance and artificiality. But in his Epistle to Donatus he mentions the need of a simple and undecorated style in the preaching of the Gospel.[1]

6. The dominant purpose of *Origen* (born 185, died 253 or 254) was the exposition of the Scriptures, that he might exhibit in them a wisdom surpassing the philosophy of the Greeks. His method was that of allegorising. He found all Christian truth in the Old Testament no less than in the New. He maintained that as the literal sense of the Scriptures was often unworthy of God, and impracticable for man, a deeper meaning must be sought. Besides the *somatic* (literal or historical) meaning he discovered a *psychic* (doctrinal and practical), and beyond that even a *pneumatic* (mystical or speculative) sense.[2] But in spiritualising as he believed the letter of Scripture, he put into it "all sorts of foreign ideas and irrelevant fancies."

In his exegetical works we are here concerned only with his *Homilies* (ὁμιλίαι), "hortatory or practical applications of Scripture for the congregation. They were delivered extemporaneously, mostly in Cæsarea in the latter part of his life, and taken down by stenographers. They are important also to the history of pulpit oratory. But we have them only in part, as translated by Jerome and Rufinus, with many unscrupulous retrenchments and additions, which perplex and are apt to mislead investigators."[3]

In spite of this allegorical method the sermons do often exhibit a fine moral and spiritual insight. A specimen of Origen's method may be given from his sermon on Jer 16[16], which has the added interest, that it describes the two ends of preaching, the converting of sinners, and the edifying of saints. Connecting with the prophetic passage the call of the disciples to become fishers of men as recorded in Matthew's Gospel, he works out the analogy in detail:

[1] See HLH, p. 9; DHPI, p. 58; KLP, p. 100.
[2] See Schaff's *Ante-Nicene Christianity*, vol. ii. p. 521.
[3] *Op. cit.*, p. 795.

"Thou hast come up from the sea, falling into the nets of the disciples of Jesus: coming forth thou changest thy soul, thou art no longer a fish, passing thy time in the briny waves of the sea; but at once thy soul changes, and is transformed, and becomes something better and diviner than it formerly was. . . . And being thus transformed, the fish that is caught by the fishers of Jesus, leaving the haunts of the sea makes his haunts in the mountains, so that he no longer needs the fishers who bring him up from the sea, but those second ones, such as are called hunters, who hunt from every mountain and every hill. Thou, therefore, having come up from the sea, forget it, come up upon the mountains, the prophets, and upon the hills, the righteous, and make there thy haunts, in order that after these things, when the time of thy departure is at hand, the many hunters may be sent forth, other than the fishers. But who could these be but those who have been appointed for the purpose of receiving the souls that are in the hills, that are no longer lying below. And see if the prophet has not mystically called out, saying these things, and offering this thought, when he says, 'Behold I send many fishers, saith the Lord, and they shall fish them; and afterwards I will send many hunters, and they shall hunt them upon every mountain, and upon every hill.'" [1]

III.

1. The victory of Christianity over paganism in the fourth century resulted in so great a change in the character of the congregations in the Christian Churches that the purpose, content, and method of preaching were necessarily affected. While outwardly more powerful, the Church was inwardly less pure. A multitude, only partially influenced in thought and life by the Christian Gospel, now pressed into the Church, and so needed to be disciplined in Christian faith and morals. To so mixed a congregation the Christian preacher had to address

[1] Quoted in DHPI, pp. 53-54. See *Origenis Opera Omnia*, ed. Caroli Delarue, *Tom Tertius*, pp. 227-228. The Writings of Origen have been in part translated in the Ante-Nicene Christian Library, vols. x. and xxiii. Edinburgh, 1869-1872.

himself, not only expounding and enforcing Christianity, but also exposing and attacking pagan superstition and corruption. It was a stern warfare, which had to be bravely and steadily waged.

(1) In order to be influenced, however, the people had to be attracted by the preacher. Hence he was tempted to prostitute his sacred calling to secure popularity. In the Greek-speaking congregations there was a keen taste for rhetoric, and the Christian preachers had to compete with the Sophists, who have already been spoken of. This tendency was confirmed by the education of the clergy, in which instruction in the art of rhetoric had had a large place. It was inevitable that Christian preaching should be more and more affected by the popular demand, and the clerical aptitude for rhetorical display. In a genuinely and intensely Christian personality the art was subordinated to the purpose of Christian preaching ; but men of shallower experience and weaker character became the slaves rather than the masters of the tool thus put into their hands. It is a proof of the cleansing and renewing power of the Christian faith that the pulpit of that age was not more secularised even than it was. This dangerous tendency is seen at its worst in one class of pulpit discourse, panegyrics of the living, in which fulsome flattery breaks all bounds of Christian judgment.

(2) One of the greatest safeguards against this peril was the close connection still maintained between the reading of the Scriptures and the sermon. In spite of the elaboration of the liturgy, the lesson kept its place in public worship, and a fixed selection of passages, called *pericopes*, was gradually introduced. While the sermon might be based on the pericope, it was not bound to it. Some of the great preachers, such as Chrysostom and Augustine, dealt with whole books in consecutive portions. On a festival, an appropriate or customary text was chosen. Despite the allegorical method of interpretation, and the rhetorical forms of the sermons, the moral and religious wealth of the Scriptures preserved Christian preaching

from the artificiality and futility into which it might have fallen.

(3) Unless in the homilies, where a verse-by-verse exposition of a portion of Scripture was given, sermons assumed a more definite form, a theme gave unity to the whole. Doctrinal and practical problems came to be discussed. At the great festivals, the sermon was necessarily closely connected with the Scripture record of the event being celebrated ; but even here the Greek orators allowed themselves to be less controlled by the details of the narrative than did Augustine. The reading of the records of martyrdom on saints' days, combined with a panegyric, further loosened the connection of the sermon with the Scripture lesson. If we may apply a modern distinction, preaching tended to become less expository and more topical. The Old Testament receded and the New Testament advanced in favour with preachers. The prophets and the psalms were still preached on in the current Christian interpretation. In contrast with the cosmology of paganism, the record of the Creation received attention. Some of the Old Testament stories still attracted, and the Old Testament types of Christ were diligently sought after ; but the Four Gospels held the first place, and the Epistles the second, in preaching.

(4) The Scriptures, however, did not alone give the content to sermons. It was the age of the Christological controversies, and preachers sought in their sermons to justify from the Scriptures the theological views which they themselves held. While a distinct confession of the faith of the Church is desirable, and its exposition and defence in the pulpit are legitimate, there is always the peril that moral and religious interests may be sacrificed to dogmatic, and that the manifold wealth of the Scriptures may not be adequately used for the enrichment of Christian experience and character. In the East especially there was an undue prominence of the controversial theological interest. While in the disputes about the person of Christ vital religious interests were involved, yet

the conception of salvation which dominated Greek thought detached Christ's work, and so His person also, from the essential moral interests. The quasi-physical deification of man, for which the Son of God was represented as having assumed human nature, was unrelated to holy living. Morality was conceived in the legal rather than in the evangelical way, and so the sermons on Christian morals did not magnify divine grace in asserting human duty, as Augustine did. In the East the extremes of genuine eloquence and artificial rhetoric were both found. In the West much less value was attached to oratory by preachers or hearers ; and it is recorded that some bishops had the doors closed, so as to prevent the departure of most of the congregation before the sermon.[1]

2. Great as were the services of Athanasius (296–372) to Christian truth, we know too little of him as a preacher to deal with him as such.[2] The three theologians who formulated the orthodox doctrine of the Trinity in the East were also noted preachers, and of their powers we have abundant evidence. (1) Of *Basil the Great of Cæsarea* (330–379), Van Oosterzee's estimate deserves quotation :

" Apart from the consideration of his excellent character and his ceaseless zeal in the defence of the orthodox Christology, he shines as an ecclesiastical orator especially, by the rare purity of his style and diction, animation of delivery, vivacity of conception, and abundance of manifold knowledge, as well of the human heart as of the nature around him. Of the last kind of knowledge, instances are to be found in his renowned Nine Homilies on the six-days' work of creation (*Hexaemeron*) ; of the other in his four-and-twenty discourses on moral subjects. . . . Basil shines even more by the magnificent and nervous character of his preaching than by its softness and tenderness."[3]

(2) The introduction and the conclusion of the second Homily in the *Hexaemeron* may be quoted as illustrating the structure of his sermons as well as his style :

---

[1] See HLH, pp. 11–15 ; DHPI, p. 60 f. ; KLP, pp. 73–80.
[2] Horne, *op. cit.*, pp. 113–129, deals with Athanasius as an instance of the royalty of the pulpit.   [3] OPT, p. 93.

"In the few words (Gn 1¹) which have occupied us this morning we have found such a depth of thought that we despair of penetrating further. If such is the forecourt of the sanctuary, if the portico of the temple is so grand and magnificent, if the splendour of its beauty thus dazzles the eyes of the soul, what will be the holy of holies? Who will dare to try to gain access to the innermost shrine? Who will look into the secrets? To gaze into it is indeed forbidden us, and language is powerless to express what the mind conceives. However, since there are rewards, and most desirable ones, reserved by the just Judge for the intention alone of doing good, do not let us hesitate to continue our researches. Although we may not attain to the truth, if, with the help of the Spirit, we do not fall away from the meaning of Holy Scriptures, we shall not deserve to be rejected, and, with the help of grace, we shall contribute to the edification of the Church of God."

Then follows an exposition of Gn 1²⁻⁵ clause by clause. The conclusion is suggested by the last clause discussed:

"But whilst I am conversing with you about the first evening of the world, evening takes me by surprise and puts an end to my discourse. May the Father of the true light, Who has adorned day with celestial light, Who has made to shine the fires which illuminate us during the night, Who reserves for us in the peace of a future age a spiritual and everlasting light, enlighten your hearts in the knowledge of truth, keep you from stumbling, and 'grant that you may walk honestly as in the day.' Thus shall you shine as the sun in the midst of the glory of the saints, and I shall glory in you in the day of Christ, to Whom belong all glory and power for ever and ever. Amen."[1]

3. His funeral sermon was preached by his friend, Gregory Nazianzen (330–390), who, in spite of inferior natural gifts and unfavourable circumstances, to his own surprise, won a commanding position as a preacher in securing the triumph of orthodoxy. (1) The secret of his combined power and charm may be found in his own confession:

"My only affection was eloquence, and long did I apply

---

[1] *Nicene and Post-Nicene Fathers*, vol. viii. pp. 58 and 65. Oxford, 1895.

myself to it with all my might; but I have laid it down at the feet of Christ, and subjugated it to the great word of God." [1]

His rhetorical art is best shown in his sermons on special occasions, but the defects of that art are also there betrayed—extravagance, artificiality, prolixity. (2) A sample of his style may be given from his eulogy on his friend Basil:

"Should we even pursue this inquiry, who, so far as my knowledge extends—and my acquaintance with him has been most intimate—who was so delightful as Basil in company? Who was more graceful in narration? Who more delicate in raillery? Who more tender in reproof, making neither his censure harshness, nor his mildness indulgence, but avoiding excess in both, and in both following the rule of Solomon, who assigns to everything its season? But what is all this compared with his extraordinary eloquence and that resistless might of his doctrine, which has made its own the extremities of the globe? We are still lingering about the base of the mountain, as at great distance from its summit. We still push our bark across the strait, leaving the broad and open sea. For assuredly, if there ever was, or ever shall be, a trumpet, sounding far out upon the air, or a voice of God encompassing the world, or some unheard of and wondrous shaking of the earth, such was his voice, such his intellect, as far transcending that of his fellows as man excels the nature of the brute. Who more than he purified his spirit, and thus qualified himself to unfold the Divine oracles? Who, more brightly illuminated with the light of knowledge, has explored the dark things of the spirit, and, with the aid of God, surveyed the mysteries of God? And who has possessed a diction that was a more perfect interpreter of his thoughts? Not with him, as with the majority, was there a failure, either of thought sustaining his diction, or of language keeping pace with thought; but, alike distinguished in both, he shewed himself as an orator throughout, self-consistent and complete." [2]

---

[1] OPT, p. 94.
[2] CME, vi. p. 301. See *Nicene and Post-Nicene Fathers*, vii. p. 417.

4. The younger brother of *Basil, Gregory of Nyssa* (*c.* 335-395), although inferior as a preacher, must also be mentioned. (1) He was so great a lover of oratory, that for a time he forsook the service of the Church for the study of rhetoric, but on his return made the art he had acquired so effective in the defence of orthodoxy that immense crowds were attracted by his preaching. In moral and religious insight, as well as fineness of feeling, he was not the equal of either his brother or their common friend. He often falls into irrelevancy and oratorical display, although his intellectual powers were conspicuous. In his fifteen *Homilies* on *The Song of Songs* he not only employs the allegorical method, but in his introduction expressly justifies it in opposition to the Antiochian school, which insisted on the literal interpretation.

(2) A sample may be given from his sermon on the Baptism of Christ :

"Abraham's servant is sent to make the match, so as to secure a bride for his master, and finds Rebekah at the well ; and a marriage that was to produce the race of Christ had its beginning and first covenant in water. Yes, and Isaac himself also, when he was ruling his flocks, digged wells at all parts of the desert, which the aliens stopped and filled up, for a type of all those impious men of later days who hindered the grace of Baptism, and talked loudly in their struggle against the truth. Yet the martyrs and the priests overcame them by digging the wells, and the gift of Baptism overflowed the whole world. According to the same force of the text, Jacob also, hastening to seek a bride, met Rachel unexpectedly at the well. And a great stone lay upon the well, which a multitude of shepherds were wont to roll away when they came together, and then gave water to themselves, and to their flocks. But Jacob alone rolls away the stone, and waters the flocks of his spouse. The thing is, I think, a dark saying, a shadow of what should come. For what is the stone that is laid, but Christ Himself ? for of Him Isaiah says, 'And I will lay in the foundations of Sion a costly stone, precious, elect'; and Daniel likewise, 'A stone was cut out without hands,' that is, Christ was born without a man. For as it is a new and marvellous thing that a stone should be cut out of the rock without a hewer or stone-cutting tools, so it is a thing beyond all wonder that an offspring should appear from an unwedded Virgin. There was lying, then, upon the well the spiritual stone, Christ, concealing in the deep and in mystery the laver of regeneration which needed much time—as it were a long rope—to bring it to light. And none rolled away the stone save Israel, who is mind seeing God. But he both draws up the water and gives drink to the sheep of Rachel; that is, he reveals the hidden mystery, and gives living water to the flock of the Church."[1]

5. The greatest orator of the Greek Church, however, was *John Chrysostom*[2] (Golden-Mouth, 347–407) (1) As a fearless preacher of truth and righteousness he enjoyed popular favour, but incurred a hostility in high quarters, which led at last to his death as he was journeying to a distant place of exile. As an exegete he is distinguished by his application of the better methods of the Antiochian school in opposition to the extravagances of the allegorising fashion of Alexandria. As an orator, though not entirely free of the defects of the rhetorical method, in which he had been thoroughly trained by Libanius, his natural gifts were entirely consecrated by his Christian devotion. He set forth his ideal of the Christian ministry in his work on *The Priesthood* (*De Sacerdotio*), in which he reveals the secret of his power as a preacher in the words ἐργαζόμενος τοὺς λόγους ὡς ἂν ἀρέσειε τῷ θεῷ ("let him frame his discourse so as to please God").[2] A passage has already been quoted which shows that he recognised the dangers of popularity, and also how he sought to guard himself against them.[3] He was more concerned about moral purity than theological orthodoxy; and while he was not uninfluenced by the prevalent asceticism, he occu-

---

[1] *Nicene and Post-Nicene Fathers*, v. p. 521. It is interesting to compare this passage with that quoted from Hippolytus, as showing how differently imagination can play about the same subject.

[2] *St. Chrysostom of the Priesthood*, translated by Bunce, London, 1759, p. 301.

[3] See pp. 64–65.

pied himself for the most part with the virtues, which do in reality belong to the Christian ideal. He frankly and boldly attacked the common vices of his age, and showed no respect of persons. Even in public affairs he intervened at some personal risk. As he himself had deeply experienced, so he could with intimate knowledge and delicate insight, present the "inner life" of the Christian. As that life was nourished by, so his theology was rooted in, the Scriptures, of which he had the knowledge of a scholar, having made himself familiar even with Hebrew. He was most skilful in the practical application of the teaching of the Bible; but we do miss a full understanding of the Pauline doctrine of grace. The stories in the Bible appealed to his æsthetic sense, and he used his art to present to his hearers some of the outstanding figures and events in the sacred narratives; but it must be admitted that his art did not always restrain him from excess, and the light and shade are overdone.

(2) His sermons were of two kinds. In his *Homilies* he dealt not only with long passages of Scripture, but even with whole books (Genesis, Psalms, Matthew, John, Paul's letters to Romans, Corinthians, Galatians, Ephesians, Timothy, Titus); excellent as these are both in exposition and application, they lack artistic structure. In his topical (theoristic) addresses ("against the Protopaschites," "concerning the statues," "against the Jews") he has a text, and uses it, but his sermon is not an explanation of it.[1] Nevertheless it is in the second kind of sermon that we can study better the rush of his eloquence. He paid great attention to the introduction, and displayed a wealth of pictures, comparisons, epigrams, observations on life, which arrested attention and secured interest. He could use the incident of the moment most happily to catch the mind of his hearers, as when he turned the attention of his audience, disturbed by the kindling of the lights of the church, to the Light of the World. He usually closed

---

[1] As we shall afterwards try to show, the synthesis of the sermon should be based on the analysis of the text.

his sermons with a doxology. While he possessed the two necessary qualities of the orator, abundance and order, he had more of the first than the second, and sometimes missed his full effect by his lack of moderation.[1]

(3) One passage may be quoted which illustrates his treatment of a vice:

"There is nothing more cruel, nothing more infamous, than the usury so common amongst men. The usurer traffics on the misfortunes of others; he enriches himself on their poverty, and then he demands his usury, as if they were under a great obligation to him. He is heartless to his creditor, but is afraid of appearing so; when he pretends that he has every inclination to oblige, he crushes him the more and reduces him to the last extremity. He offers one hand, and with the other pushes him down the precipice. He offers to assist the shipwrecked, and instead of guiding them safely into port he steers them among the reefs and rocks. Where your treasure is, there is your heart, says our Saviour. Perhaps you may have avoided many evils arising from avarice; but still, if you cherish an attachment to this odious vice, it will be of little use, for you will still be a slave, free as you fancy yourself to be; and you will fall from the height of heaven to that spot wherein your gold is hidden, and your thoughts will still complacently dwell on money, gains, usury, and dishonest commerce. What is more miserable than such a state? There is not a sadder tyranny than that of a man who is a willing subject to this furious tyrant, destroying all that is good in him, namely, the nobility of the soul. So long as you have a heart basely attached to gains and riches, whatsoever truths may be told you, or whatsoever advice may be given you, to secure your salvation — all will be useless. Avarice is an incurable malady, an ever-burning fire, a tyranny which extends far and wide; for he who in this life is the slave of money is loaded with heavy chains and destined to carry far heavier chains in the life to come."[2]

---

[1] See HLH, pp. 21–24; OPT, pp. 95–99; KHP, pp. 65–69; DHPI, pp. 86–93. Many of his sermons have been translated in The Oxford Library of the Fathers.

[2] CME, iii. pp. 309, 310.

IV.

While the East was engaged in the trinitarian and Christological controversies, and preaching was affected by the dogmatic interest, in the West attention was more directed to Soteriology; and so preaching was more evangelical and practical. Begun by Tertullian, advanced by Ambrose, this movement reached its culmination in Augustine, whose influence persisted not only in the subsequent preaching of the Catholic Church, but even through the Reformers in Protestantism.

1. A few sentences must suffice for Ambrose (340–397) [1] before we turn to "the Chrysostom of the West," whose conversion was one of the worthiest fruits of his labours. (1) Dependent as he was for much of his matter on Philo, and especially Basil, Ambrose nevertheless in his sermons, which for the most part were worked up into treatises, displayed a genuinely independent Christian personality, practical, forceful, constant, courageous, with a fuller understanding of the secret of saving grace than was shown by the Greek fathers. One characteristic incident may be mentioned regarding the truly great bishop. When the Emperor Theodosius, who had shed the blood of many innocent persons in Thessalonica, sought communion, the bishop refused with the words:

"How wilt thou lift up in prayer the hands still dripping with the blood of the murdered? How wilt thou receive with such hands the most holy body of the Lord? How wilt thou bring to thy mouth his precious blood? Get thee away, and dare not to heap crime upon crime."

The Emperor was so impressed that he submitted to the bishop's discipline.[2]

(2) Augustine's testimony must be added:

"To Milan I came, to Ambrose the Bishop, known to the whole world as among the best of men, Thy devout worshipper; whose eloquent discourse did then plentifully dispense

---

[1] HLH, pp. 27–28; DHPI, pp. 98–100; KHP, 101–102.
[2] Schaff's *Nicene and Post-Nicene Christianity*, pp. 963–964.

unto Thy people the fatness of Thy 'wheat,' the gladness of
Thy 'oil,' and the sober inebriation of Thy 'wine' (Ps iv. 7,
civ. 15). To him was I unknowingly led by Thee, that by
him I might knowingly be led to Thee. That man of God
received me as a father, and shewed me an Episcopal kindness on my coming. Thenceforth I began to love him, at
first indeed not as a teacher of the truth, of which in Thy
Church I wholly despaired, but as a person kind towards
myself. And I listened diligently to him preaching to the
people, not with that intent I ought, but, as it were, trying
his eloquence, whether it answered the fame thereof, or
flowed fuller or lower than was reported; and I hung on his
words attentively; but with regard to the matter was but a
careless and scornful bystander; and I was delighted with
the sweetness of his discourse, which, as far as concerns
manner, was more learned, but less sparkling and flattering
than that of Faustus. Of the matter, however, there was no
comparison, for the one was wandering amid Manichæan
falsehoods, but the other most wholesomely taught salvation. But 'salvation is far from sinners' (Ps cxix. 155),
such as I then stood before him; and yet I was drawing
nearer by little and little, and unconsciously." [1]

2. We may now turn to Augustine (354—430) himself.[2]

(1) "'If I might leave one bequest,' said Dr. Pusey, 'to
the rising generation of the clergy, who have, what I have
only had incidentally, the office of preachers, it would be in
addition to the study of Holy Scripture, which they too
studied night and day, study the fathers, especially St.
Augustine.' No truer word could have been spoken. There
is something so essentially great and broad about the soul
of a man like this, that, however stormy his life, however
fierce the conflict through which he passed, however intense
the controversies in which he was engaged, we seem to stand
on the mountain-top of truth as we take our place at his
side, with the heaven clear above us and the mists rolling
beneath our feet. Of the other two illustrious Africans, to
whom he stands in direct succession, Tertullian has the
fervour of Augustine without the serenity, Cyprian the
saintliness without the breadth." [3]

---

[1] *Confessions*, v. 13.

[2] See HLH, pp. 28–42; KHP, pp. 103–109; DHLI, pp. 100–104.

Simpson's *Preachers and Teachers*, p. 80. Many of Augustine's
Homilies have been translated in The Oxford Library of the Fathers.

He also stands in the great evangelical succession between Paul and Luther, and so belongs to Protestantism no less than to Roman Catholicism.

(2) Surpassingly great as is his historical importance as a believer, theologian, and churchman, here we can deal with him only as a preacher. Endowed with a great intellect, commanding wide learning of the philosophical schools as of the Holy Scriptures, exercising an extraordinary power of moral and spiritual discernment which reached the secret depths of the human soul, exceptionally skilful in the use of reasoning, a master of language, thoroughly trained in the rhetorical art—all these manifold gifts were the obedient instruments of a passionate, potent personality, developed to maturity by an experience which, through the grace of God, had passed from deepest tragedy to fullest triumph. As an orator he may have been inferior to Chrysostom, and the West cared less for oratory than the East; but if preaching be " truth through personality," [1] he had made his own the truth of the Gospel even more fully than had the other, and his, too, was an even greater personality.

(3) About four hundred of his sermons have been preserved, arranged in four classes—*de Scripturis* (on texts of Scripture), *de tempore* (festival sermons), *de sanctis* (in memory of apostles, martyrs, and saints), and *de diversis* (on various occasions); some he himself dictated, others were taken down by his hearers. Besides these are a series of sermons included in his exegetical works, as on the Psalms, the Gospel of John, the First Epistle of John.[2] of the theology which these sermons contain, it is impossible within the limits which must be here imposed to speak. Of his exegesis, Schaff says :

" Augustine deals more in lively, profound, and edifying thoughts on the Scriptures than in proper grammatical and historical exposition, for which neither he nor his readers had the necessary linguistic knowledge, disposition, or taste.

---

[1] See Introduction, pp. 8, 9. [2] See Schaff, *op. cit.*, p. 1015.

He grounded his theology less upon exegesis than upon his Christian and churchly mind, saturated with Scriptural truths." [1]

As regards the Old Testament, he could read the New Testament out of it by the use of the allegorical method, in accordance with his own saying, "Novum Testamentum in Vetere latet, Vetus in Novo patet." While his conception of faith fell far short of the Pauline idea of personal union with Christ, and did not go beyond a confident assent and submission to the teaching of the Scriptures and the Church, yet he was nearer Paul in his experience of the saving grace of God than any other of all the fathers. He was closely drawn to the Fourth Gospel, both by his philosophical interest in its Logos doctrine, and by its emphasis on love to God and man, so accordant with his own spirit.

(4) His rhetorical art differs from that of the Greeks. His imagery is simple and striking, and he drives his meaning home with fewer strokes.

" One recognizes how well he describes himself when he compared the orator with a man eager for the combat, who wins his cause by fighting with a sword gilded and set with precious stones, not because it is gilded, but because it is a weapon." [2]

He is a master of antithesis and epigram, in which wit and wisdom are conjoined, and delights even in rhyme and assonance. A few examples may be given:

" Vetus homo in timore est, novus in amore " (The old man fears, the new loves). " Præcedet spes, ut sequatur res " (Hope goes first, that fact may follow). " Non vincit nisi veritas, victoria veritatis est caritas " (Only truth conquers, truth's victory is love). " Ubi amor, ibi trinitas " (Where love, the Trinity is). " Deo servire vera libertas est " (To serve God is true liberty).

(5) One of his writings demands fuller notice. In his *De doctrina Christiana* he has left " a compend of exegetical

---

[1] *Nicene and Post-Nicene Christianity*, p. 1015.
[2] HLH, pp. 41–42.

theology for instruction in the interpretation of the
Scriptures according to the analogy of the faith,"[1] in which
he has developed a homiletic theory. In the first book
he shows that a comprehension and exposition of the
Scriptures should be the preacher's end and task ; while
the preacher must aim at edification, he must not neglect
the real meaning of the writers, as such neglect, even
for a practical object, involves the danger of arbitrariness,
and so injures the faith. The second and third books deal
with the principles and rules of exegesis, and show that
Augustine attached great importance to exposition as the
work of the preacher. The fourth book treats homiletics,
especially the theory of pulpit eloquence, which he distinguishes from the rhetoric of the schools. The Christian
preacher must seek the wisdom which will enable him to see
with "the eyes of the heart the heart of the Scriptures ";
and in the Bible itself he can find the examples of wisdom
and eloquence, unlike those of any of the rhetorical schools.
Having grounded his theory on the Scriptures, he next
discusses the conditions of lucidity and intelligibility, and,
following Cicero, defines the orator's task as threefold,
docere, delectere, and *flectere*. He accepts the current distinction of the manners of speech, *submissum, temperatum*,
and *grande*, and quotes Cicero's saying :

"Is erit eloquens, qui poterit parva submisse, modica
temperate, magna granditer dicere." (He is eloquent, who
can speak the small humbly, the middling with measure, the
great grandly.)

While he recognises that the Christian pulpit is always
concerned with the great things, yet he insists that
to avoid monotony the Christian preacher must not be
always talking in the grand style, but must aim at variety.
His experience as an orator appears in his saying :

"Facilius submissum (genus dicendi) solum, quam solum
grande diutius tolerari potest, commotio quippe animi

---

[1] Schaff, *op. cit.*, p. 1011. This treatise is translated in vol. ix. of the
Works, edited by Dods, Edinburgh.

quanto magis excitanda est, ut nobis assentiatur auditor, tanto minus in ea diu teneri potest, cum fuerit quantum satis est excitata." [1]

Corresponding to the three kinds of speech there are three kinds of hearing, *ut intelligenter, ut libenter, ut obœdienter audiatur* (intelligent, willing, and obedient). He himself was a master of the grand style, as he sought to move men deeply and strongly by the great things of the Gospel.[2]

(6) One passage may be quoted as illustrating both his theology and his exegesis. The text is Mt 20^{30}, and this is how he deals with the words, "Jesus passeth by.'

After mentioning many facts of the earthly life which have passed by, he continues his argument: "Now He dieth no more, death hath no more dominion over Him. And His divinity abideth ever, yea, the immortality of His body now shall never fail. But, nevertheless all those things which were wrought by Him in time have passed by: and they are written to be read, and they are preached to be believed. In all these things, then, Jesus passeth by" . . . "Now upon these passing works is our faith built up. For we believe on the Son of God, not only in that He is the Word of God, by whom all things were made: for if He had always continued in the form of God, equal with God, and had not emptied Himself in taking the form of a servant, the blind men would not even have perceived Him, that they might be able to cry out." [3]

V.

1. The preaching of the following centuries was imitative rather than original. While the influence of Augustine was still dominant, emphasis was increasingly laid on good works and ritual observances, and the attachment to the Scriptures was less close. The Greek Fathers exercised an influence in the West, not only in theology,

---

[1] The humble mode of speech by itself can be borne longer than the grand by itself, since the more the emotion of the mind is to be excited, so that the hearer may agree with us, so much the less can it be so kept, when it has been excited enough.

HLH, pp. 29–31.   [3] WGSI, pp. 60–64.

but in a greater tendency to employ all sorts of rhetorical devices in the pulpit. The change in the attitude to the Scriptures, while a gain as regards the form of the sermons, was distinctly a loss as regards the religious and moral worth of the contents. The homily was replaced by the topical (thematic) discourse, already in favour with the best Greek preachers. This tendency was confirmed by the growing attention to the Christian year. The ecclesiastical festivals determined the subjects to be dealt with. As the ritual became more extended and important the sermon (*sermo*) became shorter (*brevis admonitio*) and fell into the background.[1]

2. Of preachers in the West only a few claim mention. *Leo I. the Great* (died 461) illustrates the combination of the influence of Augustine and the Greek Fathers, and also the growing hierarchical tendency. *Peter of Ravenna* (died 451) was so highly esteemed as a preacher that he won the surname *Chrysologus*; but the sermons which have been preserved do not, for our modern judgment, justify that epithet. *Maximus of Turin* (died 465) was noted for his readiness as an *extempore* speaker, and his sermons are interesting for the word pictures they offer of the moral and religious conditions of the period. *Cæsarius of Arles* (died 543) was not only a zealous defender of Augustine's doctrine of prevenient grace, but so slavish an imitator of his style that it is not always easy to distinguish his sermons from his master's, although he falls far short in greatness of personality. *Gregory the Great* (died 604) was distinguished, not so much for intellectual gifts as for his conscientiousness and solicitude in the discharge of his duties as " a shepherd of souls," and for his interest in the exposition of the Scriptures. In his method he does not follow Augustine so much as Origen. His sermon accompanies his text step by step. He is famous also for his treatise *De cura pastorali*, in the third book of which he gives a number of useful practical hints to preachers.[2]

---

[1] See HLH, pp. 42–44; DHPI, pp. 105–114; OPT, pp. 99–102.

[2] See HLH, pp. 44–49; DHPI, pp. 114–129; KHPI, 110–113.

3. As regards the form of the sermons during this period, the following points deserve notice. While the distinction of *homily* and *sermon* is not always maintained, the two types of preaching are the exposition of a passage of Scripture, verse by verse and clause by clause, and the treatment of a subject (the *thematic* or *topical* sermon). The latter, however, had not yet become fully synthetic in structure. An orderly arrangement is, as a rule, found only where the rules of the ancient rhetoric are followed. Digressions and irrelevances are found even in the greatest preachers. Attention was given to the introduction in order at once to secure interest. An illustration or comparison was often used; but sometimes the preacher was content with a reference to the lesson. While in the East the conclusion was invariably a doxology, often quite arbitrarily attached, in the West greater freedom was claimed. Augustine especially shows a great variety in the close of his sermons: sometimes he does end with a call to prayer. While this use of the Amen at the end rests on apostolic practice, it is not allowed to become a mere formality. When it would be inappropriate, neither Augustine nor Leo end with the Amen. The hearers are generally addressed as "brethren," or "my brethren," or even as "beloved." [1]

[1] See HLH, pp. 49–51.

CHAPTER IV.

PRIEST, MONK, AND FRIAR: SCHOLASTIC
AND MYSTIC.

I.

THE outstanding feature of the second period in the history of preaching in the Christian Church is that in it the Gospel was carried to the new nations which rose on the fall of the Roman Empire, and that the common people began to hear the Word of God in their own mother tongue. Irenæus had in the neighbourhood of Lyons preached to the Celts in their own speech; Augustine assumed, however, that the heathen would themselves come, without messengers being sent to them, to listen to Latin preaching; but the Celtic and Teutonic tribes would not have been won had not the more excellent way of vernacular evangelisation been attempted.[1]

1. It was not the Western or Roman, but the Eastern or Greek Church which first sent missionaries to Scotland. (1) St. Rule (Regulus), an Eastern monk, according to the legend, visited St. Andrews in 369 and converted the Picts in the neighbourhood. In 400, St. Ninian, who was of English parentage, after a visit to Rome and instruction from St. Martin of Tours, came to Galloway and built a church at Whithorn, from which as a centre the Southern Picts were evangelised. About thirty years later St. Palladius came from Rome in order to draw tighter the bonds between Scotland and the Western Church. Scottish Christianity became missionary in St. Patrick, who, carried captive to Ireland, preached the Gospel there. The debt

[1] HLH, pp. 52-53.

of Ireland to Scotland was repaid by St. Columba, who gathered around him in the Island of Iona a religious community which did more for the spread of the Gospel throughout Scotland and also the north of England than had hitherto been done. Columba died in 597. His followers, the Culdees, possessed many peculiarities, for the preservation of which they had to contend against Romanising influences; but this interesting story lies beyond the scope of this volume.[1]

(2) We have no remains, however, of the preaching in the mother tongue, but Dr. Ker records that in the Advocates' Library of Edinburgh there is "an old volume which contains the *Instructiones Sancti Columbani*, not of Columba but of a later disciple of his school, who visited France, Switzerland, and the north of Italy, and preached both in Latin and the vernacular. The *Instructiones* are generally brief, giving probably little more than the line pursued . . ."

"There is not much of what we should call profound or fresh thinking, but it is very earnest, very practical, and close up to the condition of the hearers; and it must have sounded fresh enough to the ears of those wild Scots and Picts, who, not long before, had been practising barbarities upon poor provincials whose wailing cries have come down to us."[2]

2. The doubt regarding the genuineness of the sermons ascribed to Columba, which were addressed to monks, and so do not represent his missionary preaching, extends to a discourse ascribed to Gall. (1) To Boniface, whose Anglo-Saxon name was Winfrid (born about 680, martyred 755), the preacher of the Gospel in Germany, are ascribed fifteen sermons, the authenticity of which Cruel has attempted to prove; but his arguments have been met by Hahn. Not quite so doubtful is the judgment regarding the sermons of Eligius (born about 588, died about 658), who was Bishop

---

[1] See Walker's *Scottish Church History*, pp. 3-10; Robinson's *The Conversion of Europe*, pp. 68-84; Macewan's *A History of the Church in Scotland*, i. pp. 1-115.

[2] KHP, p. 53.

of Noyon, and as a preacher laboured for the sound conversion of the baptized Franks, and even reached Flanders
and Friesland.   The sermons are addressed to a constituted
church, and the reference in them to vernacular preaching [1]
shows that this was not the rule, but the exception.[2]   " From
the fragments of his sermons which have been preserved,"
says Robinson—

" we see that he had frequent occasion to warn his hearers
against the observance of heathen customs.   Thus he writes :
' He is a good Christian who putteth not his trust in amu-
lets or inventions of the devil, but placeth all his life in
Christ alone. . . . But, above all things, I adjure you not
to observe the sacrilegious customs of pagans, nor to consult
in any trial or difficulty soothsayers, fortune-tellers, or
diviners, for he who doeth this evil thing forthwith loseth
the grace of baptism.   Let there be amongst you no resorting
to auguries, or sneezings, or observance of the flight or
singing of birds, but rather when you set out on a journey
or undertake any work, sign yourselves in the name of
Christ, repeat the Creed and the Lord's Prayer with faith
and devotion, and no enemy shall be able to hurt you.   No
Christian will take note of the day on which he leaves home
or returns, for all days are made by God.   No Christian
will wait for a particular day or moon before commencing
any undertaking, nor on the first of January will join in
foolish or unseemly junketings or frivolity or nocturnal
revellings. . . . Let no one regard heaven or earth or stars
or any creature at all as deserving of worship.   God alone
is to be adored, for He alone created and ordained all
things.' [3]   In other sermons he portrays graphically the
scene which he anticipates will be enacted at the Day of
Judgment, when those who have despised and rejected
Christ will be condemned to perdition." [4]

(2) The Anglo-Saxons were evangelised by an Augustine

[1] " Rustico sermone vos alloquimur," Mgn. 87. 612.

[2] See HLH, pp. 54–55.

[3] After the quotation this note is added—"See *Vita Eligii*, ii. 16 ;
Migne, *P.L.* lxxxvii. col. 528 f.   The authorship of this sermon is not
certain, and has been attributed by some to Cæsarius of Arles (*ob.* 542)."

[4] *The Conversion of Europe*, by C. H. Robinson, pp. 326–327.   This book
may with advantage be consulted for fuller details regarding the preaching
of the Christian missionaries in Europe.

(not the Church father) whom Gregory the Great was led, in 596, to send by the incident so familiar that it need not be repeated. Augustine's follower, Wilfrith, came into conflict with the Culdees of Iona at Whitby.[1] Montalambert, in his *Monks of the West*, p. 608, makes the following statement:[2]

"It is then to the monks, scattered as missionaries and preachers over the country, or united in the numerous communities of episcopal cities and other great monastic centres, that must in justice be attributed the initiation of the Anglo-Saxons into the truths of religion. . . . They were expressly commanded to teach and explain to their flocks in the vernacular tongue, the Decalogue, the Lord's Prayer, the Apostles' Creed, and the sacred words which were used in the celebration of the mass and the administration of baptism; to expound to them every Sunday, in English, the Epistle and Gospel of the day, and to preach, or instead of preaching, to read them something useful to their souls. . . . From this spring these homilies in Anglo-Saxon which are so often to be met with among the manuscripts in our libraries, and which are by several centuries of an earlier date than the earliest religious documents of any other modern language."

(3) A quotation from Robinson brings before us the occasion, the content, and the effect of one of these missionary addresses:[3]

"In or about 775 an English missionary, Lebuin . . . determined to appeal in person to the Saxons at their annual gathering at Marklum (Markelo) in Saxony, near the R. Weser. Arrayed in priestly garments, with an uplifted cross in one hand and a copy of the Gospels in the other hand, he presented himself to the Saxons as they were about to offer sacrifices to their national gods, who, amazed at his courageous bearing, gave him at first an attentive hearing. The following are the words of his address as recorded by his biographer: 'Hearken unto me, and not so much to me as to Him who speaks to you through me. I declare unto you the commands of Him whom all things serve and obey.

---

[1] KHP, pp. 111–112.
[2] Quoted in DHPI, p. 136. See note 3 for further details.
[3] *The Conversion of Europe*, pp. 383–386.

Hearken, attend, and know that God is the Creator of heaven
and earth, the sea, and all things that are therein. He is
the one, only and true God. He made us, and not we ourselves, nor is there any other beside Him. The images
which ye think to be gods, and which, beguiled by the
devil, ye worship, are but gold, or silver, or brass, or stone,
or wood. . . . God, the only good and righteous Being, whose
mercy and truth remain for ever, moved with pity that ye
should be thus seduced by the errors of demons, has charged
me as His ambassador to beseech you to lay aside your old
errors, and to turn with sincere and true faith to Him by
whose goodness ye were created. In Him you and all of us
live and move and have our being. If ye will truly acknowledge Him and repent and be baptized, in the name of the
Father, the Son, and the Holy Ghost, and will obediently
keep His commandments, then will He preserve you from
all evil, and will grant unto you the blessings of peace here
and in the life to come the enjoyment of all good things.
But if ye despise and reject His most salutary counsels, and
refuse to correct the errors of your wicked heart, know that
ye will suffer terrible punishment for scorning His merciful
warnings. Behold I declare unto you the sentence which
has gone forth from His mouth, and which cannot change;
if ye do not obey His commands, then will sudden destruction come upon you. For the King of all the heavens hath
appointed a brave, prudent, and most vigorous prince who is
not afar off, but close at hand. He, like a most swift torrent,
will burst upon you and subdue the ferocity of your hearts,
and crush your stiff-necked obstinacy. He shall invade
your land with a mighty host, and ravage the whole with
fire and sword, desolation and destruction. As the avenger
(*vindex*) of the wrath of that God whom ye ever provoke,
he shall slay some of you with the sword, some he shall
cause to waste away in poverty and want, some he shall
destroy with the misery of a perpetual captivity, and your
wives and children he will scatter far and wide as slaves, and
the residue of you he will reduce to a most ignominious subjection, that in you may be fulfilled what has long since
been predicted, " they were made few in number, and
were tormented with the tribulation and anguish of the
wicked." [1] " It would be hard," continues Robinson, " to

---

[1] Robinson adds this note—" *Vita Lebuini* ; Migne, *P.L.* cxxxii. col.
888 ff. The life was written by Hucbald of St. Amand (918–976)."

conceive a bolder address or, we must add, one less likely to appeal to the untamed warriors to which it was addressed. . . . We are not surprised to read that the closing sentences of this missionary address were received by the audience with unrestrained anger. . . . It would have fared badly with the missionary had it not been for the kindly intervention of an aged chief named Bruto. . . . His intervention proved effective, and the intrepid missionary was permitted to depart without further molestation."

3. Most of the missionaries were monks, although Eligius of Noyon, already mentioned, was an exception. (1) Within the monasteries themselves there was a good deal of preaching done, instruction and exhortation of the monks themselves by a bishop on a visit, a travelling monk, the abbot himself, or one of the brothers gifted and chosen for the task. To the nuns, the bishop of the diocese, or a monk of the related order, was the preacher. As these sermons were often given while the hearers were at their common meal, they were sometimes called *collations*.[1]

(2) It was in this sphere that the Venerable Bede (673–735) did his work as a preacher; for while he wrote poetry in Anglo-Saxon, his sermons are all in Latin. Their form is the homily, a commentary on some portion of Scripture, sometimes marred by the allegorising method of the time. To him Palmer " ascribes the introduction of the novelty of arranging his sermons according to the seasons of the ecclesiastical year." [2] One of the sermons, entitled the Meeting of Mercy and Justice, illustrates this allegorical method.[3] Its first paragraph runs as follows:

"There was a certain father of a family, a powerful king, who had four daughters, of whom one was called Mercy, the second Truth, the third Justice, the fourth Peace; of whom it is said 'Mercy and Truth are met together; Justice and Peace have kissed each other.' He

---

[1] The use of Latin in the monasteries was a sign of the cosmopolitanism of the church in that age.

[2] KHP, p. 114, note.

[3] CME, i. pp. 345–348. The sermons have not been translated. The best edition of his works is Dr. Giles' (London, 1843–1844. 12 vols.).

had also a certain most wise son, to whom no one could be compared in wisdom. He had also a certain servant, whom he had exalted and enriched with great honour; for he had made him after his own likeness and similitude, and that without any preceding merit on the servant's part. But the Lord, as is the custom with such wise masters, wished prudently to explore, and to become acquainted with the character and the faith of his servant, whether he were trustworthy towards himself or not; so he gave him an easy commandment, and said, 'If you do what I tell you I will exalt you to further honours; if not, you shall perish miserably.'" The servant disobeys, and is handed over to tormentors. Mercy takes pity on him, and pleads for him; but Truth and Justice withstand her; and Peace flees far off. The father consults his wise son, who with Mercy undertakes to solve this problem, and he does. Man is saved, and the sisters are reconciled. "Thus, therefore, by the Mediator of men and angels, man was purified and reconciled, and the hundredth sheep was brought back to the fold of God. To which fold Jesus Christ brings us, to whom is honour and power everlasting. Amen."

4. In the previous period the duty of preaching was for the most part discharged by the bishop; but as his diocese increased in size, it became impossible for him personally to exercise the necessary ministry; parishes were formed and parochial clergy were appointed. This development began in France in the sixth century, was most marked in the ninth, and appears as complete in the tenth century. Thus to the missionary and cloistral preaching was added the parochial. (1) This was generally on a much lower level, as the clergy were often very ignorant, and sometimes even immoral. Efforts at improvement were, however, made; Chrodegang, Archbishop of Metz, in 762 issued his *Regula Canonicorum*; and in the 44th canon required preaching in all the churches in his diocese, twice a month at least, and, if possible, on every Lord's Day and fast day, and enjoined that it should be made intelligible to the people.[1]

(2) But the great reformer of the Church in France

[1] DHPI, pp. 134–135.

and in Germany was Charlemagne. Gregory the Great
had required that every priest should be a preacher, and
the Council of Toledo in 633 had for this end required
a knowledge of the Scriptures. In his *Capitularia*,
Charlemagne showed his concern for the character and
efficiency of the clergy, and especially their capacity as
preachers. In his general admonition of 23rd March 789
he describes himself as

"'a devoted defender and humble helper of the holy church,
. . . reminds the shepherds of the churches of Christ and
the leaders of His flock with moving words of their duty,
with care and unceasing exhortation to lead the people of
God to the pasture of eternal life; he there also indicates
the essential content of preaching briefly and formally in
dependence on the symbol. With emphasis he insists at
the same time in accordance with his interest in the
Christian moral education of the people, that the preachers
should hold before the vicious the eternal torments, and
encourage to virtue by pointing to the kingdom of heaven.
The impression of this sermon-like imperial admonition is
heightened at the close by a solemn prayer, 'Peace to the
preachers, grace to the obedient, and glory to our Lord
Jesus Christ. Amen.'" [1]

The priests were expected to be able to read and explain
the Gospel, and to understand the homilies of the Fathers,
of which they were even encouraged to make liberal use.

(3) Paul Warnefrid, called Paulus Diaconus, was
entrusted with the task of bringing together "the best
flowers out of the beautiful meadows of the Fathers,
that those who were unable to preach might read them."
This collection bore the name of the *Homiliarium*, and the
arrangement followed the Church festivals and seasons.
The passage apportioned for each day on which the homily
was based was called the pericope; and from this in
England as on the Continent the text is often to the
present day selected. As each homily began with the
words *Post illa verba textus*, "after these words of the text,"
sermons came to be called *Postils*; and *postillare* was

[1] HLH, p. 56.

often used instead of *prædicare* in mediæval Latin. The unintended effect of the provision of this crutch was that the clergy ceased to use their own limbs, by being content to read the sermons instead of making any attempt to preach themselves. They became more lazy, ignorant, and incapable. Further, as the homilies were in Latin, the common people did not understand them. The third Council of Tours in 813 A.D. tried to remedy this evil by requiring that the homily should be translated into the vernacular.[1]

(4) Two other contributory causes of the decline of preaching may be mentioned. Even the leaders of the Church were so much in the grip of traditionalism, that they could not hold to the Holy Scriptures the relation of intelligent apprehension and spiritual appreciation which is essential to truly Christian preaching. Although *Alcuin* (died 804) revised the Vulgate, and *Rabanus Maurus* (776–856) wrote commentaries, this defect was not corrected. Superstitions also became more rife in the adoration of saints and relics, and ritualism displaced preaching. Even the reforms of Charlemagne strengthened the hold of the liturgy, and weakened preaching by the dependence on the symbol and the Fathers enforced. Such being the general conditions, it is not necessary to deal in detail with any of the preachers.[2]

5. But the unoriginal and parasitic character of the preaching till the twelfth century may be briefly illustrated. Rabanus Maurus in his *de clericorum institutione* reproduces Augustine's *de doctrina christiana.* While *Haymo* (died 853), his friend, aims at a clear and thorough interpretation of the text, and thus is a fruitful preacher; yet he is always guided by patristic authority, especially that of Augustine and Bede. To the *Homiliarium,* already mentioned, must be added the *speculum ecclesiæ* of Honorius Scholasticus (a German of the early part of the twelfth century), the *deflorationes patrum* of Abbot Werner of Ellerbach (died 1126), the second being, however, dependent in large measure on the first, and the collection made by

[1] KHP, pp. 117–119.   [2] HLH, pp. 58–59.

Florus of Lyons. Honorius has this significance for the form of preaching, that he makes more prominent the *exordium* (introduction) and the *thema* (subject); and that he provides the allegorical method with new material in the ancient mythology. A book, dealing with animals, called the *Physiologus*, which in the early centuries appeared in Alexandria, offered a new source of illustration,[1] which became very popular. Fables and legends attracted the multitude and thus were freely used; the allegorical treatment- tended to be stereotyped. Not till the rise of Scholasticism did the sermon lose its old form as a homily, and assume a more logical structure with distinct and expressed divisions.[2]

II.

1. "He who realizes the living place which preaching, in its most vital forms, has ever taken in the spiritual life of the Church will need no further assurance of its great importance. He will not fail to note that the preacher's message and the Church's spiritual condition have risen or fallen together. When life has gone out of the preacher it is not long before it has gone out of the Church also. On the other hand, when there has been a revived message of life on the preacher's lips there comes as a consequence a revived condition in the Church itself. The connection between these two things has been close, uniform, and constant."[3]

This general statement has a striking illustration in the period of history we have now reached:

"The lowest period in the life of Christianity, and therefore in preaching, was from 800 to 1200 A.D. Thereafter it began to rise, though with many fluctuations, and the revival took different forms in preparation for the Reformation."[4]

---

[1] A Welsh preacher of a former generation had a famous sermon on the Ark, in which many of the animals were "spiritualised"; a like method was applied by a Scotch preacher to the plagues of Egypt.

[2] See HLH, pp. 58–63.

[3] Brown's *Puritan Preaching in England*, p. 7.   [4] KHP, p. 124.

The conditions for this advance can be traced to the eleventh century. The new nations of Europe became more conscious of their own worth, less dependent on the past, and more confident for the future.

The foundations of the intellectual structure in philosophy and theology, which we call Scholasticism, were laid in the labours of Lanfranc (died 1089) and Anselm (1033–1109). The Church was being cleansed, and so strengthened by the reforming work of Hildebrand (1020–1085). A great stimulus was given to thought and life by the Crusades; for not only was the religious zeal of Christendom aroused, but contact with the Saracens, who were distinguished alike in science and philosophy, resulted in a revival of learning: for instance, Aristotle came to be better known, and so to exercise a dominant influence in scholasticism.[1] In 1095 the Council of Piacenza heard an appeal from the emperor of the East, Alexius Comnenus, for support against the Saracens. Although the Pope, Urban II., and the Council lent a willing ear to the request, yet it was only at the later Council at Clermont that the Pope's eloquence awakened the necessary enthusiasm, which then was diffused by the bishops on their homeward journeys. But, while the princes were making arrangements, a multitude of 40,000 men started under the leadership of Peter the Hermit. According to the legend, he saw Christ Himself in a dream, was entrusted with a command to the Pope that all Christendom should be summoned to wrest the Holy Sepulchre from the hands of the infidels, and was then commissioned by the Pope to preach throughout France and Italy to arouse the common people. Into the history of the Crusades it is not necessary to enter, but attention may be called to the part played in them by popular preaching, such as that of Peter.[2]

2. The duty of preaching the Second Crusade in 1146 in France, Italy, and Germany fell to the greatest preacher of this century, Bernard of Clairvaux (died 1153). (1) We

---

[1] DHPI, pp. 182–184; KHP, pp. 121–123.
[2] Kurtz's *Church History*, ii. pp. 14–20.

are not concerned with him as a powerful ecclesiastic or famous theologian, still less as a heresy hunter, but as a preacher. He bears a striking resemblance to Augustine. Not his equal as scholar or thinker, he is often nearer the very heart of the Gospel. While influenced by Neo-Platonism, which came to him through the Pseudo-Dionysius, his piety remained distinctly and intensely Christian; his mysticism was saved from the common peril by his personal passionate devotion to Jesus in His earthly humiliation.

(2) In his sermons on the *Song of Songs* he seeks to lead the monks of his own order into the intimate relation of the individual soul to Christ as the Bridegroom; this analogy has its serious dangers, which Bernard did not altogether escape; for heavenly devotion cannot use the language of earthly passion with entire safety. He has seven sermons on the first verse: "Let him kiss me with the kisses of his mouth." In the eighty-sixth sermon of the series, on which he was engaged for eighteen years, he had reached only the first verse of the third chapter. He has 125 sermons on various subjects, and a great number on the holy seasons; most commonly read are his seven Advent sermons, in which, while expressing his loving joy in the Incarnation of the Son of God, he often betrays a tendency to Mariolatry, which goes far beyond anything to be found in Augustine, as the following sentences show:

"Let us also endeavour to ascend by her to him, who descended to us by her; to come by her into the grace of him, who by her came into our misery. By thee we have approach to the Son, O blessed creator of grace, generator of life, mother of salvation, so that he who is given to us by thee, by thee may receive us." [1]

Yet from the same lips falls the assurance that it is faith which justifies before God:

"It is altogether because of the gentleness, which is preached in thee, that we run after thee, Lord Jesus, hearing that thou dost not spurn the poor, thou dost not treat harshly the sinner. Thou didst not treat harshly the thief

---

[1] See II. Min. 183. 43, quoted in H. H. p. 66.

confessing, not the sinful woman weeping, not the woman of Canaan beseeching, not the woman taken in adultery, not the man sitting at the receipt of custom, not the tax-gatherer beseeching, not the disciple denying, not the persecutor of the disciples, not even those who crucified thee. . . . Thou art as able to justify, as abounding to forgive. Wherefore whosoever, contrite for his sins, hungers and thirsts for righteousness, believes in thee, who dost justify the ungodly, he *also justified by faith alone will have peace with God.*" [1]

It is his apprehension of the love of Jesus in his earthly life, and his surrender of his heart and life to that love, which make him a link in the evangelical succession of Paul, Augustine, Luther, Wesley. His mysticism represented the living piety of the Middle Ages in contrast with ecclesiastical ritualism and scholastic intellectualism.

(3) As regards the form of his sermons, they are not merely a series of comments on the text of Scripture, at least not his sermons on festivals, but aim at a certain organic unity. He even sometimes, at the beginning, indicates the main thoughts and the *divisions* of the sermon, even if in the sermon itself the structure is not made evident. Hering [2] and Dargan [3] give the same illustration from the first Advent sermon: "Diligently weigh the reasons for the coming and seeking, namely, who it is that comes, whence, whither, for what purpose, when and how." The last head he has to postpone for another sermon; the term sermo or speech, and not homily or talk, is therefore applicable. The language is that of the orator, and worthily clothes elevated thought and inspired feeling. Possibly in him we can detect already the distinctive merit of the French genius.

(4) Here is an example of how he preached the Second Crusade:

"If it were announced to you that the enemy had invaded your cities, your castles, your lands; had ravished

---

[1] Sermons on Canticles 22[8] quoted in Latin in HLH, p. 64.
[2] HLH, 66, note 2.
[3] DHPI, p. 212.

your wives and your daughters, and profaned your temples, which among you would not fly to arms? Well, then all these calamities, and calamities still greater, have fallen upon your brethren, upon the family of Jesus Christ, which is yours. Why do you hesitate to repair so many evils—to revenge so many outrages? Will you allow the infidels to contemplate in peace the ravages they have committed on Christian people? Remember that their triumph will be a subject for grief to all ages, and an eternal opprobrium upon the generation that has endured it. Yes, the living God has charged me to announce to you that he will punish them who shall not have defended him against his enemies. Fly then to arms; let a holy rage animate you in the fight, and let the Christian world resound with these words of the prophet, 'Cursed be he who does not stain his sword with blood.' If the Lord calls you to the defence of his heritage, think not that his hand has lost its power. Could he not send twelve legions of angels, or breathe one word, and all his enemies would crumble away in dust? But God has considered the sons of men, to open for them the road to his mercy. His goodness has caused to dawn for you a day of safety, by calling on you to avenge his glory and his name. Christian warriors, he who gave his life for you, to-day demands yours in return. These are combats worthy of you, combats in which it is glorious to conquer and advantageous to die. Illustrious knights, generous defenders of the Cross, remember the example of your fathers who conquered Jerusalem, and whose names are inscribed in heaven; abandon then the things that perish to gather unfading palms, and conquer a kingdom which has no end." [1]

3. For English readers, a special interest attaches to the Anglo-Saxon homilies which have been preserved.[2] Bede's sermons have come down to us in Latin, and so offer no indication of preaching in the mother-tongue. As Charlemagne interested himself in preaching in his empire, so did King Alfred (871–901) in his realm. He himself translated Gregory the Great's book on pastoral theology; and to his reforming zeal are due the collections we have of Anglo-Saxon sermons. They do not show any originality, but a dependence on Latin sermons (Gregory, Bede, and

[1] CME ii. pp. 37–38.   [2] HLH, pp. 67–68.

others). The Blickling Homilies (so called after the place where they were found), edited by Morris for the Early English Text Society (London, 1880), belong to about 971. The homilies of Ælfric, a learned Benedictine monk, known as the Grammarian, and probably identical with an archbishop of York of that name (1023–1051), have been edited by Thorpe for the Ælfric Society, under the title of *The Homilies of the Anglo-Saxon Church* (London, 1844). They are valuable from a linguistic standpoint as " a pure model of the beautiful Saxon mother-tongue, and on that account alone are of the highest significance." [1] One passage from a sermon by Ælfric on the Paschal Lamb may be given :

" That innocent lamb which the old Israelites did then kill, had signification after ghostly (spiritual) understanding of Christ's suffering, who unguilty shed his holy blood for our redemption. Hereof sing God's servants at every mass—

'Agnus dei, qui tollis peccata mundi, miserere nobis.'

That is in our speech, Thou Lamb of God, that takest away the sins of the world, have mercy upon us. Those Israelites were delivered from that sudden death, and from Pharaoh's bondage, by the lamb's offering, which signified Christ's suffering : through which we be delivered from everlasting death, and from the devil's cruel reign, if we rightly believe in the true redeemer of the whole world, Christ the Saviour. The lamb was offered in the evening, and our Saviour suffered in the sixth age of this world. This age of this corruptible world is reckoned unto the evening. They marked with the lamb's blood upon the doors, and the upper posts, Tau, that is the sign of the Cross, and were so defended from the angel that killed the Egyptian's first-born child. And we ought to mark our foreheads and our bodies with the token of Christ's rood, that we may be also delivered from destruction, when we shall be marked both on forehead and also in heart with the blood of our Lord's sufferings. Those Israelites ate the lamb's flesh at their Easter time, when they were delivered, and we receive ghostly (spiritually) Christ's body and drink his blood when we receive with true belief that holy housell (sacrament).

---

[1] Schoell in Herzog, i. p. 185, quoted in DHPI, p. 170.

That time they kept with them at Easter seven days with great worship, when they were delivered from Pharaoh and went from that land. So also Christian men keep Christ's resurrection at the time of Easter these seven days, because through his suffering and rising we be delivered, and be made clean by going to his holy housell (sacrament), as Christ saith in his Gospel, Verily, verily I say unto you, Ye have no life in you except ye eat my flesh and drink my blood." [1]

This sermon is of theological interest, as it was printed and translated in the reign of Elizabeth to prove that, as regards the Supper, the ancient Church of England held the same doctrine as the Reformers. [2]

4. A monastery which gained distinction for the preaching of its monks was that of St. Victor of Paris, founded by William of Champeaux in 1108. The cosmopolitanism of the Mediæval Church is shown in the fact that of the two most famous preachers of this monastery, Hugo (died 1141) and Richard (died 1173), the one was a Saxon and the other a Scotsman. While both were mystics, they combined mysticism with scholasticism, Hugo in a higher degree even than Richard, for, while the second divided the soul's ascent to God into three stages—cogitation, meditation, contemplation—the first divided each of these stages again into two, so reaching six steps, the highest of which was a religious ecstasy above reason. [3] The sermons of both suffer from the extravagances of scholasticism.

III.

1. Of vital significance for the history of preaching is the rise of the mendicant orders, or the friars. When the papacy in Innocent asserted its supremacy at the Fourth Lateran Council in 1215—

---

[1] LELR, pp. 22–23.
[2] Observe in the quotation the qualifying *ghostly* of the reception of Christ's body.
[3] DHPI, pp. 216–218.

"Rome had conquered, yet the victory was gained at the expense of religion, as the innumerable sectaries showed who sought guidance beyond the Church, and listened to a Gospel no priest would proclaim. Heresy was rampant, because the Church had turned from Christ to the world, and her servants had not gone forth into the highways and byways of Christendom, to teach the people the orthodox creed and to lead them into truth. Innocent himself was not ignorant of the perversion of the Church, and when the mendicants appeared and offered, though they were not all priests, to instruct the people in the knowledge of the Bible and the doctrines of theology, he did not seek to crush them, but retained them as obedient servants. Thus it happened that when religion was impotent in the hearts of the people, the friars arose and stirred it into life and strength; and when the Church was a worldly institution, and her priests had departed from the spirit of Christ, these friars devoted themselves to the missionary labour to which He had consecrated Himself. Their ideal was noble, their aim the loftiest, while yet they retained the zeal and piety of their founders; but ere many years had passed after their recognition as Orders, the Church succeeded in binding them to her own worldly uses. Rome profited by their foundation. Her dominion over the ecclesiastics of any land might perish through the combination of a national clergy; but such a combination, she saw, was less likely to be formed if the mendicants who had broken worldly ties acted as her emissaries. Her political power might suffer with the death of the great pope to whom the earth seemed given for a possession; but it might be saved if the mendicants, wandering in all countries, preached the Gospel of papal supremacy. Many were the offices of the friars. They spread throughout the world, filling the seats of learning, attaining ecclesiastical pre-eminence, serving as directors of kings, acting as instructors of the people; now reviving religion, now quickening church life, and preserving for Rome a semblance at least of that power which Hildebrand had sought and Innocent wielded, retaining for her a fragment of that dominion which the one had seen in vision and the other had beheld extending from sea to sea."[1]

---

[1] Herkless, *Francis and Dominic*, pp. 13–15. See also Brown's *Puritan Preaching in England*, pp. 15–27.

Seldom has the power of preaching been proved as it was by the friars.

2. St. Francis of Assisi (1182–1226) is one of the most beautiful, gracious, and attractive figures in the history of the Christian Church. He has been compared with Gautama the Buddha, and there is a close resemblance. While our reverence forbids our comparing him to Jesus, yet few, if any, have followed more closely in the Master's steps than, according to his understanding, did this disciple. At his conversion he resolved to give up everything, and wholly to follow Christ in poverty, humility, and love. Soon after, in the year 1209, Christ called him to preach and heal, without any provision for his needs, even as the Twelve had been commanded to do. At once he obeyed; and, clothed in "the brown woolen gown, tied with a rope," the dress of the poorest, and barefooted, he entered on his mission. He won converts; and, although he had no wish to found an order, yet those who gathered around him, and were sent out by him two and two, soon formed a brotherhood, the rule of which was in the words from the Gospels in which Francis himself had received his call to serve. The relation of the order to the papacy does not here concern us, as our interest is in its preaching and ministry to the people. Even although churches were put at the disposal of Francis, he preferred to preach in the open air to the crowds who gathered around him. His style of preaching was like his surroundings. Although he was not altogether free of the superstitions of the age, a subtle intellectualism or a rigid dogmatism was quite foreign to him, and he preached Christ out of the fulness of his own heart, and called men to follow Christ, even as he himself did.

As the brotherhood grew in numbers, its field of labour widened. It did not confine its labours within Christendom. Syria was visited by brother Elias, and Francis himself tried, although at first he failed, to carry the Gospel to the Mohammedans of the East and Morocco. It is uncertain whether he did reach the Moors in Spain.

Several stories are told about visits he afterwards paid to Moslem lands.[1]

3. At the time heresy was widespread in England, France, Germany, Belgium, Italy itself. Of the numerous sects, united only in their opposition to Rome, only one here calls for mention, the Waldenses.

"Peter Waldo of Lyons, with whose name the Waldensians are associated, seeking to lead the life in Christ, distributed his goods to the poor and began to preach the gospel. Causing a translation of parts of the New Testament, and also of 'Sentences' from the Fathers, to be made, he distributed these by the hands of disciples sent out, two by two, to teach and to preach. Poverty and simplicity of religious ceremony were the distinctive works of the Waldensians. They did not spare the reputation of the clergy, and being subjected to persecution, appealed to Pope Alexander III., who approved their poverty but condemned them for preaching. The time had not come for sanctioning an irregular ministry. A few years later, at the Council of Verona, Pope Lucius III. excommunicated them as heretics. This condemnation, however, did not end their progress." [2]

The Waldensian Church still exists, and is taking a large share to-day in the evangelisation of Italy. It is probable that Francis was not ignorant of and uninfluenced by them in founding his order, which shows many points of resemblance. Probable also is it that Dominic, the founder of the second great order, was led by them, as well as by the more extreme sects, to use preaching in the interests of the Church.

4. Dominic (born 1170 in the Castilian village of Calaruega), as the assistant of Azevedo, Bishop of Osma in 1203, on the return journey to Spain from Rome, was brought into close contact with the heresy prevalent in Southern France. The sect which was most dangerous to the church was the Cathari, called Patarines in Italy and Albigenses in Languedoc. Dominic and Azevedo, laying aside all ecclesiastical state and assuming the guise of

[1] See Herkless, *op. cit.*, pp. 16–38 ; DHPI, pp. 247–252.
[2] Herkless, *op. cit.*, pp. 84–85.

poverty, devoted themselves, despite the indifference of the
bishops, to missionary labours to strengthen the Church,
and to refute, when they did not succeed in converting,
the heretics.   Dominic proved himself a very powerful
preacher, and his life was imperilled, as the heretics
dreaded his influence.   The miracles ascribed to him need
not detain us.   Around him there gathered a number of
men, eager if not altogether capable of sharing his
labours against the heretics.

"With papal permission, therefore, they ordained competent men, wherever they could be found, and thus was
associated, not an Order, but a company to meet heretical
with orthodox doctrine.   While many of the Cathari were
restored to the faith, real progress was slow, since the charge
was constantly preferred that clerics, high and low, were
everywhere disgracing their calling." [1]

The papacy, men said, preferred the sword to the
word as a weapon; and in 1208 the cruel and shameful
crusade against the Albigenses took place.   In this violent
repression there is no evidence that Dominic took any
part, and an early biographer gives this account of him:

"St. Dominic, left almost alone with a few companions
who were bound to him by no vow, during ten years upheld
the Catholic faith in different parts of Narbonne, especially
at Carcassonne and Fanjeaux.   He devoted himself entirely
to the salvation of souls by the ministry of preaching, and
he bore with a great heart a multitude of affronts, ignominies,
and sufferings for the name of Jesus Christ." [2]

It is not proved that he was ever appointed to, or
exercised the office of an Inquisitor, although after his
death the Dominicans (the *Domini canes*, the Lord's
hounds) were most devoted agents of the Inquisition.
One would be glad to think that he wished to use no
carnal, but only spiritual weapons in the fight for the faith.
What is certain is that he did found an order, the
members of which were to be not only popular preachers,
but also learned theologians, a combination which at the

[1] Herkless, *op. cit.*, p. 89.   [2] Quoted by Herkless, *op. cit.*, p. 90.

present day is regarded by many persons as impracticable. On this subject, however, a few sentences may be quoted :

" One significant fact about this thirteenth century movement," says Dr. Brown,[1] " is that while aiming at what some would call mere popular preaching, it allied itself with an enlightened love of learning. The scientific speculative spirit of that time, so far as it was imbued with religious feeling, was powerfully influenced by leading Franciscans and Dominicans. As in the first century the greatest missionary, the Apostle Paul, was also the greatest theologian, so in the thirteenth century the most effective teachers of the people were the most ardent metaphysicians and theologians. Among them we find the great schoolmen of the continent—Albertus Magnus, Bonaventura, and Thomas Aquinas; also the great English schoolmen— Alexander of Hales, John Duns Scotus, and Roger Bacon."

The order of Dominic obtained the papal sanction in 1215 on condition of an alliance with one of the existing orders; and the Rule of Augustine was adopted. The story of the order need not be followed further. Worn out with his labours, and regardless of his health, Dominic died at the age of fifty, in 1221. Ominous as the word Dominican afterwards became, we cannot doubt the founder's true intent.

5. To the Franciscan order belonged the two most famous preachers of their time, Antony of Padua (c. 1195–1231) and Berthold of Regensburg (c. 1220–1272). Antony was born in Lisbon; fired with missionary zeal by seeing at Coimbra the remains of two Franciscan missionaries who had been martyred in Morocco, he abandoned the Augustinian order, and, becoming a Franciscan, sailed for Africa, seeking there martyrdom. Recognising in a serious illness God's leading, he left Africa for Italy, the home of the Franciscan movement. For ten years he preached in Italy with growing fame. For the last two years of his life he exercised his ministry of preaching at Padua. The report runs that sometimes thirty thousand people thronged to hear him, as he preached

[1] *Op. cit.*, pp. 23–24.

in the open air with great power and abundant fruit. No complete sermon of his has been preserved; and, even if any of the outlines of sermons which bear his name are authentic, they cannot reveal to us the secret of his power. While using the allegorical method in the interpretation of the Scriptures, he is guided by the scholastic analytical method of theology in his arrangement of the matter, and illumines his treatment by effective illustrations from the world and the life around him.[1]

6. Berthold of Regensburg (Ratisbon in Bavaria) preached to the common people from Austria to the Rhine and even Switzerland, and northwards to Thuringia and Franconia, for twenty years. He did not in any way oppose himself to the teaching of the Church; but he insisted, without any of the reservations which lowered the practice of the Church, on " true repentance, honest confession, and strict or severe penance," in short, complete satisfaction. While not attacking the absolution of the Church, he was opposed to the sale of indulgences. The sins of greed and meanness, luxury and self-indulgence, he ruthlessly denounced; and the common people heard his attacks on the rich and mighty gladly. But he did not spare the vices of the people; and dealt alike with high and low, rich and poor:

" He has a Bunyan-like power of using quaint similitudes, and can still be read with interest for his parables and comparisons. No church could hold the multitudes that flocked to hear him, and he preached in the market-places and fields to thousands, reckoned by the fifty or the hundred—vague numbers, but telling of the immense popularity of the man, and of the growing desire to listen to Christian truth when presented plainly in the mother-tongue." [2]

Simple and natural as his preaching appeared, a closer scrutiny shows the intention and the method of the trained orator. His lively imagination probably explains his arbitary treatment of the Scriptures. To use a modern distinction, his sermons are not expository but topical; and

[1] See DHPI, pp. 252-256.   [2] KHP, pp. 127-128.

the subject is generally very loosely attached to the text. The divisions, too, are often very fanciful.[1]

7. That the Franciscan order paid attention to the theory as well as the practice of preaching, is shown by the small book of Bonaventura on *The Art of Preaching*. We may place alongside of it the work of Hubert de Romanis, General of the Dominican Order, entitled *De Eruditione Prædicatorum*, of which Dr. Brown gives an account:

"He speaks of preaching as above the mass and all liturgical services. 'For' says he, 'of the Latin Liturgy the laity understands nothing; but they can understand the sermon; and hence by preaching God is glorified in a clearer and more open manner than by any other act of worship.' This work of Hubert's on preaching may be described as epoch-making, appearing as it did after long centuries of comparative silence. It sets forth to the members of the Order the obligation under which they were placed to preach the Gospel; the gravity and dignity of this great work; and the qualifications necessary for its effective discharge. Of all spiritual exercises in which monks employed themselves, preaching was set forth as the highest, and whoever possessed the talent for it, was bound to cultivate it to the utmost. . . . While thus urging the importance of preaching, he also set before the members of the Order the most effective way of doing it, and the best way of making the most of themselves as preachers. 'Though,' says he, 'the talent for preaching is obtained through the special gift of God, yet the wise preacher will do his own part of the work, and diligently study that he may preach correctly.' He warns the brethren against making a mere display of their own ingenuity and eloquence, as, for example, deriving the theme of their discourse from a text altogether foreign to the matter in hand. Such devices, he thinks, are more likely to excite derision than promote edification. As for those who looked more to fine words than true and noble thoughts, they seemed to him to be like people who were more concerned to display their beautiful dishes than to provide food for their guests."[2]

---

[1] HLH, pp. 69–71. The best edition of his sermons is that of Pfeifer, Vienna, 1862, 1880. A translation into modern German was made by Göbel in 1849.

[2] *Op. cit.*, pp. 17–19.

Dr. Brown also mentions a book on preaching by Guibert of Novigentum.

8. The greatest theologian of the Mediæval Age, who is still regarded as the authoritative teacher in the Roman Catholic Church, was Thomas Aquinas (1225–1274); but he too was a preacher acceptable to the people. His preaching is thus described by Broadus:

"Amid the immense and amazing mass of his works are many brief discourses, marked by clearness, simplicity, and practical point. He is not highly imaginative nor flowing in expression; the sentences are short, and everything runs into division and subdivision, usually by threes. But while there is no ornament and no swelling passion, he uses many homely and lively comparisons, for explanation as well as for argument." [1]

Dargan extracts from an English translation of some of his sermons,[2] the outline of two on the same subject and text:

"The Mystical Ship, Matt. viii. 23. Four things are to be considered in this Gospel: (1) The entering of Christ and his disciples into a ship; (2) the great tempest in the sea; (3) the prayer of the disciples; (4) the obedience of the storm to the command of Christ. Morally we are taught four things: (1) To enter into holiness of life; (2) that temptations rage after we have entered; (3) in these temptations to cry unto the Lord; (4) to look for a calm according to his will. The next sermon continues the same subject and shows how a ship symbolizes holiness. I. The Material: (1) The wood represents righteousness. (2) The iron, strength. (3) The oakum, by which leaks are stopped, temperance. (4) The pitch, charity. II. The Form: (1) Smallness at the beginning represents grief for sin. (2) Breadth of the middle, hope of eternal joy. (3) Height of stern, fear of eternal punishment. (4) Narrowness of keel, humility. III. The Uses: (1) To carry men over seas: in holiness we go to honour. (2) To carry merchandise: in

---

[1] *History of Preaching*, p. 106 f., quoted in DHPI, p. 241.

[2] *The Homilies of S. Thomas Aquinas upon the Epistles and Gospels for the Sundays of the Christian Year*, translated by John N. Ashley. London, 1873.

holiness we carry good works. (3) To make war: in holiness we fight against the demons." [1]

It is ingenious and interesting preaching; and this sermon at least would not justify Ker's too sweeping judgment regarding the influence of the *Summa Theologiæ*:

"The preaching founded on it addresses itself to the intellect rather than to the heart or conscience, and to the intellect of the Schools rather than to common intelligence and reason." [2]

His preaching generally was scholastic in content and method, and yet there is evidence that he was popular.

9. During the Middle Ages, scholasticism and mysticism were blended in varying proportions: Hugo and Richard of St. Victor, who have already been mentioned, were more mystical than scholastic; Albertus Magnus and Thomas Aquinas were much more scholastic than mystical. Bonaventura (1221–1274), the "doctor seraphicus," has been described as "the greatest scholastic among the mystics, and the greatest mystic among the scholastics." [3] The outline of a sermon on the Life of Service [4] may be given:

Christ in the Gospel offers us "four very notable things . . . namely, the Cross in the chastisement of our evil natures; His Body in Sacramental Communion; the Holy Ghost in mental unction; the Penny in eternal remuneration." The reasons for taking up the Cross are four: (1) "the irrefutable example of our Lord Jesus Christ"; (2) the "invincible help" of the Lord; (3) the "inviolable privileges of those who bear the marks of the Lord Jesus"; and (4) "a reward that cannot be lost."

The sermon is full of quaint fancies and strained analogies. He developed the mystic teaching both of St. Bernard and the Victorines by the scholastic method of subtle refinements and distinctions, and yet an intensely religious spirit gives life to the dry bones.

10. Bonaventura and his predecessors had moved within the range of ecclesiastical orthodoxy; but in the

[1] DHPI, pp. 241–242. [2] KHP, p. 125.
[3] DHPI, pp. 273–276. [4] CME ii. pp. 149–151.

fourteenth century there appeared what may be described as a speculative development of mysticism.—(1) The first of the succession was Meister Eckhart (died 1327). He started from the conception of God in the Pseudo-Dionysius and borrowed much also from Thomas Aquinas; but he carried out all the logical consequences of the conception of God as undefined and undefinable reality. His speculation, however, was inspired by an intense inward, world-renouncing piety, even as was Spinoza's. His pantheistic expressions sprang out of his passionate desire to escape from self and to be united to God. It is this "inwardness" which attracted many at a time when the religion of the Church had become external and mechanical; many appreciated the piety who could not apprehend the philosophy.[1]

(2) Less speculative and more practical was John Tauler (1290–1361), who influenced Luther in the same way as William Law afterwards influenced John Wesley. At Strasburg he

"filled the immense cathedral with crowds, and preached the Gospel fervently when the black death raged in 1348." He "was strongly influenced by Nicolas von Basel, a Waldense," and used his "wonderful power on behalf of the oppressed, and against the avarice and luxury of clergy and laity, not sparing even the Pope."[2]

The aim of all his preaching is the "unmaking" of man that he may be "made again" in God; and the means he urges is the Cross, by which alone, willingly accepted and submissively endured in imitation of Christ, perfection can be attained. While there is an ascetic aspect in the morality he enjoins, he places love above contemplation: he practised what he preached in ministering to the plague-stricken. While he shows little art as an orator, his speech is vitalised by his spirituality, reverence, and solicitude.[3]

[1] HLH, pp. 71–73.   [2] KHP, pp. 125–126.
[3] HLH, pp. 73–74. The following extract illustrates the inwardness of his piety: "How, children, would a man attain to such a point that the

(3) Less great a personality, but a more poetic and artistic preacher, was Henry Suso (1295–1366), of whose preaching Dargan gives us a suggestive description :

"His soft and sentimental nature made him the idol of the nunneries and of the devout women in all ranks."[1]

IV.

The mystics represent the unconscious revolt of the soul against mediæval religion in the Church : in them we have the first stirrings of a new life. More explicit expression to the "divine discontent" was given by four men, who may be described as heralds of the dawn.

1. The greatest of these was John Wyclif (between 1320 and 1330–1384). (1) He first came into prominence as the champion of national feeling against papal aggression. This made him also the opponent of the mendicant orders, who, as we have already noted, were the zealous servants of the Papacy. With his political and theological activities we are not concerned, but with his preaching, of which he made effective use in this conflict.[2]

outward things should not hinder the inward workings of the soul, that would be indeed above all a blessed thing ; for two things are better than one. But if thou find that the outward work hinders the inward workings of the soul, then boldly let it go, and turn with all thy might to that which is inward, for God esteemeth it far before that which is outward. Now we priests do on this wise ; for during the fast days in Lent we have many services, but at Easter and Whitsuntide we shorten our services and say fewer prayers, for the greatness of the festival. So likewise do thou when thou art bidden to this high festival of inward converse ; and fear not to lay aside outward exercises, if else they would be a snare and hindrance to thee, except in so far as thou art bound to perform them for the sake of order. For I tell thee of a truth, that the pure inward work is a divine and blessed life, in which we shall be led into all truth, if we can but keep ourselves pure and separate, and undisturbed by outward anxieties. . . . By such exercises, with love, the soul becomes very quick to feel God's touch, far more so than by any outward practices of devotion" (*History and Life of the Reverend Doctor John Tauler, with Twenty-five of his Sermons*, translated by Susanna Winkworth (London, 1857), pp. 345–346).

[1] DHPI, p. 280.

[2] His sermons have been preserved both in Latin (ed. Loserth, *Johannis Wyclif sermones*, 4 vols., London, 1887–1890) and English (Th. Arnold, *Select English Works of John Wyclif*, vol. i., 1869 ; vol. ii., 1871). Hering

At Oxford he was noted as a schoolman, "in philosophy second to none, in the training of the schools without a rival"; but "from subtle disputations he passed into politics. He was the brains of the party who sought in Parliament and elsewhere to resist the papal claims. Hitherto reformers had attempted to accomplish their purposes from within, and would have resisted outside interference. Wyclif introduced a new thing into the mediæval world by calling upon the State to reform an unwilling clergy. Next he laboured to effect the revival of religious life by the restoration of simple preaching, 'a humble and homely proclamation of the gospel,' and the distribution to the people of the Word of God. He struck hard at the current methods of the pulpit, the endless logical distinctions and divisions, 'the subtle hair-splitting which the apostles would have despised,' the rhetoric, legends, and poetry which men substituted for the bread of life. Finally, he felt that the souls of men were being sacrificed to an overgrown sacramental system, at the roots of which he struck by his attack on the doctrine of transubstantiation. In all these aspects—Schoolman, Politician, Preacher, and Reformer—Wyclif was the foremost man of his age, the range of whose activities was not less remarkable than the energy with which he pursued his aims."[1]

(2) In this warfare Wyclif used as one of his weapons the Bible, which he had translated from the Vulgate into the language of the people. Although the Church did not condemn the translation, it put hindrances in the way of the circulation; and yet the greater difficulty was the lack of the press to provide abundant cheap copies. This drove Wyclif to adopt another means to reach the people.

---

notes a difference in the character of the sermons. The Latin are thoroughly scholastic in method, and were probably delivered before young theologians. The English represent popular preaching, delivered as recorded, or preserved only in outlines (HLH, pp. 75-76).

[1] Workman's *The Dawn of the Reformation*, vol. i. ; *The Age of Wyclif*, pp. 113-115.

" He had unconsciously copied the methods of St. Francis, and fallen back on the lost secret of the friars. From Oxford, as from Assisi two centuries before, Wyclif, like Wesley four centuries later, had sent out as early as the year 1377 his order of ' poor priests,' who in the highways and byways and by the village greens, sometimes even in the churches, should win the souls of the neglected. These Biblemen were not laymen, as is so often assumed. The silence of Wyclif's enemies is sufficient proof of the contrary; even Courtenay only calls them ' unauthorised preachers,' *i.e.* clerics without a bishop's licence. Some, no doubt, like Wesley's Holy Club, were men of culture, students attracted by his enthusiasm; the majority, especially after his expulsion from the University, were simple and unlettered clerks whom Wyclif's keen eye had detected among his parishioners at Lutterworth—' an unlettered man,' he said, ' with God's grace can do more for the Church than many graduates ' (*Dialogues*, 54). Clad in russet robes of undressed wool, without sandals, purse, or scrip, a long staff in their hand, dependent for food and shelter on the goodwill of their neighbours, their only possession a few pages of Wyclif's Bible, his tracts and sermons, moving constantly from place to place—for Wyclif feared lest they should become ' possessioners —not given ' to games or to chess,' but ' to the duties which befit the priesthood, studious acquaintance with God's law, plain preaching of the word of God, and devout thankfulness,' Wyclif's ' poor priests,' like the friars before them, soon became a power in the land. How great must have been the influence of ' these wolves in sheep's clothing,' as Courtenay called them, is evident from the panic-stricken exaggeration of Knighton, ' that every second man you met was a Lollard.' " [1]

(3) The sermons of Wyclif himself, while inspired by a noble zeal for reform, in their religious quality do not equal those of Augustine or Bernard, nor even the best products of mysticism. The details of the Scripture narrative he makes available for popular edification by the allegorical method. For instance, the seven loaves are the Four Gospels and the three divisions of the Old Testament, the few fish are the New Testament epistles, the people resting on the ground are people humbly disposed to hear

[1] *The Age of Wyclif*, pp. 207–209.

the word of God, the seven baskets of fragments are the sermons with which afterwards the people are to be nourished, the four thousand is the totality of the righteous, which is marked by the four cardinal virtues.[1]

(4) The following passage from a sermon on the Two Fishings of Peter (Lk 5) not only illustrates his method and style, but also conveys his ideas of preaching:

" Two fishings that Peter fished betokeneth two takings of men unto Christ's religion, and from the fiend to God. In this first fishing was the net broken, to token that many men ben converted, and after breaken Christ's religion; but at the second fishing, after the resurrection, when the net was full of many great fishes, was not the net broken, as the Gospel saith; for that betokeneth saints that God chooseth to heaven. And so these nets that fishers fishen with betokeneth God's Law, in which virtues and truths ben knitted; and other properties of nets tellen properties of God's Law; and void places between knots betokeneth life of kind (nature), that men have beside virtues. And four cardinal virtues ben figured by knitting of the net. The net is broad in the beginning, and after strait in end, to teach that men, when they ben turned first, liven a broad worldly life; but afterward, when they ben deeped in God's Law, they keepen them straitlier from sins. These fishers of God shulden wash their nets in this river, for Christ's preachers shulden clearly tellen God's Law, and not meddle with man's law, that is troubly water; for man's law containeth sharp stones and trees, by which the net of God is broken and fishes wenden out to the world. And this betokeneth Gennesareth, that is, a wonderful birth, for the birth by which a man is born of water and of the Holy Ghost is much more wonderful than man's kindly (natural) birth. Some nets ben rotten, some han holes, and some ben unclean for default of washing; and thus on three manners faileth the word of preaching. And matter of this net and breaking thereof given men great matter to speak God's word, for virtues and vices and truths of the Gospel ben matter enow to preach to the people." [2]

---

[1] HLH, pp. 75–77.

[2] LELR, pp. 72–73. Besides the book by Workman already referred to, Carrick's *Wycliffe and the Lollards* (The World's Epoch-Makers) may be mentioned.

2. It is probable that Wyclif's influence was more prominent and potent abroad than at home; for, through the personality of John Huss (1369–1415), the reform movement in Bohemia was decisively affected by his ideas. Huss was so entirely dependent on Wyclif, that he often reproduced his teaching in his very words. His distinction is that not only did he widen the range of his master's influence, but even set the seal of fidelity to his teaching by his death as a martyr. While his advocacy of Wyclif's doctrine involved him in difficulties with his ecclesiastical superiors, what brought down on him the condemnation of the Papacy was his opposition by word and writing to an indulgence granted in 1412 by the pope, John XXIII.

"His most staunch supporter was a Bohemian knight, Jerome of Prague, who had studied at Oxford, and returned in A.D. 1402 an enthusiastic adherent of Wiclif's doctrines. Their addresses produced an immense impression, and two days later their disorderly followers, to throw contempt on the papal party, had the bull of indulgence paraded through the streets, on the breast of a public prostitute, representing the whore of Babylon, and then cast into the flames."

Even after his excommunication

"he spread his views all over the country by controversial and doctrinal treatises in Latin and Bohemian, as well as by an extensive correspondence with his friends and followers." [1]

He did not cease preaching, however great the peril to himself. The Hussite propaganda continued after his martyrdom, and was dreaded by the Church even in the time of Luther. Here is a glimpse into the past, given by a contemporary:

"Once Dr. Martin spoke these words to Dr. Eck, when hard pressed, upon John Huss, 'Dear Doctor, the Hussite opinions are not all wrong!' Thereupon said Duke George, so loudly that the whole audience heard, 'God help us, the pestilence!' and he wagged his head and placed his arms akimbo." [2]

---

[1] Kurtz, *Church History*, vol. ii. pp. 208–209.

[2] Quoted by Lindsay, *History of the Reformation*, vol. i. p. 238.

3. Savonarola (1452–1498), even as Huss, was a martyr for righteousness' sake.   (1) Horne has dealt with him as one of the Rulers of Peoples:

"Three great facts determined the form of his ministry, the shameless corruption in the Church, the open profligacy and sinful luxury of the ruling classes, and the renaissance of art and learning. Savonarola's sensitive temperament was profoundly affected by all these signs of the times. It was his cross to live and bear witness in days when the princes of the Church outvied, in greed and lust and passion, the princes of the State. He was one of many who fled to the cloister as to a sanctuary, to escape the contagion of the plague of immorality. He was driven across the Apennines to Florence by the scourge of war wielded by the merciless hand of an arrogant and ambitious 'Vicar of Christ' who actually died of grief and rage because of the conclusion of peace."

At first the Renaissance affected the pulpit for evil rather than good, as

"it bred affectation of learning. It had its fruit in the scholastic temper and speech. It enriched the artificial orations of windy rhetoricians with obscure and sometimes even obscene illustrations from the classics." [1]

On account of the depraved taste such preaching encouraged, Savonarola at first failed to win popularity. The new learning, however, helped him to understand the Scriptures better, and freed him from bondage to the traditions of the Church ; and yet so absorbed was he by his practical duty of fighting against the evils of his age, that he never found the opportunity to think out for himself a consistent theological position. Rejecting all the art of rhetoric, he at last conquered by his natural eloquence :

"The great moving discourses which swept all Florence subsequently into the cathedral to sit at Savonarola's feet were surprisingly simple and direct and scriptural, but the passion of the preacher expressed itself in the irresistible rush

---

[1] *The Romance of Preaching*, pp. 152–153.

of his flaming sentences which no soul could face and remain unscathed." [1]

The style of his sermons has been criticised as immoderate and too vehement; but they had the merit that many more correct utterances lack, they achieved a great, if not enduring, change in the thought and life of a city:

"No man has ever failed," says Horne, "in the Christian ministry who has inspired a whole people, even for an hour, to aspire to be subject to the sovereignty of Christ." [2]

(2) George Eliot, in *Romola*,[3] gives a description of Savonarola's preaching.

"The sermon here given," it is explained in a note, "is not a translation, but a free representation of Fra Girolamo's preaching in its more impassioned moments."

The conclusion of the sermon and the account given of its immediate effort may be quoted as enabling us to realise more vividly than a prosaic historical narrative could, the character and influence of his preaching.

"'Listen, O people, over whom my heart yearns, as the heart of a mother over the children she has travailed for! God is my witness that but for your sakes I would willingly live as a turtle in the depths of the forest, singing love to my Beloved, who is mine and I am his. For you I toil, for you I languish, for you my nights are spent in watching, and my soul melteth away for very heaviness. O Lord, thou knowest I am willing—I am ready. Take me, stretch me on thy cross: let the wicked who delight in blood, and rob the poor, and defile the temple of their bodies, and harden themselves against thy mercy—let them wag their heads and shoot out the lip at me; let the thorns press upon my brow, and let my sweat be anguish—I desire to be made like thee in thy great love. But let me see the fruit of my travail—let this people be saved! Let me see them clothed in purity; let me hear their voices rise in concord as the voices of the angels; let them see no wisdom but in thy eternal love, no beauty but in holiness. Then they

---

[1] *The Romance of Preaching*, p. 156.   [2] *Ibid.* p. 161.

[3] Book II. chapter xxiv. : *Inside the Duomo.*

shall lead the way before the nations, and the people from the four winds shall follow them, and be gathered into the fold of the blessed. For it is thy will, O God, that the earth shall be converted into thy law; it is thy will that wickedness shall cease and love shall reign. Come, O blessed promise; and behold I am willing—lay me on the altar; let my blood flow and the fire consume me; but let my witness be remembered among men, that iniquity shall not prosper for ever.' During the last appeal, Savonarola had stretched out his arms and lifted up his eyes to heaven; his strong voice had alternately trembled with emotion and risen again in renewed energy; but the passion with which he offered himself as a victim became at last too strong to allow of further speech, and he ended in a sob. Every changing tone, vibrating through the audience, shook them into answering emotion. There were plenty among them who had very moderate faith in the Frate's prophetic mission, and who in their cooler moments loved him little; nevertheless, they too were carried along by the great wave of feeling which gathered its force from sympathies that lay deeper than all theory. A loud responding sob rose at once from the wide multitude, while Savonarola had fallen on his knees and buried his face in his mantle. He felt in that moment the rapture and glory of martyrdom without its agony." [1]

4. In France a reforming spirit was shown by John Gerson (1363-1429), the Chancellor of the University of Paris. While still held fast by the scholastic and allegorising methods of his time, in his preaching he was scriptural, experimental, and practical; and without fear or favour exposed the abuses of the clergy. In one of his sermons he speaks very wisely about the aim of preaching:

"Many believe that sermons should be delivered only that the people may learn and know something that they did not know before. Hence their scornful saying, 'What is preaching to me? I already know more good than I am willing to do!' But these people are in error; for sermons are not delivered for this reason only, that one may learn something, but also for this reason, to move the heart and

---

[1] Prof. P. Villari's *Life and Times of Savonarola* has been translated into English by his wife. It contains selections from his sermons. M'Hardy's *Savonarola* (The World's Epoch-Makers) may also be mentioned.

inclination so that they shall love, desire, and accomplish that which is good. Therefore the apostle desires not so much that one should learn what is in Christ, as that he should be like-minded with him. They, however, who attend sermons only to learn something new are like those of whom the apostle writes, that they are ever learning and yet know nothing." [1]

5. These four men, with a few others, such as Geiler of Kaisersberg (1445–1510), John Veghe (d. 1504), and John Staupitz (d. 1524),[2] held the promise of a better future at a time when preaching had fallen very low in its quality, although it had not lost its influence, but was used very effectively to further the interests of the Papacy, to commend the indulgences on sale, to assail all who were suspected of heresy, and even at times to revive the failing zeal of Christendom against its ancient enemy the Turk.[3] (1) Towards the end of this period some attention was given to homiletic theory by such writers as Henry of Langenstein, Jerome Dungersheim, Ulrich Surgant, and Nicholas of Clemanges. They deal with the *exordium* or introduction, and then the statement of the subject, which is attached either to a text, given first in Latin and then in German, or to the passage, generally from the Gospel, for the day. In the divisions of the sermon the text does not guide, but practical considerations connected with the subject. Even when the text is taken into account, the allegorical method prevents its proper exposition, and the suggestions of the text are seldom brought into any organic unity.[4]

(2) Ker [5] gives a description of the four kinds of preaching which were common : (*a*) Sermons were read from one of the current collections such as the *Gesta Romanorum*, the *Lumen Animæ*, and the *Dormi Secure* ("Sleep at ease"). (*b*) "The more learned preached

---

[1] Quoted in DHPI, p. 333.
[2] See HLH, pp. 80–84 ; DHPI, 334–335.
[3] HLH, pp. 78–80.
[4] See HLH, pp. 84–85, and DHPI, pp. 304–305.
[5] KHP, pp. 142–144.

sermons of a Scholastic type, full of plays upon words and
ridiculous conceits. Erasmus gives an account of one
which he heard from an old theologian who 'looked so
wise that you thought Duns Scotus had come to life again.'
He took the word 'Jesus' as his text, and showed what
wonders it contained. It is declined in three cases, Jesus,
Jesum, Jesu; wherein we have manifestly an image of the
Trinity. Then the first of these ends in *s*, the second
in *m*, the third in *u*; which is a deep mystery, *summum,
medium, ultimum*. Further, if Jesus is divided into two
equal portions, *s* is left in the middle, which in Hebrew
is ש, *sin*, and this in the language of the Scots (Scotorum
opinor lingua) signifies *peccatum*; it is thus implied that
Jesus takes away the sin of the world. The custom of
those preachers was to have an introduction, which they
called *præambulum*, as far from the text as possible, so as
to keep the hearers in suspense, and make them say,
Quo nunc se proripit ille? Where is the man rushing to
now?" (c) The monks especially dealt with legends of
the saints "of the most trifling and irreverent kind."
(d) "Others again amused their hearers with ridiculous
anecdotes, and acted the part of comedians and jesters.
In this the parish clergy showed as much skill as the friars.
Their extravagances would be almost incredible, if we had
not the authority of grave and trustworthy writers who
give the names and parts of the sermons of some of the
preachers. Maillard, Menot, and Barletta were noted in
this department." In one of the sermons of Barletta a
story is told, which is current still, and has been assigned
to an innumerable company of preachers:

"A certain priest, in celebrating the mass, observed a
woman who seemed much touched, and freely wept as he
intoned the service. After it was over he spoke to the
woman and asked the cause of her emotion, and she told him
it was his voice, which reminded her tenderly of her recently
deceased ass." [1]

It was because the mediæval type of religion had exhausted

[1] See DHPI, pp. 302-304.

its vitality and vigour, that the common preaching sank so low. A few there were who shone as gleams in the darkness, and gave promise of the dawn of a better day, in which Christ the Head of His Church, never forgetful of His promise of continued presence, again found men and women hungering and thirsting for Him, and some chosen vessels in whom He could again prove Himself the Bread from Heaven and the Water of Life.

CHAPTER V.

REFORMERS AND DOGMATISTS.

I.

At the Reformation a new period in the history of preaching began, for new thought and life seek an outlet in the spoken word. Protestantism, by its very nature, gives a place and a power to public speech on the concerns of the soul which Roman Catholicism does not. The group of great preachers in the Roman Catholic Church of France, who will be dealt with in a subsequent chapter, had felt the quickening influence of Protestantism. Without that challenge there would not have been any such revival of preaching in Roman Catholicism.

1. Foremost among the heralds of the recovered Gospel stands Luther himself (1483–1546).[1] (1) Most unwillingly, and only in obedience to the head of his monastery, he began to preach first in the dining-hall of the cloister at Erfurt, and then in the small church of the cloister at Wittenberg. Some of his earliest sermons are scholastic compositions in Latin on the mysteries of the creed; but soon he was preaching in German as often as four times a day on such practical subjects as the Ten Commandments, the Lord's Prayer, Repentance, and the True Life; and the freshness and frankness of his speech quickly attracted attention, commanded interest, found favour with most of the people, but also provoked the opposition of some of the ecclesiastics. The traditional forms were for a time retained, even when the contents marked his breach with the past. But soon even the style was changed; and he himself has described the change:

[1] See HLH, pp. 86–100; KHP, pp. 147–167; DHPI, pp. 384–391.

"When I was young, and especially before I was acquainted with theology, I dealt largely in allegories, and tropes, and a quantity of idle craft: but now I have let all that slip, and my best craft is to give the Scripture, with its plain meaning; for the plain meaning is learning and life."[1]

From 1516 onwards he was influenced, both as regards the thought and the language of his sermons, by his growing familiarity with the German mystics. In his controversy with Rome his powers of popular argument and appeal rapidly developed. His sermons on the Ten Commandments and the Lord's Prayer were published, and by their wide circulation extended his influence beyond the borders of Germany. His sermons on a great variety of subjects, yet all directed towards the one purpose of presenting the truth of the Christian Gospel and of exposing the errors of Romanism, were circulated from one end of the land to the other, and everywhere moved the heart and reached the conscience of the multitude. When to these sermons were added, in 1520, the three chief tracts of the Reformation,[2] it became clear that this one man was bringing about, by the convincing and converting power of his words, spoken and written, a fresh era in the history of the Christian Church.

"There had been nothing like it," says Ker,[3] "since the day of Pentecost. On his way to Worms, to meet the Diet, he could not escape from the crowds. At Erfurt,

---

[1] Quoted in note, KHP, p. 152.

[2] The three treatises—*Address to the Christian Nobility of the German Nation respecting the Reformation of the Christian Estate, Concerning Christian Liberty, On the Babylonish Captivity of the Church*, together with *A Short Catechism, The Greater Catechism*, and *the Ninety-Five Theses*—have been translated by Wace and Buchheim, under the title *Luther's Primary Works*, London, 1896.

Thirtie-Foure Speciale and Chosen Sermons, Discovering the Difference between Faith and Workes, of Luther's, were translated and published in London, 1649. His *Commentary on the Galatians*, in 1644 and 1741; and *On Psalms of Degrees*, in 1687. See Lindsay's *History of the Reformation*, vol. i., and his *Luther and the German Reformation*.

[3] KHP, pp. 152–153.

where he had commenced in the little refectory, the great
church was so crowded that they feared it would fall. At
Zwickau, the market-place was thronged by 25,000 eager
listeners, and Luther had to preach to them from the
window." Amid all his other labours "he continued to
preach all his life long, though broken in health—in this,
too, like Knox—and so enfeebled that he often fainted from
exhaustion. But to the end he retained his wonderful
power. The last time he ascended the pulpit was on
February 14th, 1546, a few days before he died."

(2) His one aim was to present the Gospel in expounding the Holy Scriptures. At Easter, 1519, he began
a continuous exposition of the Four Gospels and the book
of Genesis. In 1520 he began in Latin, but then continued in German, a collection of sermons on the portions
of Scripture appointed to be read in public worship, which
served as an example and help to less gifted preachers,
and as an abounding spring of edification to the people.
He himself regarded this book, called *Die Kirchenpostille*,
as his best work. Doctrine drawn from the Scriptures
was here combined in a living, fruitful unity with practical
application to the needs of believers and of the Church
alike. As the time demanded, the great truths, for which
the Reformation stood against Romanism, were constantly
declared; but when necessary the harder problems of
Christian theology were also faced. The appeal generally,
however, was to the heart and the will rather than the
intellect. While he retained the allegorical method of
exposition, his sense of reality and his intimacy with the
very core of the truth of the Scriptures, freed him from
bondage to it. As regards form, there was no endeavour
to give the sermon an organic unity; but, as in the ancient
homily, the passage was expounded verse by verse. In his
language nature spoke rather than art; it was simple,
fresh, abounding, strong, and manly.[1] Into the details
of his later activities as a preacher in correcting error
within the Protestant churches and instructing them in
truth and duty, it is not needful for our purpose now

[1] See HLH, pp. 91-96.

to enter.[1] Suffice it to say that it was he who put the
sermon in Protestantism in the place held by the mass
in Roman Catholicism; and made preaching the most
potent influence in the churches of the Reformation.

(3) The views on preaching of so great a master of
the craft are full of interest. In 1504 Reuchlin had
published his treatise *De Arte Prædicandi,* and in 1534
Erasmus his *Ecclesiastes s. Concionator Evangelicus.* Luther's
views, though more valuable than those of either of the
classical scholars, were never systematically presented, but
must be gathered from his letters and Table-talk.[2] The
summary which Ker gives[3] must be further condensed into
a few sentences. Placing preaching as the most important
part of public worship, even above the reading of the
Scriptures, he insists that it must be rooted in and draw
its authority from these. The subject of preaching is " the
glory of God in Jesus Christ "; where that is not, the
preaching is not only worthless, but even harmful—a
betrayal of souls. While the sermon should be attached
to a text, it should not attempt to deal with all that the
text may suggest, but should lay hold of its main thought,
and stick to that. For "fine introductions or brilliant
perorations" he has no use. Instruction and impression
(the work of the *dialecticus* and *rhetor*) are the preacher's
sole concern, but the proportions of these may vary.
Clearness and simplicity of style is what he insists on.
While many of his sermons have come down to us, few, if
any, were written out by himself; and those which were
reported by others, he did not even revise. He had no
care at all for his own literary fame. It is probable, therefore, that the form in which we have most of his sermons
does not do him full justice. Imperfect though the trans-
mission of much of his preaching may be, of the greatness
of the preacher there is more than sufficient proof.

---

[1] See HLH, pp. 96–100.

[2] This, according to KHP, p. 153, has been done by Nebe in his
Geschichte der Predigt.

[3] KHP, pp. 154–158.

(4) One short passage from a sermon on Gal 4$^{1\text{-}7}$ may be quoted, as not only giving simply and firmly, but in a very brief compass, the substance of his preaching:

" But here perhaps thou wilt say : What is needful to be done ?   By what means shall I become righteous and acceptable to God ?   How shall I attain to this perfect justification ? The Gospel answers, teaching that it is necessary that thou hear Christ, and repose thyself wholly on him, denying thyself and distrusting thine own strength ; by this means thou shalt be changed from Cain to Abel, and being thyself acceptable, shalt offer acceptable gifts to the Lord.   It is faith that justifies thee.   Thou being endued therewith, the Lord remitteth all thy sins by the mediation of Christ his Son, on whom this faith believeth and trusteth.   Moreover, he giveth unto such a faith his Spirit, which changes the man and makes him anew, giving him another reason and another will.   Such a one worketh nothing but good works. Wherefore nothing is required unto justification but to hear Jesus Christ our Saviour and to believe in him.   Howbeit these are not the works of nature, but of grace.   He, therefore, that endeavours to attain to these things by works, shutteth the way to the Gospel, to faith, grace, Christ, God, and all things that help unto salvation.   Again, nothing is necessary in order to accomplish good works but justification ; and he that hath attained it, performs good works and not any other." [1]

2. As might be expected, Luther exercised a potent influence on the preaching of his companions and disciples both as regards the content and the character of the sermons.   The Holy Scriptures were expounded in accordance with his evangelical principles, and preaching in Protestantism became much more directly dependent on the Scriptures than it had been in Roman Catholicism.   Sometimes a continuous exposition of a book of the Bible was given, e.g., by Brenz in his Latin homilies on Luke and Acts (1534); sometimes selected passages only were dealt with, as by J. Mathesius in his *Postilla Prophetica* (preached 1559, printed 1588).   The use of Luther's translation of the Bible became more general ; the allegorical method fell

[1] CME vii. 412.

into disuse, but a minute typology made all the Old Testament still available for the declaration of the Gospel. As
Protestantism was still engaged in opposing its truth to
Roman Catholic error, the preaching was necessarily for
the most part doctrinal, and liberal use of this effective
weapon was made in this warfare. While the common
people needed very elementary instruction from the pulpit,
this was not deemed sufficient for the children, and special
sermons were preached to them. Brenz probably composed the Nürnberg collection of sermons for children,
which appeared in 1533. Even as regards the choice of
language, Luther was followed; but the mantle of the
great Elijah did not always fit the lesser Elishas. Gradually the simple and strong common speech of Luther
was displaced, however, by an ambitious pulpit rhetoric;
and in the heat of controversy evangelical truths were
exaggerated in a morally offensive way, against which
Urbanus Rhegius had in 1544 to utter words of serious
warning.

3. A few of the notable names alone need to be mentioned. *Urbanus Rhegius* combined power of popular
appeal with a rich theological culture; *Agricola* and
Linck showed the influence of the mysticism which had so
deeply affected Luther himself at one stage of his growth
in knowledge and grace; *Nicolas Amsdorf* was mighty in
controversy. Most distinguished of all, and marked by
independence, was *Brenz* (1499–1570), the Reformer of
Würtemberg, who was no less concerned about the duties
of life than the articles of faith. Among preachers who
reached the common people were *Veit Dietrich* of Nürnberg,
Bugenhagen of Wittenberg, and *John Mathesius* (1508–
1565). Two features on the development of Lutheran
preaching must be mentioned. First of all, the sermon
was brought into closer relation with the worship, in which
attention was again given to the great days of the Church
year, so that the sermon often began with a reference to
the occasion. When the mass for souls was abolished, the
funeral sermon took its place. In connection with the

death of a notable person this tended to become a panegyric, going beyond the bounds of good taste.[1]

4. While Luther was the more prominent, he was not the
sole reformer.   *Zwingli* (1484–1531), who led an independent movement, was great as theologian and as preacher;
in him more than in Luther the Renaissance brought its
gifts to the Reformation.   Not by the path of religious
experience as was Luther, but by his studies of the Scriptures and the Fathers he was led to his revolt against the
tyranny of Rome over the human reason and conscience.
From 1518 he exercised his gifts as a preacher in the
interests of Reform.   He expounded the Gospel of Matthew
in order to present the life and work of Jesus, the Acts of
the Apostles as the picture both of the spread of the
Gospel and what the Church should be, the First Epistle
to Timothy as showing the true Christian way of life, the
Epistle to the Galatians as the type of the Apostolic
saving faith, and the Epistle to the Hebrews as the source
of our knowledge of the mission and the benefits of Christ.
While these sermons have not been preserved, there is contemporary evidence that they exercised a very great
influence.   The treatises he published show that he
combined with his humanistic culture the genuine evangelical doctrine and the scholarly exposition of the Holy
Scriptures.   His use of the Swiss dialect of German confined the effectiveness of his preaching to his own countrymen, while his theology exercised an influence on Protestant
thought generally.[2]

5. Later in date, but greater in influence, was John
Calvin (1509–1564).   (1) A Frenchman by birth, his
greatest work on which his fame mainly rests was done in
Geneva, in French Switzerland.

"Calvin, in his intellectual qualities," says Fisher,
"differed widely from Zwingli, but he gave to the Swiss
or Reformed theology its mature form, and completed a
work which his forerunner had commenced.   Nevertheless,

---

[1] See HLH, pp. 100–107.
[2] See HLH, pp. 107–110, and DHPI, pp. 400–415.

he had little sympathy with the personal traits of Zwingli, and Dorner is right in saying that there was, all things considered, more affinity between him and Luther and the Lutheran exposition of the Gospel, than there was with Zwingli and the Zwinglian theology taken as a whole. The religious experience of Calvin corresponded essentially to that of Luther. Distress of conscience and a sense of helplessness were followed by peace of mind through trust in the wholly undeserved grace of the Gospel." [1]

The first edition of the *Institutes of Theology* was published in Latin in 1536 as an apology for the French Protestants. His genius as a dogmatic theologian there displayed at once set him beside Luther and Zwingli as one of the leaders of the Reformation. In the same year he visited Geneva, and his help was claimed by Farel, the leader of the new movement there. His reluctance to enter public life, due to his love of study, was at last overcome by "the terrible adjuration" of Farel:

"You have no other pretext for refusing me than the attachment which you declare you have for your studies. But I tell you, in the name of God Almighty, that if you do not share with me the holy work in which I am engaged, he will not bless your plans, because you prefer your repose to Jesus Christ." [2]

He was not disobedient to the heavenly vision; and from this time on to the end of his life, with one brief interval, he ruled the city, with his pulpit as his throne.

(2) In the exercise of this ministry, he added to his fame as a theologian that of an expositor, and combined both with a statesman's mastery of practical affairs. He has been described as the *orateur exegète*; for not only did his scholarly exposition of the Scriptures ever issue in practical application, but in both alike there was a fervour of feeling and force of will which sought through the conscience to move to action. While Calvin no less than

[1] *History of Christian Doctrine*, p. 298.

[2] Beza's *Life* (old French ed.), p. 22, quoted in DHPI, p. 445 ; *Calvin's Commentaries* were published by the Calvin Translation Society in Edinburgh, 1847 f.

Luther found the Gospel of salvation in the Scriptures, his emphasis fell on God's demand, and Luther's on God's pity and mercy. More systematically even than Luther, he set himself to expound the Holy Scriptures, the Old Testament no less than the New, as he maintained the identity of the true religion in both the old and the new covenant. Rejecting the allegorical method, by means of typology he linked the two stages of the divine revelation.

(3) As he preached without manuscript, his sermons had to be taken down as delivered.

" In the Preface to the Sermons on Deuteronomy, the deacons relate that the deceased Ragueneau (Raguenier) had since 1549 devoted himself to the task of reporting Calvin's sermons ' de mot à mot ' by the use of specially invented abbreviations, so that only a few words had escaped him. He himself then made a fair copy, and handed it over to the deacons, in order that the word of the great teacher might build up and strengthen the poor strangers of the reformed faith, the number of whom in France grew day by day. The proceeds of the printing were to be used for the benefit of the poor." [1]

It is in this way a large number of his sermons has been preserved.

(4) Horne has placed Calvin between Savonarola and John Knox as one of *the rulers of peoples*,[2] and thus describes Calvin's preaching :

" Students of Calvin's sermons and writings will see for themselves how admirably the instrument he employed was adapted to the kind of constructive work he set out to do. Members of congregations will note with relief that he evidently believed in short sermons; indeed, he had no patience, as he said, with a prolix style. Men have called him by almost every depreciatory epithet, but, those fifty-three octavo volumes notwithstanding, nobody will truthfully call him ' wordy.' Seldom will you read anywhere discourses with less of illustration or ornamentation which are yet more penetrating and pertinent. There are no

---

[1] HLH, p. 111, note 2.
[2] *The Romance of Preaching*, pp. 169-170.

chasings on the blade of his sword. It is plain, keen steel, and with what an edge! Calvin's style of address was, we are told, somewhat slow and measured. For one thing, he was a martyr to asthma, and often breathless in the pulpit and before the Council. It can be said of him, as it can be said of very few, that he spoke literature. Strong, stately, lucid, nervous, his sentences carry you forward from point to point of his argument. Little wonder that the French school-books of to-day should point to Calvin as one of the supreme masters and even makers of the French language, and should describe his style as an ' admirable instrument of discourse and of affairs.' It is remarkable that one who was so scholarly in all his tastes should be the determined champion of extempore preaching. Indeed, he went as far as to declare that the power of God could only pour itself forth in extempore speech. . . . He never ceased to insist that out of the fulness of the heart the mouth must speak."

6. Closely associated with Calvin was the Reformer of Scotland, John Knox (1505–1572), who "united to the statesmanship of Calvin the fiery eloquence of Savonarola." [1]

At his grave, according to Calderwood, the Regent Morton said, " Here lyeth a man who in his life never feared the face of man." Yet Knox always spoke of himself as a coward by nature, and brave and strong only by grace. (1) He, too, shrank from the ordeal of preaching, and was got into the pulpit at St. Andrews in 1546 by the solemn importunity of John Rough, who exhorted him " to refuse not his holy vocation . . . as you look to avoid God's heavy displeasure." Such was the impression at once made by his preaching that his hearers said to one another, " Master George Wishart spak never so plainelye, and yet he was brunt; even so will he be." [2] Not the stake was his lot, but a French galley for nineteen months. It was on his return to Scotland in 1559 that he became by his word the ruler of the Scottish people, and, in spite of the opposition of the Court, established Protestantism

[1] Horne, *op. cit.*, p. 171.
[2] Lindsay's *History of the Reformation*, ii. 285. See *John Knox*, by Taylor Innes. " Famous Scots " Series.

of the Calvinistic type in Scotland. No reckoning can be made of the debt his country owes to him. We may look at him and hear him in the pulpit through the eyes and ears of a contemporary, James Melville.

"Of all the benefits I had that year (1571) was the coming of that most notable prophet and apostle of our nation, Mister John Knox, to St. Andrews. I heard him teach there the prophecies of Daniel, that summer and winter following. I had my pen and little book, and took away sic things as I could comprehend. In the opening of his text, he was moderate the space of half an hour; but when he entered to application, he made me so grue and tremble that I could not hold the pen to write." He wielded this power when in bodily weakness, for he had to be helped to the church and even lifted into the pulpit, "where he behoved to lean at his first entrie . . . but ere he was done with his sermon he was so active and vigorous that he was like to ding (beat) the pulpit into blads (pieces), and fly out of it."[1]

He was assuredly an illustration of the *ingenium perfervidum Scotorum*. That his fervour sometimes passed the bounds of courtesy and consideration may be allowed. It was to his disadvantage in the eyes of men that he had to deal sternly, and even harshly, with a young and charming queen; but he shrank from no task, however trying, to which the interests of the Gospel summoned him. Savonarola and Calvin each ruled a city; Knox ruled a nation, and his influence has been even more permanent than theirs.

(2) While Knox was much engaged in controversy, and when needful smote hard and spared not in his preaching, he could address himself to believers for their comfort and encouragement. With what directness and simplicity he indicates the motive, and with what care and clearness he arranges the matter of his sermon on *The First Temptation of Christ* (Mt 4¹)!

"The cause moving me to treat of this place of Scripture is, that such as by the inscrutable providence of God fall

---

[1] Quoted by Horne, *op. cit.*, pp. 174–175.

into divers temptations, judge not themselves by reason thereof to be less acceptable in God's presence. But, on the contrary, having the way prepared to victory by Jesus Christ, they shall not fear above measure the crafty assaults of that subtle serpent Satan; but with joy and bold courage, having such a guide as here is pointed forth, such a champion, and such weapons as here are to be found (if with obedience we will hear and unfeigned faith believe), we may assure ourselves of God's present favour, and of final victory, by the means of Him who, for our safeguard and deliverance, entered in the battle, and triumphed over his adversary, and all his raging fury. And that this being heard and understood, may the better be kept in memory, this order, by God's grace, we propose to observe, in treating the matter: First, what this word temptation meaneth, and how it is used within the Scriptures. Secondly, who is here tempted, and at what time this temptation happened. Thirdly, how and by what means He was tempted. Fourthly, why He should suffer these temptations, and what fruits ensue to us from the same."[1]

(3) It is true that this is one of only three written sermons which have been preserved, and it is possible that, when he spoke, the disposition of his matter was not always as orderly as this. In the conclusion there is an interesting reference to the conditions of composition:

"But for bringing of the examples of the Scriptures, if God permit, in the end we shall speak more largely when it shall be treated why Christ permitted Himself thus to be tempted. Sundry impediments now call me from writing in this matter, but, by God's grace, at convenient leisure I purpose to finish, and to send it to you. I grant the matter that proceeds from me is not worthy of your pain and labour to read it; yet seeing it is a testimony of my good mind toward you, I doubt not but you will accept it in good part. God, the Father of our Lord Jesus Christ, grant unto you to find favour and mercy of the Judge, whose eyes and knowledge pierce through the secret cogitations of the heart, in the day of temptation, which shall come upon all flesh, according to that mercy which you (illuminated and directed

---

[1] WGS, i. 173-174. His works, edited by Laing, were published in 2 vols., in Edinburgh, 1846.

by His Holy Spirit) have showed to the afflicted. Now the God of all comfort and consolation confirm and strengthen you in His power unto the end. Amen." [1]

Even these few sentences show another and more attractive aspect of Knox than usually appears.

7. There were many preachers of the Reformation in other parts of Europe, as in Italy and Spain on the one hand, Holland, Denmark, Norway and Sweden on the other, as well as Austria, Bohemia, and Poland; and an account of some of them may be found in Dargan's *History of Preaching*, vol. i. pp. 451–472; but to deal with them in detail would not serve our present purpose. We shall in the next chapter return to the contrast in England of the preaching of Anglican and Puritan; here may be mentioned, however, one of the pioneers and martyrs of the Reformation in England, the most powerful and popular preacher of the age, Hugh Latimer (about 1490–1555).[2] (1) At first a vehement opponent of the Reformation, he was won by the personal influence of Bilney; and soon attracted attention as a frank and bold champion of the new views; but his ability and tact on several occasions warded off from him threatened ecclesiastical censure. The persistence of his enemies brought him to the Tower in the closing months of Henry VIII.'s reign. During the reign of Edward he was free, and used his freedom to preach the truth he loved. On Mary's succession he refused to seek safety in flight, as he might have done, and he and Ridley completed their confession at the stake. His last words are familiar to all :

"Be of good comfort, Master Ridley, and play the man; we shall this day light such a candle by God's grace in England as I trust shall never be put out."

Although Latimer did not write his sermons, a number of them were reported by Augustine Bernher, a Swiss, who

[1] WGS, pp. 200–201.

[2] *Sermons and Remains of Bp. Latimer*, with biographical sketches compiled from Foxe and other sources, edited for the Parker Society by the Rev. G. E. Corrie, Cambridge, 1844–1845.

acted as his secretary ; and these reports allow us to judge of his qualities as a preacher.[1]

(2) A characteristic passage may be quoted — his description of the busiest prelate in England :

" Well, I would all men would look to their duty, as God hath called them, and then we should have a flourishing Christian Commonwealth. And now I would ask a strange question. Who is the most diligentest bishop and prelate in all England, and passeth all the rest in doing his office ? I can tell, for I know him who he is ; I know him well. But now methinks I see you listening and hearkening, that I should name him. There is one that passeth all the other, and is the most diligent prelate and preacher in all England. And will ye know who it is ? I will tell you. It is the devil. He is the most diligent preacher of all others. He is never out of his diocese, he is never from his cure ; ye shall never find him unoccupied, he is ever in his parish ; he keepeth residence at all times, ye shall never find him out of the way ; call for him when ye will, he is ever at home ; the diligentest preacher in all the realm, he is ever at his plough ; no lording nor loitering may hinder him, he is ever applying his business ; ye shall never find him idle, I warrant you. And his office is to hinder religion, to maintain superstition, to set up idolatry, to teach all

---

[1] Horne thus characterises Latimer as a preacher. "The essential Protestant faith captured the ear and the heart of sixteenth-century London, through the pithy pregnant Saxon speech of Latimer, with his command of laughter and tears. He presented the citizen in the street with a plain man's religion. He spoke it as simply, I say it with reverence, as the Saviour spoke to the peasants in the fields of Judæa, or the fishermen by the Galilean lake. He did not so much appeal to the theologically trained mind ; and he certainly did not appeal to any sense of ecclesiastical authority. He appealed to common sense ; he appealed to the instincts of the multitude. He appealed to their love of justice and of humanity. There never was a more human being than Hugh Latimer. The people well know the men who love them, believe in them, and understand them. The sheep hear the voice of the true shepherd. . . . Latimer's preaching is oratory stripped of all that is meretricious, and oratory that is not sterilised by conventionality. No timid, stilted pulpiteer, who has never learned that grace is more than grammar, and that to win your hearers you may break every pulpit convention that was ever designed by a sleek respectability to keep our volcanic Gospel within the bonds of decency and order, will ever capture the soul of a great city, or speak with a voice that will ring in the hearts of a free people " (*The Romance of Preaching*, pp. 190–191).

kind of popery. He is as ready as he can be wished for to set forth his plough, to devise as many ways as can be to deface and obscure God's glory. Where the devil is resident, and hath his plough going, then away with books, and up with candles; away with Bibles, and up with beads; away with the light of the Gospel, and up with the light of candles, yea at noon days. Where the devil is resident, that he may prevail, up with all superstition and idolatry, censing, painting of images, candles, palms, ashes, holy water, and new service of men's inventing, as though man could invent a better way to honour God with than God Himself hath appointed. Down with Christ's cross, up with Purgatory pickpurse,—up with Popish Purgatory, I mean. Away with clothing the naked, the poor and impotent, up with decking of images, and gay garnishing of stocks and stones; up with man's traditions and his laws, down with God's will and His most holy Word. Down with the old honour due unto God, and up with the new god's honour. Let all things be done in Latin. . . . And in no wise they must be translated into English. Oh that our prelates would be as diligent to sow the corn of good doctrine, as Satan is to sow cockle and darnel." [1]

8. While the Reformers themselves were too much concerned about the matter of preaching to pay attention to the form, the theory of preaching was not in this period altogether neglected. Mention has already been made of books by Reuchlin and Erasmus. (1) Of Erasmus' *Ecclesiastes*, Hering gives the following brief description :

" He has, after a beautiful estimate, evangelical in tone, of preaching and the calling of the preacher, sketched with fervour a picture of the virtues of a true preacher, and has offered, in a homiletic theory, which attaches itself to ancient rhetoric without denying the pecularity of Christian preaching, many fine observations and suggestions in order at last, in his teaching on the matter of sermons, with a total disregard of the achievement of the Reformation to take up a standpoint, in which ecclesiastically orthodox propositions are set side by side with a humanistic moralism." [2]

---

[1] LELR, p. 151 ; the *Sermons and Remains*, pp. 70-71.
[2] HLH, 114.

Worth noting is the summons which the first part contains to the Church to send missionaries to heathen, Jews, and Mohammedans.

(2) Luther's companion, Melanchthon, was also a humanist; and from the same standpoint as regards the ancient rhetoric, but with the new appreciation of the Gospel, he delivered a course of lectures on preaching. His own sermons, however, follow the homiletic method of the other Reformers. *Hyperius* (1511–1566, Andrew of Ypres), a Reformed theologian, "offered his age a comprehensive Homiletic." While recognising what distinguishes Christian preaching from ancient rhetoric, and taking into account what prophets, apostles, and fathers have to teach, he borrows many elements from the rhetoric and dialectic of the ancients. He gives special attention to the gathering of the material. His humanism, and especially his admiration for Chrysostom, stand in the way of his giving a homiletic theory wholly in accord with the new evangelical standpoint, which he aims at maintaining. His counsels, however, are thoroughly practical. (*a*) The sermon is to be adapted to the capacity of the hearers. (*b*) The theological questions which excite curiosity rather than provide edification are to be avoided. (*c*) The doctrines taught are to be confirmed from the prophetic and apostolic writings. (*d*) Time, Place, and Hearers are to be considered in deciding whether doctrinal explanation is suitable or not. (*e*) In confirmation of what is taught only the canonical writings are to be employed. (*f*) The proofs used are to be simple and direct. (*g*) Preference is to be given to the simple sense. (*h*) Figurative language is to be used sparingly, types and allegories very seldom, and never for proof. (*i*) The mode of expression should not provoke contradiction. (*j*) When a doctrine is taught, it should be practically applied both in regard to the Church as a whole and the individual conscience.[1] Do not these counsels remind us that the book was written for an age of doctrinal controversy, when there was the danger

[1] HLH, pp. 115–117.

of preaching becoming too dogmatic and polemical ?   When
the fervour of the Spirit had departed, these two features
became unduly prominent, and preaching lost its living
force.

II.

As we have watched the flow of the tide of religious
thought and life at the Reformation, so must we glance, as
briefly as we can, at the ebb in Germany.

1. The decline of the pulpit began even in the second
generation. Not only did the contents of the sermons
become more dogmatic and controversial, but even the form
became more abstract and artificial. Doctrine displaced
the Scriptures; learning was paraded rather than life
expressed.

" Where are now," asked Scriver, " the fiery tongues and
the glowing hearts of the apostles ? Where is the glad
spirit of Luther ? Where are those drunken with the love
of God, and the heralds of the great deeds of God ? "[1]

We should do the age an injustice if we assumed that the
men themselves were as lifeless as the subjects and style of
their preaching. Even John Gerhard, the great dogmatic
theologian of the Lutheran Church, is affected by the
fashion of the hour. The hymns and prayers reveal a
piety the sermons fail to express.

" It is," says Hering, " as if then amid the severest
visitation of our fatherland the confessing faith renewed
its original strength in singing and praying, while this was
denied to it for the word of witness, for the proclamation in
the sermon."[2]

2. Some illustrations of this general statement may be
added :

" The preaching which resulted," says Ker, " became in
many cases of a scholastic kind, dry and hard and formal,

---

[1] Quoted in HLH, p. 118.
[2] HLH, p. 118. In KHP, pp. 168-173, will be found a brief and clear
account of the conditions, outward and inward, of the age.

full of endless disputes. One well-known volume of sermons, for example, preached in 1658 by Jacob Andreä of Esslingen, is divided into four parts, for the four quarters of the year; the first against the Papists, the second against the Zwinglians, the third against the Schwenkfeldians, who were the mystics and perfectionists of that time, and the fourth against the Anabaptists. When such heresies had all been dealt with, preachers turned to the early Christian age, and in their sermons the Patripassians, the Nestorians, and the Valentinians rose and fought again, like the dead at Châlons." [1]

The homiletic theory of the period did not correct, but increased, the evil. Hyperius, who has already been mentioned, failed to exercise a lasting influence, and found no worthy successor. Andreas Pancratius

" receives the credit of being the inventor of the synthetic mode of preaching, which was called after him, the *Pancratian*. It was, however, in use long before, as it could not but be, only he brought it more fully into notice. . . . Now there were found out endless methods, which were discussed in special treatises. As many as twenty-five are reckoned up in the scholastic style—*methodus paraphrastica simplex, methodus paraphrastica mixta, methodus zetetica*, etc. There were also methods named after the different universities—the *Wittenberg method*, the *Jena method*; and methods were imported from other countries—the *English method*, the *Dutch method*; books being published with these titles as recommendations. Exact rules were laid down for the treatment of texts; sometimes three introductions, *special, more special, most special*, were recommended, with five different kinds of applications. Nature was sacrificed to art; texts were stretched out on the rack, and dealt with, not according to their contents or the wants of the people, but according to the method of some particular homilete or university. The formalism of the dogmatic theology of the time thus found its way into the manner of preaching, and the attempt to improve sermons by such means only made them worse." [2]

---

[1] KHP, p. 173.

[2] KHP, pp. 175-176. This quotation is given so fully, as the warning it conveys is so necessary to preachers at all times, and weight is added to it because the words are those of a great preacher.

Some preachers felt the weariness and unprofitableness of this kind of preaching, and tried to gain freshness for their preaching by seeking subjects other than Scripture texts or doctrines. Sermons were preached on hymns, or emblems, such as a rose, a lily, or honey, which were dealt with by a fanciful allegorical method; or proverbs, from which practical applications to common life were made.

"There were sermons on the dressing of the hair, tobacco smoking, and so forth. Scarcely one of the subjects chosen by our sensational advertising preachers had not its prototype more than two hundred years ago in Germany."[1]

Thus, when men had lost the skill to draw from the fountain of living waters, did they hew out for themselves cisterns, broken cisterns, that can hold no water.[2]

3. Luther himself had been much influenced by German mysticism, and the leaven remained in the religious thought and life of the country. The Lutheran mysticism, however, differed from the Mediæval, in that evangelical verities were recognised and expressed in it. It exercised a wholesome influence on preaching, and was a preparation for the movement of pietism. The peril of an exaggerated subjectivism was seen in Valentin Weigel (died 1588), for whom the significance of Christmas and Easter alike was the rebirth of the soul, and the inner experiences of the believer seemed more important than the outer revelation of God in Christ. Evangelical doctrine was quickened by mystical experience in John Arndt (1555–1621).

"For preaching and popular edification," says Ker, "he is the foremost figure between Luther and Spener, and has, more than any other of that time, the characteristics of our Puritans—of men like Baxter and Rutherford and Bunyan, though without Bunyan's genius."[3]

His principal book is *Das wahre Christentum* ("The true Christianity").

"His avowed aim in writing it was (1) to draw the minds of students and preachers away from combative and

---

[1] KHP, p. 177. [2] Jer 2¹³. [3] KHP, p. 178.

scholastic theology; (2) to lead good Christians from a formal to a fruit-bearing faith; (3) to bring them from the mere science and theory of Christianity to the enjoyment and the practice of it; (4) to show the meaning of a Christian life as indicated by the apostle's words, 'I live; yet not I, but Christ liveth in me.' "[1]

Although influenced by Arndt, Valerius Herberger (1562–1627) differs from him in mode of preaching. He illustrates a fashion of the hour in revelling in imagery, regardless of good taste. In contrast to him, Joachim Lütkemann (1608–1655) was free of all such trifling, and preached forcefully; even for some of his hearers his earnestness seemed harshness. A sharp critic of the conditions in the Church in the interests of a more living and inward piety was Henry Müller (1631–1675), who, however, in his homiletic form favoured the current artificiality. A man of independent, original mind, belonging to no party, keen in observation, bold in utterance, endowed with the gifts of humour and sarcasm, and using all his powers for the betterment of the morals of the people, was Balthasar Schupp (1610–1661).[2] These names are evidence that even in this period of barren scholasticism and arid polemics the pulpit of Germany could still claim some living witnesses of Christian truth and grace; and these continued the evangelical succession until the religious revival of the seventeenth century, which is known to us as German pietism.

"For a whole century," says Ker, "after the death of the leaders of the Reformation, Germany was in a state of spiritual hardness and coldness of the most distressing kind. . . . Yet a genuine revival came in the course of the seventeenth century." Thus the period " may teach us never to despair of the revival of religion in any country."[3]

---

[1] KHP, pp. 178–179.   [2] HLH, pp. 118–131.   [3] KHP, p. 180.

CHAPTER VI.

THE ANGLICAN AND THE PURITAN, THE CHURCHMAN AND THE NONCONFORMIST, THE EVANGELICAL AND THE MODERATE.

I.

1. In his letter to Somerset, Calvin said of the Church:

"There is too little of *living preaching* in your Kingdom. . . . You fear that levity and foolish imaginations might be the consequence of the introduction of a new system. But all this must yield to the command of Christ which orders the *preaching* of the Gospel."[1]

Moderate reform under the guidance and control of the civil power—that was the policy in England; individual enthusiasm must be restrained and repressed. At the beginning of Elizabeth's reign preaching was even for a time forbidden, and for a long time there was a lack of preachers. Homilies were provided and appointed to be read. The first collection of these was issued in the reign of Edward for "the staying of such errors as were then sparkled among the people." Among the contributors were Cranmer, Ridley, Latimer, and Butzer. The second collection appeared under Elizabeth in 1562. These homilies were distinctly Protestant in content and tone, affirming both the formal and the material principle of the Reformation, the authority of the Scriptures and the doctrine of justification by faith. While there were good and godly, serious and earnest men among the leaders of the movement, yet there was lacking a personality great enough to control and direct by moral and religious influence instead of State regulation.[2]

[1] Quoted by Horne, *op. cit.*, p. 170.   [2] See DHPI, pp. 473–481.

2. The attempts by Queen Elizabeth to repress free speech in the pulpit, and to limit preaching to the reading of homilies, evoked a protest from Archbishop Grindal in 1577, an offence for which he was set aside from the exercise of his office. His views on freely spoken sermons and read homilies are worth remembering.

"Now, when it is thought that the reading of the godly Homilies, set forth by public authority, may suffice, I continue of the same mind I was when I attended last upon your Majesty. The reading of Homilies hath his commodity, but is nothing comparable to the office of preaching. The godly preacher is termed in the Gospel *fidelis servus et prudens qui novit famulitio Domini cibum demensum dare in tempore*; who can apply his speech according to the diversity of times, places and hearers, which cannot be done in Homilies; exhortations, reprehensions and persuasions are uttered with more affection, to the moving of the hearers, in Sermons than in Homilies. Besides Homilies were devised by the godly bishops in your brother's time, only to supply necessity, for want of preachers, and are by the statute not to be preferred, but to give place to Sermons, whensoever they may be had; and were never thought in themselves alone to contain sufficient instruction for the Church of England. If every flock might have a preaching pastor, which is rather to be wished than hoped for, then were reading of Homilies altogether unnecessary."[1]

3. Hugh Latimer has been dealt with in the preceding chapter, as he comes before the division of English Protestantism into the Anglican and Puritan type, and has a claim to be placed alongside of the notable preachers of the Reformation, even although his influence was not so great or so enduring as theirs. Richard Hooker (1553–1600) may be taken as a typical Anglican. The controversy in which he was involved against his will with his colleague, Walter Travers, at the Temple, of which in 1585 he became Master, led to the writing of the classic apology for Anglicanism, *The Laws of Ecclesiastical Polity*. Characteristic of his tolerant, conciliatory spirit and his reverence for his spiritual ancestry is his plea for the

[1] LELR, pp. 180–181.

kindly judgment of Roman Catholics in his sermon, entitled
" A Learned Discourse of Justification, Works, and How
the Foundation of Faith is overthrown." [1]

" I have proved heretofore, that although the Church of
Rome hath played the harlot worse than ever did Israel, yet
are they not, as now the synagogue of the Jews, which
plainly denieth Christ Jesus, quite and clean excluded from
the new covenant.   But as Samaria compared with Jerusalem
is termed *Aholah,* a church or tabernacle of her own; contrariwise, Jerusalem *Aholibah,* the resting place of the Lord;
so, whatsoever we term the Church of Rome, when we compare her to reformed churches, still we put a difference, as
then between Babylon and Samaria, so now between Rome
and heathenish assemblies.   Which opinion I must and will
recall; I must grant, and will, that the Church of Rome,
together with all her children, is clean excluded; there is no
difference in the world between our fathers and Saracens,
Turks or Painims if they did directly deny Christ crucified
for the salvation of the world.   But how many millions of
them are known so to have ended their mortal lives, that
the drawing of their breath hath ceased with the uttering of
this faith, ' Christ, my Saviour, my Redeemer Jesus.'   And
shall we say, that such did not hold the foundation of
Christian faith? . . . Forasmuch, therefore, as it may be
said of the Church of Rome, she hath yet ' a little strength,'
she doth not directly deny the foundation of Christianity.
I may, I trust without offence, persuade myself, that
thousands of our fathers in former times, living and
dying within her walls, have found mercy at the hands of
God."

This charity does not, however, loosen his hold on the
Reformation principle of justification by faith alone.

" Indeed many of them in former times, as their books
and writings do yet show, held the foundation, to wit, salvation by Christ alone, and therefore might be saved.   For God
hath always had a Church among them, which firmly kept
his saving truth.   As for such as hold with the Church of
Rome, that we cannot be saved by Christ alone without
works; they do not only by a circle of consequences, but

---

[1] This was preached in the first year of Hooker's Mastership of the Temple.

directly, deny the foundation of faith; they hold it not, no
not so much as by a slender thread." [1]

4. Very soon the influence of the Renaissance as well
as the Reformation appeared in the preaching of the
Anglican pulpit.

(1) "The sermons of Andrewes (1555–1626)," says Dargan, "are at times artificial and stilted in tone, and often over-
loaded with learning and Latin quotations, not free from the
whimsical fancies of the age, but weighty in thought, exhaustive in treatment, and much occupied with careful
exposition of Scripture; but his exposition is sometimes
vitiated, both by polemical bias and the play of fancy." [2]

John Donne (1573–1631) enjoyed great popularity as
a preacher, but his sermons also are marred "by the affec-
tations and pedantry and straining for effect which were
common to the age." [3] An Anglican with Puritan sympathies was Joseph Hall (1574–1656), who was counted
"in character, learning and eloquence" [4] one of the greatest
preachers of his age. We must pass over other noted
preachers, to deal more fully with one, Jeremy Taylor
(1613–1667), who holds a foremost place in the devotional
literature not only of his own Church, but of his nation,
and who also deserves remembrance as a preacher.
In his *Liberty of Prophesying* (1647) he tried to reconcile the contending factions in the Church on the basis,
not of the Bible itself, but of the Apostles' Creed, and
pleaded for toleration while recognising the authority of
the State. His *Holy Living* (1650) and *Holy Dying*
(1651) are recognised as religious classics. As a preacher,
Hering takes him as the illustration of the change which
came over English preaching in the seventeenth century.
He is "a brilliant author-preacher, who is as prodigal with
his wealth of anecdote 'as an Asiatic queen with her

[1] Everyman's Library. Hooker's *Laws of Ecclesiastical Polity*, i. pp. 32,
34, 35.
[2] DHP ii. p. 150. Simpson, however, speaks very highly of Andrewes,
Preachers and Teachers, pp. 116–120.
[3] DHP ii. p. 151.   [4] DHP ii. p. 153.

pearls.' In contrast to Latimer, who grips life, he makes full use of the treasures of the classics, and his speech also is of that exalted style, which is more suitable for an audience of patricians than for a popular congregation." [1]

(2) A passage on *Married Love* from one of two sermons on "The Marriage Ring," in which he gives wise counsel to the married, will serve to illustrate his style:

"It contains in it all sweetness, and all society, and all felicity, and all prudence, and all wisdom. For there is nothing can please a man without love; and if a man be weary of the wise discourses of the Apostles, and of the innocency of an even and a private fortune, or hates peace or a fruitful year, he hath reaped thorns and thistles from the choicest flowers of Paradise; for nothing can sweeten felicity itself but love. . . . No man can tell but he who loves his children how many delicious accents make a man's heart dance in the pretty conversation of these dear pledges; their childishness, their stammering, their little angers, their innocence, their imperfections, their necessities are so many little emanations of joy and comfort to him that delights in their persons and society; but he that loves not his wife and children feeds a lioness at home, and broods a nest of sorrows, and blessing itself cannot make him happy: so that all the commandments of God enjoining a man to love his wife are nothing but so many necessities and capacities of joy. She that is loved is safe, and he that loves is joyful. Love is a union of all things excellent; it contains in it proportion, and satisfaction, and rest, and confidence; and I wish this were so much proceeded in that the heathens themselves could not go beyond us in this virtue and in its proper and its appendant happiness. Tiberius Gracchus chose to die for the safety of his wife; and yet methinks to a Christian to do so should be no hard thing; for many servants will die for their masters, and many gentlemen will die for their friend; but the examples are not so many of those that are ready to do it for their dearest relatives, and yet some there have been. Baptista Fregosa tells of a Neapolitan that gave himself a slave to the Moors that he might follow his wife; and Dominicus Catalusius, the Prince

---

[1] HLH 135. See DPH ii. pp. 155–159, and Simpson, *op. cit.*, pp. 131–132.

of Lesbos, kept company with his lady when she was a leper;
and these are greater things than to die." [1]

II.

1. We are fortunate in having a volume on *Puritan
Preaching in England* from the pen of the biographer of
John Bunyan, the Rev. Dr. John Brown. He quotes from
a contemporary a description of the manner of preaching
of one William Bourne, a preacher in Manchester early in
the seventeenth century.

"He seldom varied the manner of his preaching, which
after explication of the text was doctrine, proof of it from
Scripture, by reasoning and answering more and more
objections; and then the uses, first, of information, secondly
of confutation of Popery, thirdly of reprehension, fourthly of
examination, fifthly of exhortation, and lastly of consolation." [2]

This suggests a very dreary performance. In contrast may
be placed two short passages of "that eloquent divine of
famous memory, Thomas Playfere" (about 1561–1609),

"who was Lady Margaret Professor of Divinity at Cambridge
in Queen Elizabeth's time, and afterwards Court preacher to
King James. In a sermon entitled 'The Pathway to Perfection,' based on Philippians iii. 14, he begins by saying that
as Solomon went up six steps to come to his great throne of
ivory, so must we ascend six degrees to come to this high
top of perfection. He therefore proceeds to divide his text
into six parts. On that part which deals with the Apostle's
forgetting those things which are behind, Playfere says:
'He that remembers his virtues has no virtues to remember,
seeing he wants humility, which is the mother virtue of all
virtues. For this is the difference between the godly and
the wicked; both remember virtues, but the godly remember other men's virtues, the wicked remember their own.
Wherefore though thou have conquered kingdoms yet crake
not of it as Sennacherib did; though thou hast built Babel
yet brag not of it as Nebuchadnezzar did; though thou hast
rich treasures yet show them not as Hezekiah did; though
thou hast slain a thousand Philistines yet glory not in it
as Samson did; though thou give alms yet blow not a

---

[1] LELR, p. 288.   [2] *Puritan Preaching in England*, p. 60.

trumpet; though thou fast twice a week yet make no words
of it (remember it not, but) 'Forget that which is behind.'"[1]

This extract suggests artificiality; but genuine feeling,
in spite of some rhetorical extravagance, breaks out in
a sermon on "Heart's Delight," on the text "Delight thyself in the Lord."

"Nay, I cannot hold my heart for my joy; yea, I cannot
hold my joy for my heart; to think that He which is my
Lord is become my Father, and so that He which was
offended with me for my sin's sake, is now reconciled to
me for His Son's sake. To think that the High Majesty
of God will one day raise me out of the dust, and so that I
who am now a poor worm upon earth shall hereafter be
a glorious saint in heaven. This, this makes me delight
myself in the Lord, saying, O Thou that art the delight of
my delight, the life of my life, soul of my soul, I delight
myself in Thee, I live only for Thee, I offer myself unto
Thee, wholly to Thee wholly, one to Thee one, only to Thee
only. For suppose now, as St. John speaketh, the whole
world was full of books, and all the creatures in the world
were writers, and all the grass piles upon the earth were
pens, and all the waters in the sea were ink: yet I assure
you faithfully all these books, all these writers, all these
pens, all this ink would not be sufficient to describe the
very least part, either of the goodness of the Lord in himself,
or of the loving-kindness of the Lord towards thee."[2]

2. Nearly all the makers of the Puritan movement
were university men, and most of them Cambridge men.
For nearly fifty years Laurence Chaderton (about 1536–
1640) preached in Cambridge as afternoon lecturer at
St. Clement's Church; and when he thought of resigning,
on account of his age, more than forty Christian ministers
wrote asking him to carry on his work, as each of them
had been brought to Christ by his ministry. Dr. Brown
describes him as "an almost ideal preacher."[3] Through
his own brother-in-law, Ezekiel Culverwell, his influence
reached a youth of eighteen, "John Winthrop, afterwards

---

[1] *Puritan Preaching in England*, pp. 61, 62.
[2] Quoted by Brown, pp. 62, 63.   [3] P. 69.

better known to the world as Governor Winthrop."[1]
Through William Perkins (died 1602), "a Puritan preacher
of more than ordinary spiritual power," he affected the life
both of John Cotton, who did a great work in Boston,
New England, and of John Robinson (about 1576–1625),
whose name and fame are linked with the Pilgrim Fathers.[2]

These illustrations show how expansive like the
mustard seed, and pervasive like the leaven, the preacher's
influence may be. He cannot measure the greatness of
his own work, and in few cases can it be traced. William
Perkins gave a series of addresses to divinity students and
preachers in Cambridge on " The Calling of the Ministry,
describing the Duties and Dignities of that Calling," of
which Dr. Brown gives a summary[3] which cannot here be
reproduced, but one short passage may be quoted, as it
describes the preacher's twofold function as prophet and
as priest.

"Every true minister is a double interpreter—God's
interpreter to the people by preaching to them from God,
and the people's interpreter to God, laying open their wants,
confessing their sins, craving pardon and forgiveness for,
and in their names giving thanks for mercies received, thus
so offering up their spiritual sacrifices to God."[4]

For this task he needs the tongue of the learned, and
he can have this tongue only as he has human learning
and divine knowledge, as well as being inwardly taught
by the Holy Ghost. One condition of this equipment is
that he labour for sanctity, and holiness of life. Himself
saved and sanctified, he must preach for the salvation and
sanctification of others. Perkins then shows how the
prophet is made by a discussion of the vision of Isaiah,
offering an exposition that is full of insight and suggestion.

[1] P. 70.

[2] P. 71. Horne devotes one of his lectures to "Founders of Freedom :
John Robinson and the Pilgrim Fathers " ; and seeks to show that in the
preaching of Robinson the Pilgrim Fathers found instruction and inspiration
for their enterprise, quoting as his warrant Seeley's saying, "Religion alone
can turn emigration into Exodus" (*The Romance of Preaching*, pp. 198–199).

[3] Pp. 73–83.   [4] P. 74.

3. One of the greatest preachers in the period of the greatest literary luxuriance and brilliance in the history of England, and reproducing its characteristics, was Henry Smith (1550–1593), who was spoken of as the silver-tongued, " and therefore, as Thomas Fuller says, only one metal below Chrysostom, the golden-mouthed, himself." As lecturer at St. Clement Danes, London, from 1587, he quickly gained the fame of " prime preacher of the nation." Free of the artificiality in form, and the dogmatism in tone, which characterised many preachers, he reached the common people without any attempt at pandering to low tastes.   Simplicity, and not vulgarity, was his aim.

" There is a kind of preacher," he says, " risen up of late which shroud and cover every rustical and unsavoury and childish and absurd sermon under the name of the simple kind of teaching.   But indeed to preach simply is not to preach rudely, nor unlearnedly, nor confusedly, but to preach plainly and perspicuously that the simplest man may understand what is taught, as if he did hear his name."[1]

He describes the hearers as well as preachers of his time.

" One is like an Athenian, and hankereth after news; if the preachers say anything of our armies beyond the sea, or Council at home, or matters at Court.   Another cometh to gaze about the church; he hath an evil eye, which is still looking upon that from which Job did avert his eye.   And another cometh to muse : so soon as he is set he falleth into a brown study ; sometimes his mind runs on his market, sometimes on his journey, sometimes of his suit, sometimes of his dinner, sometimes of his sport after dinner, and the sermon is done before the man thinks where he is.   Another cometh to hear, but so soon as the preacher hath said his prayer he falls fast asleep, as though he had been brought in for a corpse, and the preacher should preach at his funeral."[2]

This frankness, keenness, directness and vividness appear in his frequent character sketches.   How solemn

[1] Quoted by Brown, p. 85.   [2] *Idem*, pp. 85–86.

and searching his words could be this description of remorse shows.

"There is a warning conscience and a gnawing conscience. The warning conscience cometh before sin, the gnawing conscience followeth after sin. The warning conscience is often lulled asleep, but the gnawing conscience wakeneth her again. If there be any hell in this world, they which feel the worm of conscience gnaw upon their hearts may truly say that they have felt the torments of hell. Who can express that man's horror but himself? Nay, what horrors are there which he cannot express himself? Sorrows are met in his soul at a feast; and fear, thought and anguish divide his soul between them. All the furies of hell leap upon his heart like a stage. Thought calleth to fear; fear whistleth to horror; horror beckoneth to despair, and saith, Come and help me to torment the sinner. One saith that she cometh from this sin, and another saith that she cometh from that sin, so he goeth through a thousand deaths and cannot die." [1]

4. Even greater as a Puritan preacher than Henry Smith was Thomas Adams (died *after* 1630), "the Shakespeare of the Puritans." "While Adams is not so sustained as Jeremy Taylor, nor so continuously sparkling as Thomas Fuller, he is surpassingly eloquent, and much more thought-laden than either." While doctrine of the Calvinistic Evangelical type had a large place in his preaching, he did not overlook morals and manners. He insists on both learning and piety in the preacher, and warns him against seeking the applause of men. In a sermon on the Fatal Banquet he anticipates Bunyan in describing the vanity of human desires and efforts. The following sentences explain why he was likened to Shakespeare:

"Oh, how goodly this building of man appears when it is clothed with beauty and honour! A face full of majesty, the throne of comeliness wherein the whiteness of the lily contends with the sanguine of the rose; an active hand,

---

[1] Quoted by Brown, pp. 88–89.

an erected countenance, an eye sparkling out lustre, a
smooth complexion arising from an excellent temperature
and composition. Oh, what a workman was this, that could
raise such a fabric out of the earth and lay such orient
colours upon dust."

Aware of man's dignity, he is moved by the tragedy of
man's sin and refusal of God's grace.

" Come then, beloved, to Jesus Christ, come freely,
come betimes, the flesh calls, we come ; vanity calls, we
flock; the world calls, we fly; let Christ call early and
late, He has yet to say, ' Ye will not come unto Me that ye
might have life.' " [1]

5. More typical of the Puritan school, which was more
doctrinal in form, and in spirit more experimental and
evangelical, than either Smith or Adams, was Dr.
Thomas Goodwin (1600–1679). The character of his
preaching was determined by the nature of his experience.
From deep conviction of sin he was delivered by firm
assurance of grace. This inward change at once banished
the ambition he had cherished to win popularity by the
" vainglorious eloquence" cultivated by some preachers
at the university, and brought him to the resolution that
he would " preach wholly and altogether sound and wholesome words, without affectation of wit and vanity of
eloquence." At the end of his life he could say : " I have
preached what I thought was truly edifying, either for
conversion or bringing them up to eternal life." Dr.
Brown regards as characteristic of his preaching, and so
outlines the argument of a sermon on " The Heart of
Christ in Heaven to sinners on earth." The purpose of
this sermon, he says, " was to make intensely real to the
men to whom he spoke the Christ who had gone beyond
the region of sight into the heavens—to make them feel
that He was as closely one with them in sympathy and
personal relations of helpfulness as though they could look
into His face." [2]   The argument may be summarised in one
sentence. The living Christ is the same in character and

[1] Brown, *op. cit.*, pp. 89–95.   [2] *Op. cit.*, pp. 100–114.

purpose as the historical Jesus; and what He is in heaven that as universally present He also is to us on earth.[1]

6. After 1662, Puritanism survived under the name of Nonconformity. Hering mentions as the representatives of what he calls " the ascetic tendency," to which also he ascribes an influence on German pietism, Richard Baxter (1615–1691) and John Bunyan (1628–1688). To each of these Dr. Brown devotes a lecture. John Bunyan's *Pilgrim's Progress* is one of the classics of English literature, but here we must think of him only as a preacher.

" John Bunyan is chiefly thought of," says Brown, " as a Dreamer of wonderful dreams, but he was also, as his contemporaries have told us, one of the most living preachers England has ever known. His own intense religious experience largely aided his genius in this. As he tells us himself, he had tarried long at Sinai to see the fire and the cloud and the darkness, that he might fear the Lord all the days of his life upon earth, and tell of his wonders to others. So that when, in after days, he spoke with kindling eye and tongue of fire the things that he had seen and felt, men bent to his words as the cane bends to the wind. No piler-up of mere rhetoric was this Dreamer of Bedford, but one deeply learned in the lore of human souls, heaven-taught in the great and wonderful art of laying hold of men." [2]

His idea, which he largely realised, of the preacher is given in his description of the picture Christian saw in the house of the Interpreter.

" Christian saw the picture of a very grave person hang up against the wall; and this was the fashion of it. It had eyes uplift to Heaven, the best of Books in his hand, the law of Truth was written upon his lips, the world was behind his back; it stood as if it pleaded with men, and a crown of gold did hang over its head." [3]

Bunyan has the Christian minister in view in his description of Evangelist, the porter Watchful, Greatheart,

[1] HLH, p. 137.
[2] *Op. cit.*, p. 133. See *Life of John Bunyan*, by John Brown, D.D., London, 1885.
[3] P. 135.

and the Shepherds of the Delectable Mountains, Knowledge, Experience, Watchful, and Sincere. As a preacher, "he was a master of grand and noble Saxon speech";[1] he aimed at simplicity and directness; he sustained the interest of his hearers, never becoming dull; he confined himself to permanent and universal truths, the central themes, and "spoke of them with an honest ring of clear conviction."[2] So familiar are, or should be, his writings, that no illustration of his subjects or style need be given.

7. Richard Baxter is enshrined in history as the Kidderminster Pastor, for it is for his faithful and successful work in that then unpromising place that he should be remembered even more than for his writings, one of which, *The Saint's Everlasting Rest*, may be mentioned as a religious classic.

"There have been three or four parishes in England which have been raised by their pastors to a national, almost a world-wide, fame. Of these the most conspicuous is Kidderminster; for, Baxter without Kidderminster would have been but half of himself; and Kidderminster without Baxter would have had nothing but its carpets."[3]

While he was a model as a pastor in his care of souls, it was his preaching that transformed the town. A godless people were turned to godliness. The carpet-weavers became deeply versed in theology, but better still, were marked by their spirituality and sanctity. The people repeated his sermons in their lives with like effect.

"The holy, humble, blameless lives of the religious sort was a great advantage to me," says Baxter himself. "The malicious sort could not say, Your professors here are as proud and covetous as any. But the blameless lives of godly people did shame opposers, and put to silence the ignorance of foolish men, and many were won by their good conversations."[4]

---

[1] P. 145.   [2] P. 154.
[3] Dean Stanley, quoted by Brown, p. 169.
[4] Quoted by Brown, p. 171.

Nature had not given him any advantage as a preacher, except a glowing eye and a moving voice. He combined " vigorous intellect and vehement speech " with " a devotion pure and ethereal, a benevolence ardent and sincere," and an unfailing earnestness. His own weak health made very real to him the unseen future. He says of himself :

" Doing all in bodily weakness, as a dying man, my soul was all the more easily brought to seriousness, and to preach as a dying man to dying men ; for drowsy formality and customariness doth but stupefy the hearers and rock them asleep. It must be serious preaching which must make men serious in hearing and obeying it." [1]

He advises preachers to feel ever that necessity is laid upon them in study and labour alike.

8. Although George Fox (1624–1691) is not even mentioned in the Histories of Preaching the writer has consulted, his name cannot be altogether passed over. From his twelfth year employed by a shoemaker and shepherd, his youth was passed in inward struggles, and in his nineteenth year he began to denounce the clergy of the Church for selling the word. Abandoning his earthly calling, clothed in leather, amid hardships, perils, and persecutions, as " a man of sorrows " he moved about the country preaching his own doctrines—" Christ in us," " the Unction from above," and " the Inner Light." In six years he had gathered companions around him, in spite of all attempts to suppress the movement. Three years later he found a home in the Manor of Swarthmoor ; and here was founded the community, nicknamed Quakers, calling itself the Society of Friends. He employed his frequent imprisonments for writing, and so continued to influence the movement. In its interests, too, he visited North America, the West Indies, and Germany. His mysticism retained a Christian character, but was not altogether free of fanaticism. To regard him, however, as only affording an interesting object of study in religious pathology would be to misunderstand him. With all his eccentricity, he must be

[1] Quoted by Brown, p. 177.

regarded as " a man of the spirit " raised up for a work
needing to be done.

III.

Dr. Brown maintains that "any study of Puritan
preaching in the seventeenth century would be incomplete
without some reference to that small body of remarkable
men known as the 'Cambridge Platonists,' or, the 'Sect
of Latitude Men,' or the 'Latitudinarians' as they were
variously called; including Benjamin Whichcote, Ralph
Cudworth, Nathaniel Culverwell, John Smith, and Henry
More," since "though separating themselves from much
that was distinctively Puritan, they yet started from Puritanism and were greatly influenced by it."[1] This school
attempted to reconcile reason and revelation, Christianity
and philosophy; but they failed to exercise any wide or
lasting influence on either religious or speculative thought.

1. One of the hearers whom Whichcote inspired was
John Tillotson (1630–1694), who became Archbishop
of Canterbury in 1691. Hering[2] mentions him as the

[1] P. 114.

[2] HLH 136. Simpson in his *Preachers and Teachers*, pp. 106–107, offers
an estimate of him worth quoting. "Tillotson, in fact, represents more
fully, perhaps, than any other English divine, the religious appeal most
consonant with the spirit and ideas of the middle-classes among his fellow-
countrymen—in fact, of the typical Englishman. Springing from a class
and county which have no vein of mysticism, and where the dictates of a
common sense, which is taken as coincident with reason, are more highly
valued than the impulses of an exalted spirit, there is something solid, not
to say tangible, in these views of religion which he most forcibly recom-
mends. He is no prophet nor expounder of mysteries. He moves more
easily among the normal effects of religion than in the contemplation of God,
or the realization of Christ or the spiritual life. The very phrases, the very
turns of expression which he adopts are those with which we are still familiar
in the speech of sober and undemonstrative Britons. What is personal,
direct, intimate, he instinctively avoids. He will speak of 'professing the
Christian religion' where a Spurgeon might speak of 'closing with Christ.'
Jesus is 'the author of the doctrine' rather than 'the friend of sinners.' On
Good Friday he 'considers the sufferings of Christ as a proper means of
salvation,' instead of preaching the Gospel and leading burdened souls to the
foot of the Cross. There is a studied moderation in his commendation of
the example of Christ."

most noble representative of the new type of preaching in which the emphasis fell on reason rather than faith, moral character rather than religious experience, and, under the influence of science and philosophy, the Christian message was rationalised and moralised. Such was his fame as a preacher that his sermons were translated into German and French, and won the praise of Mosheim and the admiration of Voltaire. Bishop Burnet said of him:

"He was not only the best preacher of the age, but seemed to have brought preaching to perfection; his sermons were so well liked that all the nation proposed him as a pattern and studied to copy after him." [1]

His subjects, however, do not awaken our interest, nor his style suit our taste to-day.

2. While representing the same tendency, Robert South (1633–1716) may be regarded as even a greater preacher than Tillotson. Henry Rogers assigns him a very high place.

"Of all the English preachers, South seems to furnish in point of style the truest specimen of pulpit eloquence. His robust intellect, his shrewd common sense, his vehement feelings, and a fancy always more distinguished by force than by elegance, admirably qualified him for a powerful public speaker. His style is everywhere direct, condensed, pungent. His sermons are well worthy of frequent and diligent perusal by every young preacher." [2]

Dr. Brown appears to endorse this opinion, and adds in confirmation of it a reference to one of his sermons.

"There is a sermon of his in which he pours scorn on the florid declamation, the mere tinsel rhetoric which some people think to be so very fine. He mentions no names, but you can see that he is speaking for the especial benefit of his illustrious but too fanciful and ornate contemporary Jeremy Taylor. The passage is worth quoting: 'I speak the words of soberness,' said St. Paul, 'and I preach the Gospel not with the enticing words of man's wisdom.' This was the way of the Apostle's discoursing of things sacred.

---

[1] Quoted by DHP ii. p. 165.   [2] *Idem*, p. 167.

Nothing here of 'the fringes of the north star'; nothing 'of nature's becoming unnatural'; nothing of the 'down of angels' wings' or 'the beautiful locks of cherubims'; no starched similitudes introduced with a 'Thus have I seen a cloud rolling in its airy mansion,' and the like. No—these were sublimities above the use of the apostolic spirit. For the Apostles, poor mortals, were content to take lower steps, and to tell the world in plain terms that he who believed should be saved, and that he who believed not should be damned. And this was the dialect which pierced the conscience and made the hearers cry out, Men and brethren, what shall we do? It tickled not the ear, but it sunk into the heart, and when men came from such sermons they never commended the preacher for his taking voice or gesture, for the fineness of such a simile or the quaintness of such a sentence; but they spoke like men conquered with the overpowering force and evidence of the most concerning truths, much in the words of the two disciples going to Emmaus: 'Did not our hearts burn within us while He opened to us the Scriptures'? In a word, the Apostles' preaching was therefore mighty and successful, because plain, natural, and familiar, and by no means above the capacity of their hearers; nothing being more preposterous than for those who were professedly aiming at men's hearts to miss the mark by shooting over their heads."[1]

This is admirable criticism for every age. But South himself showed more mind than heart.

3. While these preachers opposed themselves to the increasing deistic tendency, yet they had not a little in common with it.

"The same tendencies," says Fisher, "which produced the Latitudinarian movement led, in minds of a different cast and training, to the development of Deism, and gave rise to the Deistic controversy. There were minds less appreciative of the need and the nature of Christianity. There were special co-operative influences, among which was the effect of the Copernican discovery upon the views taken of Scripture and its effect, along with that of the philosophy of Bacon, and of the new studies in natural science, upon the general mood of feeling. This new mood

---

[1] *Op. cit.*, pp. 175–177.

may be described, for the lack of a better term, as rational-
istic. Deism in its English type did not, like the Epicurean
theory, deny the Providence of the Deity. It cast aside the
belief in a special revelation, and of course the reality of
denied miracles. The Latitudinarians sought for the basis
of the religious creed in the truths held in common by the
various contending Christian, or at least, Protestant bodies.
The Deists did the same in reference to the different forms
of religion, including the Christian. The value of the Bible
is made to consist in its republication, but without supernatural sanction, of the principles of natural religion, ascertainable and ascertained by 'the light of nature.'" [1]

4. The controversy does not require our close attention,
but it is necessary to remember that it was a potent
influence on the religious thought and life of England,
depressing spiritual vitality and decreasing moral vigour
alike. Amid such conditions we cannot look for, and we
do not find, great preaching. A few names, however, call
for mention. We must mention first of all Bishop Butler
(1692–1752). The conditions under which he did his
work have been described by Canon Simpson in his study
of Butler's *Sermons*.[2]

" Men laughed at ideals, and scorned enthusiasms. They
knew no measure of excellence but that of material comfort,
no standard of value but that of personal advantage. The
aristocracy were devoted to cynicism and clothes; the
middle - classes immersed in commerce; the proletariat
steeped in gin. If religion was ever near to extinction in
this country it was then. As the brotherhood of man was
discounted by a cool self-love, so the love of God was deemed
an extravagant enthusiasm by a temper that mistook itself
for sober Reason. . . . There were no problems. For the
fashionable there were routs, for the merchants wealth, for
the multitude enough to eat and too much to drink. And
so the world wagged." [3]

As Butler's own words in his advertisement of his
famous work *The Analogy* show, he was acutely sensitive

[1] *History of Christian Doctrine*, pp. 371–372.
[2] *Preachers and Teachers*, v. pp. 145–173.
[3] *Idem*, pp. 146–147.

to the contemptuous rather than hostile attitude of the "people of discernment" to Christianity. To the "unmitigated individualism" of its morals he opposed a conception of the relation of the individual to society, which is being now forced on our recognition.

"The greatness of Bishop Butler," says Simpson, "consists in this, that, when the developments of the nineteenth century were yet unborn, when neither biological science nor industrial disorganization nor religious revival had emphasised the social principle, he reaffirmed, against the prevailing sentiment of the age, and by vigorous application of the very method by which his contemporaries endeavoured to establish their 'reasonable' view of life, the great truth rooted deeply in human nature, the basis alike of moral relationships and social unities and submission to a Living Will larger than the purposes of men, which St. Paul had expressed in the words 'We are members one of another.'"[1]

For him the benevolence which recognised the claims of fellow-men was bound to, nay even rooted in, the piety which submitted to the Will of God.

"Human nature is so constituted," he says, "that every good affection implies the love of itself. It becomes the object of a new affection in the same person. Thus, to be righteous, implies in it the love of righteousness; to be benevolent, the love of benevolence; to be good, the love of goodness; whether this righteousness, benevolence, or goodness be viewed as in our mind, or in another's. And the love of God, as a being perfectly good, is the love of perfect goodness contemplated in a Being or Person. Thus morality and religion, virtue and piety, will at last necessarily coincide, run up into one and the same point, and *love* will be in all senses *the end of the commandment.*"[2]

His contribution to ethical theory is contained in fifteen sermons, which are hard to read, and must have been even harder to hear. The difficulties they present are not altogether due to their subjects, but to the defects of Butler's style, as well as the too great closeness of his reasoning. While he cannot be taken as an example of an

[1] *Idem*, p. 158.   [2] Quoted by Simpson, *op. cit.*, p. 173.

effective preacher, yet his contribution to the thought and life of his age was so weighty, that he cannot be passed over in a history of preaching. Few, if any, sermons have been so much studied as his have been.

5. Contemporary with Butler, but illustrating the Puritan or Nonconformist as he does the Anglican type, were two Independent preachers whose names are still held in honour, Isaac Watts (1674–1748)[1] and Philip Doddridge (1702–1751). They represent the quiet and sober evangelicalism, which had not yet caught the glow of the Evangelical Revival, and may therefore be mentioned here. Watts is best known as a hymn writer, but his sermons do not show the qualities one would expect, for they are not poetical nor even emotional. They do not show him as a great preacher. Doddridge is noted for his work as the teacher of many preachers in his Academy, first at Kibworth near Leicester, and then at Northampton,[2] and for his well-known work on experimental religion, *The Rise and Progress of Religion in the Soul*. "His sermons," says Dargan, "are judicious rather than weighty in thought, evangelical in theology, clear in order and style, but with no special unction or eloquence."[3] His work as an educationalist deserves lasting remembrance. "Doddridge was great not only in his own Academy at Northampton, but in his influence in the country generally. In his day, to mention Northampton Academy was not merely to speak of the best educational centre in the country, it was also to speak of a new education."[4] The students were encouraged in the study of French that they might become familiar with the great French preachers. Of the kind of teaching given the same writer says: "Indeed the Tutors

[1] *The Life of Isaac Watts*, by Thomas Wright, London, 1914.

[2] Admission to his Academy was not confined to students for the Ministry; but boys preparing for other professions were also admitted. The sons of clergy and lay members of the Established Church were sent because the education was better and cheaper than at the Universities. There was careful moral supervision, and no "undue influence" was exerted to effect any change of religious opinion. (See *Dissenting Academies in England*, by Irene Parker, M.A., pp. 83–84.)

[3] DHP ii. p. 331.   [4] Parker, *op. cit.*, p. 101.

seem to have been desirous not of cramming their students with facts, but of educating them and of training them to think, and what is more, to express their thoughts in their own tongue." [1]

IV.

1. Across the Border there was in the eighteenth century a movement which resulted in a similar contrast of types among the Scottish preachers, that between the Evangelicals and the Moderates. As this movement began before the Evangelical Revival in England, and was due to the influence of a book, *The Marrow of Modern Divinity*, which, although the authorship is unknown, belongs to the Puritan type in England, it falls to be mentioned in this connection.

(1) Of the book which had so great an influence on the preaching of Scotland, either by commanding assent or provoking antagonism, the modern editor, the Rev. Dr. C. G. McCree, writes:

"The design of the treatise is to elucidate and establish the perfect freeness of the Gospel salvation; to throw wide open the gates of righteousness; to lead the sinner straight to the Saviour; to introduce him as guilty, impotent and undone; and to persuade him to grasp, without a moment's hesitation, the outstretched hand of God's mercy." [2]

(2) Thomas Boston (1676–1732) was ordained in 1699 to the charge of Simprim in Berwickshire; but his mind was in difficulty and doubt about the Gospel. It was this book from England which brought him theologically out of darkness into light, when he found it in 1770 in the house of one of his parishioners. In 1717 he was led to speak to others about it, and in 1718 it was reprinted. Its influence spread so rapidly that in 1720 the General Assembly of the Church of Scotland condemned its teaching on five matters as contrary to the Holy Scriptures, the Confession of Faith, and the Catechisms. A remonstrance from the "Marrow" men, as they were called, against this decision was dismissed in 1722, and the previous action

[1] P. 103.   [2] P. xv, ed. published by Bryce, 1902.

was confirmed and explained. The controversy need not be followed further, but its issue was the first Secession in 1733. The opponents of the book were hyper-Calvinists.

"The Calvinism of the *Marrow*, on the other hand, was broad, catholic, liberal. The Marrow men, both in England and Scotland, dwelt much upon the love of God for the whole world, the offer of Christ to every sinner. . . . Believing the Gospel offer was for all, that to mankind sinners the call and overture of divine love are to be addressed, the moderate Calvinists of the eighteenth century were animated and dominated by the missionary spirit of Christianity." [1]

Among the " Marrow " men were noted preachers such as Boston himself, and the brothers Erskine, Ebenezer (1680–1756) and Ralph (1685–1752). Of their work in Scotland a general description must suffice.

"The Ministers of the Church of Scotland who were evangelical in creed and evangelistic in preaching, proclaiming a gospel of good tidings of great joy to all people, were preachers whom the common people heard gladly. They secured large audiences wherever they ministered, and on communion occasions they gathered immense crowds to their open-air services. To the Marrow men and those who lighted their torches at the same altar fire we owe the maintenance in Scotland of the evangelistic and evangelical succession at a time when the dominant party in the Church of Scotland, becoming heartless in a high and dry hyper-Calvinism, abandoned theology for morality, and so drifted into moderatism." [2]

(3) A sample of the kind of preaching of these men is afforded by Boston's series of sermons on *The Fourfold State of Man* (1712). In the opening sentences of the first sermon he clearly states his intention.

"There are four things very necessary to be known by all that would see heaven. First, what man was in the state of innocence as God made him. Secondly, what he is in the state of corrupt nature as he had unmade himself. Thirdly, what he must be in the state of grace as 'created in Christ Jesus unto good works,' if ever he be made a par-

---

[1] *Idem*, pp. xxviii, xxix.   [2] *Idem*, pp. xxix, xxx.

taker of the 'inheritance of the saints in life.' And, lastly, what he should be in his eternal state as made by the Judge of all, either perfectly happy or completely miserable, and that for ever. These are weighty points that touch the vitals of practical godliness; from which most men and even many professors, in these dregs of time, are quite estranged. I design, therefore, under the divine conduct to open up these things and apply them."[1]

Much of the theology is now antiquated; the form of the sermons is scholastic to the extreme; there is a lack both of imagination and illustration; and yet the fervent feeling gives them living power.

(4) When just entering on his work, Boston wrote a *Soliloquy on the art of Man-Fishing*.[2] The account he gives of the occasion of writing it is worth quoting, as it reveals the preacher's true aim.

"The occasion thereof was this — January 6, 1699, reading in secret my heart was touched with Matt. iv. 19, 'Follow Me, and I will make you fishers of men.' My soul cried out for accomplishing of that to me, and I was very desirous to know how I might follow Christ so as to become a fisher of men, and for my own instruction on that point I addressed myself to the consideration of it in that manner. And, indeed, it was much in my heart in these days, not to preach the wisdom of mine own heart, or produce of my own gifts, but to depend on the Lord for light that I might, if I could have reached it, been able to say of every word, 'Thus saith the Lord.'"[3]

This meditation on his craft by a master of it is still worthy of the study of his fellow-craftsmen.

2. The Moderates were opposed to all enthusiasm, which they regarded as fanaticism. They insisted on moral character rather than religious experience; but as their morality had no deep roots, so it bore no rich fruits. They attached much importance to good taste and literary excellence.

(1) One of the extreme instances of this tendency was

[1] Quoted in DHP ii. pp. 336–337.
[2] Published by Alexander Gardner, 1899.   [3] *Op. cit.*, p. 11.

Alexander Carlyle (1722–1805), who can be described only as a cultured, capable and respectable worldling, for whom the ministry was "the clerical profession," and who prized above all the admiration which his oratory evoked among his genteel hearers.[1]

(2) To the same school belonged Dr. Hugh Blair (1718–1800). He combined the duties of a parish in Edinburgh with the professorship of Belles Lettres at Edinburgh University. His lectures in Rhetoric were very popular, and for many years were regarded as the best text-book on the subject. A man of finer character than Carlyle, his preaching was of the same type.

"His sermons are cold presentations of the accepted Christian doctrines and ethics, without the warmth of evangelic earnestness or the driving power of great conviction. There is want of vitality, and the elegance which characterizes them has passed away along with the starched frills, powdered wigs, and buckled knee-breeches of that age."[2]

In Scotland, as in England, there was need of religious revival, although in each there was a "remnant."

[1] DHP ii. p. 339. [2] P. 341.

CHAPTER VII.

ORATORS AND COURTIERS.

I.

1. PREACHING is more appreciated and exercises greater influence in Protestantism than in Roman Catholicism; and there can be no doubt that the classic period of the Roman Catholic pulpit in France had as one of its antecedents the influence of the French preachers of the Reformation. It was inevitable that much of this preaching was polemical, directed against Roman Catholicism, in defence of the Reformed theology. This controversy worked less injuriously on religious life than in Germany; and as regards the form of the sermons, French tact and taste saved preaching from the commonness and coarseness into which elsewhere controversy fell. Hering distinguishes two periods in Protestant preaching in France.

"In the first controversy comes much to the front; the development of thought attaches itself closely to the text, and endeavours, if at all, to get beyond the analytical-exegetical method to a grouping arrangement, and to a structure which attaches itself to the thoughts of the Biblical passage." . . . "This epoch passes slowly over into the other, in which the synthetic displaces the disjointed analytic method, and instead of the labour to explain the Bible comes the endeavour to seize a main thought in the text, and to unfold it." [1]

It is this tendency to a more artistic form which prepares the way for the classic period of the French pulpit.

---

[1] HLH, p. 132. Hering refers in a note on p. 131 to the work of Vinet, *Historie de la Prédication parmi les réformés de la France au 17 siècle.* Paris, 1860.

2. One of the most vigorous opponents of Roman Catholicism was Pierre du Moulin (1568–1658). In his preaching there was no oratory; it was simple and popular. The eloquence of Moses Amyraut (1596–1664) excited the admiration even of Roman Catholics, and impressed such critical hearers as Richelieu and Mazarin in favour of the persecuted Protestants. Jean D'Ailly (1595–1670) was regarded in his Church as the greatest man since Calvin; although he is as vehement a controversialist, he is also a greater stylist than his predecessors. To the transition between the two periods belongs Jean Claude (1619–1687). Even his opponents spoke of " ce fameux M. Claude," and the great Bossuet dreaded his logical powers. He already was influenced by the conditions which produced the classic French oratory. Among the exiles from France after the revocation of the Edict of Nantes (1685) who carried this influence with them, the most noted was P. Dubosc (died at Rotterdam 1692), of whom Van Oosterzee gives a very high estimate.

" After Louis XIV. had on one occasion listened to him pleading the cause of the Protestants, he declared that he had that day heard the most eloquent man of his Kingdom. As an orator he rendered to Calvinism no less important services than did Claude as a controversialist ; and when he was banished, England, Denmark and Holland vied with each other in seeking the honour of affording him an asylum. The seven volumes of his discourses present equally fine proofs of invention, as of arrangement and action. In him was made manifest anew how much an extensive theological knowledge, when its results are applied with tact, contributes to the effectiveness of preaching. A plastic form is here combined with abundance of material, and if the orator in some passages shows that he has taken Basil as a model, he nevertheless still survives Dubosc." [1]

A suggestive criticism is offered by Hering:

" His practical interest is above all directed to the moral impression, while polemics fall into the background.

---

[1] OPT, pp. 129–130.   See also HLH, pp. 147–149.

Although for this purpose he is helped by his rich culture, his knowledge of men and of the world, yet he stands behind the Catholics, whom casuistry and the confessional gave a multitude of individual applications, in their ability to deal with the special cases and circumstances; a defect of the Protestant preaching of the time generally."[1]

3. A still more famous name is that of Jacques Saurin (1677–1730), on whom the influence of the great Catholic preachers is evident. While Hering regards him as not the equal to the Catholic orators, although greater in respect of his evangelical message, Vinet asserts that not only is he the greatest of the Protestant preachers, but he is even not inferior to any of the Catholic masters of the pulpit. He was, however, an unequal preacher, sometimes insipid, prolix, irrelevant, but often and quickly he soared from these lower levels of thoughts and speech into the loftiest heights of a rare eloquence, sustained by a genuine inspiration of "living faith and joyful hope."[2] An illustration of his style may be given from a sermon on The Effect of Passion (1 Pet 2^1).

"O deplorable state of man! The littleness of his mind will not allow him to contemplate any object but that of his passion, while it is present to his senses; it will not allow him, then, to recollect the motives, the great motives, that should impel him to his duty; and when the object is absent, not being able to offer it to his senses, he presents it again to his imagination clothed with new and foreign charms, deceitful ideas of which make up for its absence, and excite in him a love more ardent, than that of actual possession, when he felt at least the folly and vanity of it. O horrid war of the passions against the soul! Shut the door of your closets against the enchanted object, it will enter with you. Try to get rid of it by traversing plains, and fields, and whole countries; cleave the waves of the sea, fly on the wings of the wind, and try to put between yourself and your enchantress the deep, the rolling ocean, she will travel with you, sail with you, everywhere haunt you, because wherever you go you will carry yourself, and

---

[1] HLH, p. 149.   [2] OPT, p. 131.

within you, deep in your imagination, the bewitching image impressed." Change of earthly objects, he then by a number of illustrations shews, can bring no satisfaction; and hence his conclusion :

"Let us shorten our labour. Let us put all creatures into one class. Let us cry 'vanity' in all. If we determine to pursue new objects, let us choose such as are capable of satisfying us. Let us not seek them here below. They are not to be found in this old world, which God has cursed. They are in the 'new heavens and the new earth.'"[1]

II.

1. While the preaching of the Reformed Church in the seventeenth century showed the influence of classical culture, yet it was excelled by the Roman Catholic pulpit oratory, which in turn soon began to affect the style of preaching not only of the Protestants of France, but even of Germany.[2] The French language is marked by its lucidity; the French people possess a quality which can be expressed only by their own word *esprit*; quickness of feeling, lightness of touch, fineness of taste, a ready wit, vivid imagination, all combined to produce the brilliance of the classic orators. In their art they were under the influence of ancient models. The appeal was not to the common people, but to the King and his Court, for whom preaching was an æsthetic interest. The King chose the preachers at Versailles, and rewarded them with his compliments; in the correspondence as well as the conversation of the Court the merits of the orators were discussed. We should do injustice to the preachers themselves, however, if we assumed that the favour and applause of the King and Court were all that they sought in their endeavours. Doubtless they hoped and strove to use their gifts as orators for the higher end of influencing the King, and through him the Court and the nation, for their moral and religious good. A minor motive for the Catholic orators was the desire to excel their

---

[1] CME ix. pp. 145-146.
[2] See *Great French Sermons*, ed. by O'Mahony, London, 1917.

Protestant rivals in the art of the pulpit.   But even when
we have tried to be as generous in our judgment of their
intentions as we can, we are forced to admit that there was
not a little in their methods which now offends.   In their
panegyrics and funeral sermons there was an exaggerated
patriotism ; and their flattery went beyond the bounds of
good taste, and sometimes even became blasphemous.   This
national enthusiasm was allied even in the pulpit with
Roman Catholic fanaticism.   These orators provoked and
exulted in the persecution of their Protestant fellow-
countrymen.   They all approved the revocation of the
Edict of Nantes, and rejoiced in any humiliation of a
Protestant State.   Such preaching could not fail to be
injurious to morality as well as religion, and its influence
did not retard, but rather stimulated the process of national
deterioration, which one hundred years later found its judgment in the French Revolution.   But with " the wood, hay,
stubble," there were mingled in these sermons to the King
and his Court " gold, silver, and precious stones."   Vices were
boldly and frankly denounced ; solemn warnings were uttered
against piety from unworthy motives.   The duties of a king
even were openly and earnestly declared.   But such is the
perversity of human nature.   The courtiers gained a malicious pleasure in listening to exhortations addressed to their
sovereign, and found enjoyment in the eloquent denunciation of the vices which they had no intention whatever of
abandoning.[1]

2. While a statement of the general characteristics of
the period may be made, yet individual differences must
be recognised ; and each of the preachers must be separately treated.   In Jules Mascaron (1643–1703) and
Esprit Fléchier (1632–1710) the art of the orator had
not yet found its full development.[2]   The itinerant
preacher, Jacques Bridaine (died 1767), excelled the
even famous preachers in his avoidance of flattery, and
his courage in exposing sin and its penalty.[3]   François
de Salignac de la Mothe Fénelon (1651–1715) stands

[1] See HLH, pp. 137–142.   [2] HLH, p. 142.   [3] OPT, p. 132.

apart, more attractive in personality, if less oratorical in style. The summit of the eloquence of the age is reached by three preachers, Jacques Bénigne Bossuet (1627–1704), the Bishop of Nîmes and Meaux, Louis de Bourdaloue (1632–1704), the Jesuit father, and a little later in date than these contemporaries, Jean Baptiste Massillon (1663–1742), an Oratorian, with leanings to the Jesuits.[1]

3. Bossuet first claims notice. (1) He was in his home as well as in his course of training brought under the influence of the Holy Scriptures, and their thought and language greatly and lastingly affected his preaching more as regards the style than the contents. Into the forms of prophetic speech he pours his own ardour and imagination. A diligent student of the Fathers, he learned much from Augustine and Chrysostom. The third factor in his development as a preacher was humanism, the culture of the Renaissance. The native intensity and impetuosity of his personality fused all these elements into a glowing mass, which, however, shone rather than warmed.[2] Van Oosterzee compares him to "a broad mountain stream, which with thundering roar rushes down from the heights, and carries away everything which would offer resistance."[3] His usual method of preparation was to make a rough draft only, and to leave to the moment the filling out and shaping of his sermon ; a proof of his extraordinary power as a speaker. His art appears more fully in the funeral orations, which he afterwards worked over with great care, now holding himself in and then letting himself go as his mastery of his craft required. A learned theologian, a vehement controversialist, a consummate courtier, a supreme orator, his is not the eloquence of the life which is hid with Christ in God. Tested by this, his oratory often sounds hollow, and feels cold. (2) His funeral sermon on the Death of the Grande Condé is an example of his use of the pulpit for the unstinted praise of the great, and

[1] See HLH, pp. 142–147 ; DHP, ii. pp. 82–117 ; OPT, pp. 131–134.
[2] See HLH, p. 143.   [3] OPT, p. 131.

yet in the following passage he justifies himself for so doing with masterly skill.

" Let us try, then, to forget our grief. Here an object greater and worthier of this pulpit presents itself to my mind; it is God, who makes warriors and conquerors. ' It is Thou,' said David unto Him, ' who hast trained my hand to battle, and my fingers to hold the sword.' If He inspires courage, no less is He the bestower of other good qualities, both of heart and mind. His mighty hand is the source of everything; it is He who sends from heaven generous sentiments, wise counsels and every worthy thought. But He wishes us to know how to distinguish between the gifts He abandons to His enemies and those He reserves for His servants. What distinguishes His friends from all others is piety. Until this gift of Heaven has been received, all others not only are as naught, but even bring ruin on those who are endowed with them; without this inestimable gift of piety what would the Prince de Condé have been, even with his great heart and great genius ? No, my brethren, if piety had not, as it were, consecrated his other virtues, these princes would have found no consolation for their grief, nor this pontiff any confidence in his prayers, nor would I myself utter with conviction the praises which I owe to so great a man. Let us, by this example, then set human glory at naught; let us destroy the idol of the ambitious, that it might fall to pieces before this altar. Let us to-day join together (for with a subject so noble we may do it) all the qualities of a superior nature; and for the glory of truth, let us demonstrate, in a prince admired of the universe, that what makes heroes, that what carries to the highest pitch worldly glory, worth, magnanimity, natural goodness—all attributes of the heart; vivacity, penetration, grandeur and sublimity of genius—attributes of the mind; would be but an illusion were piety not a part of them—in a word, that piety is the essence of the man. It is this, gentlemen, which you will see in the for ever memorable life of the most high and mighty Prince Louis de Bourbon, Prince de Condé, first prince of the blood." [1]

4. It was in 1669 when Bossuet had reached the height of his fame, and withdrew from Paris to his diocese of Condom, that the Jesuit father, Bourdaloue, by his

[1] WGS ii. pp. 86–88.

eloquence captured the French aristocracy. At six in the morning servants were sent to secure places for the afternoon service. His sermons were taken down as preached, and were published without his authority, He died before he had carried out his intention to revise them for publication. For thirty-four years he held his audiences spellbound whenever he opened his lips.

(1) " Bourdaloue," says Feugère, " addresses himself much more to the reason than to the imagination and the emotions. . . . If sometimes his tone became more tender or more passionate, these are exceptions which seem unintended. One could even say, that the more a subject lent itself to pathos, the more was Bourdaloue on his guard against it." [1] He excelled Bossuet in the orderly arrangement and the logical cogency of his sermons. " He is—*Sit venia verbo*—as compared with this royal eagle, as the royal serpent which with velvet coils slowly surrounds the object of its prey, softly, indeed, but in such a way that the captured animal can no longer escape. He convinces you, but—without carrying you with him; through the intellect he seeks the way to the heart, but frequently he does this in a manner which reminds you rather of the accomplished barrister than of the preacher pleading with unction from on high." [2]

His expression went beyond his impression; and eloquence tended to drop to rhetoric. With his intellectual vigour he combined moral seriousness. His training as a Jesuit in casuistry gave him masterly skill in dealing with moral issues. He was bold enough not only to depict vices generally, but to denounce the evil customs of his own age. He held up the Court of Herod as a mirror in which the Court at Versailles might see itself. In this respect he recalls Chrysostom.[3]

(2) In a sermon on the Passion of Jesus Christ, Bourdaloue expounds 1 Co 5^{22-24}. In dealing with *Christ Crucified the power of God*, he thus explains that death :

[1] *Bourdaloue, Sa Predication et son temps*, Paris, 1888, p. 64, quoted HLH, p. 144.

[2] OPT, pp. 131–132.   [3] See HLH, pp. 143–145.

" He died, then, only because He willed to die (Isa. liii. 7), and even in the manner He willed to die. And this, says St. Augustine, is what the God-Man alone could do; this is what shows forth, even in death, the sovereign independence of God. It is hereon I base another proposition, namely this, that the Death of Jesus Christ, if we consider it closely, was not only a miracle, but the most singular of all miracles. And why? Because, instead of dying as other men die out of weakness, out of violence, out of necessity, He died by the effort of His own absolute power; so that as Son of God and God Himself, He never exerted that absolute power more supremely than at the moment in which He consented that His most blessed soul should be separated from His body. And for this theologians give two reasons. In the first place, they say, Jesus Christ being exempt from all sin and absolutely impeccable, He could not but be naturally immortal; whence it follows that His body and His soul, which were united hypostatically with the Divinity, could not be separated from each other but by a miracle. It was, then, of necessity that Jesus Christ in order to effect this separation, should, so to speak, do violence to all the laws of ordinary providence, and that He should employ all the power which God had given Him for the destruction of that beautiful life which, although human, was at the same time the life of a God. Secondly, because Jesus Christ, in virtue of His Priesthood, was pre-eminently the High Priest of the New Law, none but He could or should offer to God the Sacrifice for the redemption of the world and immolate the Victim destined for that Sacrifice. Now, this Victim was His own Body. None then but He was to offer this Sacrifice, none but He had the power necessary for such an act. The executioners who crucified Him were indeed the ministers of the justice of God, but they were not the priests who were to sacrifice this Victim to God. For this a High Priest was needed who should be holy, innocent, spotless, separated from sinners and endowed with characteristics peculiar to Himself (Heb. vii. 26–28)." [1]

5. Thirty years elapsed between the appearance in Paris as preachers of Bourdaloue and Massillon.[2]

---

[1] *Great French Sermons*, pp. 10–12.

[2] Hering refers in a note on p. 145 to a monograph by Blampignon in two volumes. Paris.

(1) As a boy he was interested in pulpit eloquence, and attracted attention by the vivacity with which he was able to reproduce a sermon he had heard. The oratory of Bourdaloue taught him to correct his faults, but he made no man his model. He aimed, not at the oratory of the imagination and the intellect, but the eloquence of the heart. He impressed by his seriousness and his modesty. Less majestic than Bossuet, and less polished than Bourdaloue, he showed more spiritual unction as, like Barnabas, a son of consolation. Yet he could also search the conscience of his hearers, and make them see themselves as they really were. Thus he laboured in Paris for twenty years. Twice, in 1701 and 1704, he preached to the Court at Versailles. He, by his frank and bold speech, moved even the king to discontent with himself; but what does discount the value of the fact as a testimony to his power is that the king was growing old, and was under the influence of the bigoted Madame Maintenon. In the funeral sermon for Louis XIV. he allowed himself to follow the fashion of the panegyric without the restraint which might have been expected from him. More worthy of him, however, were the fatherly educative counsels which he addressed to the eighteen years old king, Louis XV., in Lent, 1718. His addresses as bishop to the clergy of his diocese show him as zealous to make his brethren worthy of their calling in the cure of souls. Though himself a preacher, he does not give any prominence to the duty of preaching.

"We should compare him," says Van Oosterzee, "by preference, not to a brilliant meteor, but to a moon veiled with fleecy clouds, which sheds a kindly light over a wide prospect."

He adds this qualification to his praise, and his words are worth repeating, as they point to the common defect of the French pulpit of the classic period, and a danger which threatens every preacher:

"We are afraid that even he too often sought to recommend himself to the refined tastes of his hearers, rather than to their awakened conscience, and that here too the courtier stood only too often in the way of the orator, and the orator in that of the preacher of the Gospel in the proper acceptation of the term."[1]

(2) However doubtful we may be of the propriety of using the pulpit in the season of Lent to give advice to a young king instead of preaching Christ Crucified, and of at any time adopting such a method of education, yet the content and spirit of the counsels are admirable.

" Sire, always regard war as the greatest scourge with which God can afflict an empire; seek to disarm rather than to conquer your enemies. God has entrusted to you the sword only for the safety of your people, and not for the misfortune of your neighbours. The empire over which heaven has set you is vast enough; be more zealous to assuage its miseries than to extend its borders; put rather your glory in redressing the misfortunes of past wars than in undertaking new ones; render your reign immortal by the happiness of your people more than by the number of your conquests; do not measure the justice of your undertakings by your power, and do not forget that in the most righteous wars, victories always bring after them as great calamities for States as the most sanguinary defeats."[2]

(3) Characteristic of his own disposition is the saying addressed to his clergy:

" It is not always the great talents which imply in us the greatest virtues. They make us more useful to men, but they do not always make us more acceptable to God; they advance his work in others, but they often retard it in ourselves."[3]

His description of the restless and reckless priest is true of all times:

" They undertake everything. All that has the appearance of being good inspires and impels them, nothing appears impossible to them, and nothing seems to them to be in the place where it should be. They would wish to

---

[1] OPT, p. 132.

[2] Blampignon, i. p. 275, quoted in HLH, pp. 146–147.

[3] *Op. cit.*, i. 125, quoted HLH, p. 147.

change everything, to displace everything. They begin by putting into general confusion all they touch under the pretext of putting it again in order. Restless, narrow, rash, venturesome, if only they are doing something, they are pleased with themselves, and think that they are fulfilling all righteousness. They rashly hurl themselves against the most delicate and difficult situations which deserve to be most carefully handled, are most exposed to great and grievous consequences, and are most capable even of baffling the most masterly prudence and skill; and when they have got out of this scrape where they come to grief and offer the public a spectacle always unbecoming for a clergyman, they go with the same foolhardiness to deal with some other undertaking which offers them no less danger, and promises them no less confusion." [1]

While these illustrations reveal to us the man, they do not show us the preacher when he most moved the hearts of men.

(4) The concluding passage of a sermon on *The Woman that was a Sinner* (Lk 7³⁷⁻³⁸) may serve as an example of his art in the pulpit.

"By her sins Mary Magdalene had been degraded in the eyes of men; they beheld with contempt the shame and the infamy of her conduct, and the Pharisee is even astonished that Jesus Christ should condescend to suffer her at His feet. For the world which authorises whatever leads to dissipation never fails to cover dissipation itself with infamy; it inspires and approves all the passions, yet it always blames all the consequences of them; its lascivious theatres resound with extravagant praises of profane love, but its conversation consists only of biting satires upon those who yield themselves to that unfortunate tendency; it praises the graces and charms that light up impure desires, and it loads you with shame from the moment that you appear inflamed with them. Such had been the afflictions by which the passions and the debaucheries of our sinner were followed; but her penance restores to her more honour and more glory than had been taken away from her by the infamy of her past life. This sinner, so despised in the world, whose name was not mentioned without a blush,

---

[1] *Op. cit.*, ii. 129, quoted HLH, p. 147.

is praised by Jesus Christ for the things which even the world considers as most honourable, for generosity of sentiments, kindness of heart, and the fidelity of a holy love; this sinner, whose scandal was without example in the city, is exalted above the Pharisee; the truth, the sincerity of her faith, of her compunction, of her love, merits at once the preference over a superficial, pharisaical virtue; this woman, whose name was concealed as if unworthy of being uttered, and whose only appellation is that of her crimes, is become the glory of Christ Jesus, a triumph of grace and an honour to the Gospel."[1]

6. The personality of Fénelon, as revealed in his writings, commands our affection as none of the great orators can do.

(1) As only two of his sermons on special occasions have been preserved, we cannot compare him with them, or estimate what he was capable of as a preacher. With his controversy with Bossuet we are not here concerned; nor yet with the consequences of it as regards his ecclesiastical position. The doctrine of Quietism, which he defended, may be illustrated by a passage from a sermon on *Simplicity and Greatness.*

" If we desire that our friends be simple and free with us, disencumbered of self in their intimacy with us, will it not please God, who is our truest friend, that we should surrender our souls to him, without fear or reserve, in that holy and sweet communion with himself which he allows us? It is this simplicity which is the perfection of the true children of God. This is the end that we must have in view, and to which we must be continually advancing. This deliverance of the soul from all useless, and selfish, and unquiet cares, brings to it a peace and freedom that are unspeakable; this is true simplicity. It is easy to perceive, at the first glance, how glorious it is, but experience alone can make us comprehend the enlargement of heart that it produces. We are then like a child in the arms of its parents, ' we wish nothing more; we fear nothing'; we yield ourselves up to this pure attachment; we are not anxious about what others think of us; all our motions are free, graceful, and happy. We do not judge ourselves, and we

---

[1] *Great French Sermons*, pp. 220–221.

do not fear to be judged. Let us strive after this lovely
simplicity; let us seek the path that leads to it. The
farther we are from it, the more we must hasten our steps
towards it. Very far from being simple, most Christians are
not even sincere. They are not only disingenuous, but they
are false, and they dissemble with their neighbour, with God,
and with themselves. They practise a thousand little arts
that indirectly distort the truth. Alas! every man is a liar;
those even who are naturally upright, sincere, and ingenu-
ous, and who are what is called simple and natural, still
have this jealous and sensitive reference to self in everything, which secretly nourishes pride, and prevents that true
simplicity, which is the renunciation and perfect oblivion of
self." [1]

Such a type of preaching would not lend itself to oratory.
It lacks passion, since it aims at self-repression, and the
power of passion; to its sense of truth the art of oratory
must be an offence.

(2) Fénelon is of greater importance for our present
purpose as a writer on homiletics than as a preacher. In
his youth he wrote his Dialogues concerning *Eloquence in
General; and particularly, that kind which is fit for the
Pulpit*, and later he returned to the same subject in
*A Letter to the French Academy, concerning Rhetoric,
Poetry, History, and a Comparison between the Ancients
and Moderns*.[2] One passage, giving his view of the purpose
and the method of eloquence from the *Letter*, may be
quoted.

"We must not judge so unfavourably of eloquence as to
reckon it only a frivolous Art that a declaimer uses to
impose on the weak imagination of the multitude and
to serve his own ends. 'Tis a very serious Art; designed
to instruct people; suppress their passions, and reform their
manners; to support the laws; direct public Councils; and
to make Men good and happy. The more pains a haranguer
takes to dazzle me by the artifices of his discourse, the more
I should despise his vanity. His eagerness to display his

---

[1] CME vi. pp. 111–112.

[2] A translation of both works was made in 1722 by William Stevenson,
M.A., and published in London, 1722; Glasgow, 1750.

wit would in my judgment render him unworthy of the least admiration. I love a serious preacher, who speaks for my sake, and not for his own; who seeks my salvation, and not his own vainglory. He best deserves to be heard who uses speech only to clothe his thoughts, and his thoughts only to promote truth and virtue. Nothing is more despicable than a professed declaimer, who retails his discourses as a quack does his medicines."[1]

In dealing with poetry he expresses his preference for simplicity in style.

"There's much gained by losing all superfluous ornaments, and confining ourselves to such beauties as are simple, easy, clear, and seemingly negligent. In poetry, as well as in architecture, all the necessary parts should be turned into natural ornaments. But that which serves merely as an ornament is superfluous; lay it aside; there will be nothing wanting; vanity is the only sufferer by the loss. An author that has too much wit, and will always show it, wearies and exhausts mine. I don't desire so very much. . . . So many flashes dazzle me. I love a gentle light that refreshes my weak eyes. I choose an agreeable poet that adapts himself to common capacities; who does everything for their sakes; and nothing for his own."[2]

It is a surprise to find that in his Dialogues he advocates the analytic homily rather than the synthetic sermon.

"The further I enquire into this matter, the more I'm convinced that the ancient form of sermons was the most perfect. The primitive pastors were great men; they were not only very holy, but they had a complete clear knowledge of religion, and of the best way to persuade men of its truth, and they took care to regulate all the circumstances of it. There's a great deal of wisdom hidden under this air of simplicity, and we ought not to believe that a better method could have been afterwards found out."[3]

This conclusion which cannot claim assent, must not hide from us the great value of his discussion of the subject.

7. The Roman Catholic and the Reformer pulpit of

---

[1] Pp. 229-230 of the translation mentioned in previous note.
[2] *Ibid.*, pp. 254-255.   [3] P. 177.

France, because subject to the same conditions, display similar characteristics. There is not in the Protestant preachers the same glow of religious feeling as at the Reformation. Without abandonment of the Calvinistic theology, there is a less vital relation to it. Without rationalism, there is a tendency to rationalising, and the ethical interest becomes more prominent than the experimental testimony. While it might appear as if the arts of oratory were more in keeping with the splendour of the Roman Catholic ritual than the simplicity of the Protestant message, yet, divided as they were from most of their countrymen in matters of faith, these Reformed preachers remained Frenchmen, subject to the same literary influences. In their controversy with Roman Catholicism and their defence of their own creed, they had to learn from the enemy, and to acquire the same arts of persuasion as their pulpit rivals. The results, religious and moral, of this classic period of the French pulpit bring home the conviction that the art of oratory as savouring too much of " the wisdom of the world " may often be a hindrance rather than a help to " the foolishness of preaching,"[1] which it has pleased God to use for the salvation of men, for the end may be forgotten in the means. When oratory is subordinate to " the holy enthusiasm " of the Spirit-filled believer, then it may become the eloquence which touches hearts and changes lives.

It must be added, however, that the resounding fame of the French preaching was carried into other lands, and there exercised a wholesome influence on the form of the sermon and in raising the standard of taste. In preachers of the nineteenth century, even in Germany, such as Theremin and Frederick William Krummacher that influence may still be traced. The synthetic type of sermon supplanted the analytic, and the attachment to the Holy Scriptures was replaced by a closer contact with current interests in the subjects chosen.

[1] See 1 Co 1[18-25].

CHAPTER VIII.

PIETISTS, RATIONALISTS AND MEDIATORS.

I.

1. In a previous chapter the decadence of the German pulpit after the great Reformation period was described and reference was by anticipation made to the man, through whom the Spirit of God came to breathe life "in the Valley of the dry bones." [1]

(1) " It has sometimes been said," says Ker, " that Spener was the reformer of the life of the German church, as Luther was the reformer of its doctrine. This may place him too high, but it is certain that he was the most remarkable theological figure in Germany during the seventeenth century, and that he began a movement in the German Church which long survived him, and which exercises an effect even on our country and our time." [2] " Through Philipp Jacob Spener (1635–1705) and August Hermann Francke (1663–1727)," says Hering, " Pietism gained the importance of a religious appearance, which by its intensive insistence on the vitality of faith, on the new birth and the Christian passion for consecration, rose far above the orthodoxy of the 17th century." [3] " Spener," says Van Oosterzee, " did succeed in recalling to life the spirit of Luther and Arndt in many a pulpit, and in making the preaching a powerful embodiment of the *theologia regenitorum.*" [4]

(2) The deep piety which he afterwards showed and preached was fostered in him by godly parents, by familiarity with the Bible, and devout literature, such as Arndt's *True Christianity* and some of Baxter's writings.

[1] Ezk 37[1-14].   [2] KPH, p. 183 ; see pp. 183–198.
[3] HLH, p. 151 ; see pp. 151–158.   [4] OPT, pp. 121–122.

The life and work of the Reformed Church in Geneva, where he studied for a year, made a deep impression on him. "He was also moved by the fiery preaching of Labadie, so different from the stiff and formal methods which then prevailed in Germany." [1] On his return to Germany, his promotion in the Church was rapid. His influence spread over the whole of Germany. His labours were almost incredible. He excited violent antagonism no less than secured passionate attachment.

(3) In his *Pia Desideria*, or Pious Wishes, his position is most briefly defined.

"(1) The larger circulation of the Word of God, and private meetings of Christians for the study of it. (2) The diligent exercise of the Christian priesthood—*i.e.*, the co-operation of the members with the minister for prayer and edification. (3) The earnest conviction that knowledge is not enough in Christianity, and that we must also have life and action. (4) A right bearing towards unbelievers, so as to carry on discussion with heart-felt love, and to seek not merely to answer them but to gain them and do them good. (5) Such a course of theological training as will make students feel that they should progress in heart and life as much as in learning. (6) A new way of preaching, in which the great aim will be to show that Christianity consists in the inner or new man, whose soul is found in faith, with the fruits of a good life as the results." [2]

(4) While devoted to Luther, and desiring in all things to be Lutheran in his theology, his emphasis is other than Luther's.

"Like Luther he preaches the Gospel as a message of grace; but he more than the other emphasises the importance of making with the benefit of redemption and the consolation of faith a proper impression on the heart, of touching the conscience and commending the following of Jesus. If Luther's preaching of faith is a restoration, a comfort of the frightened conscience by the grace of for-

---

[1] KHP, p. 187. Ker in a note on p. 199 gives an account of Jean de Labadie.

[2] *Idem*, pp. 189–190.

giveness, Spener's ultimate object is consecration with the warnings, characteristic of pietism, against false comfort from grace; and in the acuteness and purity of the moral judgment and sentiment, the knowledge of the heart, and the Christian wisdom of life, in the caution with which he pursues that task is to be found the great and good part of his preaching. This its essential tendency, when one looks at it as a whole, throws into such predominance the preaching of penitence and consecration rather than the testimony of faith, and gives such prominence to the demand for conversion and the new birth, that in this already one becomes aware of the difference between him and Luther; and that not the less on account of the difference which separates him from later pietism. He at least did not wish to give absolutely an affirmative answer to the question whether it is necessary to know the time and hour of one's conversion."[1] In him the emphasis on subjective experience is not yet exaggerated.

To produce the inward change of contrition, conversion, and consecration was the object of his preaching. With a view to the last he dealt often with the moral duties of the Christian, but never as a moralist merely.

(5) Not only did he always seek the contents and the warrant of his message in the Holy Scriptures, but it was no less the aim of his preaching to make the Bible familiar to, and so a dominant influence in the life of the Christian people. He chafed under the limitation imposed by the prescribed selection of passages for use in public worship, as forbidding his use of the whole Bible, but especially as not giving adequate opportunity for dealing with matters so important as the new birth. He tried to get over this difficulty in two ways. He seized on some aspect of a Gospel narrative, which served his particular purpose, even if it were in itself quite subordinate, and made that his sole subject; or he made use of the introduction to explain other passages, even in a course of sermons a whole epistle, regardless of the abandonment of the unity of the sermon which this involved. When a passage was suitable, he would give a practical exegesis of it, dwelling even on

[1] HLH, pp. 152–153.

the explanation of single words according to the original text.

(6) How little importance he attached to homiletic theory his own confession shows. "From the time onwards, when I had learned to grasp in some measure the *realia* I set aside all the *technica* and *oratoria præcepta* so that I scarcely have any more remembrance of all such artificialities. . . . The matter must always give me the method, and this so to speak changes always as the materials differ." [1] In practice, however, his sermons usually assumed the same structure. An introduction (sometimes even two, a general and a special) was followed by the statement of the subject. An exposition of the passage led up to the chief doctrine and the practical lessons. Lastly came the application in warning or comfort. The sermon closed with a long prayer. He was prolix, unable on his own testimony to be brief, often preaching for two hours. There was no brilliance, nor poetry, nor passion; but he held his audiences by his sincerity and earnestness, the freshness of the truth he presented, and the variety of his use of the Holy Scriptures. His practice was to write out his sermons carefully; after only three readings his excellent memory enabled him to deliver almost exactly what he had written without the use of any notes. While he was ready to take up into his sermon thoughts which came to him in the pulpit, he inserted them afterwards into his manuscript. He had a distrust of extempore preaching, which he had himself tried for a time.

(7) Hering shows the artificiality and prolixity of his sermons by giving an account of a sermon on *Fidelity in the Preacher's Office*, based on Jn 16$^{5-15}$.[2]

"In the *introduction* he starts from the spiritual character of the Kingdom of Christ according to John 18^{36}. As all its members are spiritual, therefore this Word does not belong only to the preachers, but they must in a special

---

[1] *Theol. Bed.* iv. p. 228.   Quoted HLH, p. 156.
[2] HLH, pp. 156–157.

sense be spirituals,[1] who have still an advantage in ministerial arrangements. Now comes the *theme*; *the official duty and fidelity of the teachers and preachers,* Hymn and Prayer— The Explanation of the Gospel; I. *the foundation,* it is an office of the spirit, 2 Cor. 3[6]. Sp. explains briefly the statements of the passage regarding the Spirit, His procession, His connection with the work of Christ (John 7[39]). His working (vv.[7. 13]); II. *the duties*: 1, to teach (to lead into all truth); 2, to punish (to convince inwardly); 3, to comfort; 4, good and holy example: III. the *fruit*: 1, from the side of God, that Christ is thereby glorified; 2, from the side of man; to be led into all truth and then to lead others into it. (Now Sp. weaves in as well a similar exposition according to John 10)—The 'main doctrine' considers the official duty and fidelity of the preacher. I. *The foundation of the fidelity* consists—1, in this, that the clerical office is not a human office, but an office of the Holy Ghost; it has to do *with the Word of God,* which comes from the Spirit, and its living recognition, which only the Spirit of God can give; also all the gifts of the preacher's office spring from the Holy Ghost; accordingly the person who fulfils the office must have the Spirit dwelling in him; lastly, it belongs to the office of the Spirit, that it is He who calls thereto; 2, the *call* does not always come immediately from God, but also through men; but not without the inner call. This call is a foundation of fidelity. II. As regards the *duties,* they demand—1, first of all generally a consciousness of being Christ's servant and steward of his mysteries; 2, the special duties, to teach, to warn, to punish, *i.e.,* powerfully to convince, to comfort; also to dispense rightly the seals of the Word, the Sacraments; to present to the congregation a good example; to follow the individual with care for his soul. III. *The Fruit*: 1, God's Honour; 2, the blessedness of the hearers and the preachers themselves. IV. *The Means of this fidelity*: 1, generally God's word; 2, witnessing holy baptism; 3, the Holy Supper; 4, Prayer; 5, the Cross. Special Means: diligent consideration of the heavy responsibilities, as of the splendid promises. V. Only two *hindrances to fidelity here*: fleshly wisdom and the love of the world,— Thereon admonition, consolation, and closing prayer."

Long as this summary is, it is worth quoting, as it not

---

[1] The German word for a clergyman or minister is a *spiritual*; there is here a play on the word.

only shows us the method of the preacher, but also his motives, his purposes, and the manner of his fulfilment of his calling.

2. Next to Spener as a leader in the movement of Pietism stands August Hermann Francke (1663–1727).

(1) "In point of form," says Van Oosterzee, "Francke stood above Spener; as regards spirit and depth not below him; and, though Francke's sermons were a little longer than those ordinarily listened to, they did not fail to hold captive a numerous audience. Like his predecessor, he was specially concerned about the application, and for the defects which, as judged by the standard of later times, might perhaps be discovered in the homilete, amends were made by the excellence of the preacher." [1]

Although he used none of the arts of the orator, he had a natural eloquence which made a deep impression. While his early ambition to be a learned man was lost in his aspiration to be wholly surrendered to God, he made good use of his learning in expounding the Scriptures; but unlike Spener he wove his exposition of the passage into his development of his theme. In opposition to orthodoxy, but with Spener's approval, his explanation of words, based on a study of the original languages, prepared the way for a revision of Luther's translation. In him scholarship was allied not with piety only, but also with philanthropy. He founded the Orphan House at Halle, where he was both a professor at the university and the minister of a town church.

"He also set up," says Ker, "a great Apothecary Institute for supplying medicine and medical advice, and an establishment for printing the Bible in different languages, and other books for the people. These buildings still excite the wonder of everyone who visits Halle, and the remarkable little book in which he tells how they were raised, *The Footsteps of God in the Building of the Orphan House at Halle*, may well be reckoned among the classics of Christian faith." [2]

---

[1] OPT, p. 122. See also HLH, pp. 158–159, and KHP, pp. 201–207.
[2] KHP, pp. 204–205.

(2) These wider interests influenced his preaching. He preached on the care of the poor. He was one of the foremost advocates of the Danish mission in Tranquebar. In this respect he was in advance both of Luther and Spener. By his presence and influence the university became a fountain of living truth and grace for all Germany. The number of theological students rose to twelve hundred, and they perpetuated and diffused their teacher's life and work wherever they went as pastors. The journeys which for the sake of his health he had to make were used by him to secure adherents, and to conciliate opponents of the movement. At his death, worn out with his labours, it seemed as if a spring-time which would pass into a summer of religious revival had come to Germany; but the movement proved less enduring than might have been hoped.

(3) Before glancing at the reasons for this disappointment of hopes, a sketch by Ker of one of Francke's sermons may be given, which will justify the statement of his superiority to Spener as regards form.

"Luke viii. 4–16.—The Parable of the Sower. *Introduction*; Not enough to hear the word of God, we must take heed of what and how we hear, and ask if we are bearing fruit from it. *Theme stated*; How are we to act so that the Word of God may come to a true, ripe, and rich fruit. *Short prayer bearing on the subject*. I. A man must learn to know the right seed, and that by looking to the Good Sower, Jesus Christ. It is in His Word, the Word of God, specially the Gospel Word. 'Thy sins are forgiven Thee.' This is the beautiful and precious little seed which when falling into the sinner's heart brings the sweet and joyful message of grace, and springs up in the soul as righteousness and peace and joy in the Holy Ghost. We also know the right seed by its power. Man's seed cannot overcome sin or fill the heart; power comes only from Christ's hand. II. A man must see that the field is prepared. Here the husbandman may be taken for a copy, and the parable followed. (1) The heart must be free from the hard wayside surface; the thinking, speaking, or doing of evil makes the ground so hard that the seed cannot enter; there must come the plough of the law, the stern plough of Sinai. (2) The heart must

be freed from the rock below the surface. The understanding often takes the seed and talks of it; the fancy takes it
and is pleased with it; while the heart beneath is rocky and
callous. The heart must be broken—a contrite heart. The
rock must be pierced. We need repentance to open it for
the seed, and for this we must plead with God who alone
can take away the hard and stony heart. (3) The heart
must be free from thorns and thistles, *i.e.*, the worldly mind,
the love of worldly pleasures, the anxiety of worldly cares,
which deprive the seed of room for growth. Therefore pray
the Lord that He may tear out such thorns and thistles,
clearing the field for the precious seed. III. A man must
work and wait for the seed to grow. Here, again, the
husbandman is our example with his harrows and his roller
waiting through weeks and months in sunshine and rain, in
drought and frost, in weariness and fainting of heart, till the
grain is ripe. Therefore (1) the Word must be kept in the
heart, not in the memory only, hidden there and pondered.
Parents, hide the word in your children's hearts. (2) It
must be commended in faith and prayer to God, who is the
God of the harvest, of the early and latter rain. (3) It must
be waited for. It does not grow in a day, at least in its
fulness. It needs the cross, and often many crosses to drive
it in and cover it up. (Then follow words of sorrow for the
small spiritual harvest in Germany after so many years of
waiting, and the sermon closes with a suitable prayer.)"[1]

3. With two such leaders it is surprising that pietism
did not stay the full tide of rationalism in Germany. Ker
suggests three reasons for the failure of pietism. (1) Its
intellectual interest was too narrow, being focused almost
entirely on the inner Christian life, and it neglected the
art of popular effective speech. (2) It was too subjective
and introspective, and the spiritual experiences so observed
were reported in a language which, real as long as emotion
was intense, became affected when feeling had subsided.
(3) While at the beginning, in Halle especially, there was
considerable activity directed outwards, the adherents of
the movement afterwards and elsewhere tended to separation, to the formation of small self-righteous and self-
satisfied societies which assumed a censorious and

[1] KHP, pp. 219-221.

uncharitable attitude to the world around.[1] While this judgment must be passed on the movement as a whole, what was best in it was continued in two notable men, Johann Albrecht Bengel (1687–1752) and Count Nikolaus Ludwig von Zinzendorf (1700–1760).

"These are the two offshoots from the Pietism of Spener and Francke," says Ker, "which gave it a permanent interest and influence—the school of Bengel led to a deeper and more comprehensive study of the Bible, and the school of Zinzendorf and the Moravian Brethren transformed the *ecclesiolæ* of Spener into an *ecclesia* that exercised an important influence on the Church and the World."[2]

4. With the great work of Bengel as an expositor of Scripture in his famous *Gnomon* and other books, we are not at present concerned; but only with him as a preacher.

(1) "His preaching was thoroughly evangelical, though he did not dwell upon conversion as constantly as did the Pietists. 'That doctrine,' he says, 'is very important; it is the finger-hand of the clock, but we must also remember the round dial-plate—all duties in their turn.' His preaching was also more expository than that of the body of Pietists, and had therefore more of the breadth and variety of Scripture. His weakness, if we can call it so, was that he dealt rather frequently with prophetical chronology. He fixed, *e.g.*, upon 1836 as the year when a great catastrophe would befall the Kingdom of evil—a catastrophe still delayed."[3]

(2) More important still as a preacher, but dependent on Bengel as his teacher, although more potently influenced even by Böhme, was Friederich Christoph Oetinger (1702–1765), who may be described as a Christian theosophist. Although he indulged in speculation even in the pulpit, yet he knew how to make his speech popular, and far and wide quickened religious thought and life. For his thinking was attached very closely to the Holy Scriptures, and not less decisive for his language were the sacred writings. He was a decided opponent of the rationalising of his time.

[1] KHP, pp. 210–217. [2] KHP, pp. 236–237. [3] KHP, p. 228; see pp. 225–229. HLH, pp. 173–174.

Bengel and Oetinger were the dominant influences in the Würtemberg type of pietism—which did not form a separate community, but like a leaven pervaded the whole people. The ideas of Oetinger were carried further by Philipp Matthäus Hahn (1739–1790), who developed a scriptural and yet speculative Christology in representing the reign of Christ as a new creation, the glory of which should far exceed that of the thousand years' reign. In M. F. Christoph Steinhofer (1706–1761) the influence of Bengel combined with that of Zinzendorf to form a personality full of unction as a preacher.[1]   The influence of this pietism has continued in Würtemberg to the present day, where, besides attendance at the ordinary church services, fellowship meetings are used as a means of grace.[2]

5. Count Zinzendorf, whose family, old and noble, had been compelled to leave Austria for Germany on becoming Protestant, came to Halle at the age of ten, and for six years there was under the influence of Francke.

(1) " At an early age he became decided in his religious life, and he never swerved till he died. He was a man of lively fancy and poetic temperament, with considerable power of judgment, which, however, was ready to be carried away by his ardour and restless activity. His devotion to the Gospel took the form of an intense personal love to the Saviour sometimes marked by an over-sweetness and familiarity which made his hymns distasteful to Bengel, whose depth disliked great demonstrativeness. Bengel and Zinzendorf are men who shew in what different moulds Christianity may be cast; the one full of thought and regulated feeling, the other full of impulse, demonstrative expression and action."[3]

(2) In 1722 he was led by Christian David to befriend the persecuted community of "Bible Christians," or Moravian Brethren, and to afford them an asylum in the village he built for them, and to which was given the name *Herrnhut*, the Lord's watch. The Brethren were hence known in Germany as *Herrnhüter*, "the Lord's Watchmen." To the

---

[1] See HLH, pp. 174–176.   [2] KHP, p. 229, note.
[3] KHP, pp. 232–233 ; see HLH, pp. 170–172.

interests of this community Zinzendorf devoted the rest of his life. He travelled far and wide, not only in Europe, but even in America, to spread the movement. Crowds, drawn from all classes, gathered to hear him preach. He preached salvation through Christ as not only outward forgiveness, but as inward renewal, with an earnestness and insight that gave him power over human hearts. There are two facts about the Moravian community of special interest. Not only were the Moravians the first to send out missionaries as an essential function of the Church, but they even regarded the Church itself as a whole as committed to mission work at home and abroad. It was a Moravian, Peter Böhler, "who revealed to John Wesley the way of God more perfectly,"[1] and Methodism borrowed much from the Brethren.

6. Another centre of pietism in the West of Germany was in Elberfeld and Barmen. (1) Here Gerhard Tersteegen (1697–1769), a cultured layman, exercised a wide-spread and deep-rooted influence. Beginning as an ascetic hermit, he passed through great inward struggles to a more friendly attitude to the Church: by the practice of the presence of God and constant self-discipline he fitted himself to be the guide of the inner life of many, especially when he founded at Otterfeld, in the "Pilgrim's Hut," a brotherhood which in a common life devoted itself to prayer, labour and joy in God. His influence as a preacher spread far beyond this community; and his sermons, "Spiritual crumbs, fallen from the Lord's Table," published shortly before his death, perpetuated the spirit of his piety, which influenced especially Gottfried Menken (1768–1831), and which still remains in the Wupperthal.[2]

(2) Other representatives of the more spiritual movement, even when rationalism was dominant, who are mentioned by Ker, are Jung Stilling (1740–1817), who by his correspondence was a helper of many in the higher life; Lavater[3] (1741–1801), a pastor of Zurich, best known for his theories and researches on physiognomy, but

[1] KHP, p. 237.   [2] HLH, pp. 177-178.   [3] KHP, pp. 267-268.

still more worthy of remembrance as one who hungered and
thirsted for the living God, and who boldly confessed Jesus
Christ as Lord in a circle of unbelieving friends; Johann
Georg Hamann [1] (1730–1788), a philosophical thinker of
great power who held fast the belief in Divine revelation,
and whose counsels to many in distress of soul won him
the title of the Wise Man of the North, even as Oetinger
was called the Wise Man of the South.

Matthias Claudius (1740–1815), who, while emphasis-
ing feeling in religion, as did Jacobi, yet maintained the
need and worth of God's Word as the support of religious
feeling, was less the mystic than either Stilling or Lavater
and less the philosopher than Hamann, and may best be
described as an old pietist and Puritan with modern culture.   It was by such men as these that the faith of many
who were grieved by the prevalent rationalism, and who
feared even that the evangelical piety might succumb to
its withering influence, was sustained.   They were the
watchmen who gave the assurance, that the night would
pass and the dawn break.[2]

II.

1. In a previous chapter the fact was noted that the
Latitudinarian movement in England had a historical
connection with Puritanism; so it was also with Pietism
and Illuminism or Rationalism.   Thomasius and Wolff, the
leaders of the German "Enlightenment," worked at the
same high school with Francke.[3]   For the reasons already
stated, the later movement to a large extent superseded the
earlier.   The buds of spring were nipped by the frosts of
winter.   Between the two movements, however, stands
Johann Lorenz Mosheim (1693 or 4–1755), orthodox in
doctrine but "moderate" in feeling.   Not only was he
the most learned man, but he was also the most popular
preacher of his age.   He did not reach the masses, but
rather the cultured classes; and yet the congregations he

[1] KHP, pp. 269–275.   [2] KHP, pp. 276–285.   [3] HLH, p. 159.

atttacted were often so large as to require that soldiers
should be present to keep order. His practice as a
preacher was based on a theory which he expounded in
lectures on Homiletics, published after his death. "A
sermon," he says, "is a discourse in which, following the
guidance of a portion of Scripture, an assembly of Christians, already instructed in the elements of religion, is
confirmed in knowledge or roused to zeal in godliness."[1]
He does not, be it observed, take account of missionary or
evangelistic preaching; "edification" of those already in the
Church is the object, and this must determine what shall
be included or excluded, to enlighten the mind, or quicken
the will. As regards the form, he lays down these rules:

"That it should be in keeping with the dignity and
importance of the subject; that it should be lively and have
as much ornament as does not interfere with clearness; and
that the language should as far as possible be that which is
used in ordinary life among cultivated people."[2]

So great a contrast was there between his method and
style of preaching and that current, that multitudes were
charmed by his eloquence. He belongs to the same type
as the "classic" French preachers; and his preaching
lacked permanent influence just as did theirs. He was
lucid, but superficial; he was eloquent, but not fervent;
his reasonableness and seriousness did not sound the depths
of God or man. He was too fluent; and so his sermons
assumed an inordinate length, e.g., his funeral sermon for
Frederick II. fills eighty-three printed pages.[3]

[1] Quoted KHP, pp. 242-243.   [2] KHP, p. 243.
[3] HLH, p. 166; see pp. 164-167. He mentions as examples of the
influence of the new intellectual conditions, not primarily on the content,
but the form of preaching, Johann Jacob Rambach (1693-1735) and Johann
Gustav Reinbeck (1683-1741); and describes them as the first-fruits of this
movement (pp. 162-164). As instances of increasing influence on content
as well as form, he gives two younger contemporaries of Mosheim, Jh.
Friederich Wilhelm Jerusalem (1707-1789) and A. F. Wilhelm Sack
(1703-1786). The second imitated Tillotson, and followed the Reformed
French preachers in taking short sayings as his texts (pp. 167-169). The
contrast of the two positions (the orthodox and the rationalist) is clearly
presented in Ker's quotation from Reinhard's *Geständnisse* in his note on
pp. 286-287.

2. The enlightenment in Germany was but part of a wider movement.

"In Scotland, Hume was writing his *Essay* against miracles, and Blair was the great preacher. In England, it was the age of the deists who followed Tillotson, the English Mosheim; and the old Presbyterian church of Howe, Baxter, and Henry was passing along the road of culture and progress, to drop one after another of the Christian doctrines, till it became the church of Taylor of Norwich, Price, and Priestley, and the sparse Unitarianism of our day. In France, Voltaire had taken the place of Pascal and Bossuet, and, worse than Voltaire, the materialism of the Encyclopædists was sowing the seeds of the Revolution." [1]

The object of the Illuminism was to make everything, Christianity itself, appear "reasonable" to the knowledge and intelligence of the age. It was assumed that nature had endowed man with certain simple truths about God, duty and destiny; and the Christian revelation itself had to be brought within the bounds of this natural religion.

(1) Thomasius applied these principles not only to science and philosophy, but also to religion and even preaching.

"Since all knowledge had this alone as its object to distinguish the true from the false, the good from the bad, to learn how one may understand to live rightly and usefully, it seemed natural and justified, to place instruction about religion, preaching, under this application. The tendency to moralising which first became popular in England, could only be strengthened by the German Illumination in respect of securing the utility of preaching, inasmuch as the religious was employed as a means of virtue." [2]

[1] KHP, p. 245.

[2] HLH, p. 160. See pp. 160-162. "Most of this School," says Ker, "took to 'moral preaching.' Sometimes they changed the language of the Bible, in order to make it, as they said, more rational. For conversion or regeneration, they spoke of amendment of life; for justification, of forgiveness on condition of repentance; for the Holy Spirit, of the exercise of the higher reason; for the atonement of Christ, of the spirit of sacrifice which He has taught us by His example, and so on" (p. 247).

The "Moderate" movement in Scotland shows the same characteristics.

(2) To the form of preaching Wolff contributed the demonstrative method. Formal logic found its way into the pulpit. Apprehension was to be secured by clear definition, and conviction wrought by rigid inference. That religion by its very nature and object refuses to be forced into the *Procrustes* bed of logical method was not realised; because the piety of the time was itself so superficial. The Wolffian philosophy affected even the language of the pulpit. While French and English influences did not succeed in imparting to German all the excellences of these tongues, and German prose remained not swift and light-winged, but slow and heavy-footed, it did gain greater lucidity and intelligibility. Gottsched became dictator as regards the language to be used in the pulpit, and lent it that insipidity which characterised it long after the great poetic revival in the literature.[1]

3. In the absence of religious life to sustain the aspiration and endeavour of the pulpit, a lamentable degradation soon appeared. The language, in aiming at sublimity, became bombastic. Paul was patronisingly described as "the enlightened teacher of the Gentiles." The principle of utilitarianism dominated the pulpit; "refinement and enlightenment" were to be brought within the reach of the common people.

"There appeared," says Van Oosterzee, "during the second half of the eighteenth century 'agricultural' discourses, 'nature sermons and field sermons,' homiletic commendations of vaccination (end of eighteenth century), silk-worm culture, etc. Who has not heard of the Christmas sermon on the stall-feeding of cattle; of the Epiphany sermon on listening to good counsels; of the Palm Sunday sermon on the damaging of trees; the Easter sermon on the benefit of a walk (the travellers to Emmaus); the Pentecost sermon on drunkenness, etc.? not to speak of a Maundy-Thursday discourse 'on the making of a good will'; or another on the exciting theme, 'how wise and beneficial the arrangement, that death is placed not at the beginning, but at the end of life.' The 'sermons on texts taken from

---

[1] HLH, pp. 160–161.

nature,' by J. L. Ewald (died 1822) and others, in which, *e.g.*, the storm, the eye, the tongue, etc., supplies the theme to be treated of, were of this kind, still the best." [1]

4. Amid such conditions no great preaching is to be expected; but a few of the notable preachers may be mentioned. (1) Johann Joachim Spalding (1714–1804) [2] offered a defence of the ministry against the assaults of unbelief in his book on the *Utility of the Office of the Preacher*. The preacher's duty is to instruct and improve his hearers. He should not teach theology, the metaphysical doctrines which the common people cannot understand and of which they can make no good use; such as the Trinity, the two natures of Christ, the atonement. All moral duties are to be enforced by diligent presentation of the teaching and example of Christ.

Ker gives a Sketch of a Sermon by Spalding on Luke 11[33-40]—Simeon and Anna in the Temple.

"The whole life of a Christian can, and should be, the service of God.

I. The whole life can be divine service, for—

    1. Every benevolent deed in God's name is service.
    2. The common work of life, with the feeling of religion, is service.
    3. The pleasures of life, when innocent and God-grateful, are service.

II. Our whole life should be divine service, for—

    1. All our life belongs to God, as its Author and Owner.
    2. All our life may thus be made true happiness." [3]

(2) George Joachim Zollikofer (1730–1788) was considered "the Cicero of the pulpit" in his own age. He was a topical preacher; his subjects often had very little connection with his text, the exposition of which he ignored, and were at the circumference of Christian morals

---

[1] OPT, p. 124.

[2] See KPH, pp. 248–250; also HLP, pp. 187–190. Spalding was involved in a controversy with Herder, which will afterwards be noted.

[3] KHP, p. 260.

rather than at the centre of Christian faith. Style and delivery, however, were faultless, and so he enjoyed a great popularity.[1]

(3) Frank Volkmar Reinhard[2] (1753–1812) had so great a fame, that in the common opinion he was held to be the greatest preacher since Luther. He strove for something more satisfying to the soul than the thought of his own time ; but could not escape from it. Preaching evengelical doctrines, he lacked the spiritual fervour which gives them power. An account which Ker gives of his method of preparation is interesting enough to justify quotation.

" He worked out each sermon with the greatest care. First he sketched a scheme in which the chief thoughts were outlined in logical order, and on this he set great value, both for its own sake and as an aid to his memory. His memory for words was very weak, and, despite all the exercise he gave it, did not improve. But he had a memory for the logical outline, and he constructed his discourses accordingly, filling up the parts of the plan as a painter might do with a sketch. The committing of the sermon was to him the most disagreeable part of his work. But he did not shirk it. Beginning on Monday, he committed a section every morning, so that on the Saturday the whole sermon was fast and firm. While he was committing one thus piecemeal, he was working out another, and by the time he had the first committed, the second was ready in his desk. The sermon, in his view, is a piece of art, to which, as to its outer form, both logic and rhetoric must contribute, but logic is the more important. Its thoughts must come up in regular order, group themselves in proportion, and lead to proper conclusions. The language should be suited to this, simple, clear, pointed. The preacher must never forget that he is above all a teacher ; he who makes it his chief aim to awaken and move robs his office of much of its value, for if we are to reach the heart, it must be through the understanding." [3]

Unhappily it must be added what the understanding

[1] See KHP, pp. 250–252 ; also HLH, pp. 196–197.
[2] See HLH, pp. 202–205, and KHP, pp. 252–259.   [3] KHP, 257–258.

of the time accepted was not capable of reaching and moving the heart.

(4) Joh. Caspar Häfeli (1754—1811) began as a follower of Lavater, but violently changed to extreme rationalism, and only his eloquence remained to link together the two periods. A similar revolution took place in Fried. Wilh. Abraham Teller (1734–1804). Faith for him was only a stage preparatory for knowledge in the sense of the Enlightenment. Hence his advice to preachers is: "In religion men need to be enlightened, always more enlightened, and they cannot get too much enlightenment." With good moral intentions his preaching was religiously impotent. At the Church festivals he advised that history and doctrine should be quickly passed over for the sake of the practical lesson. The visit of the wise men (Mt 2^{1-12}) shows how we may give and take good advice. It was along such a downward path that preaching went to the depths of degradation, already described, in which it lost not only Christian, but even religious character, and was concerned only about earthly business and worldly prudence.[1] Contrary to the general practice of this volume, a larger number of individual preachers has been referred to, but in each case to illustrate some characteristic, condition, or consequence of the two movements under discussion.

III.

1. The opposition between pietism and rationalism could not remain permanent: a reconciliation must be sought between revelation and reason as the final authority on religion. A promise of a better day was given by Johann Gotfried Herder (1744–1803), who was "preacher and poet, theologian and many-sided author."[2] He aspired for a spirit-filled preaching, but did not soar above the enlightenment, the spiritual poverty of which he felt. His youth was influenced by pietism, and Hamann as well as Kant affected his development as a thinker. (1) At the

[1] HLH, pp. 197–200.   [2] HLH, p. 186 ; see pp. 185–187.

very beginning of his activity as a preacher he sketched his ideal in his small book, *God's Speaker*. " God's Speaker ! great in quietness, solemn without poetic splendour, eloquent without Ciceronian periods, powerful without the bewitching arts of the drama, wise without learned sophistication, and captivating without politic cleverness." [1] He required in the preacher sincerity and simplicity, no assumption and no artificiality ; but preaching based on experience, intuitive, confident and inspiring confidence, awakening the sense of God's presence, and promoting a morality that had its roots in religion.   This ideal remained his during the whole of his distinguished and influential career as a preacher.   To the influence of Hamann probably was due his loving appreciation of the stories and persons in the Holy Scriptures.   He delighted in the humanness of the Bible as showing God's condescension.   He did not, however, altogether detach himself from his environment, and may be described as " an Illuminist with his Bible in his hand."   In his *Provincial Leaves to Preachers* (1773–1774), he attacked with all the intellectual resources at his command, " Spalding's attempt to lay a firm ground for the certainty of salvation and the importance of the office of the preacher in morality."   His guiding idea is God's education of mankind in piety by a progressive revelation, in which the Bible is rooted, and of which it forms a part. Accordingly the business of preaching is the proclamation of this revelation, and not teaching wisdom or virtue by argument.   For him moralism was one-sided in regarding religion only as a motive of morality ; piety as relationship to God both in the Bible and in human history ever touched a responsive chord in his sensitive soul.   Nevertheless, he himself did not make the Gospel of the reconciling love of God in Christ central in his own preaching ; but a " humanity transfigured by pious morality, of which Jesus is regarded and presented for imitation as the archtype and mediator, forms the content of his own sermons." [2]

(2) In spite of his living interest in history, he does

---

[1] HLH, p. 186.   [2] HLH, pp. 190–192.

not always succeed in making it valuable for religious life. An opponent of moralism, he shows his greatest power when he is dealing with moral issues. In sermons on special occasions the distinctively Christian is often lost amid the generally religious reflections. His sermons were cast in the form of homilies, although based on a full outline; and the delivery was living, sometimes fiery, sometimes quiet, as in talk, made more effective by full-toned voice and expressive face, but without any gestures. While he disappointed those who from his early defence of the Bible expected a scriptural expositor, yet by his poetic genius he did impart vital reality to the Bible and the religious history of mankind, and by his influence carried religious thought beyond the narrowness of pietism and the shallowness of rationalism.[1]

(3) A characteristic passage on *The Meaning of Inspiration* may be quoted. Having shown that as speech is a sign of human imperfection, God does not speak, he next explains how God reveals Himself.

" Now, if we suppose that God wished to reveal himself to man, and yet otherwise than in his essential nature, how else could he do it but by human agency? How can he speak to man otherwise? to imperfect men, otherwise than in the imperfect, defective language in which they can understand him, and to which they are accustomed? I use far too inadequate a comparison for our purpose, when I say that a father speaks to a child only in a childish way; for between them both there still exists a relationship. Father and child are yet both akin, who can think no otherwise than by words, and have a common language of reason. But between God and men there is no correspondence; they have, as it were, nothing at all in common as a basis of mutual understanding. God must, therefore, explain himself to men altogether in a human way, according to our own mode and speech, suitably to our weakness, and the narrowness of our ideas; he cannot speak like a god, he must speak altogether like a man." The use of human agency involves other limitations. " Now this religion has been revealed in an Eastern land; how, then, could it be

---

[1] HLH, pp. 193-194.

revealed except in a manner intelligible to Orientals, and consequently in those forms of thought prevalent among them? Otherwise God would have failed entirely in his object. Our Bible, therefore, carries upon every page of it all the traces of Oriental habits of thought." The Bible must, therefore, be interpreted by our own thinking. "Believe me, my hearers, it is no tenet of religion to abjure thinking. It is rather its decay and the decay of humanity." If we think about our religion, it "serves also for the education of our time, and that which has already so far exalted the human understanding would continue to elevate it, and with it our virtue, our humanity, our bliss. Happy times! happy world!"[1]

2. A theologian and preacher of greater endowments and wider and more enduring influence was Friedrich Daniel Schleiermacher (1768–1834),[2] who combined piety and philosophy, culture and faith, the power of the thinker, and the gifts of the speaker in so great a personality, that he marks the beginning of the most fruitful epoch of religious thought in Germany.

(1) At first, in his *Speeches* on religion (1799), he appealed to the class which had been most affected by the Illumination. He showed that "the pious consciousness of entire dependence belongs essentially to the human consciousness, when it rightly understands itself." It is impossible to estimate the number of those to whom he made religion significant and authoritative as it had never been before. In his theology he vindicated the claim of faith, and reconciled it with the rights of knowledge. In his preaching, to which much of his commanding influence was due, he gave the central position to Christ as the Sinless Saviour, the Mediator between God and man, because of the unique potency of His consciousness of God, which He communicates to others. Laying stress on religious emotion in the relation to God through Christ, he

[1] CME vii. pp. 37–41.

[2] Dr. Selbie has offered a *Critical and Historical Study* of Schleiermacher (London, 1913); and Dr. Cross has given a condensed presentation of his chief work, *The Christian Faith* (Chicago, 1911). See HLH, pp. 209–212, and KHP, pp. 288–303.

always related piety to the tasks of the individual believer and the Christian community, for he was a "practical mystic."

(2) Educated at a Moravian school, "his heart was with Pietism"; a student at Halle, under the influence of Semler and other rationalist teachers, "his mind was with Illuminism"; and these two elements in him were never quite fused into an inward unity. Perhaps for that very reason he was the better able to prepare for, if not finally to perform, their synthesis. Ker, judging him from a more conservative theological position than prevails to-day, bears this testimony concerning him:

"There can be no question as to the deep sincerity, earnestness, and lofty character of Schleiermacher, nor as to the fact that he struck a deadly blow at the old rationalism by his deeper views of sin and redemption, and his more exalted conception of the work of Christ; but his was a position that could not be maintained. He himself was wounded in the heel by the arrow of doubt. The shifting sands of restless criticism that were blowing about him prevented him from seeing clearly the real and the positive. Yet, after all, his face was not towards rationalism, but away from it. It is this that marks the difference between men, not so much where they stand as whither they are looking and going, and teaching others to go; and Schleiermacher was the man who made the Church turn from the theology of the surface understanding to the deeper theology of religious feeling and faith."[1]

(3) He had a distinct conception of what preaching should be. The source of the sermon is the inward experience, the religious feeling of the preacher, stimulated and confirmed by the Bible; and the subject must be Christian; the person and the influence of Christ must be applied in manifold ways to life and duty. The purpose is not conversion, for the Church is not a missionary agency, but the confirmation of the faith which it is to be assumed the congregation already possesses. Not instruction, on the one hand, nor impulse to action on the other, is to be

[1] KHP, p. 295.

the purpose, but the stimulation of the religious emotions by the presentation of the object of faith. In seeking the heightening of feeling, he was himself often led to a process of reflection which strained rather than stirred. While insisting that each sermon should have a text, his treatment was topical rather than expository; having got out of the text the subject wanted, he was no more concerned about it. As his aim was neither exposition nor instruction, but the movement of the heart, he attached no importance to logical structure. What matters in his view is that the preacher himself gets the tone proper to his subject, and by mutual sympathy the tone of the preacher is imparted to his hearers. The sermon should be a homily or conversation, a dialogue of the preacher and the Scriptures on the one hand, and a dialogue of the preacher and his congregation on the other; what by inquiry of the Scriptures he gains he imparts by questioning his hearers as to their needs and wishes. The style suitable for the sermon is not the poetic, but animated and elevated prose, moderate and modest in the delivery.[1]

(4) His preaching was neither reading nor recitation from memory of what had been written, but *ex tempore* speech after much and careful meditation. His language often fails to be concrete, and loses power and charm because it lacks close touch with the Scriptures, especially the Old Testament. Whatever defects a close scrutiny may detect, they do not diminish his greatness.

" It was not a school that he founded," says Otto Braun, " but an epoch. He is a great man, for he cannot be replaced. From his writings and deeds there confronts us radiant, a pure and complete humanity. In him a cheerful gentleness was combined with active manliness, and both united to form a harmony of the inner man that issued in a selfless devotion to the highest aims. Schleiermacher's greatest work was his own life."[2]

3. Among other preachers we may distinguish several tendencies.

[1] See KHP, pp. 296–303.   [2] Quoted by Selbie, *op. cit.*, p. 27.

(1) In the steps of Schleiermacher followed the *Mediating School*, which aimed at the reconciliation of religion and science, faith and reason; its most distinguished representatives in the pulpit were Karl Immanuel Nitzsch (1787–1868) and Friederich August Tholuck (1799–1877). Of the second Ker says : " While he lived he was probably the best preacher in Germany, and when he died it was felt that one of the finest-moulded Christian natures had left the world." [1]

(2) The succession of pietism was maintained in Würtemberg by Ludwig Hofacker (1798–1828), who, by his simple, direct, earnest, intense, sympathetic and urgent preaching, without any arts of oratory, moved multitudes, as an ambassador of God beseeching men in Christ's stead to be reconciled. Claus Harms (1788–1855) was the instrument of revival in the North of Germany, as from deep personal conviction he preached frankly and boldly the Christian Gospel as Luther had conceived it. Compared with Hofacker, " he was not so searching, arresting, subduing in spiritual power, but more broadly human and fresh, having a quaint fancy and a love for old confessional forms—an eloquent Matthew Henry." [2]

(3) While both these preachers held fast the teaching of the Scriptures, the content and form of their preaching was not so completely dominated by it as that of Rudolf Stier (1800–1862) and Friederich Wilhelm Krummacher (1796–1868). [3] There were popular preachers of many schools in Germany in the nineteenth century ; but they must be passed over, as the present purpose is to illustrate important movements in, and characteristic types of, preaching, rather than to give an account of preachers, however eminent or influential.

[1] KHP, p. 319 ; see pp. 308–325.
[2] KHP, p. 342 ; see pp. 328–345.   [3] KHP, pp. 348–365.

CHAPTER IX.

EVANGELISTS AND MISSIONARIES.

I.

1. A MOVEMENT, similar in some respects to German pietism, but of far greater and wider influence, was the Evangelical Revival in England, which is comparable in its importance for the religious life of the country with the Reformation.[1] What it meant for the national history may be stated in the words of a historian who speaks with special authority on the subject. Dr. J. Holland Rose is contrasting the political situation in France and England.

"The relations of religion to democracy at the time of the French Revolution offer a curious contrast to those which are noticeable in the life of England at the same period. The following reasons for that contrast may be suggested. In the first place the National Church in England had held a secure place in the hearts of Englishmen ever since the time of the glorious Revolution of 1688; and though the eighteenth century witnessed a decline in her activity and an alarming increase in the stipends and sinecures enjoyed by the higher clergy, still these abuses were slight compared with those of the Church of France. Further, the Wesleyan revival then began powerfully to influence the Established Church for good; and the work of many devoted preachers brought home to the people a vital knowledge of evangelical truth. Further, the names of Clarkson, Wilberforce and John Howard will remind the reader of the close connexion between evangelical religion and philanthropy in our land. Thus, whereas in France the philanthropic movement was mostly the work of Voltaire and the philosophers, in England it was an offshoot of reviving religious zeal."[2]

---

[1] See HLH, pp. 178–183. Horne, *The Romance of Preaching*, pp. 217–251.
[2] *Christ and Civilization*, p. 440.

As was shown in a previous chapter, the religious life of the country in the eighteenth century had lost vitality and vigour as a result of the Illumination. Irreligion and immorality went hand in hand throughout the land. Among dissenters as well as churchmen the salt had lost its savour; exceptions there were, as God leaves not Himself without witness in any age of the history of the Church; but speaking in general terms it is no exaggeration to say that religion was at the lowest ebb, when Wesley and Whitefield turned the tide to full flood.

2. John Wesley (1703–1791)[1] was deeply religious from his youth. (1) At Oxford he became the soul of the small society, founded by his brother Charles, among some seriously-minded students for the cultivation of the devout life. Their nickname, Methodists, was afterwards adopted by the world-wide community which, as a result of his preaching, came into being. Yet before he could become the human instrument of the Divine Spirit in the Evangelical Revival he needed a fresh experience of the Divine grace for himself. After his return from America in 1738 he was in great depression of spirit; he met Peter Böhler, who had come to start a Moravian society in London.

"The Wesleys, having met Böhler at the house of a Dutch merchant, rendered him such services as his position in a strange land appeared to require. John Wesley procured him lodgings, Charles Wesley taught him English. By way of return, Peter Böhler taught both John and Charles Wesley the meaning of faith. In a letter to Zinzendorf he diagnosed their case as follows:—The elder was a good-natured man, who knew that he did not properly believe on the Saviour, and was willing to be taught, while the younger was very much distressed in mind, but did not know how he should begin to be acquainted with the Saviour."[2]

They both had intellectual belief and practical obedience; what they lacked was the trust of the heart, the

---

[1] See DHP ii. pp. 315–326. See bibliography there.
[2] F. J. Snell, *Wesley and Methodism*, p. 53.

comfort and the joy of the assurance of salvation. On the necessity of this Böhler insisted; and the possibility of the instant possession of this he asserted. It was at one of the meetings of the Moravians, on 24th May 1738, while Luther's Preface to his *Commentary on Romans* was being read, that John Wesley "felt his heart strangely warmed," and that he became sure "that his sins were freely forgiven." This emotional crisis had both intellectual and practical consequences: it gave new content to his theology, and fresh motive to his ministry.

(2) He soon parted from his teacher on the question of works; while teaching that justification is by faith alone without works, he could not accept fully the Moravian quietism, and insisted on works as not negligible, but as the necessary fruit of saving faith. For no less than in conversion did he see the work of the Holy Spirit in sanctification.

"This faith in the living power of the Holy Spirit, not anything ascribed to unaided human agency, was the secret of the emphasis which was laid on Assurance as a privilege attainable by all believers. From the same source sprang the Wesleyan doctrine of Perfection. All believers may attain to a perfection, which, however, is not a *legal* but a *Christian* perfection. It is a state where love to God and man reigns continuously, where there are no presumptuous sins, yet where there are still involuntary negligences and ignorances, transgressions of the perfect law, for which, therefore, forgiveness through the Atonement is requisite."[1]

The Spirit of God, received through faith in Christ, both assures forgiveness and secures holiness; imparts the grace of God and the power for goodness; cancels the miserable past and guarantees the blessed future; quenches fear and enkindles hope; saves from death and hell and makes sure life and heaven; brings a full and free salvation.

(3) This type of theology has its perils; and emotional satisfaction may be felt where no personal transformation

[1] Fisher, *History of Christian Doctrine*, p. 392.

has taken place: the claim of perfection even in the restricted sense of rightness of purpose may result in a lack of moral sensitiveness regarding what are deemed trivial failures.   Nevertheless its quickening, arousing, and renewing influence when preached by one who, like John Wesley, had been made a new creature [1] by it, cannot be doubted or denied.   His zeal for evangelism led him, as it afterwards led James Morison, to revolt against Calvinism, and the restriction of salvation to the elect, and to affirm the universality of God's grace towards sinful mankind. His Arminianism, however, laid stress more on God's grace and less on man's faith than some representatives of this school have done, and has been rightly described as "on fire."   It kindled a flame which spread swiftly and far.

3. Before dealing with Wesley's preaching, an account must be given of his fellow-labourer, George Whitefield (1714–1770).   (1) While admiring the piety of the members of the "Methodist Club" at Oxford, and even taking part in their godly exercises, he sooner than John Wesley discovered that his deepest need was not met. His change from darkness to light may be described in his own words:

"About the end of the seventh week, after having undergone innumerable buffetings of Satan and many months' inexpressible trials by night and day under the spirit of bondage, God was pleased at length to remove the heavy load, to enable me to lay hold on His dear Son by a living faith, and by giving me the spirit of adoption, to seal me, as I humbly hope, even to the day of everlasting redemption." [2]

This was in 1736.   (2) On 27th June his first sermon was preached in the church in Gloucester, where he had been brought up.

"As I proceeded," he says, "I perceived the fire kindle till at last, though so young and amidst a crowd of those who knew me in my childish days, I trust I was enabled to speak with some degree of gospel authority.   Some few mocked, but most seemed for the present struck; and I

[1] 2 Co 5[17].   [2] Quoted DHP ii. p. 309; see pp. 307–315.

have since heard that a complaint was made to the bishop that I drove fifteen mad the first sermon. The worthy prelate wished that the madness might not be forgotten before next Sunday." [1]

4. On his return from America in 1738 he had deep joy in observing the change in his two friends the Wesleys. (1) Denied access to the churches by the suspicion and hostility of the clergy, he began in February 1739 to preach in the open air to the colliers at Kingswood, near Bristol. It was with difficulty that he persuaded John Wesley to join him, as the ecclesiastical conservatism of the latter made him reluctant to preach outside of a church. On Monday, 2nd April, however, Wesley did preach at Kingswood to about three thousand people, and thus began a ministry that lasted fifty-two years. His reason for the new departure may be given in his own words:

"God in Scripture commands me, according to my power to instruct the ignorant, reform the wicked, confirm the virtuous. Man forbids me to do this in another's parish; that is, in effect to do it at all, seeing I have now no parish of my own, nor probably ever shall. Whom shall I hear, God or man? . . . I look upon all the world as my parish; thus far I mean that, in whatever part of it I am, I judge it meet, right, and my bounden duty to declare unto all that are willing to hear the glad tidings of salvation. This is the work which I know God has called me to; and sure I am that his blessing attends it." [2]

Well was it for England and the world that the new message was forced to adopt the new method, as it thus reached an innumerable multitude who would otherwise have been untouched.

(2) Except when on visits to America, Whitefield made field-preaching his chief work till 1769. Wesley was spared to continue his manifold labours till 1791, when on 23rd February he preached his last sermon. On Sundays he usually preached three times, and held other services besides; during the week he liked to

[1] DHP ii. p. 310.   [2] Quoted DHP ii. 319; cf. Acts 13[46].

preach at five o'clock in the morning, so that the working people might hear him before their day's toil began.
In his *Journal* he records that up to 21st April 1770, he
had ridden over a hundred thousand miles on horseback.
In 1741 there was "a sharp contention" between Wesley
and Whitefield, as between Paul and Barnabas,[1] as Whitefield had remained a Calvinist, and was offended by
Wesley's Arminianism. Before death they were reconciled, and Wesley did due honour to his companion in his
funeral sermon. While Whitefield's movement is preserved
in the Countess of Huntingdon's Connexion, Wesley's
assumed much larger proportions and a much wider
diffusion; and against his wishes, as he remained a loyal
Churchman, he was forced by the logic of facts to make
provision for its continuance in the separate society which
bears his name. One feature of Wesleyan Methodism
deserves mention: the pastoral care for the individual
converts which is assured by the class meeting. This
religious revival did not waste and lose itself in transient
emotionalism, although there was often excess of emotion
with abnormal psychical conditions; but found permanent
embodiment in a Christian community "zealous of good
works."[2]

5. What were the sermons which reached and changed
multitudes? Of John Wesley's sermons Horne writes:

"As evangelistic discourses they are most significant and
most surprising. The evidences of a mind steeped in classical
culture, and keenly alive to the thought of his time, abound
on almost every page. Every perusal of them leaves me
wondering what it was in them that pierced the consciences
of the most hardened sinners to the quick. There is nothing
sensational in this evangelism. There is plain dealing.
There is much practical, sensible and serious exhortation as
to the sins that corrupt men's lives and harden their hearts.
Of rhetorical fireworks there is not a trace. We are less
impressed by the vehemence than by the calm strength of
them. Yet certain it is that when this man preached, the
world knew that the hour of battle had sounded. Those

---

[1] Acts 15[39]. [2] Tit. 2[14].

scenes of fury, which belong now to English history, and in which Wesley's life was again and again in peril, are the tribute to the power of his message. If he had been arguing for a verdict before a society of learned men, he could hardly have reasoned more closely or employed more classical illustrations. . . . Even as Wesley was singularly fine and pure in controversy when he was being assailed by a multitude of scurrilous pens and pelted with gutter-epithets, so, also in the warfare which he waged with error and evil in almost every market-place in the land, he was content to use the Gospel weapons of Truth and Love, and, as the smoke cleared from the battlefield, it was seen that he and his forces were in possession of the best strategical positions." [1]

6. To Wesley, Whitefield was a great contrast. "We may accept the almost universal verdict that for dramatic and declamatory power he had no rival in his own age, and no superior in any age." [2] Although he used the art of the orator, which he possessed almost to perfection, his purpose was not to please, but to convert by arousing to the highest point the passions of love, hope and fear. While he cast the spell of his eloquence over the cultured and the noble, not them alone did he seek to reach, but

"the miners and the puddlers and the weavers; the masses of neglected and ignorant artisans and field labourers, to whom clergymen and ministers had ceased to appeal, and for whom in all the land there existed no passionate sympathy, until George Whitefield arose and spoke to them, in a voice often choked with tears, of death in sin, and life in Christ." [3]

His deep conviction and intense emotion was allied with "a large command of vivid, homely, and picturesque English, and an extraordinary measure of the tact which enables a practised orator to adapt himself to the character and disposition of his audience." [4]

7. An example of Wesley's preaching, which will illustrate both content and manner, may be taken from a sermon on *The Poverty of Reason* (1 Co 14^{20}). After

---

[1] *The Romance of Preaching*, pp. 236-237.
[2] *Ibid.*, p. 238.   [3] *Ibid.*, pp. 240-241.
[4] Lecky, quoted by Horne, p. 239.

several classical allusions (Latin and Greek in the original tongues) he states his argument:

"Reason, however cultivated and improved, cannot produce the love of God, which is plain from hence; it cannot produce either faith or hope, from which alone this love can flow. It is then only, when we 'behold' by faith 'what manner of love the Father hath bestowed upon us' in giving His only Son, that we might not perish, but have everlasting life, that 'the love of God is shed abroad in our heart by the Holy Ghost which is given unto us.' It is only then, when we 'rejoice in hope of the glory of God,' that we 'love him because he first loved us.' But what can cold reason do in this matter? It may present us with fair ideas; it can draw a fine picture of love; but this is only a painted fire. And further than this reason cannot go. I made the trial for many years. I collected the finest hymns, prayers, and meditations which I could find in any language, and I said, sang, or read them over and over, with all possible seriousness and attention. But still I was like the bones in Ezekiel's vision: 'The skin covered them above, but there was no breath in them.' And as reason cannot produce the love of God, so neither can it produce the love of one's neighbour; a calm, generous, disinterested benevolence to every child of man. This earnest, steady goodwill to our fellow-creatures never flowed from any fountain but gratitude to our Creator. And if this be (as a very ingenious man supposes) the very essence of virtue, it follows that virtue can have no being unless it spring from the love of God. Therefore, as reason cannot produce this love, so neither can it produce virtue. And as it cannot give either faith, hope, love, or virtue, so it cannot give happiness, since, separate from these, there can be no happiness for any intelligent creatures. It is true, those who are void of all virtue may have pleasures, such as they are; but happiness they have not, cannot have. No:

> 'Their joy is all sadness;
>   Their mirth is all vain;
>   Their laughter is madness;
>   Their pleasure is pain!'

Pleasures? Shadows! Dreams! Fleeting as the wind! Unsubstantial as the rainbow! As unsatisfying to the poor gasping soul

> 'As the gay colours of an eastern cloud.'

None of them will stand the test of reflection; if thought comes, the bubble breaks!"[1]

8. The closing appeal of Whitefield's sermon on "The Kingdom of God" (Ro 14[7]) illustrates his manner.

"My dear friends, I would preach with all my heart till midnight to do you good, till I could preach no more. Oh that this body might hold out to speak more for my dear Redeemer! Had I a thousand lives, had I a thousand tongues, they should be employed in inviting sinners to come to Jesus Christ! Come, then, let me prevail with some of you to come along with me. Come, poor, lost, undone sinners, come just as you are to Christ, and say: If I be damned, I will perish at the feet of Jesus Christ, where never one perished yet. He will receive you with open arms; the dear Redeemer is willing to receive you all. Fly, then, for your lives. The devil is in you while unconverted; and will you go with the devil in your heart to bed this night? God Almighty knows if ever you and I shall see one another again. In one or two days more I must go, and perhaps I may never see you again till I meet you at the Judgment Day. Oh, my dear friends, think of that solemn meeting; think of that important hour when the heavens shall pass away with a great noise, when the elements shall melt with fervent heat, when the sea and the grave shall be giving up their dead, and all shall be summoned to appear before the great God. What will you do then if the Kingdom of God is not erected in your heart? You must go to the devil—like must go to like—if you are not converted. Christ hath asserted it in the strongest manner: 'Verily, verily, I say unto you: Except a man be born again he cannot enter into the Kingdom of God.' Who can dwell with devouring fire? Who can dwell with everlasting burnings? Oh, my heart is melting with love to you. Surely God intends to do good to your poor souls. Will no one be persuaded to accept of Christ? If those who are settled Pharisees will not come, I desire to speak to you who are drunkards, Sabbath-breakers, cursers, and swearers — will you come to Christ? I know that many of you come here out of curiosity; though you come only to see the congregation, yet if you come to Jesus Christ, Christ will accept of

---

[1] CME x. pp. 230–231. Wesley's *Works* are published in 14 vols. by the Wesleyan Conference Offices.

you. Are there any cursing, swearing soldiers here? Will you come to Jesus Christ, and list yourselves under the banner of the dear Redeemer? You are all welcome to Christ. Are there any little boys or girls here? Come to Christ, and he will erect his Kingdom in you. There are many little children whom God is working on, both at home and abroad. Oh, if some of the little lambs would come to Christ, they shall have peace and joy in the day that the Redeemer shall set up his Kingdom in their hearts. Parents, tell them that Jesus Christ will take them in his arms, that he will dandle them on his knees. All of you, old and young, you that are old and grey-headed, come to Jesus Christ, and you shall be kings and priests to your God. The Lord will abundantly pardon you at the eleventh hour. 'Ho, every one of you that thirsteth.' If there be any of you ambitious of honour, do you want a crown, a sceptre? Come to Christ, and the Lord Jesus Christ will give you a kingdom that no man shall take from you."[1]

9. To the Evangelical Revival also is due the organisation of lay preaching as an important auxiliary of the work of the ordained ministry.[2] (1) Men were crying out for the Bread from Heaven and the Water of Life; and there were not enough fully trained preachers to carry the divine provision for hungering and thirsting souls. In 1738 Joseph Humphreys began to help Wesley. In June 1739, John Cennick had to take the place of a young man who was to have read a sermon, but failed to appear. Wesley would not forbid his preaching. His reluctance to allow Thomas Maxfield, a companion and servant of his

[1] CME x. pp. 243, 244.

[2] Among ministerial helpers of John Wesley and George Whitefield may be mentioned Charles Wesley (1708–1788), who only for a short time devoted himself to the itinerant ministry, but was the "sweet singer of Methodism"; John William Fletcher (1729–1785), the vicar of Madeley, and superintendent of the seminary for training preachers established by the Countess of Huntingdon at Trevecca, an ardent controversialist in defence of Arminianism yet devout in spirit, lovable and beloved; Rowland Hill (1745–1833), who on account of his itinerant ministry was refused ordination, and at last found a permanent sphere of influence at Surrey Chapel, where many flocked to hear his earnest and evangelical, but original and oft quaint preaching, vivid in imagination, relieved by wit and humour, and intense in conviction, coming, as Sheridan described it, "hot from the heart." (See DHP ii. 326–329.)

brother Charles, was only overcome by the evidence of the
Spirit's presence and power in him, which drew the confession: "It is the Lord; let Him do what seemeth Him
good."

(2) In his *Further Appeal to Men of Reason and
Religion*, he defended his use of such agency on the ground
of the manifest divine approval shown in the abounding
fruit of these labours. He asserted their competence in
the one thing needful, their personal experience of the
Gospel they preached; and, scholar as he was, carried his
appeal to the court of Church history. Despite prejudice
and opposition, and to begin with even his own inclinations,
he continued to use all who were willing and fit to spread
the good news of salvation.

(3) John Haime, the dragoon, became a kind of chaplain to his regiment, and his influence spread throughout the Army, as the Commander-in-Chief, the Duke of
Cumberland, gave him permission to preach anywhere.
Howell Harris (1714–1773), who was refused ordination,
was the Apostle of Wales, and, though much persecuted,
saw his native land thoroughly changed. The movement
crossed the Atlantic in the person of Philip Embury, who
was aroused from his despondency and inactivity by Barbara
Heck, to preach the first Methodist sermon in New York.
His hands were strengthened by Captain Webb, one of
Wesley's converts. These were but the first-fruits of an
abundant harvest of lay endeavour which has been an
untold blessing to mankind.[1]

II.

1. The religious revival of the eighteenth century was
not confined to the Methodist community. (1) While
Whitefield cannot be claimed as the founder of the evangelical school in the Church of England, it felt his stimulus.
John Newton (1725–1807),[2] the friend of Cowper, had no

---

[1] See Telford's *A History of Lay Preaching*, chap. v.
[2] See DHP ii. pp. 306–307.

great gifts nor much art as a preacher, but his own deliverance from a very sinful life gave him power in the pulpit in dealing with those who were feeling the pangs of remorse. William Wilberforce (1759–1833) as an orator and statesman illustrates the influence of evangelicalism in philanthropy and politics. Wesley's Arminianism lessened his direct influence on the older dissenting Churches, Presbyterian, Baptist and Independent; but as many of the converts found their way into the membership of these Churches, there was a quickening of their religious life.

2. In 1740 Whitefield came into contact with the movement in New England, which had begun in 1734 as a result of the preaching of Jonathan Edwards (1703–1758), and which after a pause had been renewed in 1839. "The 'Great Awakening' was accompanied by the advocacy of Calvinistic doctrines and attacks upon Arminianism," which with Arian and Socinian opinions was held to be responsible for growing religious laxity. Not only was Edwards the leading preacher of this movement, he was its theologian, and the author of the modified Calvinism, known as "New England Theology." "Edwards is an example of that rare mingling of intellectual subtilty and spiritual insight, of logical acumen with mystical fervour, which qualify their possessors for the highest achievements in the field of religious thought." These contrasts appear in his books on *The Will* and on the *Spiritual Affections*; as we turn from the one to the other "it is like passing from the pages of Aristotle to a sermon of Tauler."[1] It is with his preaching we are here concerned.

"His sermons were thoughtful and argumentative, yet plain and searching. They were delivered, with little or no action, from the manuscript, but with that manifest depth of conviction and of feeling which has been likened to 'white heat.'"[2]

His wife noted the contrast between him and White-

---

[1] Fisher's *History of Christian Doctrine*, p. 395.
[2] Fisher's *The History of the Church*, p. 525.

field, who aimed at stirring the emotions. Unlike as the two men were, for a time they laboured together, and revivals resulted in many places in New England.

"Physical manifestations—trances and the like—sometimes occurred while the revival preachers delivered their discourses. Other exhibitions of strong emotion, as tears and audible exclamations, were not infrequent."[1]

The movement met with opposition even as did Wesley's labours in England; and Edwards himself recognised that there was unhealthy excitement, and that many converts fell away, and yet approved it as a work of the divine grace.

3. A previous chapter has dealt with the "Marrow" movement in Scotland, with its issue in the Secession, and the contrast between Evangelicals and Moderates. We now deal with the influence of the Evangelical Revival in Scotland.

(1) John Maclaurin (1693–1754) was in correspondence with Jonathan Edwards, but his evangelicalism avoided all revivalist extremes. The translator of Van Oosterzee's *Practical Theology* says of him : "His one sermon on Gal 6^{14}, if it were the only one in the two little volumes of his 'Remains,' would alone suffice to rescue himself and the age in which he lived from oblivion."[2] Blaikie is reported by Dargan as saying of it "that it is rather a treatise than a sermon."[3] John Erskine (1721–1803), a cousin of the founders of the Secession Church, had some correspondence with Wesley, although doctrinally more in sympathy with Whitefield. Walter Scott, whose parents belonged to Erskine's church, has described him in his novel of *Guy Mannering*.[4] Not eloquent, he brought learning and ability to the service of a message which he himself describes : "Christ Crucified and salvation through Him ; the law as a schoolmaster to bring men to Christ ; and exhorting the disciples of Jesus to adorn his doctrine

---

[1] Fisher's *The History of the Church*, p. 525.   [2] P. 140.
[3] DHP ii. p. 342.   [4] The passage is quoted DHP ii. p. 343.

by the conscientious performance of every duty, ought to be chief subject of our sermons." [1]

(2) Early in the nineteenth century there was formed in the Church of Scotland the Evangelical Party to oppose the dominant Moderatism. The leader was Dr. Andrew Thomson, who in 1814 became minister of St. George's Church in Edinburgh. His preaching there soon made a great change.

"Religion was not in disrepute at the time of Dr. Thomson's appointment. . . . Some earnestness there was in connection with one or two congregations, which had recently obtained ministers of evangelical belief, faithful gospel preaching, and consistent Christian walk and conversation. But the general atmosphere was extremely worldly, cold, and indifferent; and church-going, as a rule, was attended to very much because it was generally considered a proper thing to be done. . . . But the preaching of Dr. Thomson was like a bombshell falling among the people. Not only did he give constant prominence to the distinctive gospel doctrines of grace and redemption by an atonement, but in terms of great directness and plainness of speech he denounced the customs of a society calling itself Christian; and in a marvellously short time, by his zeal and faithfulness under God, a remarkable change was effected in the habits and pursuits of many of his people." [2]

Into the ecclesiastical conflict which resulted from the religious awakening we cannot now enter, but must note in it the close association of the claim of the Church's spiritual independence with the belief in evangelical doctrine.

4. The greatest personality in the movement which resulted in the formation of the Free Church of Scotland in 1843 was Dr. Thomas Chalmers (1780–1847),[3] who was thinker, teacher, pastor, philanthropist, leader and preacher, whom it is no exaggeration to regard as the greatest man next to John Knox in the religious thought and life of Scotland.

[1] Quoted DHP ii. p. 343.

[2] Maclagan's *History of St. George's*, quoted in Walker's *Scottish Church History*, p. 130.

[3] See DHP ii. pp. 487–495.

(1) There is a link between him and the Evangelical Revival in England. He entered on his ministry as a Moderate, not worldly in aim, genuinely conscientious in the discharge of his duties, but not possessed by the " holy enthusiasm " which afterwards glowed in him as a steady flame. On the 24th December 1810 he began to read Wilberforce's *Practical View of Christianity*.

"'As I got on in reading it,' he says, ' I felt myself on the eve of a great revolution in all my opinions about Christianity.' Many things had prepared him to receive the light—a long illness, family bereavements, lines of study which he had been providentially led to pursue, and other things. But through all the Spirit of God was guiding him ; and when at last he rose above the mists, he soon compelled the country to recognize his mission as that of the great religious leader of his age." [1]

(2) Confining ourselves to Chalmers as a preacher, it must be admitted that neither in appearance nor voice and manner was he specially qualified to excel in the pulpit. His sentences were long, and he read his sermons. And yet he put into the delivery the force and fervour of free speech ; and the mastery of the man, thinker and believer asserted itself over his hearers. He had one peculiarity, in which a noted preacher of to-day bears him a striking likeness : he repeated the same idea with a great variety of expression. Robert Hall states this fact with a touch of exaggeration.

" Did you ever know any man who had that singular faculty of repetition possessed by Dr. Chalmers ? Why, sir, he often reiterates the same thing ten and twelve times in the course of a few pages. Even Burke himself had not so much of that peculiarity. His mind resembles . . . a kaleidoscope. Every turn presents the object in a new and beautiful form, but the object presented is still the same. . . . His mind seems to move on hinges, not on wheels; there is incessant motion, but no progress." [2]

---

[1] Walker's *Scottish Church History*, p. 133.
[2] Works of Robert Hall, vol. iii. p. 79 f., quoted DHP ii. p. 492.

His powers as an expositor are seen in his sermons on Romans, and his scientific attainments in his *Astronomical Discourses*.

(3) The most famous sermon is that on *The Expulsive Power of a New Affection*, and a short extract from this great utterance may justify the inclusion of Chalmers among the evangelists.

"Nothing can exceed the magnitude of the required change in a man's character—when bidden, as he is, in the New Testament, to love not the world ; no, nor any of the things that are in the world—for this so comprehends all that is dear to him in existence as to be equivalent to a command of self-annihilation. But the same revelation which dictates so mighty an obedience places within our reach as mighty an instrument of obedience. It brings for admittance, to the very door of our heart, an affection which, once seated upon its throne, will either subordinate every previous inmate, or bid it away. Beside the world it places before the eye of the mind Him who made the world, and with this peculiarity, which is all its own—that in this Gospel do we so behold God as that we may love God. It is there, and there only, where God stands revealed as an object of confidence to sinners—and, where our desire after Him is not chilled into apathy by that barrier of human guilt which intercepts every approach that is not made to Him through the appointed Mediator. . . . It is when He stands dismantled of the terrors which belong to Him as an offended lawgiver, and when we are enabled by faith, which is His own gift, to see His glory in the face of Jesus Christ, and to hear His beseeching voice, as it protests goodwill to men, and entreats the return of all who will to a full pardon, and a gracious acceptance—it is then that a love paramount to the love of the world, and at length expulsive of it, first arises in the regenerating bosom. It is when released from the spirit of bondage, with which love cannot dwell, and when admitted into the number of God's children, through the faith that is in Christ Jesus, the spirit of adoption is poured upon us—it is then that the heart, brought under the mastery of one great and predominant affection, is delivered from the tyranny of its former desires, and in the only way in which deliverance is possible." [1]

[1] WGS iv. pp. 66–67.

5. Two other names may be mentioned.

(1) "The oratory of a heart penetrated with the vital truths of the Gospels," says Van Oosterzee, "found one of its noblest exponents, of this or any other age, in the person of the youthful Robert Murray M'Cheyne (died 1843), whose 'Memoir and Remains' and 'Additional Remains' (by his friend, Andrew Bonar) have passed through numerous editions, and whose influence continues to exert itself with blessed results both far and near even to the present day." [1]

(2) That unhappy genius, Edward Irving (1792–1834), took London by storm, but soon lost his popularity, and strayed into devious paths.

" He produced an excitement," says Dr. Stoughton, "which, from the extent to which it prevailed, the class of persons it affected, and the prophetic fervour which it displayed, rose to the importance of a national event. . . . He spoke to men at large, to people of fashion in particular. Never since George Whitefield had anyone so arrested attention; and Irving went far beyond Whitefield in attracting the respectful, even the admiring, notice of lords, ladies, and commons. His name was on every lip. Newspapers, magazines, and reviews discussed his merits; a caricature in shop windows hit off his eccentricities." [2]

6. Two movements of religious revival in Scotland claim brief notice. In dealing with the *History of Congregational Independency in Scotland*, Dr. James Ross makes this statement:

"It is significant that most of the churches of this order came into existence within the short period of four years, from 1794 to 1798, thus indicating that there must have been some common causes of their origin, or rather of the state of mind and religious feeling of which they were the expression." "The origin" of most of these churches can be directly "traced to the great evangelistic movement that took place in Scotland during the last few years of the century, and with which the names of the brothers Haldane,

---

[1] OPT, pp. 140–141. This was written in 1878. In the boyhood of the writer of this volume the memory of M'Cheyne was still fragrant in Scotland.

[2] Quoted by DHP ii. pp. 484–485.

and Messrs. Campbell, Rate, Aikman, and others are associated. Robert Haldane has placed on record that ' he was aroused from the sleep of spiritual death by the excitement of the French Revolution.' " [1]

It was when his wish to go to India as a missionary was thwarted by the refusal of the East India Company, that he resolved to give himself and his means to work in his motherland. A few sentences from the *Missionary Magazine* will suffice to indicate the kind of ministry exercised.

" The advantages of missionary schemes both in England and Scotland have remarkably appeared, not only in exciting the zeal of Christian people to send the Gospel of Jesus to the dark places of the earth, but to use means to extend its influence at home. With this view a missionary journey has been undertaken in the northern part of Scotland, not to disseminate matters of doubtful disputation, or to make converts to this or that other sect, but to endeavour to stir up their brethren to flee from the wrath to come, and not to rest in an empty profession of religion. Accordingly they are now employed in preaching the word of life, distributing pamphlets, and endeavouring to excite their Christian brethren to employ the talents committed to their charge, especially by erecting schools for the instruction of youth. . . . That their object may be misrepresented they have no doubt. It has already been said that they are going out with a design of making people dissatisfied with their ministers; but they can appeal to the great Searcher of hearts that they are determined in their conversation and preaching to know nothing but Jesus Christ and Him crucified." [2]

The converts won by this preaching found so little encouragement and help in the existing Churches that they were driven to form small groups in order to sustain by prayer and study of the Scriptures their new life, and out of these grew the Independent Churches.

7. In time these Churches got fixed in their theological tradition, and were not ready to welcome any new light.

[1] Pp. 42–44.   [2] Quoted by Ross, *op. cit.*, p. 51.

Their most noted leader, Dr. Ralph Wardlaw (1799–1853),[1] was a moderate Calvinist; he held that the atonement of Christ has universal sufficiency, but that its efficiency is limited to the elect whom the Spirit of God moves by a special influence to exercise the faith that receives the gift of God.[2] When James Morison (1816–1893) and others were led by their evangelising zeal in presenting a full and free salvation to all men, to break the hampering fetters of Calvinism, the old movement opposed itself to the new. Nine students were expelled from the Glasgow Theological Academy in May 1844 for sympathising with the heresy that not only is the atonement sufficient, but that it is also efficient for all who believe, as God withholds His enabling Spirit from none. It was in a religious revival due to his evangelising efforts that James Morison [3] was led step by step to abandon his Calvinism, until he reached the position of the three Universitalities, that God loves, Christ atones for, and the Spirit works in all; and the preaching of this truth by himself and others continued the effective means of religious revival. Expelled for this view from the Secession Church in 1841, he and those like-minded formed the Evangelical Union in 1843, which sought to make an evangelical theology practical in evangelistic effort.

8. Later in the nineteenth century the outstanding evangelist was Dwight L. Moody (1837–1899),[4] who visited Britain in 1873. For two years and three months he laboured from one end of Great Britain to another, moving by his simple, artless, yet sincere and powerful preaching a vast multitude to decision for, and consecration to Christ. Other evangelists have come and gone; but this was the last of the great revival movements, unless in the mission field, to which we now turn.

[1] See DHP ii. p. 482.
[2] See Ross, op. cit., pp. 125–136.
[3] See The Life of Principal Morison, by Wm. Adamson, D.D. (cc. v.–xx.).
[4] See his Life, by his son, W. R. Moody.

III.

1. Amid all the defects and failures of the Christian Churches, the nineteenth century shines with an unquenchable glory as the period of world-wide foreign mission work. The evangelist at home and the missionary abroad are inseparable, for where there is the enlightened zeal of the one there must also be the constraining motive of the other. In the previous chapters the closeness of this connection has been illustrated; but now we meet with its most conspicuous instance. The missionary as well as the philanthropic movement of the beginning of last century was one of the blessed fruits of the Evangelical Revival. Wesley's saying : " I look upon all the world as my parish," is the inspiring watchword of the effort to carry the Gospel to the ends of the earth.

(1) In the first period of missions the Roman Empire was evangelised: in the second period the nations of Europe were christianised, although in a very superficial fashion. The records of the Reformation are very disappointing as regards this sacred charge of the Christian Church. Roman Catholicism showed greater zeal for propaganda than did Protestantism. Whatever we may think of his methods, Xavier's labours demand that his name be remembered; and still more Raimund Lull's. The missionary character of the Moravian Brethren has already been noted. The work of John Elliot (1604–1690) and David Brainerd (1718–1747)[1] among the Red Indians must not be forgotten. But the world-wide movement of to-day has first on its roll of honour William Carey (1761–1834).

(2) In 1784 the Northamptonshire Association of Baptist Ministers resolved to invite the Churches to join in united prayer not only for religious revival at home, but also for the spread of the Gospel abroad. " Let the whole interest of the Redeemer be affectionately remembered and *the spread of the Gospel to the most distant parts of the habit-*

[1] See Smith, *Short History of Christian Missions*, pp. 136–138.

able globe, be the object of your most fervent requests."[1]   On
this occasion Andrew Fuller (1754-1815),[2] a noted
expositor, theologian and preacher, delivered a sermon
on *Walking by Faith*.   When the Baptist Missionary
Society was formed in 1792 he became its first secretary,
and it owed much to his leadership.   From 1787, William
Carey, after reading Cook's *Voyages Round the World*, began
to cherish the desire to go as a missionary to Otaheite; but
his zeal was at first repressed even by Andrew Fuller with
the remark : " If the Lord should make windows in heaven,
then might this thing be."   The Spirit of God could not
be quenched by discouragements in him, and through him
others were convinced.   In 1793, Dr. Ryland, who at first
opposed his project, confessed : " I believe God Himself
infused into the mind of Carey that solicitude for the
salvation of the heathen which cannot be fairly traced to
any other source."   On the 2nd October 1792, Carey
preached at Kettering on Is 54[2, 3] : " Enlarge the place of
thy tent, and let them stretch forth the curtains of thy
habitations : spare not, lengthen thy cords, and strengthen
thy stakes ; for thou shalt break forth on the right hand
and on the left ; and thy seed shall inherit the Gentiles,
and make the desolate cities to be inhabited "; and uttered
his two famous mottoes, " Expect great things from God ;
attempt great things for God."[3]   Such was the impression
made that those who heard the sermon founded the Baptist
Missionary Society.   A short time before, Carey had
published his " *Enquiry into the Obligation of Christians to
use Means for the Conversion of the Heathens* ; in which
the Religious State of the Different Nations of the World,
the Success of Former Undertakings, and the Practicability
of Further Undertakings, are considered "; and thus some
of his hearers were prepared for the impression made.

(3) It was fitting that Carey himself should be the
first missionary ; but he went not to Otaheite as he had
desired, but to Bengal.   The East India Company opposed

---

[1] Quoted by Smith, *Short History of Christian Missions*, p. 156.
[2] See DHP ii. pp. 332-335.   [3] Smith, *op. cit.*, p. 157.

all missionary enterprise, and it was under the Danish flag at Serampore that Carey and the two colleagues who joined him, *Marsham* and *Ward*, in scholarship no less than in preaching, laid the foundations of Indian Missions. For forty-one years without break Carey laboured in Bengal, and died there, at the age of seventy, on 9th June 1834.

2. Carey and the Baptist ministers he influenced were responsive to the Spirit of God, who was imparting the impulse to this new form of service to many besides themselves. (1) Dr. Haweis, chaplain to the Countess of Huntingdon, was also stirred to interest by the account of Captain Cook's voyages, and made several attempts, which, however, were at the time frustrated, to send missionaries to the South Seas. In 1793 the *Evangelical Magazine* was started "to arouse the Christian public from its prevailing torpor, and excite to a more close and serious consideration of their obligations to use means for advancing the Redeemer's Kingdom."[1] As showing the catholicity of the enterprise, it may be noted that the editor, the Rev. John Eyre, was a Churchman, and one of the chief supporters was the well-known Independent preacher, Matthew Wilks. Dr. Haweis and Dr. Bogue of Gosport now associated themselves with the enterprise; and the outcome was the foundation of the London Missionary Society, on an inter-denominational basis, in 1795. Dr. Bogue in the sermon preached on the occasion declared that his hearers had been attending "the funeral of Bigotry"; and added the fervent prayer: "May she be buried so deep that not a particle of her dust may be ever thrown upon the face of the earth."

(2) The first mission undertaken was to the South Seas. In 1796 the *Duff* under Captain James Wilson, with thirty men missionaries, besides some wives and children, sailed to the sound of the hymn, "Jesus, at Thy command we launch into the deep." The troublous and even tragic experiences of this missionary party cannot be told in detail. After long delay the dawn began to

[1] Quoted by Horne, *The Story of the L.M.S.*, p. 4.

break; and the victory of the Cross had begun in some
of the islands, when one of the great missionaries of the
Society arrived. John Williams (1795–1839) reached
Tahiti in 1817; he had the aspirations of the pioneer.
"For my part, I cannot content myself within the narrow
limits of a single roof";[1] and he pushed on from island to
island, preaching the Gospel, winning converts and starting
churches, until his death on Erromanga. He multiplied
his own labours by the employment of native Christians as
missionaries, many of whom have since shared the glory of
martyrdom with him.

3. The Society for the Propagation of the Gospel,
which had been at work in America since 1700, became
a world-wide missionary agency in 1821. The Evangelical
party in the Church of England in 1799 started the
Church Missionary Society. (1) Most famous of the early
Anglican missionaries in India was Henry Martyn (1781–
1812), who was aroused to interest by the experience of
Carey, and who in 1806 landed as a chaplain in Calcutta.
He at once began the study of Hindustani, Hindi, Persian,
and Arabic, and within five years had translated the New
Testament into the first of these languages. Pushing on
into Persia in 1811, he had in a few months translated
the greater part of the New Testament into that language
also. As he was returning home by Asia Minor, he died
at Tokat, worn out by his labours and perils. Short as
was his career, although he won only one convert, his
personality made a deep impression.[2] At Cambridge he
had graduated as Senior Wrangler; and Sir James Stephen
describes him as he was before the missionary call gave
unity to his life.

"A man born to love with ardour and to hate with
vehemence, amorous, irascible, ambitious, and vain; without
one torpid nerve about him; aiming at universal excellence
in science, in literature, in conversation, in horsemanship,
and even in dress; not without some gay fancies, but more

---

[1] Quoted by Horne, p. 42.
[2] See Robinson, *History of Christian Missions*, p. 84.

prone to austere and melancholy thoughts; patient of the most toilsome inquiries, though not wooing philosophy for her own sake; animated by the poetical temperament, though unvisited by any poetical inspiration; eager for enterprise, though thinking meanly of the reward to which the adventurous aspire; uniting in himself, though as yet unable to concentrate and to harmonize them, many keen desires, many high powers, and much constitutional dejection—the chaotic materials of a great character."[1]

What the sacred passion made out of this material the brief record of his life shows, and at his death Lord Macaulay was constrained to offer him this tribute:

> "In manhood's early bloom
> The Christian hero found a pagan tomb;
> Religion, sorrowing o'er her favourite son,
> Points to the glorious trophies which he won.
> Eternal trophies, not with slaughter red,
> Not stained with tears by hapless captives shed;
> But trophies of the Cross."[2]

4. Alexander Duff (1806–1878), a Scottish Presbyterian, made a new departure in missionary policy; he sought to influence the higher castes of India by means of schools offering a liberal education in the English language. From 1830 to 1863 he worked on these lines in Calcutta. "His converts were not numbered by thousands, or even by hundreds, but they included a large number of high caste Hindus whose brilliant mental gifts and whose strength of character have exercised an immense influence upon their fellow-countrymen in North India."[3]

A marked contrast was the work of Ringeltaube,[4] who was one of a party of six missionaries whom the L.M.S. sent in 1804. He laboured with great success till 1815 among the pariahs and outcasts of Travancore, a country in which missionary work has made marvellous progress.

5. The American Board of Commissioners for Foreign Missions was formed in response to a challenge from four

---

[1] Quoted by Horne, *The Romance of Preaching*, pp. 223–224.
[2] *Ibid.*, p. 227.   [3] Robinson, *op. cit.*, p. 89.
[4] See Horne's *History of the L.M.S.*, pp. 93–97.

students, who asked " whether they may expect patronage and support from a missionary society in this country, or must commit themselves to the direction of a European society ? " [1]

The most famous afterwards of the four was Adoniram Judson, who, when refused the opportunity of work in Calcutta, which he reached in 1812, went on to Burma, where he landed at Rangoon in 1813. As on the voyage he became a Baptist, the American Baptist Missionary Union was formed in 1814 to support him. In seven years he baptized ten converts. During the war with England in 1823 he suffered much hardship for twenty-one months in prison. He died in 1850. "Judson believed in peregrinating as opposed to concentrated mission work, and was doubtful as to the value of missionary schools. His legacy to those who came after him was the inspiration of a devoted life and the translation of the Bible into Burmese." [2]

6. "A Chinese politician who held one of the highest positions under the new republican government, in answer to the question, When did the Chinese revolutionary movement begin ? replied : On the day that Robert Morrison the missionary landed in Canton. The start of Protestant missions in China, notwithstanding the fact that the earliest Protestant missionaries were wholly devoid of political aims, was, in fact, the introduction of a new factor into the political life of China, the far-reaching results of which can now be seen." [3]

(1) It was in 1807 that Morrison (1782–1834) [4] was sent by the London Missionary Society and landed at Macao. Amid disappointments, difficulties and dangers which would have daunted most men, he persevered in secretly acquiring the language, preparing a grammar and dictionary, and translating the Scriptures. From Macao he had to remove to Canton, as permission for his colleague Milne to reside was refused. In 1813 the whole of the New Testament was printed. While Morrison remained

[1] Smith, *op. cit.*, p. 178.   [2] Robinson, *op. cit.*, p. 153.
[3] *Ibid.*, *op. cit.*, p. 181.   [4] See Horne, *op. cit.*, pp. 121-141.

at Canton, Milne removed to Malacca, where greater freedom for the work could be secured, and the projected college could be founded. As interpreter for the East India Company, not as missionary, Morrison was allowed to visit Peking, and so increase his knowledge of China. He had little opportunity of winning converts, as all his work had to be done as secretly as possible, but in 1814 his first convert, Tsae A-Ko, was baptized. While in England in 1824 and 1825 he presented the Chinese Bible to King George IV.

"In June 1834 he prepared his last sermon on the text, 'In my Father's house are many mansions.' It was to show how much of the joy of the eternal Home would 'consist in the *society formed there*; the *family* of God, from all ages and out of all nations.' . . . On July 31st the pioneer Protestant missionary to China passed peacefully to his rest."[1]

Small as was the Chinese Christian community that mourned his loss, he laid in his scholarly labours the foundations of modern missionary work in China.

(2) In the footsteps of Morrison as a Chinese scholar followed James Legge (1815–1897),[2] who in 1840 became head of the college at Malacca, which was soon removed to Hong-Kong, and who in 1876 was appointed Professor of Chinese Language and Literature at Oxford, and translated the Chinese classics into English.

(3) For more than fifty years Griffith John [3] (1831–1912) laboured at Hankow. He devoted himself to evangelisation and the writing of books for the Chinese. One who still more largely contributed to the creation of a Chinese Christian literature was Dr. Timothy Richard,[4] first Chancellor of the Imperial University founded in 1900 at Shansi by the Chinese Government.

(4) In Mongolia a mission was attempted in 1817–1841,[5] but its evangelisation began with the coming of James Gilmour in 1870. About his book *Among the*

[1] Horne, p. 141.   [2] See Robinson, p. 194, and Horne, p. 309 ff.
[3] Robinson, p. 194, and Horne, pp. 326–328.   [4] Robinson, p. 196.
[5] See Horne, pp. 141–145.

Mongols (1882) the reviewer in the *Spectator* said: " Robinson Crusoe has turned missionary, lived years in Mongolia, and written a book about it."[1]   Incredible were the hardships, severe the strain, and small the encouragement of the work, but undaunted the resolution, and quenchless the hope of the worker.   His story is one of thrilling interest. After his death in 1891 the small Christian community at Ch'ao Yang wrote of him to his orphan boys :

" Pastor Gilmour in his preaching and doctoring at Ch'ao Yang, north of the Pass, truly loved others as himself, was considerate and humble, and had the likeness of our Saviour Jesus.   Not only the Christians thank him without end, but even those outside the Church (the heathen) bless him without limit."[2]

7.   Reference has already been made to John Williams. The spread of the Gospel in the islands of the Pacific has been more rapid than in any other part of the world, and owes much to the labours and sufferings of native evangelists.   (1) In 1871 Bishop Patteson was murdered on Nukapu Island, one of the Santa Cruz group; "he was credited with being able to speak forty of the Melanesian dialects."[3]   (2) In 1858, J. G. Paton, a Scottish Presbyterian, began work in Tanna in the New Hebrides.   In 1906 he thus describe the results: " Our dear Lord has given our missionaries about 20,000 converts, and the blessed work is extending among the other cannibals. . . . In one year 1120 savages renounced idolatry and embraced the worship and service of Christ."[4]

(3) Although the Rev. W. G. Lawes was the first missionary of the L.M.S. to settle in New Guinea in 1874,[5] it is his colleague, the Rev. James Chalmers, who joined him in 1877, after ten years' labour in Raratonga, who in public regard holds foremost place among the pioneers in that island.   "Tamate," as he was called by the islanders, exercised a marvellous personal influence.

[1] Quoted by Horne, p. 383.   [2] *Ibid.*, p. 393.
[3] Robinson, p. 455.   [4] Quoted by Robinson, p. 457.
[5] See Horne, pp. 394–412.

"No white man had ever had a more wide and varied knowledge of the mainland of New Guinea, or visited more tribes, or made more friends, or endured more hardships, or faced more perils."[1]   R. L. Stevenson knew him well, and wrote of him to his mother: "I shall meet Tamate once more before he disappears up the Fly River, perhaps to be one of the unreturned brave; he is a man nobody can see and not love.   He has plenty of faults like the rest of us, but he is as big as a church."[2]   This foreboding (if such it was) was fulfilled.   On 7th April 1901, Tamate and his whole party were slain and eaten by the savages at the Aird River.

8. Were this volume a history of missions, a chapter would be devoted to the Martyr-Church of Madagascar; where through many years of persecution the Gospel was spread and the Church grew by the reading of the Scriptures and the witness of the converts.   We must pass the island, however, to the continent of Africa.[3]

(1) One of the most fruitful of missions has been that in Uganda.   It was in response to an appeal from the traveller Stanley in 1875 that the first missionaries were sent out.   "Within two years of their start two of the original party of eight had been massacred, two had died of disease, and two had been invalided home.   One of the remaining two, Alexander Mackay, an engineer, became the real founder of the Uganda Church."[4]   The company of Christians was soon called to pass through the fiery furnace of persecution; and the founder, in constant hardship, suffering and peril, sustained their faith and courage by his words and example.   The numbers continued to increase.   The first bishop, James Hannington, was murdered as he was journeying to his diocese.   It is wonderful that Mackay himself did not suffer martyrdom.   Worn with his cares, labours and sorrows, he died on 8th February 1890.   Twenty years later the number of

[1] George Robson, *The Pacific Islanders*, p. 292, quoted by Robinson, p. 463.
[2] *Ibid.*, p. 463.   [3] See Horne, pp. 171–199.   [4] Robinson, p. 348.

Christians had risen to 70,000. A letter which he addressed to the Christians of Uganda carries us back in language as well as spirit and content to the Apostolic Age.

"We, your friends and teachers, write to you to send you words of cheer and comfort, which we have taken from the Epistle of Peter the apostle of Christ. Our beloved brothers, do not deny our Lord Jesus, and He will not deny you in that day when He shall come in glory. Remember the words of our Saviour, how He told His disciples not to fear men who are able only to kill the body. . . . Do not cease to pray exceedingly, and to pray for our brethren who are in affliction and for those who do not know God. May God give you His spirit and His blessings. May He deliver you out of all your afflictions. May He give you entrance to eternal life, through Jesus Christ our Lord." [1]

On such a foundation was the Church built.

(2) Robert Moffat (1795–1883) [2] spent nearly fifty years among the Bechuana in Africa (1821–1870). He translated the whole Bible into Sechuana, and established an influential missionary centre in Kuruman, including a training school for native evangelists. By his writings and his speech, when at home, he did much to awaken interest in the spread of the Gospel in Africa.

(3) Greater in fame was his son-in-law, David Livingstone (1813–1873). [3] The world thinks of him as one of the greatest explorers; and as such "he travelled twenty-nine thousand miles in Africa, and added to the parts of the world known to civilised man nearly one million square miles." [4] He thought of himself as a missionary. "I am a missionary, heart and soul. God had an only Son, and He was a missionary. A poor, poor imitation of Him I am or wish to be. In His service I hope to live, in it I wish to die." [5] His wish was fulfilled, and he died on his knees at Ilala, to the south of Lake

---

[1] Quoted by Robinson, p. 349.
[2] Robinson, p. 317 ; Horne, pp. 72–88.
[3] See Robinson, pp. 317–320 ; Horne, pp. 232–245.
[4] Robinson, p. 319.　　　　[5] Quoted by Robinson, p. 320.

Bangweolo, on 1st May 1873. Because he loved the African, and won, as no other probably had done, the love of the African, he wanted not only to give Africa the Gospel, but to save it from the blighting curse of the slave-trade. Words cannot describe the greatness of the man, the Christian, and the missionary : to him a whole continent will for ever be a debtor.

9. A few words of justification of the inclusion of the preceding pages may seem necessary. Of the preaching of these men little has been said, because their work was done under conditions and by methods which the Christian preacher at home cannot imitate. They all made the preaching of the Gospel their aim ; but they had also to use many other ways of influencing and instructing those whom they sought to win for Christ, and most of their preaching was not in sermons from pulpits, but in talk wherever and whenever the door of opportunity opened. An interesting volume might be written on the methods of presenting the Gospel in different lands, and some materials might be gathered from biographies and missionary reports; but the task, alluring as it is, cannot be attempted now, and the writer claims no competence to discharge it. But the history of preaching would have been incomplete for the encouragement and guidance of any preacher had not the outstanding personalities in this greatest enterprise of the Christian Church in our own age been presented. Doubtless many others by their labours and sufferings no less deserve mention ; but so far as the writer's knowledge reaches and his judgment guides, the names recorded here have won the foremost places in the admiration and gratitude of the Christian Churches.[1]

[1] The notes and references in Robinson's *History of Christian Missions* and Horne's *The Story of the L.M.S.* should be consulted for the abundant literature on this great subject.

CHAPTER X.

THE REPAIRERS OF THE BREACH.

1. IN the preceding chapter some of the preachers of the earlier decades of the nineteenth century have been mentioned, as they attach themselves to the great Evangelical Revival of the eighteenth. As the Missionary Movement sprang out of that Revival, the great missionaries of the century have also been dealt with. In this chapter an attempt must be made to discuss some representative preachers of the nineteenth century, who have not been referred to in the one or the other connection. So great is the variety of type and tendency, that at first sight it appears a "forlorn hope" to bring them all under one banner : and yet, recognising that the description is but partial, and not at all exhaustive, the writer has ventured to give the definite title to this chapter, which to him does not seem inappropriate or forced, and which expresses what the pulpit specially needed to be.

2. So manifold and rapid were the changes in the thought and life of mankind during last century, that the Church did not keep its hold on the knowledge or the activity of the age. It may be that we are prone to magnify unduly what is nearest our vision, and that the breach between the Church and the world around was not wider than in many previous periods of the history of Christendom ; but that the Church was more conscious of the existence of the breach, and more concerned about the repairing of it, will not be generally denied.

3. Some of those whose names will be mentioned had no intention of departing from the familiar ways, nay, made it their endeavour to restore the old paths. Yet

even they did not, and could not, assume that the world they addressed stood unmoved and unmovable as regards Christian doctrine and practice. The passion of their protest against change was the evidence of the peril which they were forced to recognise. Others responded to the call of the hour, and were ready to go themselves and to lead others to "fresh fields and pastures new"; although not many of the influential preachers of the age represented this more advanced tendency. Most of the noted preachers sought rather the middle path of mediation between the old beliefs and the new knowledge. Without attempting rigidly to separate from one another men who had much in common, the writer feels justified for convenience of treatment in distinguishing among the preachers of the nineteenth century the conservative, the progressive, and the mediating tendency. About the placing of some of the preachers there can be no difficulty; others in the breadth of their outlook and effort defy classification. Any arrangement must be at best only an approach to, and not an attainment of, the exact truth.

I.

1. There can be no hesitation about the place to be assigned to Cardinal John Henry Newman (1801–1890).[1] (1) The Tractarian movement, of which he was *facile princeps*, was a resolute, one might almost say a desperate, attempt to arrest modern progress in the Church, and to bring it back to Mediæval or even Patristic ways.

"What was to Thomas Arnold," says Fairbairn, "the evidence of God's action in the present—viz., its enlarging liberty, widening knowledge, saner morals, purer love of truth as truth and man as man—was to Newman, who read it through the ecclesiastical changes he both hated and feared, Liberalism, or the apostasy of modern man from God, and constituted the need for bringing out of a period where God most manifestly reigned, forces and motives to restrain and order and govern the present."[2]

---

[1] See DHP ii. pp. 514–518.   [2] *Christ in Modern Theology*, 1893, p. 178.

(2) It was contrary to his own inclinations that he was thrust into the leadership of the movement; but it was inevitable.

"Never was there a religious vocation," says Sarolea, "more spontaneous and more certain. He understood that he had a care of souls as soon as he became conscious of his power to influence others. And that power he soon exhibited to an extraordinary degree. There are fifty points in Newman's life and work which have given rise to ardent controversies, but there has always been absolute unanimity on his magnetic gift in drawing to himself those with whom he came in contact. And the faculty appears all the more marvellous when we remember that it was combined with a shy and reserved disposition. . . . Never was there any man more devoid of all worldly ambition. And it was in the fitness of things that the greatest religious genius of his century, the man of whom even opponents like Gladstone only spoke in a whisper of awe and admiration, should live to the age of seventy-eight as a humble and solitary monk." [1] With that personal magnetism there was joined "an essentially sympathetic intellect," for "*he was himself highly receptive and impressionable*," and "could enter into the ideas of others. This is indeed part of his power. He has always read the human soul as in an open book." [2] The intellectualism due to the influence of Whately in his earlier years in Oxford was conquered by "the vitality of his religious and mystical temperament." [3] It was as he was preaching in St. Mary's, Oxford, for five years that his own experience deepened, and his own theology developed. Six months in Italy did still more for the unfolding of his genius. On his return in 1833 he resumed his work in Oxford, "fully conscious of his mission and delivered of his doubts." [4]

The question why Newman became a Roman Catholic is thus answered by Sarolea. "*Newman became a convert because Catholicism was adapted to his temperament, because there was a pre-established harmony between his character and the Catholic system, because his soul was naturaliter catholica.*" [5]

His career in the Church of Rome we do not need to follow.

(3) What for the present purpose is significant is, that

---

[1] *Cardinal Newman*, pp. 44-45 (The World's Epoch Makers).

[2] *Ibid.*, p. 46.   [3] *Ibid.*, p. 47.   [4] *Ibid.*, p. 51.   [5] *Ibid.*, p. 61.

it was his five years' preaching in St. Mary's, Oxford, that was the dominant influence in the Tractarian movement.

"All contemporary witnesses," says Sarolea, "both friends and opponents agree in their testimony as to the indelible impression left by these extraordinary sermons, probably unique in the annals of sacred oratory: an impression explained by the beauty of the language, lucid and direct, pure and simple, and devoid of all rhetoric; by the lofty ideals and the wonderful psychological insight into the most hidden recesses of the human soul, by the external advantages of the orator and the mysterious charm emanating from his whole personality—a musical voice, quivering with restrained emotion, a manner in turn sweet and imperious, an appearance slender and graceful, emaciated and ascetic, as a messenger from that invisible world of which he was ever speaking to his hearers. And together with the revelation of a great spiritual force there was a revolution in the doctrine. That doctrine was rather suggested than explicitly stated; but, whilst being asserted without dogmatism, the dogma was none the less novel; the orator restored the supernatural life, the Sacraments, the Visible Church, the Communion of Saints. He dwelt on the opposition between the City of God and the world, between faith and reason." [1]

(4) One characteristic passage may be quoted in illustration. It is the concluding passage of a sermon on "God's Will the End of Life," from the text, "I came down from heaven not to do Mine own will, but the will of Him that sent Me." [2]

"The world goes on from age to age, but the Holy Angels and Blessed Saints are always crying Alas, alas! and Woe, woe! over the loss of vocations and the disappointment of hopes, and the scorn of God's love, and the ruin of souls. One generation succeeds another, and whenever they look down upon earth from their golden thrones, they see scarcely anything but a multitude of guardian spirits, downcast and sad, each following his own charge, in anxiety, or in terror, or in despair, vainly endeavouring to shield him from the enemy

---

[1] *Cardinal Newman*, pp. 24–25 (The World's Epoch Makers).
[2] Jn 6^{38}.

and failing because he will not be shielded. Times come and go, and man will not believe, that that is to be which is not yet, and that what now is only continues for a season, and is not eternity. The end is the trial; the world passes; it is but a pageant and a scene; the lofty palace crumbles, the busy city is mute, the ships of Tarshish have sped away. On heart and flesh death is coming; the veil is breaking. Departing soul, how hast thou used thy talents, thy opportunities, the light poured around thee, the warnings given thee, the grace inspired into thee? Oh, my Lord and Saviour, support me in that hour in the strong arms of Thy sacraments, and by the fresh fragrance of Thy consolations. Let the absolving words be said over me, and the holy oil sign and seal me, and Thy own body be my food, and Thy blood my sprinkling, and let my sweet Mother Mary breathe on me, and my angel whisper peace to me, and my glorious saints, and my own dear father, Philip, smile on me; that in them all, and through them all, I may receive the gift of perseverance, and die, as I desire to live, in Thy faith, in Thy Church, in Thy service and in Thy love." [1]

2. Not all who threw themselves into the Tractarian movement followed Newman to Rome; many not only remained in the Church of England, but even came out into open opposition to the claims of the papacy. The most famous preacher of the High Church Party in the nineteenth century was Canon Henry Parry Liddon (1829–1890). [2]

(1) The Bampton Lectures on *The Divinity of Christ*, which on very short notice he delivered in Oxford in 1866, put him in the first rank as a learned and able theologian and an eloquent preacher. From 1870 till 1882 he was Ireland Professor of Exegesis at Oxford; and he combined with this a canonry at St. Paul's, where, when twice a year he took his turn, he preached to great crowds. A strong High Churchman, he was opposed to the Broad Church views, and declined to preach at Westminster Abbey, because Dean Stanley threw the pulpit there open to preachers of all schools. German criticisms he abhorred. His last appearance in St. Mary's, Oxford, was to denounce

[1] WGS iv. pp. 229-231.　　　　[2] See DHP ii. pp. 550-553.

the views of the *Lux Mundi* group.[1] His rigid theology and vehement polemic will affect the permanence of his influence as a teacher; but his powers as a preacher will continue to claim recognition. Learning and intellectual force were in his preaching so combined with intense conviction and personal magnetism as to give him complete mastery over his hearers. The outward graces of the orator were his also: " a handsome face, a graceful action, and a ringing voice." The one word that describes his preaching best is loftiness of style, tone, thought and feeling. " Canon Liddon," says Hoyt,[2] " brings the riches of exegesis and theology and philosophy to the pulpit, and gives to the sermon the distinction of his refined and spiritual personality."

(2) In his sermon on " Influences of the Holy Spirit," [3] he derives from the analogy of the wind and the Spirit the two characteristics of the Spirit's working, freedom and mysteriousness, and traces " the import of our Lord's simile in three fields of the action of the Holy and eternal Spirit; His creation of a sacred literature, His guidance of a divine society, and His work upon individual souls." [4] A passage may be quoted from the beginning of the second division, which sets forth the presence of the Spirit of God in the history of the Church.

"The history of the Church of Christ from the days of the Apostles has been a history of spiritual movements. Doubtless it has been a history of much else; the Church has been the scene of human passions, human speculations, human errors. But, traversing these, He by whom the whole body of the Church is governed and sanctified has made His presence felt, not only in the perpetual proclamation and elucidation of truth, not only in the silent, never-ceasing sanctification of souls, but also in great upheavals of spiritual life, by which the conscience of Christians has been quickened, or their hold upon the truths of redemption and grace made more intelligent and serious, or their lives and

---

[1] The writer was a student in Oxford at the time, and remembers the sensation produced by the sermon.

[2] *The Work of Preaching*, p. 60.   [3] Jn 3⁸.   [4] WGS vii. p. 130.

practice restored to something like the ideal of the Gospels.
Even in the apostolic age it was necessary to warn Christians
that it was high time to awake out of sleep; that the night
of life was far spent, and the day of eternity was at hand.
And ever since, from generation to generation, there has
been a succession of efforts within the Church to realize
more worthily the truth of the Christian creed, or the ideal
of the Christian life. These revivals have been inspired or
led by devoted men who have represented the highest conscience of Christendom in their day. They may be traced
along the line of Christian history; the Spirit living in the
Church has by them attested His presence and His will;
and has recalled lukewarm generations, paralysed by indifference or degraded by indulgence, to the true spirit and level
of Christian faith and life."[1] He then shows how these
movements illustrate both the freedom and the mysteriousness of the Spirit's operation. " Sometimes these movements
are all feeling; sometimes they are all thought; sometimes
they are, as it seems, all outward energy. In one age they
produce a literature like that of the fourth and fifth centuries;
in another they found orders of men devoted to preaching,
or to works of mercy, as in the twelfth; in another they
enter the lists, as in the thirteenth century, with a hostile
philosophy; in another they attempt a much needed reformation of the Church; in another they pour upon the heathen
world a flood of light and warmth from the heart of
Christendom." . . . " The Eternal Spirit is passing; and
men can only say, ' He bloweth where He listeth.' "[2]

3. The most popular preacher of the nineteenth
century was Charles Haddon Spurgeon (1834–1892).[3]
(1) Not only did he gather crowds wherever he preached,
but his printed sermons reached a far wider circle. About
two thousand five hundred of his sermons have been published, and the average sale of each was 25,000 copies; they
have been translated into many languages. He, too, stood
in the old ways, professing himself a sound Calvinist, and
denouncing in no measured terms modern expositions of
the Christian Gospel. He was neither a profound scholar

[1] GWS vii. pp. 134–135.   [2] *Ibid.*, pp. 136–138.
[3] See DHP ii. pp. 535–561; Edwards' *Nineteenth Century Preachers*,
pp. 121–130; Brown's *Puritan Preaching*, pp. 219–228.

nor an original thinker, although he was widely read, and had a very acute mind. His sermons were delivered *ex tempore*, and printed afterwards from shorthand reports. Often the immediate preparation was very short ; yet he was always living, thinking, and reading for his pulpit, so that the general preparation, to which more importance should be attached, was very thorough. It was to no empty treasury that he went to draw abounding riches for his pulpit. He was, in his own words, " always in training for text-getting and sermon-making." His constant study of the Bible supplied him with more texts than he could use. He often tried many a text before he got what seemed to him the right one. A text must lay hold on him so that he could not escape it, and he must get hold of a text so that it must speedily and surely yield up its meaning to him before he felt free to preach about it. He aimed at preaching in every sermon definite teaching on the Christian salvation ; but it was not mere theology he preached ; his truth was often embodied in a tale, and the arrow of his appeal was winged with a wise and witty saying. His wide and keen observation of life, his varied reading, supplied him with abundant illustrations of the doctrine he set forth. His exegesis, from our modern standpoint, may often have been forced ; his construction of his sermon faulty, according to rules of homiletics ; but " the common people heard him gladly," and he even impressed hearers of culture and influence.

(2) What accounts for his marvellous success ? His personal appearance was not attractive, although, as he caught fire with his message, his face shone. He had not, as far as one can learn from reports, the personal magnetism some men possess. His voice had clearness and strength, and he could be well heard in a vast building. It had not, however, the range of expression which has been so great a gain to many orators. His preaching was natural, without any pulpit affectation ; he talked with fulness and freshness of thought. He knew how to make even an ordinary subject interesting by unhackneyed exposition and illustra-

tion. "He was a speaker of superb English, a master of that Saxon speech which somehow goes warm to the hearts of men."[1] Not only was such racy English native to his genius; his early training and surroundings had been favourable to this gift, and he afterwards cultivated it by a close study of the masters of the language. The secret of his power, however, did not lie here, although these endowments might explain his popularity. He preached the Gospel of the grace of God, which men need and their hearts long for, with the distinctness and certainty which carries conviction to the hearers, because it springs out of the convictions of the preacher. He preached as himself sure that the Gospel is the power and wisdom of God unto salvation, and that is the will of God by the foolishness of preaching to save men.[2] And its ancient inexhaustible efficacy was proved as he preached.

(3) We may listen to him as he sets forth the doctrine of election as a reason for the believer's *Songs in the Night*.[3]

"If we are going to sing of the songs of yesterday, let us begin with what God did for us in past times. My beloved brethren, you will find it a sweet subject for song at times, to begin to sing of electing love and covenanted mercies. When thou thyself art low, it is well to sing of the fountain-head of mercy, of that blest decree wherein thou wast ordained to eternal life, and of that glorious Man who undertook thy redemption; of that solemn covenant signed, and sealed, and ratified, in all things ordered well; of that everlasting love, which, ere the hoary mountains were begotten, or ere the aged hills were children, chose thee, loved thee firmly, loved thee first, loved thee well, loved thee eternally. I tell thee, believer, if thou canst go back to the years of eternity; if thou canst in thy mind run back to that period, or ere the everlasting hills were fashioned, or the fountains of the great deep scooped out, and if thou canst see thy God inscribing thy name in His eternal book; if thou canst see in His loving heart eternal thoughts of love to thee, thou wilt find this a charming means of giving thee songs in the night. No songs like those which come from

---

[1] Brown, *op. cit.*, p. 225.   [2] 1 Co 1²¹⁻²⁵.   [3] Job 35¹⁰.

electing love; no sonnets like those that are dictated by
meditations on discriminating mercy. Some, indeed, cannot
sing of election; the Lord open their mouths a little wider!
Some there are that are afraid of the very term, but we only
despise men who are afraid of what they believe, afraid of
what God has taught them in His Bible. . . . But if thou
hast not a voice tuned to so high a key as that, let me
suggest some other mercies thou mayest sing of; and they
are the mercies thou hast experienced. What! man, canst
thou not sing a little of that blest hour when Jesus met
thee; when, a blind slave, thou wast sporting with death,
and He saw thee, and said: ' Come, poor slave, come with
Me '? Canst thou not sing of that rapturous moment when
He snapt thy fetters, dashed thy chains to earth, and said:
' I am the Breaker; I come to break thy chains, and set
thee free ' ? " [1]

4. A few sentences must suffice for Thomas Guthrie
(1803–1873).[2] He knew how to reach the hearts of the
common people, and he was a master of what may be called
pictorial preaching. Few preachers have so aimed at
presenting truth in a tale. " An illustration," he says, " or
an example drawn from nature, a Bible story or any
history will, like a nail, often hang up a thing which
otherwise would fall to the ground. . . . Mind the three
P's. In every discourse the preacher should aim at
PROVING, PAINTING, and PERSUADING; in other words,
addressing the Reason, the Fancy, and the Heart." [3]

There are two Scottish preachers whom the writer
heard in his youth, and to whom he is constrained to bear
his tribute. Repeated references have been already made
in this volume to the *History of Preaching* by Dr. John
Ker (1819–1886).[4] He was not only learned in the
history, but himself skilful in the art of preaching. A
man of varied culture and rare spiritual insight, he left the
impress of his personality on many of his hearers, and as
professor of Pastoral Theology in one of the Presbyterian

---

[1] WGS viii. pp. 23–25.

[2] See DHP ii. p. 530; Edwards, *op. cit.*, 56–64.

[3] Quoted by Edwards, *op. cit.*, p. 62.

[4] DHP ii. p. 571; Edwards, *op. cit.*, pp. 65–74.

Colleges, influenced the preaching in many a pulpit.   A big man in every respect, mentally, morally, spiritually, as well as physically, was Dr John Cairns (1818–1892). Rigid in his own theology, he was charitable to all men. Unaware of his greatness, he was simple and humble as a child.   Himself unmoved by the changing thought of the age, however, he failed with all his powers to influence his age as he might have done.

II.

1. One of the saddest and yet most influential ministries in the pulpit was that of Frederick William Robertson (1816–1853).[1]   (1) Desiring to fulfil his Christian calling as an officer in the army, the seeming accident of the delay in obtaining his commission led him, against his own inclinations, to acquiesce in his father's wishes that he should take holy orders.   Having once made the decision he devoted himself whole-heartedly to preparation for his work.   Opposed to the High Church movement, in revolt against the narrow evangelicalism in which he had been brought up, too ardently positive in his own faith in Christ to be at home among Broad Churchmen, he stood alone. Sensitiveness even to morbidness, about what he regarded as his own failures, and about the antagonism which his fearless advocacy of what he believed right and true aroused made his loneliness a martyrdom, and bad health increased the crushing burden that fell on him.   Yet to the end he did his work bravely and faithfully.   It was seven years after his ordination before he found the throne, from which he exercised an ever-widening rule over the spirits of men, in the pulpit of Trinity Chapel, Brighton. There he reached not only the cultured and thoughtful, but also the shop assistants and artisans of the town. Transparent in his sincerity, almost reckless in his courage, tender as any woman in his sympathy with need or sorrow,

[1] DHP ii. pp. 520–524 ; Edwards, *op. cit.*, pp. 118–120. *Life and Letters of the Rev. F. W. Robertson*, by Stopford A. Brooke. London, 1872.

blazing with anger against any wrong, the very soul of chivalry, he threw his whole personality into his preaching. Much he learned in suffering that he taught in words which reached to the depths of the soul in many of his hearers.

(2) Only one of his sermons was published before his early death after much pain; it was entitled "The Israelite's Grave in a Foreign Land," and was preached on the occasion of the public mourning for the widow of William IV. in December 1849. It was not written out before delivery, but in a condensed report for a friend after it had been preached. The sermons collected and published after his death were preserved in the same way. We do not possess any of them in full as spoken, or as revised for publication, and yet in what would appear so imperfect a form they have exercised and still exercise an indescribable influence over the choice circle of readers to whom they make their irresistible appeal. They are based on a constant and minute study of the Scriptures; they breathe the spirit of intense devoutness; they are most searching in their scrutiny of the experience and character of men; they are illumined by illustrations drawn from varied and accurate study; their arrangement is logical and thus clear and memorable; the plan is thoroughly thought out; there is no ambiguity or uncertainty about the truth taught; their theology, which excited so much suspicion and hostility, while thoroughly independent, the fruit of his own meditation, would now be regarded as liberal evangelical, having its centre in Christ the Saviour. Acceptable and attractive as is the truth, it is the personality through which it comes that gives to his preaching its enduring worth.

(3) As bringing us into close living touch with the man himself we turn to his sermon on "The Loneliness of Christ." [1]

He begins with the distinction: "There are two kinds of solitude; the first consisting of isolation in space; the other of isolation of the spirit." The first division deals with the loneliness of Christ. "The loneliness of Christ was caused

---

[1] WGS vi. pp. 113–130. The text was Jn 16³¹⁻³².

by the divine elevation of His character. His infinite superiority severed Him from sympathy; His exquisite affectionateness made that want of sympathy a keen trial." His insight into the human heart is shewn in distinguishing from Christ's loneliness the morbid sense of loneliness some people cherish, and in pressing home this test. "Is that because you are alone in the world—nobler, devising and executing grand plans, which they cannot comprehend; vindicating the wronged; proclaiming and living on great principles; offending it by the saintliness of your purity, and the unworldliness of your aspirations? Then yours is the loneliness of Christ. Or is it that you are wrapped up in self, cold, disobliging, sentimental, indifferent about the welfare of others, and very much astonished that they are not deeply interested in you? You must not use these words of Christ. They have nothing to do with you." After dealing with his wonderful discernment of the mind of Christ with one or two of the occasions of loneliness, he in the second division makes the practical application in shewing the spirit or temper of Christ's solitude.

2. From Robertson we turn to a man of equally independent mind, and yet altogether different temperament, Henry Ward Beecher (1813–1887).[1] (1) His ideal of preaching may be given in his own words as quoted by Edwards:

"To preach the Gospel of Jesus Christ; to have Christ so melted and dissolved in you, that when you preach your own self you preach Him as Paul did; to have every part of you living and luminous with Christ, and then to make use of everything that is in you . . . all steeped in Jesus Christ, and to throw yourself with all your power upon a congregation—that has been my theory of preaching the Gospel. . . . I have felt that man should consecrate every gift that he has got in him that has any relation to the persuasion of men and to the melting of men—that he should put them all on the altar, kindle them all, and let them burn for Christ's sake."

---

[1] Dargan has reserved for a third volume the treatment of preaching in the United States, so that no reference to him can be given. See Edwards, *op. cit.*, pp. 1–7. Beecher gave the first three courses of the *Lyman Beecher Lectures on Preaching* in Yale University, 1871–1872, 1872–1873, 1873–1874.

The personality is here emphasised, if not over emphasised, and it was characteristic of Beecher to give himself
with utmost freedom and force.

(2) The love of Christ dominated his theology, and his
wide knowledge and keen insight into men enabled him, as he
made it his steadfast aim, to bring home to " all sorts and
conditions of men " their need of this Saviour. He was constantly studying his Bible, the world around him, and the
men he met, reading, observing, meditating with one object,
to gather material for his pulpit. Thorough as was his
general preparation, his special preparation was very slight,
and only a pulpit genius could have ventured so to make
ready for his work. His Saturday was " a kind of active
rest-day," in which he got himself fresh and fit for the
tasks of Sunday. " His Sunday morning sermons were
prepared after breakfast, and the evening sermons after
tea." [1] Sometimes the outline of the sermon came to him
only in the pulpit. Nevertheless so great a preacher as
Phillips Brooks regarded him as the greatest preacher
in America, and he has even been described as " the
greatest pulpit orator the world ever saw." His vivid
imagination and his intense passion gave him an extraordinary dramatic power. Without exaggeration he may
be regarded as one of the greatest orators who have used
the heaven-sent gift in the pulpit. He passed through
all the horror and heroism of the Civil War, and doubtless the times helped to make the man. Great events
should find great voices. One of his greatest orations
was delivered, 14th April 1865, by request of President
Lincoln, on the occasion of the Raising the Flag over Fort
Sumter.[2]

(3) It is more consonant with the purpose of this
volume, however, to give a passage from his sermon on
" Immortality," [3] in which he develops the argument from
the human affections, and shows his tender insight into
the hearts of men.

---

[1] Edwards, *op. cit.*, p. 6.   [2] See CME i. pp. 352–374.
[3] WGS vi. pp. 3–25. The text is 1 Co 15^{19}.

"I cannot believe, I will not believe, when I walk upon the clod, that it is my mother that I tread under foot. She that bore me, she that every year more than gave birth to me out of her own soul's aspirations—I will not believe that she is dust. Everything within me revolts at the idea. Do two persons walk together in an inseparable union, mingling their brightest and noblest thoughts, striving for the highest ideal, like flowers that grow by the side of each other, breathing fragrance each on the other, and shining in beauty each for the other; are two persons thus twined together and bound together for life until in some dark hour one is called and the other left: and does the bleeding heart go down to the grave and say, 'I return dust to dust'? Was that dust then? That trustworthiness; that fidelity; that frankness of truth; that transparent honesty; that heroism of love; that disinterestedness; that fitness and exquisiteness of taste; that fervour of love; that aspiration; that power of conviction; that piety; that great hope in God —were all these elements in the soul of the companion that had disappeared but just so many phenomena of matter? And have they already collapsed and gone, like last year's flowers struck with frost, back again to the mould? In the grief of such an hour we will not let go the hope of resurrection. Can a parent go back from the grave where he has laid his children and say, 'I shall never see them more'? Even as far back as the dim twilight in which David lived, he said, 'Thou shalt not come to me, but I shall go to thee'; and is it possible for the parental heart to stand in our day by the side of the grave, where the children have been put out of sight, and say, 'They neither shall come to me, nor shall I go to them; they are blossoms that have fallen; they never shall bring forth fruit'? It is unnatural. It is hideous. Everything that is in man, every instinct that is best in human nature repels it. Is not the human soul, then, itself a witness of the truth of immortality?"

3. When Henry Ward Beecher died, Joseph Parker (1830–1902) was spoken of as his successor.[1]   (1) An eccentric and egotistic personality, his genuis in the pulpit triumphed over all obstacles. Without any training of the schools, he entered the Congregational ministry; but his powers quickly showed themselves in his first pastorate at

[1] See DHP ii. pp. 561–567 ; Edwards, *op. cit.*, pp. 101–112.

Banbury.   He was for eleven years in Manchester (1858–1869), but his name is inseparably linked with the City Temple, London (1874–1902).   The two sermons on Sunday and the noonday sermon on Thursday drew crowds of devoted hearers; and he reached a still wider circle with his books.   Besides his own more permanent congregation, he was constantly reaching by his influence the multitudes of visitors to London from all parts of the world, whom his fame attracted.   Rough and overbearing in manner as he often was, his heart was tender and gentle.   His self-conceit was often quite ludicrous; and yet was forgotten in the strength of his faith, the fervour of his feelings and the force of his speech.   Taking his own line in theology, he remained true and devoted to the evangelical verities. Unfettered by the technicalities of scholarship, he delighted in the exposition of the Scriptures, in which he displayed a very fine moral and religious discernment.   A rich imagination and a keen humour were controlled by a thoroughly masculine intellect.   While his style was often conversational, yet it could also rise to a lofty and glowing eloquence.   His fertility of mind was amazing; and his sermons were full of surprises.   The thunder and the earthquake of vehement emotion, anger or scorn against evil, sometimes expressed without due restraint, did not exclude the still small voice of comfort and entreaty.

(2) A short sample of the wooing note in his preaching may be given.   The sermon on a " Word to the Weary " [1] ends with a tender appeal :

" Did we but know the name of our pain we should call it Sin.   What do we need, then, but Christ the Son of God, the Heart of God, the Love of God ?   He will in very deed give us rest.   He will not add to the great weight which bears down our poor strength.   He will give us grace, and in His power all our faintness shall be thought of no more.   Some of us know how dark it is when the full shadow of our sin falls upon our life, and how all the help of earth and time and man does but mock the pain it cannot reach.   Let no

---

[1] The text is Is 50⁴.

man say that Christ will not go so low down as to find one
so base and vile as he.   Christ is calling for thee; I heard
His sweet voice lift itself up in the wild wind and ask
whither thou hadst fled, that He might save thee from death
and bring thee home.   There is no wrath in His face or
voice, no sword is swung by His hand as if in cruel joy,
saying, 'Now at last I have My chance with you.'   His eyes
gleam with love; His voice melts with pity; His words are
gospels, every one.   Let Him but see thee sad for sin, full of
grief because of the wrong thou hast done, and He will
raise thee out of the deep pit and set thy feet upon
the rock." [1]

One of the Boanerges could also be the Barnabas, as
this passage shows.

4. Independent as thinkers, the preachers hitherto
mentioned, Robertson, Beecher, Parker, still held the
evangelical position.   Brief reference must be made to
one who represented with conspicuous ability the Unitarian
position, Dr. James Martineau (1805–1900).[2]   Distinguished as a philosophical, theological and critical writer,
he may also claim remembrance as a preacher.   Negative
as his theological position appears to the orthodox
believer he was a man of deep devoutness of spirit.   The
two volumes of sermons, *Endeavours after the Christian
Life*, in which he gathered the fruit of his ministry in
Liverpool, are "unsurpassed for beauty and charm by his
later writings, and realise his ideal that a sermon should
be a 'lyric' utterance."   "His spoken addresses were
simpler in style than most of his literary works."   "The
delivery of his sermons was vivid and even dramatic, though
without action."

5. Without identifying their theological position with
Martineau's, mention may here be made of the brothers
Pulsford, William and John.   William in Edinburgh
(1856-1865) and Glasgow (1865–1886) and John in
Edinburgh (1867–1884) made a deep impression on many
hearers by their devout mysticism; a tendency by no

[1] WGS vii. pp. 207-208.
[2] *Dictionary of National Biography*, Supplement, iii. pp. 146–151.

means common in the pulpit to-day.[1] It may be observed, however, that the preachers who reach and move the multitude are those who hold strongly and preach clearly the Gospel of the grace of God in Christ as Saviour and Lord.

6. Although his name might almost as fitly be included in the next group, the representatives of the mediating tendency, on the whole Dr. John Caird (1820–1898)[2] may be most properly dealt with here as representing the liberal movement. (1) He began as a fervent and forceful evangelical preacher. His younger brother's influence probably led him to recast his thought in the Hegelian mould, but his later writings indicate a movement towards the evangelical position. As the writer during his student days in Glasgow had the opportunity of hearing a number of the addresses on various themes which Caird delivered as Principal of the University, he retains to this day a very vivid impression of his mastery as an orator. His range of learning, his sweep of thought, his wealth of exposition or illustration, his dignity of diction, made one of his hearers at least feel as he used to feel when listening to a grand symphony. While his fame by no means rests on one sermon, yet one of his sermons has become more famous than any other. His sermon on " Religion in the Common Life "[3] was preached in 1855 at Balmoral Castle, before Queen Victoria and the Prince Consort, and won the approval of the Royal hearers.

(2) It seems inevitable that his preaching should be illustrated by a quotation from this sermon, part of his peroration, for we may so describe the conclusion of his sermons.

"No work done for Christ perishes. No action that helps to mould the deathless mind of a saint of God is ever

---

[1] A rare spirit, who appealed only to a very small circle of choice hearers, was the Rev. S. A. Tipple of Norwood ; their enthusiasm warrants this mention.

[2] DHP ii. pp. 532–533.

[3] The text was Ro 12[11], and the treatment rests on the current misrepresentation of the first clause.

lost. Live for Christ in the world, and you carry with you into eternity all of the results of the world's business that are worth the keeping. The river of life sweeps on, but the gold grains it held in solution are left behind deposited in the holy heart. 'The world passeth away and the lust thereof; but he that doeth the will of God abideth for ever.' Every other result of our 'diligence in business' will soon be gone. You cannot invent any mode of exchange between the visible and invisible worlds, so that the balance at your credit in the one can be transferred, when you migrate from it, to your account in the other. Worldly sharpness, acuteness, versatility are not the qualities in request in the world to come. The capacious intellect, stored with knowledge, and developed into admirable perspicacity, tact, worldly wisdom, by a lifetime devoted to politics or business, is not, by such attainments, fitted to take a higher place among the sons of immortality. The honour, fame, respect, obsequious homage that attend worldly greatness up to the grave's brink, will not follow it one step beyond. These advantages are not to be despised; but if this be all that, by the toil of our hands, or the sweat of our brow, we have gained, the hour is fast coming when we shall discover that we have laboured in vain and spent our strength for naught. But while these pass, there are other things that remain. The world's gains and losses may soon cease to affect us, but not the gratitude or the patience, the kindness or the resignation they drew forth from our hearts. The world's scenes of business may fade in our sight, the sound of its restless pursuits may fall no more upon our ear, when we pass to meet our God, but not one unselfish thought, not one kind and gentle word, not one act of self-sacrificing love done for Jesus' sake, in the midst of our common work, but will have left an indelible impress on the soul which will go out with it to its eternal destiny. So live, then, that this may be the result of your labours. So live that your work, whether in the Church or in the world, may become a discipline for that glorious state of being in which the Church and the world shall become one — where work shall be worship, and labour shall be rest—where the worker shall never quit the temple, nor the worshipper the place of work, because 'there is no temple therein, but the Lord God Almighty and the Lamb are the temple thereof.'" [1]

---

[1] WGS vi. pp. 191–193.

7. In connection with John Caird, the writer is constrained to mention his brother Edward Caird (1835–1908), and with his name may be linked that of Thomas Hill Green (1836–1882). Both were teachers of philosophy, but both exercised a potent moral and religious influence on the young minds brought into contact with them. They both gave addresses on topics usually dealt with in the pulpit; but, excellent as these are, they are not the sole reason why these two thinkers should be held in grateful remembrance. There are many in Christian pulpits to-day who have abandoned the philosophy which they taught, but who are worthier preachers of the Gospel as better men because of their influence! Each had been a Socrates to those he taught.

III.

1. We may give the first place in the group of preachers who seek to offer the Gospel to the age in its own language, to Bishop Phillips Brooks (1838–1893).[1] (1) His lectures on preaching have already been quoted, and he was himself a conspicuous example of his own definition. His personality was great, a fit channel for the Gospel he preached. It was not till he had begun his work, and had passed "through a period of trial and disappointment," that he discovered himself as born for his calling because of the joy he found in it, and the powers that were brought into free and full exercise by it. He was a very hard worker, a very diligent student, reading widely "science, literature, biography, history, poetry"; but the one thing he did was to preach, using all else for this end. Edwards quotes a series of striking testimonies to his power and charm. Only one of these we may quote.

"Mr. (now Lord) Bryce, in comparing his preaching with that of Wilberforce, Spurgeon and Liddon, said, 'In all these

[1] See Edwards, *op. cit.*, pp. 8–18 ; Phillips Brooks, *Memoirs of his Life*, by Alexander V. G. Allen, London, 1898.

it was impossible to forget the speaker in the words spoken, because the speaker did not seem to have quite forgotten himself, but to have studied the effect he sought to produce. With him it was otherwise. What amount of preparation he may have given to his discourses I do not know. But there was no sign of art about them, no touch of self-consciousness. He spoke to his audience as a man might speak to his friend, pouring forth with swift yet quiet and seldom impassioned earnestness the thoughts and feelings of a singularly pure and lofty spirit. The listeners never thought of style and manner, but only of the substance of the thoughts.'"[1]

Unlike Beecher, Brooks made laborious preparation. He was always recording in his notebooks germs for sermons. On Monday and Tuesday he was gathering the material suitable for the development of the subject he had chosen. On Wednesday he wrote the plan. On Thursday and Friday he wrote out the finished sermon. By such labour he found his freedom in the pulpit. Varied as were his interests and resources, he concentrated in his preaching on the great central truths of Christianity, and to this was in large measure due his attractiveness. It is not novelty of subject, but freshness of treatment for which the pulpit calls.

(2) No fitter illustration of the spirit and the purpose of his preaching could be found than the last paragraphs of his volume on Preaching.

"It is by working for the soul that we best learn what the soul is worth. If ever in your ministry the souls of those committed to your care grow dull before you, and you doubt whether they have any such value that you should give your life for them, go out and work for them; and as you work their value shall grow clear to you. Go and try to save a soul and you will see how well it is worth saving, how capable it is of the most complete salvation. Not by pondering upon it, not by talking of it, but by serving it you learn its preciousness. So the father learns the value of his child, and the teacher of his scholar, and the patriot of his native land. And so the Christian, living and dying

---

[1] *Op. cit.*, pp. 11–12.

for his brethren's souls, learns the value of those souls for which Christ lived and died. And if you ask me whether this whose theory I have been stating is indeed true in fact, whether in daily work for souls year after year a man does see in these souls glimpses of such a value as not merely justifies the little work which he does, but even makes credible the work of Christ, I answer, surely, yes. All other interest and satisfaction of the ministry completes itself in this, that year by year the minister sees more deeply how well worthy of infinitely more than he can do for it is the human soul for which he works. I do not know how I can better close my lectures to you than with that testimony. May you find it true in your experience. May the souls of men be always more precious to you as you come always nearer to Christ, and see them more perfectly as He does. I can ask no better blessing on your ministry than that. And so may God our Father guide and keep you alway." [1]

This is written from his own heart; and he claims our reverence and affection as few of the great preachers do in the same degree, for few there are so utterly forgetful of self and mindful of their hearers as he was.

2. Archbishop William Connor Magee (1821–1891) [2] expressed his view of the function of the pulpit in the words: "The office of the preacher is to smite the rock, that the living waters may gush forth to satisfy the thirst of the age." [3] This description could be applied to himself. He desired always in his preaching, which was warmly evangelical in tone, to be the ambassador of God. Not distinguished either as scholar or thinker, he took his place in the front rank of the orators of the age. Liddon regarded him as the greatest orator; others place him only second to Gladstone or John Bright. He was an *ex tempore* speaker, believed thoroughly in this method, and commended it to others. In contrast to Magee may be mentioned Dean Frederic William Farrar [4] (1831–1903), whose preaching often tended to become rhetoric rather than

---

[1] *Lectures on Preaching*, pp. 279–281. Allenson's Handy Theological Library, 1903.

[2] See DHP ii. pp. 548–549.   [3] Quoted by Edwards, *op. cit.*, p. 88.

[4] See DHP ii. pp. 557–558; Edwards, *op. cit.*, pp. 45–55.

oratory. He had an amazing memory, had read very widely, and adorned his sermons with quotations, allusions and illustrations, which his too fertile mind suggested to him with a prodigality that seemed to know no restraint. His scholarship was not always exact, nor was his language always measured. The rush of his thoughts and feelings was allowed to carry him away, and he did not allow himself time to prune his sermons; but he was a very popular preacher, who exercised a wide influence for good. There can be no doubt that his *Life of Christ* did a great deal to diffuse among the people a vivid sense of the historical reality of Jesus.

3. The claim of Dr. Alexander Maclaren (1826–1910)[1] to be placed among the greatest preachers of the nineteenth century cannot be challenged. (1) Dargan quotes the testimony of the Bishop of Manchester in 1896. "In an age which has been charmed and inspired by the sermons of Newman and Robertson of Brighton, there were no published discourses which, for profundity of thought, logical arrangement, eloquence of appeal, and power over the human heart, exceeded in merit those of Dr. Maclaren." If the occasion, the presentation of a portrait, may have led the speaker to slight over-statement, yet a very generous estimate of the value of Maclaren's ministry is fully justified. The words of Edwards may be accepted as true and just. "He possesses in an eminent degree the true expository genius, the power of vivid and glowing illustration, a fervent and established faith joined to wide and generous culture, and an attractive and fascinating style. Keenly alive to and fully abreast of all the intellectual questions of the day, he is singularly free from any taint of modern scepticism; confident and undismayed in presence of its loud-voiced materialism."

(2) Dr. Brown, who had personal knowledge of him, gives an analysis of the causes of his success as a preacher:

[1] DHP ii. pp. 572–577; Edwards, *op. cit.*, pp. 75–87.; Brown's *Puritan Preaching in England*, pp. 263–288.

(1) "His teaching is firmly based upon and is a careful exposition of the revelation God has given to us in the Scriptures. (2) His intelligent reverence for Scripture is accompanied with, or rather grows out of his firm belief in the historical facts related in Scripture." (3) His preaching is "intensely *practical* in character," not in the sense of "ethical instruction in the duties of daily life," although that is not absent, but of "clear and definite instruction as to the rationale of the divine life in the souls of men,—its nature, its beginnings, its after developments, and the spiritual forces by which it is begun, and carried on"; in this teaching the contrast of the natural and spiritual man is emphasised; and the need of faith in Christ for the change from the one to the other is asserted. (4) Not only the substance of his preaching has given him his place, but "also the crystal clearness of his way of putting the truth before the minds of his audience. (5) The great literary and intellectual qualities of this man are suffused with intense spiritual earnestness."

(3) The methods of preparation of such a master are worth recording. He resolved at the beginning of his ministry not to write sermons, but to think and feel them, not a less but a more arduous method of preparation, and still more of delivery. A few introductory sentences were written to launch him out into the deep; but afterwards he spoke freely with only the help of jottings. The heads were also carefully worded, and the closing sentences written. In the earlier years of his ministry this method involved, however, long pauses, when he was carefully choosing the best words, and a very short sermon, when his matter gave out sooner than he expected. In later years these defects were altogether overcome.

Instead of a quotation from one of Dr. Maclaren's sermons, some sayings of his on the preacher's calling may be given.

"I have always found that my own comfort and efficiency in preaching have been in direct proportion to the frequency and depth of daily communion with God. I know no way in which we can do our work but in quiet fellowship with Him; in resolutely keeping up the habits

of the student's life, which needs some power of saying, *No*;
and by conscientious pulpit preparation. The secret of
success in everything is trust in God and hard work." [1]

In answer to an inquiry about his method of preparation he wrote:

" I have really nothing to say about my way of making
sermons that could profit your readers. I know no method,
except to think about a text until you have something to
say about it, and then to go and say it, with as little thought
of self as possible." [2]

This thinking about a text with him included, however,
careful exegesis.

" A minute study of the mere words of Scripture, though
it may seem like grammatical trifling and pedantry, yields
large results. Men do sometimes gather grapes from
thorns: and the hard dry work of trying to get at the
precise shade of meaning in Scripture words always repays
with large lessons and impulses." [3]

As Dr. Brown's analysis indicates, in Maclaren's
preaching that Christian truth is definitely conceived and
distinctly expressed, and that truth goes forth to men
through a personality genuinely and intensely Christian.

4. The writer has never met a man, or heard a
preacher, who so deeply impressed him with the sense of
greatness as Dr. Robert William Dale (1829–1895); [4] and
he cannot pretend to write about him with cool impartiality.
(1) Dale was not so much an expository preacher as
Maclaren, although he was at home in the Holy Scriptures;
but he was more explicitly doctrinal. He took a more
prominent and active part in public life in Birmingham
than did Maclaren in Manchester; his civics and politics,
however, did not lower his standard, but increased his

[1] Quoted by Brown, *op. cit.*, p. 287.

[2] Quoted by Edwards, *op. cit.*, p. 78.

[3] *Ibid.*, p. 80.

[4] See DHP ii. pp. 560–561 ; Edwards, *op. cit.*, pp. 32–44 ; Brown, *op.
cit.*, pp. 231–259. *Life of R. W. Dale of Birmingham*, by his Son,
London, 1898.

influence. His doctrinal preaching was not remote from reality, but experimental, rooted in his own inner life, and ethical, applied to the outer life of his hearers. His independent and constructive contribution to theology does not lie in his lectures on the *Atonement*, which do not come into close living touch with the thought of to-day; but in his exposition of what was distinctive of his own inner life, *fellowship with the Living Christ*; and this should make a persuasive appeal to present mystical tendencies. To the perils of negative criticism he opposes this defence of positive experience. Himself compelled to restate his own belief in terms of modern thought, he regarded it as a binding duty that he should share with others the distinctness and assurance of faith which he had himself attained. In a time more averse to doctrinal preaching than is our own, which is being driven to ask questions about the ultimate realities, he disregarded the fashion of the hour, and preached theology, not divorced from ethics, for he was one of the sanest and strongest moral forces of his age, and not presented in a technical or academic fashion, for he had a robust common sense, and a constant and intimate contact with the busy world around him; but as the interpretation of an experience of the divine truth and grace possessed by Christian believers, and possible to all, which is the source of all worthy character and good conduct; and this he offered in language which he sought to make intelligible to all his hearers.

(2) His style was influenced by Edmund Burke more than by any other writer; and in the same manner bears the marks of greatness. His sermons may be claimed as literature; but we must ask, is such a style the best fitted for the pulpit? Dr. Brown quotes Dr. Fairbairn as saying that Dr. Dale's words " though written to be spoken, are even more fitted to be read than to be heard; for his books are as firm in texture, as weighty in matter, as vigorous in expression as the concentrated thought of a strong man could make them."[1] Dr. Brown's own opinion is, however,

[1] *Op. cit.*, p. 249.

that they are less fitted to be heard than to be read, and so are not as well adapted for the pulpit as they should be. His delivery of the sermons was, as a hearer testifies, adversely affected by this mode of composition. It tended to monotony, and lack of pathos; the intellectual predominated over the emotional. On great occasions when thoroughly aroused, he could profoundly affect an audience. Often, however, he moved in a region beyond the common reach. As a student of theology the writer found no difficulty in following the course of Dr. Dale's thought; and yet he must admit that he sometimes had a feeling of oppression, as if too great a weight were being laid upon his mind. It is surely an evidence of the greatness of Dr. Dale that he himself recognised his own limitation, while realising that he could not altogether escape from it, for his habit had become a second nature.

5. Although none of the books consulted on the preachers of the nineteenth century reckons Dr. Andrew Martin Fairbairn (1838–1912)[1] among them, the writer as one of his students cannot withhold his tribute to his master. The sermons were often far too long, learned, philosophical and theological for popularity; and the preacher inclined to make his boast of what to most persons would appear his defect; he overtaxed the attention, because he overrated the intelligence of most of his hearers. His delight in description and narration, and his warm human sympathy did something to relieve the tension, and to secure in some measure a personal responsiveness, if not mental receptivity, in many of his hearers. He had no natural advantages as an orator, and his mannerisms sometimes distracted the attention; but, when he was at his best, for those who could appreciate him, his preaching was great, profoundly impressive in its range of knowledge, sweep of thought, keenness of vision, passion of conviction, and power of personality. Had he laid less stress on intellect in religion and so in preaching,

[1] See *The Life of Andrew Martin Fairbairn*, by W. B. Selbie, London, 1914.

and had he allowed as free and full exercise in his sermons
to his great heart revealed to those who knew him as to
his great mind, he would have been more effective as a
preacher.   The writer heard him on the same day preach
two sermons, which presented a striking contrast.   In the
morning he preached from his Christian heart on the
Christian Motive: "The Love of Christ constraineth us."[1]
In the evening he delivered a lecture in answer to the
question, "What think ye of Christ?"[2]   The first moved
his hearers to the depths of their inner life; the second
only bewildered most of them.   One is safe in conjecturing
that his own judgment of the respective value of the two
utterances would be the reverse of that of his hearers.
The limitation of Dr. Dale's influence by the *stateliness* of
his style has been mentioned; and yet Dr. Dale was more
experimental and practical, less historical and speculative
than was Dr. Fairbairn.   Both were great men, and the
writer who knew both well fully appreciates their greatness; more effective as preachers they would have been
had they known better how to stoop to conquer.

6. All the preachers mentioned were concerned about
repairing the breach between the Christian Gospel and the
thought of the age.   Just as, if not more serious is the
breach between the Christian Church and the toiling
masses.   Two men may be mentioned who sought to reach
the shepherdless multitude, and to bring it into the fold of
Christ.   The first of these was Hugh Price Hughes (1847–
1902).[3] He cannot be reckoned among the great preachers,
but he claims a place here as representative of the
necessary, and too long delayed, endeavour to get the
common people to hear the Gospel gladly, and to commend
the Gospel not in word only, but also in deed, by manifold
ministry to their needs of body as well as of soul.   He
was a strong and bold champion of the application of
Christian principles to public life, to the moral issues of
modern society.   The writer heard him preach twice in
Oxford, once revealing his power, and again showing his

[1] 2 Co 5[14].   [2] Mt 22[42].   [3] DHP ii. pp. 568–569.

limitation. A straight talk on personal decision, based on the words, "Sir, we would see Jesus,"[1] moved his audience of students who had no love of academic discourses, too reminiscent of their work in classrooms. A more ambitious effort to deal with the *Natural Agnosticism of the Human Heart*[2] failed of any effect. It is the former kind of preaching that the multitude needs; and that even the cultured, unless spoiled by pride of culture, also delight in. His strength lay in the speech that moves from heart to heart.

7. The second of these leaders of the Church back to the people was Charles Silvester Horne (1865–1914). (1) As one of his fellow-students at Glasgow, and then Oxford University, the writer can testify that his powers as a speaker were early acknowledged. In spite of his tendency, when excited, to overstrain his voice, there was no speaker who could move an audience of Free Churchmen to such an enthusiasm or indignation as he could. Although he excelled on the platform, yet in the pulpit also his influence was great. He left a West-end congregation to lead a new movement to recapture the masses for Christ at Whitefield's Central Mission. Many of his friends regretted that, impelled by his high sense of public duty, he added to his manifold exacting labours the burden of representing a constituency in Parliament. Whether, if he had spared himself, his life would have been prolonged, who can tell? In the midst of his work in a moment death took him; just after he had finished the delivery of the Yale Lectures on Preaching.

(2) As a personal friend from student days the writer ventures to bring to a conclusion the history of preaching in this volume by a brief summary of Horne's last lecture, entitled "The Romance of Modern Preaching."[3] He seeks to answer the question what gives preaching "a perennial fascination and glory." He offers four reasons. (*a*) "*Preach-*

---

[1] Jn 12²¹.

[2] The text, if memory does not deceive, was Ps 14¹.

[3] *The Romance of Modern Preaching*, pp. 255–292.

ing can never lose its place so long as the mystery and wonder of the human spirit remains. For we are dealing with that which is the source of all the amazing interest of life." . . . " We preachers live always in the conscious presence of the supreme mysteries." (*b*) "*Amid all changes of thought and phrase the wonder of conversion remains.*" . . . "There is not a moment of any day, in any year, when we may not rise with Christ into newness of life and walk in His ways with transfigured spirits. All this goes to make up the charm, the fascination, the rapture, the romance of the ministry." (*c*) "*We are manifestly on the eve of new application of Christ's teaching, which will revive the interest of the people in Christianity to a surprising degree.* . . . The watchword of our new century is Justice. It will create as splendid an army of prophets ; and it may very well be that, before the victory is won, men and women will have to buy the new inheritance at a great price. But buy it they will ; for the master passion in the breast of the noblest of our young men is that the will of the Father shall be done ' on earth as it is in heaven.' " (*d*) "*Over this world of military camps, bristling frontiers and armoured fleets, there is being heard to-day with new insistence the ever-romantic strains of the angels' song of Peace and Goodwill.*"

8. Does this last statement ring in our ear as a cruel mockery ? Horne did not live to witness the outbreak of war.[1] Yet he was no false prophet ; the general permanent purpose of the nations, in so far as they are Christian, is peace, and not war. If the Churches are true and brave, on the bloody battlefields of Europe will be sealed the doom of its armed camps. One cannot doubt that had he lived he would not have abated heart or hope, but would have continued the prophet of the better day, the impassioned advocate of the League of Nations. More than ever the preachers of to-day must labour as the repairers

[1] Two volumes of the Yale Lectures have appeared which take account of the war in its influence on preaching. Coffin's *In a Day of Social Rebuilding*, and Kelman's *The War and Preaching*.

of the breach in the world which, professing Christianity, has yet in mutual slaughter been disowning the sovereignty of the Prince of Peace. Even if, as the writer himself believes, war was forced on some of the nations in defence of the precious heritage of nationality, and to prevent the triumph of might over right, so that all the peoples at war are not involved in blood-guiltiness, yet inevitably much of the good gained during the last century, which to him, who, though dead, speaks to us in this hopeful forecast of the future, seemed an assured possession, must be recovered by suffering and toil. In that resurrection of the Christian Churches from among dead aims, hopes and achievements, the Christian preacher [1] must in this age, as in former ages, bear his witness to the inexhaustible power and final triumph of the Risen Lord ; must continue calling to the world around, " Awake, thou that sleepest, and arise from the dead, and Christ shall shine upon thee," [2] and send forth to the Churches themselves the summons : " Arise, shine ; for thy light is come, and the glory of the Lord is risen upon thee." [3]

[1] The writer has decided not to mention any preachers still living, owing to the greater difficulty of making a choice. An intelligent appreciation of a number of these may be found in the book entitled *Voices of To-day*.

[2] Eph 5[14].   [3] Is 60[1].

PART II.

THE CREDENTIALS, QUALIFICA-
TIONS AND FUNCTIONS OF THE
PREACHER.

INTRODUCTORY.

THE history of preaching, with which the First Part has dealt, is the necessary presupposition of any discussion of the credentials, qualifications and functions of the preacher to-day. Since he stands in a historical succession, he will recognise the responsibility of his trust, and the difficulty of his task, only as he has a distinct consciousness of this succession, and takes up into his ideal of his vocation all the elements of permanent significance and value in the previous history. But on the other hand "God fulfils Himself in many ways lest one good custom should corrupt the world," and accordingly the conception of the preacher's calling which the past yields cannot simply be transferred to the present; but in his work he must recognise the necessity of adaptation to the existing conditions, as in this sphere, no less than in others of human activity, the principle of evolution is applicable. What must as far as possible be combined are loyalty to the past and devotion to the present; and with that alliance there will surely go also guidance for the future. As far as possible, in order to emphasise the virtue of continuity, the old terms descriptive of the position and obligations of the preacher will be used, with such modification of meaning, however, as changed times may demand.

CHAPTER I.

THE PREACHER AS APOSTLE, PROPHET AND SCRIBE.

As the preacher claims to be offering men truth valid for their reason and authoritative for their conscience, he must be able to offer his credentials, he must show that he has the competence, and so the authority, to speak to men in the name of God. As it is the Gospel of Jesus Christ which he is called to preach, he must first of all be able to show that Christ Himself has entrusted His Gospel to him, and that Christ's Church has confirmed his claim; he must be an *apostle*. While the Gospel of Jesus Christ was given once for all, yet in the interpretation and application of that Gospel, the Christian preacher needs the enlightening and quickening of the Spirit of God, that he may declare the permanent and universal revelation of God as personally revealed to himself; he must be a *prophet*. This revelation of God has been preserved in the Holy Scriptures, and the personal illumination of the preacher cannot be a substitute for, but is always in dependence on his study of the Holy Scriptures; he must be a *scribe*. These three relations, *apostle, prophet, scribe*, indicate the channel through which comes to him the message for which he can claim the validity and the authority of *truth*.

I.

1. In dealing with the Christian preacher the starting-point must be the relation of Jesus to the Twelve, whom He chose, called, taught and trained, and then sent forth as the witnesses of His Gospel, and the workers for His kingdom. We are not concerned here with any ecclesiastical

figments of apostolic succession; but are simply trying to
learn from what the apostles were what the Christian
preacher should be.   As was pointed out in a previous
chapter,[1] a necessary qualification of apostleship was personal knowledge of Jesus, especially witness of the Resurrection.   The personal experience of Christ as Saviour and
Lord is also the primary qualification of the Christian
preacher.   While we must not insist on any one type of
Christian development as essential, yet we may lay down
the broad general principle that the less the religious life
of the Christian preacher is *second-hand*, dependent on the
theological traditions and pious conventions of the religious
community to which he belongs, and the more it is *first-
hand*, due to his individual consciousness of the presence
and power of the living Christ in his own soul, the fitter
will he be to bear testimony to what Christ is and what
Christ can do.   If his Christian life has been a gradual
development, he runs the risk of not recognising adequately
in the natural growth the supernatural grace of Christ
which has made, and is making him what he is.   The
necessity, sufficiency and efficiency of the grace of Christ
may not be adequately appreciated by him.   If, on the
other hand, his Christian life has had a certain and distinct
beginning in a conscious and voluntary conversion, his peril
is that he may so emphasise the supernatural act of Christ
in saving as to ignore the manifold natural channels of
this gracious activity.   Whatever be the type of his
Christian experience, the preacher will be disqualified for
his work by one-sidedness, unless he learns to live his
religious life vicariously, to live in the life of others whose
experience is unlike his own.   Sympathy and imagination,
however, should enable a man to put himself in the varied
and varying positions in which, owing to differences of
education, temperament and circumstances, men living the
same life in Christ do find themselves.   Preaching is to
be the voice, not of the preacher's individuality, with
its narrowing limitations, but of the universal Christian

[1] Pp. 48–49.

experience which testifies to the manifoldness of the truth and grace of Christ. Without desiring to qualify this statement, the writer cannot but add that to him, at least, it seems that preaching can be truly apostolic only when the note of certainty that Christ is risen is distinctly heard. Jesus as teacher and example may be the theme of Christian preaching; but that preaching will surely lack the " holy enthusiasm " of the preaching of the apostles which does not witness from personal experience that the Lord is risen indeed.[1]

2. This personal experience must, however, include the consciousness of personal vocation by Christ for the work of preaching. (1) Each of the Twelve was called; and so must the preacher know himself called. While to all Christians according to the gift of the Spirit some work in the Christian Church is appointed, this work, because so much more prominent, responsible and representative, does demand a certainty of vocation. Some men can testify to having received as distinct a call from Christ to the work of the ministry as did any of the Twelve. It may be even that contrary to their previous education, their personal inclination, and their determining circumstances, necessity was laid upon them, while recognising their unfitness, un-readiness, and the difficulties in the way of obedience, so that they dared not be " disobedient to the heavenly vision." The possibility of mistake may be admitted. There are disqualifications of capacity, character and even circum-stances, which only ignorant conceit could disregard and vain ambition could defy; but nevertheless it would be rash for another to challenge the reality of the call where it comes with such authority and urgency. All that in the one case seemed to offer a reason against the choice of this calling, may in the other combine to compel the question, whether the natural inclinations are not to be taken as God's supernatural guidance. If a man recog-nises- that the fields ripe for the harvest are needing

---

[1] Dr. Stalker devotes four of the nine lectures of his book on *The Preacher and his Models*, to St. Paul, as the representative of apostolic preaching.

labourers, and that God in His providence has made it possible for him to render such service, he may decide that it is his duty so to serve, even if there be no distinct experience of a call. In either case it is not the form of the experience which matters, but the reality of the divine guidance which is experienced.

(2) As the preacher in the Christian Church is the representative of the community, speaks for it as well as to it, to his own sense of his calling there must come the confirmation of the call of the Church. Here too there is possibility of mistake; the Church may appoint whom God has not set apart, and may refuse its acknowledgment to one who has the divine warrant. And yet the man's sense of being called, and the appointment of the man who has heard the call by the Church, are a mutual safeguard, and ordinarily the Church should satisfy itself that he who seeks its ordination can claim the vocation by God, and the man who thinks himself called, but fails to win the Church's recognition, should accept the judgment of the community in correction of his own estimate of himself. The qualifications which will be indicated in the course of these chapters are such as demand a special education of the preacher, and it is for the good of the Churches that the possibility of such an education should be placed within the reach of all who have felt the call, and in whom the Church sees the promise of fitness for the calling, without regard to financial resources or social rank. The training for the ministry should be offered freely to the poor youth, if worthy and fit.

3. It is the personal experience and the personal vocation, confirmed by the Church, which give to the Christian preacher his authority. There can be no doubt whatever that, in the early Church, the apostles claimed an authority which was conceded to them. Without any hierarchical pretensions or official arrogance, the Christian preacher also may claim authority, but an authority which imposes an obligation. The apostles had authority as the companions of Jesus and the witnesses of His Resurrection; and so the

Christian preacher has authority only as he continues the same function in the Church. (1) It is the truth and grace of Christ which he must apprehend for himself and offer to others. It is Christ, and the Christ of the evangelical history, apostolic testimony, and Church's continuous experience, and not himself, his own views and aims, that he must preach. Whatever be his own immediate contact with Christ in personal experience, yet historically he is linked to Christ by the Christian community, and it is his relation as its representative which gives him his authority, and this relation demands on his part, if his authority is not to be a usurpation, fidelity to its historic confession of Christ as Saviour and Lord. This does not mean that he is to go on repeating stereotyped phrases, or even in his own mind to preserve superseded phases of Christian belief, but it does mean that in his preaching he does declare the historic facts, the religious truths, and the moral duties which, undefined and undefinable in any creed, would command the acceptance of all Christians, and which form, nevertheless, the common treasure which believers and saints know themselves to possess.

(2) Most Christian denominations seek to secure the continuity of faith by means of subscription to a creed, but even if such subscription were desirable, as in the writer's opinion it is not, it is useless as a safeguard without the personal loyalty to the doctrine it includes on the part of those who subscribe it. No creed has yet been formed the terms of which were so unambiguous as to leave no room for variety of interpretation, and no subscription was ever so rigid as not to allow for mental reservations. Given the loyalty, the creed subscription is unnecessary; failing the loyalty, it is futile. The Christian community is a living body, and the continuity of its life cannot be maintained by such mechanical devices as creed subscription. The recognition of this fact makes not less, but more necessary the insistence on the duty of the Christian preacher to recognise fully his responsibility in his preaching to maintain with all necessary adaptation in the forms

of presentation, the faith which has linked the Christian generations to one another. Only as he recognises that he is a man under the authority of the truth can he declare the truth with authority.

4. It was the apostolic function to link historically the Christian Church to the historical Jesus, and so it is the function of the Christian preacher as an apostle to maintain the historical continuity of the Church. It is surely not in rites, customs, creeds and codes that the Christian life maintains its identity through the changing centuries, for that identity cannot be a uniformity such as these external forms alone can maintain, but must be realised in a development, to which change as well as sameness belongs. It is for the Christian preacher to receive the Christian inheritance of the past, and to adapt it in such wise to the need of his own age that it will be effective for all religious and moral ends, and will pass from him to another generation as a greatly enriched bequest. So conceived, the pulpit becomes the channel of the growing life of the Christian Church from generation to generation ; it is not an individual possession of the preacher, however great and many his gifts may be, but a common trust, and the Church's fidelity to its purpose in the world will depend on the preacher's loyalty as its representative. That there is need of, and room for, originality in the pulpit, will be shown in the subsequent discussion ; but what needs to be asserted in view of many tendencies towards an excessive subjectivity is that the Christ of the faith of the Church is a constant objective reality, and that the preacher is Christian only as he recognises and respects the distinctiveness of the faith he preaches as historical.[1]

II.

1. But if the apostolic function suggests one aspect of the Christian preacher's work, the prophetic offers us the

[1] This subject has been fully treated by Dr. Forsyth in his book, *Positive Preaching and the Modern Mind*. See pp. 71-72.

complementary aspect. The Christian preacher does not stand only in a historical succession ; he has also a spiritual equipment. The Spirit who fitted the prophets for their calling has made the Christian Church His permanent organ, and all who share the common life of the Church are subjects of the Spirit's presence and power. He who possessed the Spirit without measure has also endowed His body with a like possession.[1] The Montanist movement was an attempt to force a recovery of the external aspects of the Spirit's operation in the Apostolic Church, the abnormal psychical conditions which in some persons accompanied the "holy enthusiasm" kindled by the certainty of the Risen Living Lord ; but in suppressing Montanism, the Church tended to substitute mechanics for dynamics, organisation for inspiration. Even to-day it is necessary to insist that a genuinely and intensely Christian life will be an inspired life, not sporadic exaltations, but a constant religious and moral transformation of the spirit of man by the Spirit of God. In His Spirit the Living Christ gives Himself to be the inner life of believers. To be His is to possess the Spirit. There is an enlightening of the mind, a quickening of the heart, a cleansing of the conscience and a renewal of the will in the Christian, which is not merely natural human development, but is also a supernatural divine action.

2. While this claim of inspiration may and ought to be made for all Christians, yet there is diversity of the Spirit's operations, and some are specially endowed for distinctive service. Although the historic connection with Jesus was a necessary condition of apostleship, yet the apostles also possessed a distinctive gift of the Spirit to fit them for their leadership of the Church.[2] Next to the apostles ranked the prophets, of whose functions a previous chapter[3] also gave some account. The difference between the apostolic and the prophetic aspect of the Christian

[1] John 3[34] AV. "God giveth not the Spirit by measure *unto him*." RV. "He giveth not the Spirit by measure."

[2] 1 Co 12[28].

[3] Pp. 49–50.

ministry may be thus briefly stated. The apostle declares
the faith which has once for all been delivered as the
sacred deposit of the Christian community; the prophet
reads the signs of the times, and applies the truth as it
is in Jesus to the new needs. There is still a purpose
of God being fulfilled in human history; and that men
may co-operate with that purpose it is necessary that they
should understand it. It is to be feared that while on the one
hand rash men have far too confidently declared the decrees
and the designs of the divine providence; yet on the other
hand the Christian preacher has often shrunk from his prophetic task when God was calling him to it. Contemporary
human events have some eternal divine meaning; and this
both for guidance and encouragement the Christian Church
should seek to know, and the preacher or prophet is especially charged with the function of such interpretation.

3. It is a task full of peril. As in Israel so in the
Christian Church there may be false as well as true
prophecy.[1] National prejudices, ecclesiastical preferences,
class interests may so blind the eyes of the preacher that
he does not see the history of his own time as God would
have it understood. During recent years Christian
preachers in Germany were defending the war as necessary
and legitimate self-defence, on which the blessing of God
could be invoked. Little more than a decade ago Christian
preachers in Britain were as zealously defending the Boer
War. Now the invasion of a small country like Belgium
is a crime against humanity for those who regarded the
suppression of the Boer nation as a debt to civilisation and
even Christianity. While the man who always finds his
own country wrong is probably just as mistaken as the man
who always finds it right; yet the prophet must be specially
on his guard against confusing human prejudices and divine
principles, his own inclinations and God's inspiration of
him. Great as is the difficulty of an objective judgment
of what concerns us personally very closely, yet for the

[1] Dr. Stalker in the book already referred to deals in the fifth lecture with
the Preacher as a false prophet.

discharge of his duty the preacher must learn as in this, so in all respects to rise above and go beyond his own limitations of time and place, and so to live in the permanent and universal life of the Spirit of God, that God will find in his moral insight and spiritual discernment an unimpeded channel for the communication of His mind and will to his age and people.

4. A very important distinction between ancient and modern prophecy must be asserted. The prophet of old was the agent of a preparatory and progressive revelation, but the prophet to-day is the agent of a confirmatory and expository revelation. When Jesus made the promise of the Paraclete to His disciples, He so defined the functions of the Spirit of truth as to subordinate the revelation by the Spirit to the revelation in the Son. "Howbeit when He, the Spirit of truth, is come, He will guide you into all truth : for He shall not speak of Himself ; but whatsoever He shall hear, that shall He speak. . . . He shall glorify Me : for He shall receive of Mine, and shall shew it unto you." [1] As He the Son was wholly dependent on the Father, so would the Spirit be dependent on the revelation that He the Son had already given of the Father. The religion of the Spirit is sometimes so represented as to be a setting aside of Christ as the Saviour and Lord. If a man is convinced that the Lord hath spoken to Him something above and beyond what has already been spoken in the Son, he cannot be hindered in declaring the oracle which has been committed to him ; but it can be said with an impartial historical judgment that nothing of any value has been added by any of these new prophets to the deposit of moral and religious truth already possessed by the Church in the revelation of God in Christ. The Christian prophet claims only the humbler service of confirming and interpreting under the Spirit's influence the revelation already received.[2]

[1] Jn 16[13. 14].

[2] The preacher's inspiration has been dealt with by Dr. Horton in his book, *Verbum Dei*.

III.

1. The revelation which culminated in Christ, and the revelation which is complete in Christ, are both recorded in the Holy Scriptures. This record includes not only the narrative of the historical events in which God's purpose was fulfilled, but also the testimony to, and the interpretation of, this history in the religious life and thought of the subordinate agents of revelation, prophets and apostles. The Christian preacher both as *apostle* and as *prophet* has a dependent relation to the Holy Scriptures; and we may, retaining as far as we can the old terms, describe him as a *scribe*. He is the student and exponent of the Bible, because, alike in his apprehension of Christ and his interpretation of the mind and will of God, he cannot know and understand the revelation of God apart from the Holy Scriptures. This dependence is confessed, though often it is to be feared unconsciously and involuntarily, when the text of a sermon is given out. Thus the preacher acknowledges that what he is about to say has its source and its authority in what God has already said in Christ, or by prophets and apostles. The use of a text, then, is not an arbitrary convention which may be set aside without making any difference to the preacher and the character of the preaching. There may be rare occasions, and peculiar subjects, when the preacher may feel warranted in dispensing with a text; and this is the more honest course than to attach a sermon to a text by a *tour de force* of exegesis. But a preacher would have good ground for suspecting the adequacy of his knowledge of the Bible, or the loyalty of his preaching to Christian truth, who found it necessary frequently to depart from not only a time-honoured custom, but an authoritative principle rooted in the very character of Christian preaching as dependent on divine revelation. The contents of the Scriptures are so varied, and the wisdom, righteousness and grace therein recorded so manifold with a divine abundance, that it could be but very seldom that a preacher who was also an instructed scribe could not find in that treasure-house a warrant both for things new as well as old which he might desire to bring forth.[1] Accordingly it may be urged as strongly as possible that the preacher who does not find in the Holy Scriptures not only his themes, but even the most profitable treatment of them, is likely very soon to exhaust his stock of subjects, and to get theadbare in his treatment of them ; while, on the contrary, he who knows and understands the literature of the divine revelation and of the human redemption, has an inexhaustible source to which he can constantly return with confidence that he will not be sent empty away, but that he will find the record as abundant as the truth and grace of the Infinite God can make it.   It has pleased God that as in His Christ, so in His Scriptures His fulness should dwell—and of that fulness we may keep on freely receiving according to our desires and capacities.

2. The generally accepted results of modern scholarship in regard to the Bible raise a problem for the preacher which cannot be ignored or escaped.   (1) It is, of course, possible for a man to decide that he will keep his eyes closed to all new light on this as on other subjects ; and, if he is ignorant and dishonest enough, he may be able to go on treating the Bible in the pulpit in the traditional way.   Apart from the injury, moral as well as intellectual, of such an attitude to the man himself, and the weakness of faith which lies at the root of such cowardice in facing fact and truth, his influence over his hearers who read and think will be not to promote faith, but rather to provoke doubt and unbelief.   The Christian ministry is probably not aware to how great an extent its moral and religious authority is being undermined by a growing suspicion in the cultured class that ministers have not the courage either to acquaint themselves with any new knowledge which might disturb their theological assumptions, or, having gained some acquaintance, the sincerity to betray it lest they might disturb the tran-

[1] Mt 13^{52}.

quillity of their congregations. It is certain that a preacher cannot influence those who are doubtful of his courage and his sincerity, and that a fearless following of the truth, whithersoever it may lead, alone will command respect. It is not merely the preacher's intellectual adequacy, but even his moral integrity, which is involved in the solution of this problem.

(2) If a man has both knowledge and courage, there still remains a difficult question, which will demand all his Christian wisdom to answer: how far is he in the pulpit to deal with the results of the literary and historical criticism of the Bible? He must consider not only what he means to say, but also what his hearers are likely to understand by what he says. Truth may be so spoken as on unprepared minds to leave the injurious impression of falsehood. The denial of the Mosaic authorship of the Pentateuch, or of the unity of the book of Isaiah, to mention as instances only two of the most assured conclusions of modern scholarship, may appear to some ignorant saints (and saints are often very ignorant) in a congregation a challenge of the authority of the Bible in morals and religion as well. Some of the very best men and women in a congregation are most firmly bound by the traditional views of the Bible; and, even in the interests of accurate knowledge, their convictions, however mistaken, must not be disregarded. Courage must be combined with considerateness. The " strong " in faith in this respect must not despise the " weak "; but, at the same time, the " weak " cannot ever continue to impose their limitations on the liberty of the " strong." [1] But the adjustment of these two interests requires a judgment and tact which only the enlightening of the Spirit can give. Are there any general principles which can be laid down, while their application must always remain the obligation and responsibility of individual conscience?

(3) The following considerations are offered with some diffidence, even although there is practical experience

[1] See Ro 14 for Paul's treatment of a similar problem.

behind them.   *In the first place*, it must be maintained
that the pulpit is not the place for instruction about the
Bible, but for declaration of the truth and grace of God
conveyed in the Bible.   Special courses of lectures on
Sunday evenings on some of the critical questions may be
in some congregations not only tolerable, but even desirable ; for, if the public mind is engaged at any time by any
theological problem, it may be the duty of the preacher to
offer his own contribution to the solution.   As a general
rule, however, any parade of learning in the sermon is
offensive in the highest degree, and most of all to those
who are best able to judge its value.   In the Bible Class,
the minister may prepare the young people of his " cure of
souls " to accept the new knowledge without any loss of
the old faith.

In the second place, the exposition of a passage of
Scripture may require that the results of modern scholarship should be assumed.   For instance, the fifty-third
chapter of Isaiah cannot be made as intelligible and interesting as it should be, unless the historical situation is fully
and clearly presented.   The existence of the great prophet
of the Exile may be simply affirmed without any debate
about the unity of the Book.   Or again, the differences of
the Synoptic and the Johannine presentation of the person
of Jesus may need to be recognised in order to leave the
true impression of the life and work of Jesus ; and yet the
Synoptic question, or the problem of the authorship of the
Fourth Gospel, need not be discussed in detail.   The
influence of changing historical conditions on Paul's theology may be noted without raising any controversy about
" the husk " and " the kernel " in his teaching.   So far as
modern scholarship is an aid to an understanding, and an
appreciation of the Holy Scriptures, the preacher not only
may, but ought to, use it freely and boldly ; never in a
controversial spirit, but always with a constructive purpose.

In the third place, even when a preacher is not directly
dealing with any matters of scholarship, his treatment of
his text will show any discerning and informed hearer

whether or not he has the scholarship, and is using it. A reverent and sympathetic hearer, however well informed on these questions, does not expect nor desire that these questions should be discussed in detail in the pulpit. What such a hearer resents, and resents with good reason, is that the preacher should show by his handling of his subject either that he is ignorant of what he ought to know, or that, though not ignorant, he does not allow his knowledge to have its due influence on his method of exposition of the Scriptures. Competence and candour are legitimate demands of the pew upon the pulpit.

In the fourth place, it is possible so to present the moral and religious truth of the Bible, detached from the traditional view hitherto associated with it and in consistency with modern scholarship, that gradually and insensibly a congregation is moved from one standpoint to the other, so that it becomes detached from the traditional, and accustomed to the critical without any feeling of the loss of anything valuable for conscience or spirit. While there are prejudiced bigots of the new as well as of the old, who would like the pulpit to be aggressive either traditionally or critically, most Christian men and women desire simply to hold fast the truth as it is in Jesus, the faith once for all delivered to the saints, and are relieved to find that they can retain what alone they can value as well in the new as in the old position on all critical questions.

3. In the considerations just presented it has been assumed that modern scholarship does not affect the substance of the Christian Gospel, and this assumption must as briefly as possible be justified.[1]

(1) It will be readily conceded that questions of date, authorship, modes of composition of the writings in the Bible, do not affect matters of faith unless in so far as the credibility of the history recorded, or the trustworthiness of

[1] The question has been discussed by Dr. Forsyth, in his book already mentioned, *Positive Preaching*, pp. 106–109, as well as by Dr. (now Sir) George Adam Smith, in his *Modern Criticism and the Preaching of the Old Testament*.

the witnesses of the divine revelation is involved.   A book is not morally or religiously less or more valuable because it was written by one author or another, in one century or another.   Poetry may convey truth even more effectively than does prose; the literary character of a writing affects our method of exposition, and not the substance of its message for us.   If modern scholarship had *changed* our traditional views of the Bible in these respects only, there would be no problem about which we need trouble ourselves.   It must be admitted, however, that we are forced to face the question whether the history of the divine revelation and the human redemption as recorded in the Scriptures is substantially accurate.   Did God fulfil His purpose in the Hebrew nation progressively making Himself and His will known to man, or was the history just the same as that of any other nation, and was the difference which the records present not objective reality but subjective illusion ?   Was there no choice and call, no guidance and guardianship, no teaching and training of this people by God ?   Did Jesus exist at all, or was He, if He did exist, in reality Christ, Saviour, Lord, as He now is for the Christian faith ?   Is the New Testament the literature of an actual religious movement which was as it is there represented, or is it the result of the mythical tendency of all religion ?   Can the death and rising again of Jesus be resolved into the myth of a dying and reviving God ?   All these questions are not equally crucial for Christian faith.   The miracles of Elijah and Elisha mean far less than the miracles of Jesus; and the surrender of the records as unhistorical would involve far less loss.   The translation of Enoch is immeasurably less significant for Christian thought and life than the resurrection of Jesus.   The accuracy of the narratives in Kings does not touch us as Christians so closely as does that of the Gospels.   And when we insist on the necessity of the trustworthiness of the history contained in the Scriptures for our Christian faith, we should always recognise these distinctions between the essential and the non-essential.

(2) To the question whether we have or have not a historical revelation of God and redemption of man, modern scholarship, candid and courageous, does allow us to give an affirmative answer. Upon many subordinate matters there are, and will remain, wide differences of opinion; but the general conclusion may be hazarded that the historical reality of the Lord Jesus Christ remains unshaken, that the testimony to and interpretation of His person and work in the New Testament retains its value for Christian faith, that even in the Old Testament a preparatory and progressive revelation towards Him can still be traced. What is necessary and valuable for the moral and religious life in the Holy Scriptures has not been taken away from the Christian Church; and the preacher may use fully and freely in the pulpit the teaching of the hallowed writings.

(3) Although we must not try to answer historical questions otherwise than historically, yet from the standpoint of the preacher another consideration remains relevant. The Scriptures are self-witnessing to the moral conscience and religious consciousness. They have proved their value and their authority in Christian experience, which they have sustained, and Christian character, which they have produced. It is here that their pre-eminence in literature is seen, and it is here that the concern of the preacher lies.[1] Apart from the trustworthiness of the historical revelation of God, especially in Christ, the preacher is not primarily concerned with historical questions at all; but only with matters of faith and duty; and to moral and spiritual discernment the Scriptures remain unchanged by all the results of modern scholarship.

(4) The new knowledge we have gained about the Bible does not in the least degree lessen the demand that the preacher shall be a scribe as well as an apostle and a prophet; but it does render two valuable services to him. *In the first place*, there is a simplification of the content of

---

[1] This argument has been developed by Dr. Dale in his book, *The Living Christ and the Four Gospels*. See pp. 10–11.

his preaching as determined by the Holy Scriptures.   A
great deal in the Bible, which from the old standpoint
still possessed dogmatic authority, has now for him literary,
biographical and historical interest.   He is now not at
all concerned about defending the cosmology or anthro-
pology of Genesis, or the morality of the patriarchs or
judges.   Balaam's ass or Jonah's whale are no more
formidable obstacles in the path of faith.   He can now
confine himself to that in the Bible which does
sustain the Christian experience and produce the Christian
character.

In the second place, there is a liberation of his reason
and conscience.   The Bible does not now require him to
believe and teach what his knowledge in other spheres of
inquiry renders unintelligible and incredible.   There need
be no schism between his respect for science and his
reverence for the Bible.   He is free to follow modern
knowledge where it alone is competent to lead, and yet be
loyal to the truth and grace of God offered to him in
the Holy Scriptures.

4. The fresh light which modern scholarship throws
on the Bible imposes on the Christian preacher the obligation to study in order that he may teach according to the
best methods.   (1) *The allegorical method* is now discredited,
and yet there are preachers found who are always striving
to impose on the Scriptures another than the literal sense.
The only proper method of study is the *historical*, to use all
the resources of our modern knowledge to find out what the
ancient writer meant that his words should mean.   Far
from taking liberties with the Scriptures, this historical
method alone treats the Scriptures with the respect due
to them, for its one object is to discover the meaning in
them, and not to impose a meaning on them.   By *textual
criticism*, to discover as nearly as possible what at first
was actually written; by *linguistic study*, to fix the exact
meaning of every word, clause, sentence and passage; by
literary criticism, to ascertain what each writing tells us
about itself, its date, author, occasion, literary character

and historical value; by *historical criticism*, to test the trustworthiness of each writing in relation to the history contained in the writings as a collection, and to any other historical evidence, and to construct an intelligible record of what did actually take place from this history—this is what the historical method in its manifold disciplines attempts to do. Its ideal is to make each reader of the Bible an eye-witness of each scene, an ear-witness of each discourse, a contemporary of prophet, evangelist, apostle and even Jesus Himself. Only when this has been done can the full moral and religious significance of the writings be apprehended and appreciated. The goal is actuality, reality, truth.[1]

(2) This process of study is not for the pulpit, but the product is; for it is a fatal mistake for a preacher to suppose that in his preaching he can ignore and neglect what he learns as a student. There is a common impression that the treatment of the Bible in the pulpit by methods now ignored by scholars is for the greater profit of the hearers; and that, however valuable for scholars, this method of study of the Bible has less value for Christian believers; and accordingly a devotional and a scholarly study of the Bible are contrasted. But against this assumption two considerations must be insisted on. *In the first place*, if God be truth, that cannot be for *profit*, which is not according to *truth*. The Bible, as it is, has far greater moral and spiritual value than a preacher may arbitrarily make it appear to be. What prophet or apostle or Christ meant to say is much more worth hearing than any meaning that the preacher's fancy may put into their words. *And in the second place*, the Bible studied by the historical method is a far more interesting book than the traditional exposition can ever make it. Many who have adopted this fresh method with prejudice have come to acknowledge that the Bible had become a new book to them. If the study of the Bible is interest-

---

[1] For a full discussion of this method see Peake's *A Guide to Biblical Study*.

ing to the preacher, unless he is exceptionally unskilful, he will make it interesting to his hearers.

5. While in the last part of this book the different kinds of sermons will be discussed, it is relevant to the present subject to add, that if a preacher wants to keep his freshness, variety and attractiveness in theme and treatment alike, he will aim at being an expository preacher, not in the narrow sense of always expounding in detail a passage of scripture, but in the broad sense that even when he deals with a subject, that subject will be connected by no forced exegesis, but by natural affinity with his text, and that the context historically studied will determine his treatment of his text.   Many preachers search high and low, near and far, for ingenious divisions of their text, for varied contents for their sermons, when in the text itself taken with its context there lies close to their hand an abundance of appropriate material.   It is only by such a method of preparing his sermon that the preacher will prove himself a true and a wise scribe, rightly dividing among men the treasures of truth and grace contained in the storehouse of the Scriptures.   It is by being thus a *scribe* in dependence on the Holy Scriptures, a *prophet* directed and instructed by the Spirit of God, and an *apostle* with a personal relation to Christ Himself and in Christ to the Christian community that the preacher can assure himself that he possesses the *truth* from God, which must be the motive, the content and the warrant of his preaching, the credentials which he may confidently offer to men.

CHAPTER II.

THE PREACHER AS SCHOLAR, SAGE, SEER, SAINT.

IN the previous chapter an attempt was made to indicate in what ways the Christian preacher might assure himself of the *truth* of his preaching, in this chapter we must try to describe the *personality* of the preacher through which that truth is to be presented. Before dealing with this subject it is necessary to relate it to the preceding. (1) It is a common and persistent error which seeks in Christian life and work to magnify God by depreciating man; and in regard to preaching, the form which the error takes is this: the truth from God is represented as alone important, and the personality of the preacher as insignificant. It is even argued that the more contemptible the preacher, the greater glory to God may redound from his preaching; and some men disguise their indolence as piety, and do nothing themselves, that God through them may do all. The writer can confidently say that he has never yet heard a sermon worth listening to from a man who substituted reliance on the Spirit for preparation. It is true that often the results of preaching are quite disproportionate to the resources of the preacher, that the Spirit of God exalts the humble and abases the proud. The preacher does not preach himself, but Christ, and he seeks to hide his own personality behind the truth. Nevertheless God does not despise and reject the gifts in human personality which He has Himself bestowed, and it is ingratitude to the Giver to depreciate His gifts. As the history of preaching has shown, the great preachers have been men richly endowed, fully equipped, and thoroughly trained for

their work.   And accordingly no preacher need shrink from
the effort of making himself as complete a personality,
mentally, morally and spiritually, as the use of human
powers in dependence on the grace of God will allow him
to become, lest he should appear to magnify man rather
than God.   In personal self-development only ignorance and conceit can assume human self-sufficiency, and
fail to recognise constant and complete dependence on God,
who gives the self to be developed, and all the conditions
of its development.   We do not show humility in refusing
to make of ourselves the very most and the very best that
we can in order that we may be as fit and worthy
instruments of God's will as can be.[1]

(2) The personality of the preacher is to be developed
as fully as possible mentally, spiritually and morally.   In
the mental development we may further distinguish two
aspects : there is the gathering of as much *knowledge* as
possible, there is also the forming of as true a *judgment*
on questions of belief and of duty as we can.   We can
thus distinguish the *scholar* and the *sage*, the man of
knowledge and the man of wisdom.   But for religion
more than a true judgment is wanted ; there must
be vision of the spiritual as the real ; and this is the
gift of the *seer*.   And the end of all is the character of
the *saint*.

I.

1. As a scribe, the Christian preacher must be a
scholar in all that relates to the Bible ; but he will not be
even that unless he is a good deal more.   Much nonsense
has been talked and written about knowing the Bible
rather than about the Bible, although the contrast is a
contradiction ; for a man cannot really know the Bible
until he has learned all he can from modern scholarship
about the Bible ; and who can imagine what knowledge
about the Bible without knowledge of the Bible can

[1] Much valuable help in mental discipline will be found in Adams' *The Student's Guide.*

possibly be? A pious man may be ignorant of scholarship, and a scholar may lack piety; but this contrast is not properly expressed in the above statement. A man cannot know all worth knowing about the Bible unless he is not a man of one book. Let him follow out thoroughly any enquiry that arises from the Bible, and he will be led into far wider fields of knowledge. It is necessary for the Christian preacher who is thoroughly equipped for his task to be a man of as wide a culture as possible. The world is God's world, and the knowledge of nature and man is a study of God's works and ways. There is a revelation of God which science, history and philosophy can interpret to us, and the wider revelation will not impoverish but enrich for wise understanding the less extended and more concentrated revelation of God through the Holy Scriptures. Not that we are to use this wider knowledge merely as a handmaid to fetch and carry for our theology; it has claims upon us for its own worth.

2. It is now quite impossible for a man to claim "all knowledge for his province," and for the preacher what is important is not so much the *extent* of his knowledge as the *quality* of it. If the words may carry this distinction, he need not be so much *learned* as *scholarly*. To avoid one-sidedness it is desirable that he should be familiar with different kinds of knowledge. It is probable that the training of ministers has hitherto been too exclusively literary and linguistic with a very slight addition of philosophy. (1) There are mental and moral sciences, such as psychology, ethics and sociology, with which for the efficient discharge of his duties the preacher must be acquainted, and to their consideration we must return. In addition to these, however, it does seem very desirable that he should have some acquaintance with at least one physical science, so that its methods of observation, experiment, hypothesis, generalisation, verification, etc., may become familiar to him. If a preference may be suggested, physics or biology would seem to be of most interest and

importance as raising some of the fundamental problems to which no theologian can be indifferent.[1]

(2) His biblical studies will have familiarised him with the ways of literary and historical criticism; but it is desirable that the general history of mankind in outline at least should be known to him, so that the history recorded in the Scriptures and the history of the Christian Church with which he is familiar, should be seen in their proper background. That a preacher should know his own age should need no mention. He cannot afford to pretend the superiority of not reading the newspapers; but he should try so to read that he will not only know the gossip of the hour, but be an intelligent and appreciative observer of the main currents of the world's life, in which as prophet he should be able to discern the activity of God.

(3) Without philosophy it seems to the present writer no man can be a thinker. Without depreciating the mental discipline which may be derived from the study of *formal logic*, it seems to him that a man will learn to think best as he tries to rethink the thoughts of the world's greatest thinkers. He will discover that the last questions to which the mind is driven are just the problems which religion seeks to solve. Where the philosophical task ends, there the theological begins.

(4) Whatever he knows, or does not know, religion he must know, not only in the familiar form of the faith he himself professes, but in the manifold forms in which the spirit of man has sought the reality above, beyond and through all. Here more than in any other sphere he will find that touch of nature which makes the whole world kin. In the beliefs, customs and rites of the savage he will find the same Godward movement of man as in his own experience has met with the manward movement of

---

[1] Although the writer may expose himself to the charge of personal bias, he feels constrained to express the conviction that the requirements for the Scottish M.A. under the old regulations afforded a better general discipline than do the more recent.

God in the revelation and redemption in Christ Jesus. Of the value of literature generally much will have to be said in a subsequent chapter.[1]

II.

1. Knowledge, however extensive and varied, which is merely stored in the memory, is only an external possession; it becomes an inward gain only as judgment is developed. The three spheres in which judgment is to be exercised are the intellectual, the moral and the religious; and we may distinguish two excellences of judgment as *prudence* and *wisdom*. In his judgment the preacher must aim as a *sage* to display both these excellences in these three spheres. (1) Science, history, philosophy, the study of religion will be constantly presenting to him conclusions which require the exercise of judgment. Knowledge does not always lead to judgment; there have been only too many "learned fools." In every department of knowledge, theories are advanced, with a great parade of learning in their support, which are conclusive on only one point, the lack of judgment of their authors. While on the one hand prejudice should never stand in the way of an impartial examination of any unfamiliar view, however much it may run counter to our deeply-rooted convictions; yet, on the other hand, all things must be proved that the good may always be held fast.[2] Theology has suffered much from *obscurantism*. Theories, now generally accepted among thinkers, were at first derided as folly. We must not forget the discredit Christian theology brought upon itself by its attitude to the doctrine of evolution, or to the

---

[1] Dr. Dale in his *Nine Lectures on Preaching* devotes two to the subject of reading. After dealing with the studies which belong more immediately to the theologian and the preacher, he advocates as a corrective to one-sidedness a much wider range of reading, including even books of "a merely ephemeral popularity," so as to keep the preacher in close touch with his hearers and what interests them, and to afford a needed relief from the severer strain of his ordinary studies. See pp. 100–102.

[2] 1 Th 5^{21}.

methods of the higher criticism, and must avoid the repetition of the same mistake. On the other hand, the guardians of Christian truth are justified in examining carefully the credentials of any new claimant to rule the minds of men. A rash acceptance of any and every new theory, and the ready abandonment of any and every old conviction, which seems inconsistent, are not proofs of candour and courage, but of foolhardiness. In the Christian pulpit in recent years there has often been an indecent haste in abandoning this or that verity of the Gospel on the demand of a review article, probably written by one not competent, even intellectually, still less morally and religiously, to deal with a serious and sacred subject. Better for the preacher not to be quite so up-to-date as the cinema theatre than that he in his folly should trouble the minds and grieve the hearts of God's people by retelling the latest theory on things human or divine.

(2) The *prudence* which weighs well the arguments for or against any new view, which tests the arguments by not merely theoretical, but also practical values and interests, prepares the way for the *wisdom* which, furnished with knowledge, but always controlled by truth, at last offers its judgment for or against the new claimant. To some extent such judgment is a natural gift, as there seem to be some " born fools " (of whom not a few stray into the ministry), whom no amount of painful discipline can make anything else; but few indeed are the men altogether lacking the gift in comparison with those who do not cultivate it. None should assume he lacks it until he has done his utmost to cultivate it. Let the preacher resolve that his " I think " will always wait on his " I know "; that he will learn all he can about a subject before he even begins to form a judgment upon it; that he will not express his judgment even when formed until it has stood the test of time, and he has found no adequate reason for reconsideration; that when he expresses his judgment it will be only with such outward assurance as his inward certainty allows; and that if his judgment is one that may

disturb the convictions of others, he will keep silence, unless necessity is laid upon him to speak. While all that the preacher utters must be the truth, and there is truth in other spheres of knowledge than that which concerns him which he need not speak, it is a foolish assumption of some preachers that they are honest only as they speak everything that they know or think, whether it does or does not relate to the purpose of preaching, the sustenance of the " eternal life " of their hearers. They desire to emulate Carlyle's Teufelsdroeck as Professors of Things-in-General; thus they mistake the church for a lecture-hall, and the pulpit for a platform; and while they are troubled—and their audiences still more—about many things, they often let slip the one thing needful, and fail to choose for themselves, and help their hearers to choose the better part.[1] In an age of so manifold intellectual activity the preacher needs the prudence and wisdom to limit himself in speech to those things which alone he is called to preach.

2. What he is concerned about is goodness and godliness, duty and faith. Here he must exercise his judgment in all prudence and wisdom. He is, and must be a *moralist*. (1) The complaint of the Evangelicals against the Moderates in Scotland that they preached morality, was justified only in so far as the morality they preached was not distinctively Christian morality, and did not assume the saving work of God's grace as the necessary condition of even its possibility. The culmination of the progressive revelation through the prophets was " ethical monotheism," God one and God holy; and in the Christian religion morality is included. Love to God and love to man are conjoined as the fulfilment of all law, and in Christian life holiness no less than blessedness in God is the gift offered to men. How much of the teaching of Jesus is moral! And in the teaching of the Apostles, doctrines are never divorced from duties, and duties towards men no less than towards God. While in the subsequent history of the Christian Church the essential unity of the religious good and the moral

[1] Lk 10⁴¹, ⁴².

duty was often disregarded, and a legalist morality was placed alongside of, rather than derived from a mystical or magical piety; yet that the Christian religion enjoins a morality distinctive of itself was never in theory or in practice altogether ignored. Luther's view of Christian perfection as consisting of faith in God and fulfilment of the earthly calling, sought to recover this essential unity. In modern Protestantism, however, it is not always recognised that Christian religion is the inexhaustible source of Christian morality, and that Christian morality is the irrepressible expression of Christian religion; that Christian faith by necessity of its nature energises in love,[1] and that love's demands can be met only by faith's resources. The difference between legal and evangelical ethics lies in the failure of the one and the success of the other in maintaining this essential unity of goodness and godliness, duty and faith. If Christian morality with its infinite aspiration says, *Jube quod vis*, it is only because Christian religion with its absolute dependence says, *Da quod jubes*. This discussion is not an irrelevance, as the beginning of wisdom for the Christian moralist is the constant recognition of this organic relation of morality and religion; and he will never teach Christian morals wisely unless as " the fruits of the Spirit of God," [2] as the work of the grace of Christ in the soul of man. He will measure the Christian demand by human capacity, unless he always remembers that the Christian commands divine resources.

(2) The Christian preacher as moralist must meet a double challenge, theoretical and practical. With few exceptions moralists, whether Christian or not, until recent years, recognised the value of the moral teaching of Jesus, but now that value is challenged frankly and boldly. Into this controversy it is not necessary to enter in detail.[3] One duty it has imposed on the Christian moralist, which he has often ignored. If he is to vindicate the permanent and universal authority of the ethics of Jesus, he must

---

[1] Gal 5[6].   [2] Gal 5[22].
[3] See the writer's *Can we still follow Jesus?*

learn to distinguish the kernel from the husk. Even if we deny the position of the advocates of the exclusively eschatological character of the teaching of Jesus,[1] that His moral teaching is only an *interim ethic*, we must admit that to be effective for the time and place the form had to be adapted to local and temporary conditions. One service Tolstoy has rendered to Christian thought, in that he has shown how impractical would be a literalist interpretation of that teaching. But it is easier to make than to meet this demand to separate the kernel from the husk. While knowledge of the local and temporary conditions will greatly aid, and without that knowledge the task would be impossible, yet knowledge will not carry us all the way: to knowledge must be added judgment. With learning we must conjoin wisdom. To determine what is temporary and what permanent, what local and what universal in the morals of Jesus, requires a moral insight, and one might even say tact, which is no less real because it is indefinable. Here no rigid rules can be laid down for guidance; the guidance must come from within, from a conscience enlightened and quickened by the Spirit of God. A natural gift, too, we may here recognise possessed by some in greater measure than by others; but it is a gift that can be cultivated, and, when the conditions of development are fulfilled, imparted by God. "If any of you lack wisdom, let him ask of God, and it shall be given him."[2] But God's gifts do not fall into folded hands; and the man who has studied general ethics will have given the natural gift that cultivation which can be crowned by the supernatural grace. Such a question as that discussed by general ethics, whether the moral end is a *law* or a *good*, is one the answer to which will be of great value to the Christian moralist.

(3) The Christian moralist's task, however, is only half done when he has separated the kernel from the husk in the teaching of Jesus; he has now to give to the permanent and universal principles he has thus discovered a temporary

---

[1] See Schweitzer's *The Quest of the Historical Jesus*.   [2] Jas 1[5].

and local application, if they are to be at all useful for
present moral guidance. To do this he must know the
economic and social conditions of his own time. The
industrial revolution of last century has so altered economic
conditions, that what is comprehensively called the Social
Problem has emerged. The moral standards of the
previous stage of economic and consequent social development have proved inadequate to give the necessary
direction; and the insistent demand to-day is for a
morality which shall be adequate to the new conditions.
This is a demand which the Christian Church should
welcome, and not fear, if it is warranted in its confidence
that in the teaching of Christ it has no *interim ethic*, but
an ethic which can be made applicable always and everywhere.[1]

(4) If the discovery of the principles of Christian
morality requires wisdom, the application of these principles,
etc., to the details of conduct demands prudence, and
involves a knowledge of the conditions under which the
Christian ideal is to be realised. These conditions are the
subject of study in the sciences of economics and sociology.
It would be unreasonable to expect the preacher to be an

[1] The following may be commended for this study :

1. *General Ethics.*—J. S. Mill's *Utilitarianism* ; H. Sidgwick's *History
of Ethics and Method of Ethics* ; H. Spencer's *Data of Ethics* ; T. H.
Green's *Prolegomena to Ethics* ; Leslie Stephen's *Science of Ethics* ; J.
Martineau's *Types of Ethical Theory* ; S. Alexander's *Moral Order and
Progress* ; J. S. Mackenzie's *Manual of Ethics* ; J. H. Muirhead's *Elements
of Ethics* ; J. Seth's *Study of Ethical Principles* ; W. R. Sorley's *Ethics of
Naturalism* and *The Moral Life* ; W. Rashdall's *The Theory of Good and
Evil* and *Christ and Conscience.*

2. *Christian Ethics.*—Martensen's *Christian Ethics* ; Newman Smyth's
Christian Ethics ; Haering's *Ethics of the Christian Life* ; Dobschütz'
Christian Life in the Primitive Church ; Murray's *Handbook of Christian
Ethics* ; Strong's *Christian Ethics* ; Illingworth's *Christian Character.*

3. *Modern Social Ethics.*—*Christ and Civilization* ; Muir's *Christianity
and Labour* ; Bruce's *Social Aspects of Christian Morality* ; Peabody's *Jesus
Christ and the Social Question, The Approach to the Social Question* and
Christian Life in the Modern World ; Shailer Matthew's *Social Teaching of
Jesus* ; Rauschenbush's *Christianizing the Social Order.* There are numerous
series of books dealing with particular problems of modern society, but the
above are general discussions.

expert in these sciences; and it would be folly for him without expert knowledge to dogmatise in the pulpit on these subjects. But a preacher may be expected, in view of the present urgency of the Social Problem, to have a general knowledge of these sciences, and a detailed knowledge of the special conditions, industrial and social, under which his hearers may be expected to put into practice the principles which he teaches from the pulpit. There are complex problems with which only one with special knowledge could safely deal; but what Christian love demands in the world to-day is not so very difficult to discover, that on account of the lack of expert knowledge the pulpit can be condemned to silence on the vital issues of the hour. Adequate knowledge and the sound judgment, which a training in ethics and sociology may be helpful in securing, are the requirements for the preacher, if as the sage with both prudence and wisdom he is to meet the challenge of the age for guidance from Christian ethics.

3. A Christian congregation needs guidance as regards faith as well as duty; and so the preacher must be *theologian* as well as *moralist*. If there has been disturbance of moral standards, there has been no loss of religious beliefs. As the new industrial situation has presented a challenge in morals, so the new intellectual position in beliefs. (1) When the provinces of science and theology are correctly defined, there need not be conflict between the conclusions of the one and the convictions of the other; we now recognise that the attempts to reconcile geology and Genesis, Darwin and Moses, in regard to nature and man were vain futilities, as here there lies no good ground for quarrel. The danger from science is rather when, going beyond its province, it essays a task for which its methods do not secure it the competence, and attempts to answer the ultimate questions of reality in contradiction of the answer given by religious or Christian faith. So successful, too, have been the methods of science in its own sphere, that there is the peril of the attempt being made to apply the same methods in the sphere of the supersensible

and the supernatural where they do not apply.   Of the disturbance of faith due to the conclusions of the literary and historical criticism of the Bible enough has already been said in the previous chapter.   Philosophy may legitimately claim to answer these last questions, and may offer answers which conflict with faith's assurances.[1]   When such a conflict ensues, the Christian thinker must *first of all* make sure that what is opposed is an assurance of faith, and not an opinion of his own, which has no claim to be regarded as necessary for faith.   In the *next place* he must examine the conclusion of philosophy to discover if all the data, moral and religious as well as intellectual, have been taken into account, and have had full justice done to them ; and he will often find that the philosophy has been too exclusively intellectual, and has not recognised the practical interests of men in religion and morals.   Even if theoretically the philosophy should seem to make out its case, he may fall back on his own experience of God as saving grace in Christ, confirmed by the common experience of the Christian Church, and find there a firm foundation, when all opinions seem to be shaken.

(2) In defending and commending the Christian Gospel thus challenged, the preacher needs knowledge ;[2] but here, too, he still more wants judgment.   And the judgment which in the religious as in the moral sphere he is called to exercise is not a merely intellectual activity ; it is conditioned, and legitimately conditioned, by his personal hopes

---

[1] See the writer's *The Ritschlian Theology*, chap. iii.

[2] It is manifestly impossible to attempt here to give a list of theological books, for so varied and numerous are they.   But attention may be called to the other volumes in the series in which this volume appears.   Another series also deserves mention, *The Studies in Theology*, published by Duckworth & Co.   In this series the bibliography with which each volume is furnished affords a useful guide to the relevant literature.   Messrs. Williams & Norgate in their *Theological Translation Library* and in their *Crown Theological Library* have placed many foreign books within the reach of English readers.   The use of Hastings' *Bible Dictionary* and *Encylopœdia of Religion and Ethics* offers an almost boundless range of inquiry to the preacher.   The writer may venture to mention his own book, *The Christian Certainty amid the Modern Perplexity*, as treating very much more fully what it has been necessary to handle here in a very cursory way.

and fears, needs and aspirations; by his hunger for righteousness and his thirst for God. His moral conscience and his religious consciousness as well as his speculative intellect must be brought into play in this judgment; for neither can goodness be appreciated, nor God apprehended by a purely intellectual process; and grace can be received only in actual experience, in which the whole man is involved. That the preacher should have as wide a knowledge of theology, and its wider intellectual context in science, criticism and philosophy, is most desirable; but what is essential is that he should cultivate spiritual discernment—that he should have a keen sense of both moral and religious realities. The two are not always proportionate to one another. A man of wide knowledge even in all that pertains to theology may be singularly lacking in the wisdom which discerns what is true and worthy; and there have been humble Christian believers who had a very quick and keen sense for the things that really matter for the soul of man. If a preacher lacks this wisdom he will select themes, and so treat them that there will be little spiritual profit to his hearers, however brilliant intellectually his preaching may be. If he has this wisdom, he will not be concerned about the impression of his own ability that he may make; he will not choose the subjects of ephemeral interest and superficial value, but he will always be handling these certainties for faith which bring the soul into closest contact with and under the most effective control of the eternal divine realities of God, which enlighten, cleanse and renew the soul, and bring to the need of man the abounding resources of God. It is thus that he can prove himself a sage dowered both with earthly prudence and heavenly wisdom.

III.

1. The Christian preacher must be more than a sage, however, he must be a *seer* as well. The sage judges in morals and religion what is given to him in the divine

revelation, and the thoughts of men regarding that revelation : the *seer*, while dependent on that revelation, seeks to realise for himself in the soul's vision the reality so revealed.   We need not claim with some of the mystics a special organ for the knowledge of God apart from and above reason and conscience ; and yet there is a difference between the man who knows God as it were by report, and the man who has the perception of the reality of God.   Must we not admit that for many Christians the reality of God is a matter of evidence and inference, and not of experience ?   If the word imagination did not suggest fiction rather than fact, we might speak of the spiritual imagination for which God, Christ, the Spirit, truth, grace, holiness, glory, blessedness are not abstractions but realities, even as things seen and handled.   There is a faith which so realises the unseen that it becomes certain as is the seen.[1]   It is only to degrade this vision of the soul when hallucinations of sense are regarded as confirming its certainty, although it can find expression in figurative language as it cannot in abstract terms.   It is the danger of the moralist and the theologian that he thinks and speaks in abstractions, and so may convey to those to whom he speaks a sense of the unreality rather than of the reality of those subjects about which he is speaking.   Men do often feel that the preacher is offering them the stones of doctrines about God instead of the bread of the reality of God.   And yet he who thinks much about God need not on that account lose his inward sight of God.   Paul combined in a remarkable degree the capacity of the sage and of the seer.   The living Christ, whom his bodily eye had not beheld in the days of his flesh, is more real to him than to any of the Evangelists, except the Fourth.   It may be frankly admitted that here we are concerned with an endowment which all believers do not equally share, and that some could not by any amount of cultivation gain.   Some genuine Christians live by testimony rather than experience ; and we must

[1] He 11[1].

not depreciate them if their lives show the fruits of the Spirit of God: and yet for the preacher it is surely essential that he should have this power of realising God, and all that belongs to the life in God, and that he should be able to make his sense of the reality of God as it were contagious, so that even if his hearers do not share his vision, yet they will share the certainty which the vision gives to him. If he cannot get beyond the attitude in the prologue to Tennyson's " In Memoriam ":

> "We have but faith : we cannot know;
> For knowledge is of things we see,"

he will lack an essential condition of the highest kind of power in preaching. He must be able to say, " I know, because in inward vision I see God, real as the things of sense are."

2. The writer must confess that he has never been attracted much by the literature of mysticism;[1] for it seems to him to seek the right end by the wrong means. (1) The end of all religion is the direct contact, the intimate communion of the soul with God, such an experience of God that in intensity of feeling and certainty of thought it can compare even with sensible experience. In the measure in which a man has such a vision of God, can he testify to men the reality of God. But just as the perceptions of sense on analysis by psychology show a very complex process of mediation between the mind and the world, even so this experience of God is not immediate and altogether incapable of analysis. After the analysis is carried as far as it can be in either case, there remains an indescribable remainder. In both cases, too, there may be the sense of immediate knowledge without any consciousness of the process of mediation. Another analogy may make the matter still

---

[1] Among recent books may be mentioned Baron von Hügel's *The Mystical Element of Religion* ; Inge, *Christian Mysticism* ; Rufus M. Jones, *Studies in Mystical Religion* ; Underhill, *The Mystic Way* ; Herman, *The Meaning and Value of Mysticism.*

clearer. In the communion of living souls there is a sense of immediacy, and yet the content of their communion with one another, which gives it its value, does not consist only of the words of the moment, and the thoughts the words express, or the feelings they awaken, but includes, unanalysed, yet capable of analysis by reflection, the common life of the former years. In the same way surely the soul's communion with God not only includes the momentary experience, but has its distinctive quality determined by the whole past experience of His truth and grace.

(2) If this psychological analysis is correct, then it follows that God is not more directly known by a withdrawal into the subjectivity of the experient, but rather by an apprehension of all that is included in the objectivity of the experienced. Not by suppression of the human personality in its manifold activities, nor by absorption in the mood of the moment can the steady and clear vision of God be maintained; but surely by living life as fully as possible *sub specie divinitatis*. Nature, history, man, can all be media of this direct contact with God. To assume otherwise involves a false dualism of God and the world He has made, and in which He dwells. The mysticism which flees from the without to the within to find God, and seeks God in the within, not in the normal psychical activities, but in ecstasy, or some abnormal state, is the practical application of a doctrine of divine transcendence, which so separates God from nature and man, that He cannot be found in them. A doctrine of divine immanence should have as its practical application a seeking and a finding of God as the reality in all and through all and over all. The writer has learned more from Spinoza than from any of the mystical writers about the practice of the presence of God; and even Hegel seems to him nearer the truth as regards the vision of God than a neo-Platonic mysticism. For Christian religion especially is the reality of God mediated historically by Jesus Christ, and by that mediation not less directly or certainly known, but even possessed more fully and surely.

3. The writer must further confess that he cannot for himself follow a great deal of the advice which is given regarding the cultivation of the devout life. He even questions whether the devout life is to be isolated, and cultivated by itself and for itself. Such a practice promotes an artificial pietism rather than a natural piety. He believes rather that the whole personality in its manifold activities should be developed with Christ Godwards. He believes that there can be unceasing prayer in all interests and pursuits by maintaining the spirit of dependence on, and submission to God. He cannot distinguish a devotional study of the Bible which is not also scholarly, from a scholarly which is not also devotional. Arduous theological thought is for him also pious meditation; and the solution of problems of thought is the discovery of God Himself. That the preacher must pray much and meditate much, and hold as constant and intimate communion with God in Christ as is possible to him in order to become a seer, one to whom God is reality more certain than any of the things of sense, none would affirm more strongly than would he; but he will not venture to offer any precise rules as to how this fellowship with God is to be maintained. Of one thing he is convinced, however, that the more completely the whole of life is suffused with the light and heat of the realised presence of God, and the less devotion is kept in a place apart, the broader and stronger will the piety be. A few sentences of a master preacher may be added: "It may scarcely be needful," says Spurgeon, "to commend to you the sweet uses of private devotion, and yet I cannot forbear. To you, as the ambassadors of God, the mercy-seat bears a virtue beyond all estimate; the more familiar you are with the court of heaven the better shall you discharge your heavenly trust. Among all the formative influences which go to make up a man honoured of God in His ministry, I know of none more mighty than his own familiarity with the mercy-seat. All that a college career can do for a student is coarse and external compared with

the spiritual and delicate refinement obtained by communion with God.   While the unformed minister is
revolving upon the wheel of preparation, prayer is the
tool of the great potter by which he moulds the vessel.
All our libraries and studies are mere emptiness compared
with our closets.   We grow, we wax mighty, we prevail
in *private* prayer." [1]

IV.

1. The proof of the life hid with Christ in God is the
light that so shines before men, that they may see the
good works, and glorify the Father which is in heaven.[2]
If only the pure in heart can see God, the *saint* alone can
be the *seer*; he who beholds the glory of the Lord will be
changed into the same likeness from glory to glory,[3] the
seer will become the *saint*.   Christian experience and
Christian character are mutually dependent; they must be
developed together.   If the preacher must be one who sees
God, he must also be pure in heart.   Modern Christendom
is afraid of the word *saint*, and regards saintship as the
privilege of a select few, and not the obligation of all.
We must first of all understand that when the New Testament speaks of saints it does not mean the sinless and
perfect; the term describes the ideal and not the actuality
of believers, the destiny to which they are called in Christ
Jesus.   Such an ideal, however, imposes the constant effort
to realise it.   There must be no base content with faults
and failures: there must be eager aspiration to become all
that by the grace of Christ is attainable.   The abandonment of the pursuit of holiness, and the acquiescence in a
condition of only moral respectability is a common defect

---

[1] *Lectures to my Students—First Series*, p. 41.   A few books on the
subject of prayer may be mentioned: Carey's *Some Difficulties of Prayer*;
H. G. Moule's *Secret Prayer: The Fellowship of Silence*, ed. C. Hepher;
Poulain's *Graces of Interior Prayer*; E. Benson's *Communings of a Day*;
Mme. Guyon's *A Short and Easy Method of Prayer*; William Law's *The
Spirit of Prayer*; St. Theresa's *The Way of Perfection*; Bro. Lawrence's
The Practice of the Presence of God.

[2] Mt 5[16].   [3] Mt 5[8], 2 Co 3[18].

in Christians which brings discredit on the moral sufficiency of the grace of God in Christ Jesus; for to attempt little is to distrust much; to rest in sin is to disbelieve in grace.

2. If the preacher is to preach holiness, he must himself desire holiness, and must impress his hearers as one who is seeking after holiness. Not only does a reputation inconsistent with the sacred functions of the preacher rob his message of its life and power, but a man's character will, in spite of himself, affect the tone and content of his preaching. A consummate hypocrite may possibly give the impression of a holiness which he does not possess. Some years ago a man who had been forced to leave one pastorate after another in England on account of his bad character went to America, and for a time conducted what at least appeared to be successful meetings for the deepening of the spiritual life.[1] Religious emotionalism is not infrequently accompanied by moral weakness. While it would be rash to say that the effect of any man's preaching corresponds exactly in quality and degree with his personal character, since the Spirit of God is not limited by His human agent; yet, allowing for such exceptions as have been mentioned, we may say that the worth of a man's preaching will be measured not only by his reputation among men, but even by his character, which in countless ways affects the passion and power, the temper and tone of his preaching. Not only when preaching morals will a man betray his own moral level, but even in presenting the grace which saves from sin he will show the fineness or coarseness of his conscience by the way in which he deals with sin, by the kinds of sin which he denounces, by his emphasis on sin itself, or on the consequences of sin. Any hearer of keen moral sensibility is a judge of the preacher's moral quality, whether lofty or low, and the impression left will vary, even when there is no conscious judgment. Thus moral respectability is not enough; there must be moral truth in the inward parts for full moral

[1] Of a preacher who was indeed a brand plucked from the burning, a hearer said that he had always the smell of the fire upon him.

effect in preaching. There is a kind of "revival" preaching in which emotional effect is the object aimed at, and for which little moral demand may be made on the preacher; one hears of successful evangelists of dubious reputation, and even of the employment of these evangelists because of their success where that reputation is known. But this is a scandal which weakens the moral influence of the Christian Church. But apart altogether from the impression of the preacher's character on his hearers, any man worthy to fulfil this calling will demand of himself that though he may often fall far short of his ideal, he should honestly, earnestly and constantly endeavour to realise it, and hold no success as a preacher compensation for his own failure as a Christian man.

3. It is not necessary here to deal with the Christian character as a whole, but there are sins which do most easily beset the preacher which may be mentioned as serious hindrances to saintship, and they are mentioned just because they are far from uncommon among preachers. (1) The calling itself brings with it a secret and subtle peril to the preacher in the desire for the praise or the dread of the blame of men. Human applause may mean more than divine approval. Popularity may appear to him his heaven, and obscurity his hell.[1] A false estimate of the value of preaching prevails. Does the preacher draw? Does he please? Do his hearers praise? These are the questions asked; and not such as these: Did he utter the truth fully and fearlessly? Did he offer the grace of God tenderly and earnestly? Did he call men to repentance, faith, holiness effectively? Even if the preacher escapes the degradation of trimming his sails to catch the breeze of popularity; even if the content and purpose of his sermons remain right, yet he may very easily in preaching think rather of the ability he is displaying, and the reputation he is acquiring, than of the glory of God and the gain of man.

(2) When a man falls before the temptation of seeking

[1] See Chrysostom's warning, quoted at pp. 64–65.

and prizing popularity, another fault often appears. He gives himself "airs"; he looks down on men, it may be really abler and worthier than himself, who are not as popular as he is; he is not among his brethren as the least of all, but makes it plain that he regards himself, and expects to be regarded, as the greatest of all. The people who throng to hear the popular preacher and offer him lavishly the incense of praise, and the Press (the so-called "religious") which "booms" him are responsible for the moral deterioration of some whom they sought to make idols, but have made victims. While the preacher may legitimately aim at attracting, interesting and impressing his hearers, it must ever be for the sake of the Gospel he preaches that it may have free course and be glorified, and never for his own sake that he may be praised and idolised. The man who, despising popularity, is careless of the effect of his preaching, is not proving his superiority to the man who seeks popularity, because he is also an unfaithful servant, as he, too, is thinking more of himself than of his Gospel. The escape from this danger is on the one hand to magnify the truth and grace of God preached, and on the other to regard the preacher as not in himself sufficient or worthy for so high a calling. Devotion to Christ, which humbles in penitence and exalts only in pardon, will save the preacher from self-devotion.

(3) But popularity as a preacher brings other worldly gains besides the praise of men. It is much to be regretted that no better method of offering some recognition of the service rendered by a preacher than the paying of a fee has been devised, and still more to be regretted that the amount of the fee is often proportionate to the popularity which the preacher possesses, or at least is supposed or supposes himself to possess. One has heard even of preachers who themselves fix the fees they expect in payment for their eloquence in the service of the Gospel. One would fain believe that it is rarely that a preacher so degrades his calling as to treat it as a means of worldly gain. That preachers need to be supported, that they should be freed

from money anxieties may be conceded.   But a preacher is a profane person like Esau [1] who cares at all for the fees, and not altogether for the sacred task of preaching.

(4) A fourth peril of the preacher is that out of the pulpit he may not in his conversation and manner adorn the doctrine he preaches.   Humour is legitimate in and out of the pulpit, but there is sometimes displayed by the preacher either a flippancy or a coarseness which is a glaring contrast to the message with which he is entrusted. An artificial manner and an unnatural solemnity are not at all necessary or desirable, but a man should never so speak or behave out of the pulpit as would make it impossible for his companions to listen to his preaching with respect. He must not undermine his own authority as God's messenger.   An ungracious manner also is an offence in the preacher of the grace of God.   One hears of preachers to whom the distance of the pew from the pulpit lends enchantment, and whose spell fails on closer acquaintance. A hot temper or an overbearing manner bars the way to the entrance of the message, however eloquently delivered. The preacher in the pulpit and the man out of it should always present a harmonious unity.   The last fault which need now be mentioned is the very opposite of any of these. The preacher may invest himself with an exaggerated dignity in the pulpit where even it is ridiculous, and then he may retain his pulpit manner out of it, and so make himself still more ridiculous.   The consecrated natural human personality is best both for the pulpit and out of it.[2]

[1] He 12¹⁶.

[2] On this subject very helpful counsel can be found in Dr. Oswald Dykes' *The Christian Minister and his Duties*, pp. 55-56.   As regards ministerial manners he quotes a Frenchman, Vinet, and a German, Schweizer.   "Il faut," says Vinet, "sinon qu'on le reconnaisse pasteur, du moins qu'on ne s'étonne pas d'apprendre qu'il est pasteur."   (Even if one does not recognise him as a minister, at least one ought not to be surprised on learning that he is a minister.)   "Man nimmt das Amt," says Schweizer, "nich überall hin mit sich sondern nur das Bewusstsein in anderen Stunden vor denen, mit welchen man jetzt gesellig frei umgeht, amtlich aufzutreten."   (One does not take the office about with one everywhere, but only the consciousness of appearing at other times in that office before those with whom one now has

4. These may seem so trivial matters as scarcely to
be worth mentioning; but the holy place of a man's
character, and the holy of holies of his life in God can be
approached by others only through the outer court of his
ordinary manner and behaviour. It is true that some
preachers have avoided these occasions of offence by
isolating themselves from their fellow-men; but the writer
ventures to think that whatever may be allowable for the
genius, for the ordinary man who wants to be as good a
preacher as he can, familiar intercourse and intimate
communion with his fellow-men is a necessary condition
of his own fullest personal development. We must rid
ourselves of the Roman Catholic idea of the saint, and
must assert the Protestant position that it is in the
common life of men that saintliness is both won and
shown. To walk with Jesus among men in close
companionship with them, and to show them what He
is through likeness to Him—that is the way of saintship.
To love men, and in love to sympathise with them, and
serve them—that is the way the Master went, and
that is the way the servant should still tread. To be
with Jesus and so like Jesus—this is the Christian
experience and character, which may claim to be fulfilling
the ideal of saintship. Scholar, sage, seer, saint—this
must the personality be becoming through which the
truth is preached.[1]

free social intercourse.) (Quoted pp. 61–62.) The second lecture in Dr.
Jowett's *The Preacher: His Life and Work*, deals with the perils of the
preacher, religious as well as moral (pp. 37–69).

[1] Although the Protestant ideal of saintliness differs from the Roman
Catholic, yet the classic books of devotion, whether Protestant or Roman
Catholic, still claim devout study, e.g. *Augustine's Confessions*, the *Imitatio
Christi*, the *Theologia Germanica*, Pascal's *Thoughts*, Law's *Serious Call*,
Taylor's *Holy Living*, Baxter's *Saints' Rest*, Rutherford's *Letters*, Bunyan's
Grace Abounding. The writer ventures to add his own deep conviction
that there is a genuinely Christian asceticism, which the ministry in the
Protestant Churches would gain much by adopting. There are few ministers
who now use intoxicating liquors; but is not smoking often indulged in far
beyond the bounds of Christian temperance? Does not golf or some other
amusement claim more time than health really demands? Without asserting a double morality, one for clergy and one for laity, we may ask:

should not the man who preaches the Christian ideal of self-denial and self-sacrifice, feel under a sacred obligation to be in all his works and ways a conspicuous example of what he preaches, especially as his vocation places him in circumstances in which detachment from the world is more practicable for him than it is for most of his flock following their earthly calling? There need be no morbidness or artificiality, but freeness and fulness of life in taking up the Cross and following Christ, whose meat it was to do the Father's will (Jn 4³⁴), and who was straitened till His Baptism of self-surrender in death was accomplished.   (Lk 12⁵⁰.)

CHAPTER III.

THE PREACHER AS PRIEST, TEACHER, PASTOR AND EVANGELIST.

WE have considered the truth which is to be preached, and the personality through which it is to be preached; the end of preaching is the eternal life of the hearers, and we must now ask ourselves in what ways does the preacher through his personality so convey the truth to his hearers that the eternal life will begin and grow in them. In so far as the truth he preaches is the common good of his hearers already, and he as their representative confesses, and in confessing confirms the truth, religious and moral, which he and they together hold, he may be called their *priest*, and his sermon is an act of common worship. In so far, however, as they do not know the truth, or know it so imperfectly that they still need to learn from him what he knows as they do not, he is their *teacher*, and his sermon is his instruction of them. But the hearers in any congregation vary in experience, character, stage of moral and religious development, and thus the common truth needs to be individually applied so as to meet the case of each; in this individual care the preacher is *pastor*, and the sermon is one of the means to be employed in "the cure of souls." Within the Christian Church and still more beyond its borders are those who have not begun the eternal life; and the preacher must aim at their conversion from sin to God by presenting to them the Gospel of grace; he must be the *evangelist*; and his sermon by the Spirit's operation must seek to be regenerative.

316

I.

1. A contrast is often made between Worship and the Sermon in order to exalt the one and depreciate the other; and it is therefore necessary to deal first of all with the function of the preacher as the leader of the worship of the congregation. If we may use the term *prophet* to describe the preacher as he speaks for God to men, we may also use the term *priest* to describe him when he speaks to God for men. No sacerdotal pretensions of exclusive meditation between God and man are made in either case; but it is quite consistent with the Evangelical Protestant principles, while recognising the High priesthood of Christ and the priesthood of all believers, to lay stress on the mediation of the minister both in the name of God and on the behalf of men. But when we speak of the *priesthood* of the preacher we do not think merely of his conduct of the prayer and the praise of the congregation, for the preaching is also a priestly act: it is no less a part of the worship of the congregation. This is a view of it which is generally neglected and yet a view which is of the utmost importance, if the sermon is to be rightly conceived and worthily esteemed. The preacher not only speaks *to* the people but *for* the people; the sermon is no less a collective act through the representative of the community than are the prayer and the praise; and as the congregation participates in the one, it should no less in the other. Not only theory but practice is involved in this view of preaching.

2. The sermon has two aspects; it is a declaration either of divine truth and grace, or of human duty. It is in the first aspect not merely doctrine, but doctrine presented with gratitude and adoration; it is in the second aspect not merely precept, but precept expressive of aspiration and obedience. Its Christian character is preserved only if it is not merely a statement of opinion about belief or life, but if it is quickened by emotion, and strengthened by purpose. As communication of divine

truth and grace it involves in the speaker and hearers alike praise, as apprehension of human duty, prayer. Who can preach or hear what God is and does without blessing the Lord? Who can bid or be bidden to be holy without seeking the Spirit of the Lord? Thus the sermon does not lie outside of the worship; but it is worship of God so to declare His goodness as to be filled with praise, and so to aspire to goodness, as to be fervent in prayer for the sufficiency of His grace! If the sermon is not worshipful, and is in contrast with, and not a completion of the worship of prayer and praise, it has failed to be what Christian preaching ought to be. Man's insufficiency without God, and man's sufficiency in God—should be the dominant note in all preaching whether regarding faith or duty; and that note is not and cannot be anything else than the praise of God's grace, and the prayer of man's faith. Not only would the services of the Church by the constant recognition of this ideal by preacher and hearer alike gain harmonious unity; but the sermon especially would gain in devout and worshipful character.[1]

3. As regards the preacher, this view of the sermon would correct the excessive subjectivity from which the pulpit so often suffers. The pulpit is not the preacher's confessional nor his platform. It is not his own opinions and counsels which he is offering to men. The pulpit belongs to the Church; here is to be heard the voice of the Christian community. The preacher is the representative of the faith the Church holds, and the life that it would attain. Accordingly the preacher is not primarily teacher or master, telling the congregation what he believes and wants them to believe, how he thinks of their duty, and wishes them to do it. This lording it over God's heritage[2] is only too common an offence in the pulpit. The correction of it is the constant recognition that preacher and hearers alike possess a common gift from

---

[1] On this subject see Forsyth's *Positive Preaching*, pp. 97-99.
[2] 1 P 5³.

God in the revelation and redemption in Christ Jesus, and
that that gift, whether conceived religiously as what God
has done or morally as what man may become, is ever
jointly in gratitude and aspiration to be presented as a
living sacrifice on the altar of the worship of God.   It is
something much larger and more abiding than the
preacher's own changing opinions, or his varying moods;
and what he must beware of is merely preaching himself,
his Christian experience and Christian character, instead
of preaching the truth and grace God has given, and the
duty and destiny to which God calls the Church of Christ.
The preacher's individual peculiarities and personal preferences are out of place in this objective testimony of the
whole Church of Christ.   "We" and not "I" is the
proper pronoun for the pulpit.

4. This seems to be the most appropriate connection
in which to deal with the conduct of worship by the
preacher.   However much he may strive for objectivity
in his sermon, as preaching is truth through personality,
he will not altogether escape subjectivity.   His sermon
would lack both sincerity and intensity did he not throw
himself into it.   But this inevitable subjectivity of the
sermon should be corrected by the objectivity of the
worship.   Some preachers have held that the sermon
should dominate the worship, that the hymns and lessons
should be appropriate to the subject of the sermon, and
that in this way a unity of impression should be produced.
That there should be unity may be admitted; but what
should be aimed at is a comprehensive and not an exclusive
unity, a harmony and not a monotony.   It seems desirable
that the hymn before the sermon should prepare the minds
and hearts of the congregation for it, and the hymn after
the sermon should in song continue and complete the
impression it has made.   It is often necessary to choose
one of the lessons at least with a view to presenting to the
attention and interest of the hearers either the passage
from which the text is taken, or a passage which illuminates
the theme; this practice keeps the work of the preacher

in due subordination to the Holy Scriptures. There are occasions when it is desirable that both lessons should be so selected, in order that the agreement or the difference of the Old and the New Testament on the truth may be clearly presented. But with these qualifications the principle may rather be affirmed, that the sermon should not dominate the worship; but that in prayer and praise and reading of the Scripture any narrowness or one-sidedness of the sermon either in thought or feeling may be corrected.[1] A congregation meets in many varied moods with many different needs, and the common worship should not express only the preacher's mood, and satisfy only his needs. A preacher is of a melancholy temperament, or he has passed through some painful experiences; and he so indulges his own feelings that the shadow of his gloom of spirit falls over the whole of the service he is conducting. This is altogether wrong, for joyousness and hopefulness, courage and confidence—these are the characteristically Christian moods; and these should for the most part mark public worship. Even the sad and the suffering will be more helped by a service which is cheerful than by one that is gloomy. It is true that they must feel that the cheerfulness is not thoughtless, nor regardless of the grief there is in the world, and in their own hearts. The worship as well as the sermon must convey the assurance of the sympathy and succour of God for the distressed; but it is indecent for the preacher in his sermon, even still more in his conduct of the worship, to force his private sorrows on public notice. The leader of worship must think representatively, must feel vicariously, must act collectively, so that the service may be not his own individual devotion, but the sacrifice of praise and prayer of the whole Christian community.

5. The previous discussion forces on our attention a

[1] Dr. Dale has expressed his opinion very distinctly on the choice of hymns to the same effect. He even goes farther than the writer does, and advises contrast as well as agreement in thought and feeling between hymn and sermon, so as to avoid wearisome monotony. See his *Nine Lectures on Preaching*, pp. 277–279.

question which can scarcely be passed over altogether. At first sight it would appear as if a liturgy would best meet the demand for objectivity in the conduct of worship; by the use of a liturgy the congregation is saved from the subjectivity of the preacher. A liturgy maintains the collective and the continuous consciousness of the Christian Church; there is impressiveness in the use of the same words in worship by many separate congregations and successive generations of worshippers. But repetition tends to produce formality, and to repress the spontaneity of the devout feelings; and, just as the language of a creed gets antiquated, so will the language of a liturgy. Who can maintain that the Church of England litany always does express the religious thought and feeling of Christians to-day? Are there not many expressions in it which suggest a view of man's relation to God which we have outgrown? A liturgy would need constant adaptation, local, temporal and even occasional, to make it a true and fit expression of the devotion of a Christian community. While fully recognising the dangers, the writer's own preference is for free prayer, but free prayer which seeks to correct the errors which may result from it by *first of all* being as widely objective as can be, so as to express as completely as possible the worship of the whole congregation; and *secondly*, by using not the speech of the street of to-day, but the language, in so far as it has not become antiquated, in which believers and saints in many generations have addressed themselves to God.[1]

[1] The opinion on this subject of Dr. Dale is worth quoting.

"Before you have been very long in the ministry I think it very likely that your public prayers will occasion you great perplexity and humiliation. Your courage will, perhaps, fail altogether, and you will begin to ask whether your people would tolerate a liturgy. There is hardly a thoughtful minister of my own age, among my personal friends, who has not at times looked wistfully in that direction. Happily the traditions and instincts of our congregations have saved us from the mistake into which our weakness might have betrayed us. Reflection and experience have convinced me that it would be hardly possible to inflict a worse injury on the life and power of our Churches than to permit free, extemporaneous prayer to be excluded from our services, or even to be relegated to an inferior position. We

6. To return from this justified, because necessary, digression, we may now consider how the view of the sermon as an act of common worship affects the hearers of it. If they will regard the preacher as their representative, as offering for them in the sermon their sacrifice of gratitude and aspiration to God, it will not have for them the opposite defect that it has for him. If his danger is excessive subjectivity, theirs is excessive objectivity. They will not describe the preaching part of the service as hearing a man talk, in contrast with the other parts as worship; they will not merely admire the learning or

need not despair. We, too, have received the Holy Ghost. He did not forsake the Church when the great saints of former ages passed away, and if we rely on His inspiration and devote to the substance, the spirit, and the form of this part of the service the thought and care which it ought to receive, our difficulties will soon be diminished, and perhaps in time they will disappear altogether" (op. cit., pp. 263–264). While insisting that "prayers are not works of art, they are great spiritual acts," he advises definite preparation for the prayer as for the sermon. The preacher is not to think of himself only in this preparation, but of the congregation and the "materials of inexhaustible variety their lives present, class by class, and even as far as is possible, person by person"; he must look beyond his congregation to the Church and the Kingdom. Not only the substance, but even the form of the prayer may be thought about in this preparation. Having summoned Dr. Dale against it, it is only fair that an advocate of the use of a liturgy should be cited to state his case. The plea of an Anglican might be set aside as the result of custom, but it is a Presbyterian, the Rev. R. C. Gillie, who has recently expressed a growing desire among Free Churchmen in England. On the one hand he admits that "spontaneous utterance is the ideal best," and on the other that, "the only valid reason for change should be the desire for a deeper and more widespread devotional experience," not imitativeness or even fashion. He offers three reasons why he believes that "the time has come when the Free Churches should give some place to forms of prayer." (1) "There may be forced free prayer," when "neither the mood nor the impulse nor the language of free prayer is present." (2) "People have indubitably become more sensitive to the use of words"; ruts of phraseology offend; some petitions require very careful expression; force in prayer needs to be sought, and offence shunned. (3) In free prayer, "there is no opportunity for audible response from the listeners," and so the congregation is excluded from anything but silent participation except in the hymns. As intercession should be as inclusive as possible, and must necessarily deal with the same subjects, why not use the most beautiful forms available? He also makes a plea for the greater use of the fellowship of silence in worship. (The Free Church Year Book, 1916, pp. 73–75.)

eloquence of the preacher, or in the contrary case, censure his defects of thought and speech. He will be confessing what they believe when he preaches the Gospel; he will be expressing what they desire to be when he presents the Christian ideal. They will not be hearers of the word only, nor even doers only in the sense of trying afterwards to practise the doctrine which they have heard; they will be doers even as they hear; their gratitude and their aspiration will be taken up into the preacher's collective act in his sermon; their praise and their prayer will make that atmosphere for themselves and others, which is as the breathing of the Holy Spirit on the souls of men. The preacher well knows when he is preaching not only *to* the congregation, but *for* it; when his hearers are not only receptive passively, but so actively that he feels that his preaching is not his own solitary act, but the collective act of the Christian community in the worship of God.

7. There are two practical consequences from this conception of the sermon which may be mentioned. (1) *In the first place*, that the sermon may be the collective act of the congregation the preacher must see to it that he is expressing the thoughts, feelings, wishes which he has a right to assume as common to himself and his hearers. That does not mean that he will never impart thoughts that are fresh, or arouse feelings hitherto unstirred, or quicken resolves that are new in any of his congregation; but it does mean that he will ever move within the wide circle of the Christian revelation. Such authority as he has is as an apostle of Jesus Christ, and so his message must be within the bounds of the Name, in which his congregation is gathered as one. If a man has another Gospel to preach, let him preach it from a platform in a hall, not from the pulpit of a church, which is dedicated to the worship of Father, Son and Holy Spirit, one God.

(2) *In the second place*, if the sermon is a collective act of worship, it fulfils its end if those who hear it are inspired by it to worship, the worship of gratitude and devotion as

well as of aspiration and obedience. A sermon need not always be practical, in the narrow sense many people would assign; that is, it need not always enjoin some duty to be done. Religion is not less, but greater than morality. The fruit of Christian experience is Christian character; and a sermon that waters the roots of Christian experience in making the truth and grace of God more real and sufficient, even if it does not bear directly on Christian character, is not unpractical. If men go away adoring God, the preacher has not failed in his purpose.

II.

1. While the sermon ought to be an act of worship, in which the emotions are stirred and the will is moved, yet, as speech which expresses thought, it must address itself to the intelligence. The divine revelation has been made as truth which can be understood, and it is the function of the pulpit to interpret that revelation. It is the common faith which the preacher proclaims, and yet that common faith is but partially and imperfectly understood by many who confess it; and he must accordingly be their *teacher*. There was for a generation a strong prejudice in many Churches against the teaching function of the pulpit. Doctrinal sermons were not at all popular; congregations desired poetical, emotional or practical preaching.

(1) The revolt for a time against doctrinal preaching is intelligible, for two reasons. *In the first place*, Christian doctrine had come to be expressed in stereotyped phraseology, which, full of meaning once, had lost all the meaning it ever had; and yet many doctrinal preachers insisted on repeating the same old phrases. The repetition of these phrases showed that for the preachers themselves the realities which had once been expressed by them had become abstractions, uninteresting and ineffective for living minds. *In the second place*, the intellectual changes of last century necessitated a fresh statement of the Gospel, in

language which would be more intelligible to the hearers ; and yet some preachers believed themselves to be proving their fidelity to the Gospel when, through indolence or timidity, they insisted on repeating the old phrases.

(2) While there was an absence from many pulpits of informed and competent teaching, the profoundest problems of faith and duty were being discussed often most superficially and without adequate knowledge in reviews, magazines and the daily press. Young men and women have passed from evangelical Churches to Agnosticism on the one hand, or High Anglicanism or even Roman Catholicism on the other. The readiness with which new theological ventures have been accepted shows how many were not receiving the teaching that their education and the intellectual interests it had awakened craved. There is to-day both a desire and an opportunity for teaching in the pulpit. The sermon need not be less charged with religious feeling, nor less directed to a moral end, because the intellectual demands of the hearers are being adequately and efficiently met. In dealing in the previous chapter with the preacher as sage, some indication was given regarding the material on which an enlightened judgment needs to be exercised. Modern science and philosophy, history and criticism, the practical problems of the age, all make demands on the preacher that he shall give his hearers the guidance of the truth as it is in Jesus. Doctrinal preaching must not repeat the mistakes of the past in the use of abstract terms, in the dogmatic tone, in the impression of remoteness from living interests ; but, using the language of to-day for the life of to-day, never could it expect a warmer welcome.[1]

[1] The testimony of the pew may be added. George Wharton Pepper, the first layman who has been asked to deliver the Yale Lectures on Preaching, devotes one lecture to this subject. "As far as his own development is concerned, the preacher will do well to remember that teaching is the basis of all good preaching. It has been said to be the hidden or revealed foundation of all inspiration. But preaching is teaching and something more ; for the preacher should approach his hearers not as intelligences but as men. Truth can never be stated wholly in terms of the intellect, for the

2. That doctrinal preaching may be as effective as possible, it is desirable that the preacher should have some knowledge of the methods and principles of teaching, the ways in which knowledge, truth, wisdom may be conveyed most easily and thoroughly from one mind to another. Attention depends on interest, and interest depends on character and experience; but the interests of all the members of a church are not the same, and thus the preacher has to discover how to command the widest attention by appealing to as varied interests as he can. Again, few persons can maintain their attention very long, unless their interest is renewed from time to time; and so the preacher must change the method of argument and the motive of appeal. As the unknown hitherto will be understood and remembered only as it can be associated with what is already familiar (the principle of *apperception*), the preacher must ever be on the outlook for the points of contact between himself and his hearers. Jesus associated the new truths of the Kingdom of heaven with the old facts of nature and man.[1] It would be going beyond the present purpose to attempt even an outline of modern educational theory; but if in the sermon the teaching element is to be as effective as the present intellectual needs of many congregations demand, then it is certain that the preacher will need to qualify himself for his task

mind is a lesser thing than the truth which it strives to comprehend. But the teaching method should always be at the preacher's disposal, and his presentation of truth should be systematic and thorough. It is a good thing to train one's self to teach the lesson that is needed, whether or not it is the one in which the teacher takes the greatest interest. Especially in the case of the minister who always preaches to the same congregation, it is of great importance to present Christian teaching in its symmetry. It is easy to distort truth by a failure to preserve just emphasis and proper perspective. I wish that the observance of the Christian year were less exclusively the habit of a few communions. . . . I am not a great believer in announced courses of sermons on related topics. They are apt to be as dull, for example, as a course of lectures on preaching. But the preacher will do well to map out for his own guidance the field which it is his duty to cover in the course of a year, although his plan must be kept flexible and subject to modification at the call of opportunity " (*A Voice from the Crowd*, pp. 110–111).

[1] Mt 13⁵².

by as wide and thorough a knowledge as he can of the principles and the methods of teaching.[1]

3. Although we are primarily concerned with the sermon in the pulpit, yet it is not irrelevant to the present subject of discussion to call attention to the other tasks as teacher which have a claim on the preacher. He is to be a *doctor doctorum*, a teacher of teachers. One of the alarming symptoms of church conditions to-day is the decrease in the number of Sunday-school scholars. In the public school the methods of instruction are so much improved, that if the youth of the land are to be retained in the Sunday schools a corresponding improvement must be secured ; and all the efforts which are being made in this direction will be futile unless there is given to them not only the cordial, but even the instructed and intelligent support of the ministry; and how can a minister direct such educational effort unless he has an interest in, and a competence for it ? That he should be willing and able to train his teachers for teaching according to the improved

---

[1] In this connection mention may be made of the movement to improve on the basis of recent psychological science and pedagogic method the teaching in the Sunday schools, from which the preacher can learn a great deal. A few books may be suggested as useful for this end : Welton, *Principles and Methods of Teaching* ; William James, *Talks to Teachers on Psychology, and to Students on some of Life's Ideals* ; John Adams, *Exposition and Illustration in Teaching* ; *Primer on Teaching* ; *The New Teaching*, edited by John Adams ; Patterson du Bois, *Point of Contact in Teaching* ; *Natural Way of Moral Training*. A few sentences on only one of the subjects mentioned need be added to show what kind of help the study recommended can offer. "Voluntary attention," says James, "is an essentially instantaneous affair. You can claim it, for your purpose in the schoolroom, by commanding it in loud, imperious tones ; and you can easily get it in this way. But unless the subject to which you thus recall their attention has inherent power to interest the pupils, you will have got it for only a brief moment ; and their minds will soon be wandering again. To keep them where you have called them, you must make the subject too interesting for them to wander again. And for that there is one prescription ; but the prescription, like all our prescriptions, is abstract, and, to get practical results from it, you must couple it with mother-wit. The prescription is that *the subject must be made to show new aspects of itself; to prompt new questions; in a word, to change*" (*Talks to Teachers*, p. 103). This advice is given to teachers ; but it still more applies to preachers, as they cannot order, but must win, attention.

methods may seem to many a distraction of his efforts from his main business, the preaching of the Gospel. Even if it were, the present situation demands that, if necessary, such a sacrifice must be made, so that the young may be held for, and not lost to, the Church. But it is no such diversion of his mind from what should occupy it, for the writer is fully persuaded that a man will be more effective as a teacher in the pulpit if he has undergone this discipline. He who can interest children will know how to interest adults.

4. The contention that the writer ventures to advance contrary to common opinion is that teaching should have a larger place in preaching than it has hitherto had, and that this teaching, which necessarily in many accidents is different from that of the school, should be guided by the new recognised educational theory. It is not only possible, but even probable, that such preaching will not be widely popular, as very many persons are averse to any exercise of their minds even in listening to a sermon; and prefer vivid pictures for their imagination, vigorous excitement of their emotions, a reproduction in the pulpit of the narrow views and the shallow feelings of the crowd. Such preaching will deserve to be unpopular, if it is academic, if it reproduces the terminology of science, philosophy, criticism or theology, if the preacher lectures as professors are supposed to lecture, although a good many of them would pity themselves if they did. It must be insisted that the sermon remains the sermon, the conveyance of truth through the whole personality, and not through the abstractions of the intellect alone. It must be required of the preacher that while he does not quite use the language of the *man-in-the-street*, as preaching, even if it be conversation, must be "dignified conversation," yet he shall use words that the man-in-the-street can understand, language such as cultured men use in serious converse with one another: it must not be too literary even as it must not be too academic; it must remain speech simple, clear, strong, but always cultured.

5. That the preacher may be a teacher, there must needs be some system in his choice of themes and texts. This object will be much more fully discussed in the last part of this volume; but meanwhile only the general principle may be affirmed. Unless a man has a very comprehensive mind, and a very sympathetic heart, it is not likely that the whole range of Christian doctrine and practice will equally appeal to him; and unless he deliberately resolves not to be guided solely by his own preferences as regards either belief or duty, but to declare " the whole counsel of God," his work as teacher will be one-sided. The writer has heard of an ancient divine who was so much under the spell of the *federal* theology, that he found the covenant of works and the covenant of grace in every text and incident on which he preached: and of a more modern, to whom the universal fatherhood of God came as so great a surprise and relief, that for the rest of his ministry he preached nothing else. Some congregations might be alarmed if told that a series of sermons on the great Christian doctrines, or on the chief Christian virtues, was to be preached to them: but the risk would be worth incurring. Let not the series be too long; let it deal only with matters of primary importance, let each sermon have its own interest, and not merely as one in a series; and most congregations would come to appreciate the effort. But even if the intention to preach a series be not intimated, the preacher must in his teaching have method, so that it shall be adequate to the truth.

III.

1. Instruction is only one of the needs represented in a Christian congregation. If the preacher looking from the pulpit on the faces before him could read there the life history of each person, and the sorrows or joys, fears or hopes, disappointments or aspirations, woe or bliss which each may be experiencing, he would surely be overwhelmed by the greatness of his task. How can he so

rightly divide the word of truth that to each will be given in due season his own portion ?[1] Can he find even in the treasure-house of the Scriptures the gift which each desires and expects ?[2] A sermon must have unity and definiteness, and that necessarily involves limitation. It cannot contain explicitly the answer to all the questions which the hearers in their needs and longings are addressing to the preacher. Must he then resign himself to the grievous necessity of sending away many of his congregation dissatisfied ? Against this conclusion may be set several considerations. *In the first place*, if the preacher knows to present the Gospel of the grace of God in its fulness and freeness, he will so minister to the universal needs of the human heart that even individual necessities will be relieved in the sense of this deepest and most

---

[1] 2 Ti 2[15], Lk 12[42].

[2] The feeling of the preacher in facing a congregation in time of war has been admirably expressed by the Rev. Edward Shillito in the following poem on "Preaching in War-time" :

> "One looks at me with distant eyes
> As though far hence his treasure lies :
> Another spent last week in hell ;
> One knows to-day that she must dwell
> Alone till death ; and there are some
> Waiting for cablegrams to come :
> Before another Sabbath ends
> That soldier takes his leave of friends ;
> This is the last time he will take
> The bread and wine for Jesus' sake.
>
> When bursting shells to man proclaim
> Death's new insatiable name,—
> When in the hazard and the loss
> They dimly see the Eternal Cross,—
> When a thousand thousand voices cry,
> 'Prepare to meet Him, God is nigh !'
> What need of words from men like me,
> When all around their steps is He,
> The God who draws them by their fears,
> The God who wipes away their tears ?"

Mutatis mutandis, the situation is the same at all times as regards human need, sorrow, care and fear, although war may, as it were, focus the human tragedy.

abiding satisfaction.   Sometimes the very best a preacher
can do is to lead the individual out of the circle of his own
personal interests into the common realm of the soul's
need of God.   *In the second place*, if the preacher has a
sympathetic personality, even if his sermon does not
convey an individual message to all the hearers, the
sorrowing and tempted may find comfort and succour
even by contact with him.   If in tone he can interpret
the loving-kindness and tender mercy of the Lord Jesus
Christ, he will be ministering to the needs of men even if
his words do not explicitly convey help.   It may be possible
for one who gives himself to preaching as the work he can
do best, and who has either no time or no taste for pastoral
work, by width of sympathy and keenness of imagination,
stimulated by a study of literature in which the human
heart has found the interpretation of genius, to acquire
the gift of dealing wisely and tenderly with the manifold
needs of men.   But this is possible only to genius.   For
the ordinary man what is needed is pastoral experience and
activity.

2. The preacher, who is not a genius, must know his
people to minister to them ; he must have been much in
their homes in order to get close to their hearts.   The
man who in the interests of his pulpit neglects his pastoral
duties, unless he is quite exceptionally gifted, defeats his
own end ; for it is in the intimacy of pastoral visitation
that the secrets of many hearts are revealed to him ; and
he acquires not only the knowledge which makes his
sermons *human*, but also develops that sympathetic
personality, the value of which for the preacher has already
been noted.   The proposal sometimes made, that there
should be greater division of labour in the Christian
ministry, so that one man shall be set apart for preaching
only and another for pastoral work only, is a thorough
mistake.   The pastor's influence is reinforced by the
preacher's authority, and the message of the pulpit is made
more effective by the ministries of the home.   Profundity
of thought, intensity of emotion, brilliance of style

eloquence of delivery are all precious gifts for the preacher;
but they are surely only as "sounding brass or a clanging
cymbal"[1] if he is not in intimate, affectionate and sympathetic relation with those to whom he is preaching.
Men of very moderate ability in the pulpit have exercised
a stronger influence than men of far more abundant
talents, because of their pastoral fidelity. The man who
has won the confidence, gratitude and devotion of his congregation by his varied ministry in their common life will,
when he preaches, be listened to with a respect and responsiveness which ability alone cannot command. It is
much to be regretted that the attention given to a comparatively few eminent preachers, who can gather crowds
wherever they go, and whose doings are minutely recorded
in the "religious press," tends to foster a false ambition in
many young ministers. While we do not depreciate the
value of the great preachers to the Christian Church and
are grateful to God for their reputation and influence, we
must not overlook the importance of the quiet ministries in
the obscurer places, where the influence, if more restricted
in its range, is in many cases more intensive in its
character.

3. The pastoral duty can in part be discharged in the
pulpit. The preacher who knows the individual needs of
his hearers will be able to adapt his preaching to those
needs. As he looks around him and sees the wistful look
of those who have come from the house of mourning, he
will be better able to speak the comfort which the Christian
hope brings. If his eyes fall on the youth who has begun
with evil companions the path which ends in ruin, his
warnings will have an urgency, and his entreaties an
insistence, which if sin were to him only a general conception would certainly be lacking.

(1) It has been said that Christian preaching attracts
women rather than men, and that the pulpit is often
effeminate, and not virile. It is to be remembered that
such a statement may be an unfavourable judgment of the

[1] 1 Co 13¹.

manhood which is not attracted and a favourable judgment
of the womanhood which is.   The virility which the pulpit
is blamed for lacking may be a self-sufficiency and self-
assertiveness, to which the distinctively Christian spirit is
an offence; and may need abasement in humility and
obedience before it can develop into Christian manhood.
The effeminacy charged against the pulpit may be what
the tenderness and gentleness of Jesus appear to those
whose spirit is not fine enough in quality to appreciate
these graces.[1]   But in so far as there is any justification
for such a charge, it is a challenge to the pulpit to get into
closer touch with the manhood of the Church.   In ordinary
pastoral visitation it is probable that the minister does
come into more immediate and intimate contact with the
women than the men of the Church ; and, as his life apart
from these duties is mostly in his home, it is not impossible
that his point of view may be rather that of the woman in
the home than of the man in the world.[2]   Again it is
likely that the one view is nearer the Christian standpoint
than the other; and nevertheless he must learn to know
and understand both, even for the correction of what may
be defective in either.   The needs and aims, cares and
difficulties of the man in business, whose motive in what
appear his hard ways may be not so much to gain wealth,
as to protect from the world's cruelty the wife and children
who are his most precious possession and most sacred
obligation, need to be understood, that justice may be done
to all the good in them, even when judgment is pronounced
on what seems evil from the Christian standpoint.

(2) But here again lurks a danger.   The minister of a
suburban church may so adopt the partial view of the
social problem which even intelligent business men are
prone to take, that he may fail to reach the standpoint of
the working man.   The preacher must not take sides in

[1] Nietzsche's attack on Christian morals as servile may serve as an
illustration.

[2] This topic has been discussed by Hoyt in his book, *Vital Elements in
Preaching* : *Lecture VIII. A Man's Gospel.*

the pulpit ; but he must know both sides in these disputes which divide society, and he must so preach the Christian ethics that the business man and the working man alike may feel that the position of each is not only understood, but judged with the judgment of a pastoral solicitude.

(3) In recent years the social problem has been forced into such prominence that there is little danger of its not receiving due attention in the pulpit. The peril rather is that the preacher may forget that in spite of the industrial revolution, and the social transformations which this involves, in its deepest experiences humanity remains unchanged. Birth and death, union of hearts and bereavement, the joy or the sorrow of motherhood, the care or hope of fatherhood, the smiles of youth and the sighs of age, all always abide. And the Christian Gospel is concerned with the cleansing and hallowing of the whole of this common life of man. We hear of courses on *Questions of the Day*; these are both necessary and desirable. But only a small part of the soul of man is concerned with questions of the day ; there are questions of yesterday, and to-day, and for ever which are the same, and which lie far nearer the heart of the life of man. The preacher cannot afford to treat these common and constant interests of mankind as beneath his notice ; for the character and spirit of man are more affected by these than by the questions of the day. As pastor [1] then, the preacher must, himself living the vicarious life of which mention has already been made, and so able to make his own the varied experience of his people, make his preaching of the Gospel a ministry

[1] Dr. John Watson has called his volume on preaching, *The Cure of Souls*, and the title would have led one to expect that he would devote himself mainly, if not solely, to this side of the preacher's work ; but he gives only one chapter to the *Work of a Pastor*. Disappointing, too, is his advocacy of the proposal which has already been condemned, that a congregation should have two ministers, a pastor and a preacher. Bad for pastor and preacher alike is the one-sidedness of development which in support of that proposal he seems to approve with somewhat rhetorical exaggeration. His description reads almost like a caricature (p. 171). A statement worth noting in regard to the solicitude of the ideal pastor for individual souls is made on p. 173.

of comfort, hope, encouragement, warning, pleading, and if need be judgment as well as mercy, so that each hearer will be made to feel that he, just as he is, is being cared for with watchful, wise and tender love.

4. Living is after all the best instruction about life. *Experientia docet.* And yet we must not ignore the service that science can render. Psychology [1] will never by itself make a pastor : only by shepherding can a man become a shepherd. It would be well if in the ministry there could be an apprenticeship, as there used to be in most trades. But while a man must become a master in his calling by the exercise of it, the study of psychology can be useful in making familiar with the workings of the mind, the heart, and the will, in introducing to a wider circle of human experience and character than the sphere of labour of most

---

[1] Dr. Stalker in his *Christian Psychology* advocates the direct use of psychology as well as ethics, and other subjects which the preacher has studied in the pulpit itself (pp. 9–10). How necessary psychology is to the preacher in order that he may adapt his message as closely as can be to the thought and life of to-day has been shown with German thoroughness in Niebergall's book, *Wie predigen wir dem modernen Menschen?* (How shall we preach to the modern man ?) In the first part he makes an investigation into *motives* and *quietives*. In the second part he discusses man from two points of view, psychological and ethnological (*Volkskundliches*). In the last part, in view of the results of the previous discussion, he indicates what the message for to-day should be. To reproduce his discussion in detail would defeat the very purpose for which attention is being called to his work, *i.e.*, not to offer results which the preacher can appropriate for himself without labour, but to suggest a method of investigation which he should follow out for himself. The preacher should ask himself such questions as these : Does the doctrine of the Atonement appeal to the modern conscience ? If not, why not ? Is the defect in the doctrine or in the conscience ? Does the preaching of heaven or hell move men as it once did ? Who, if any, can still be reached by such an appeal ? It is not enough that the preacher is sure that he himself has the truth. He must find out how he can make his hearers know and feel that that which is truth for him is truth for them, making not merely a theoretical demand on their minds, but mainly a practical demand on their wills. This is one of the most profitable kinds of study in which a preacher could engage, using all helps, such as Niebergall's book, within his reach, but pursuing the inquiry for himself, as on the one hand no man should simply borrow his message from another, and on the other hand the differences of audiences are so great that only a separate study of each can secure the closeness of application desired.

preachers affords them.   This study of psychological text-
books may be usefully supplemented by as wide an
acquaintance with the literature, novel or drama, which
deals with human life.   The mere scientific jargon of
psychology is not only out of place in the pulpit, but however necessary it may be, has even a repellent effect on
the student.   And yet exact observation and accurate
explanation of the ways of the soul of man have a very
great value, when vitalised by experience.   Literature
especially is essential to the preacher's equipment as
widening his sympathy, making keener his insight, affording
him illustrations of the subtle and secret, wonderful and
enthralling movements of the inner life of man.   But this
psychological interest must never be allowed to become
theoretical or æsthetic only ; it must ever be subordinated
to the desire and purpose to bring the abounding grace of
God into closest touch with the manifold needs of men.

IV.

1. The sermon has been described as the confession of
the common faith and duty of the Christian community ;
and till now in this discussion it has been assumed that
the preacher is addressing himself to those who themselves
accept the Gospel, to whom he is to give a fuller knowledge
and a deeper understanding, or whose manifold needs he is
to meet from its abounding resources.   And it is of the
utmost importance that the preacher should ever regard
himself as both representative and servant of the Christian
community.   The constant recognition of his dependence
and obligation will correct the defect of egotism which is
a danger of one thrust into a position of such prominence
and importance.   But as the Church does not exist for
itself, but as the body of Christ, through which He may
carry on His work in the world, so the preacher cannot
limit himself to the Christian community.   He must seek
in his preaching to address himself to those who are as yet

without and not within the Christian fellowship : he must be an *evangelist*. So important is this work, and so often are its claims overlooked, that it is necessary to deal with it more fully.

2. There are pulpits from which an appeal to the unconverted would come as a shock to the respectable and (must we not even add ?) self-righteous congregation. There are preachers who assume either that all their hearers have been converted, or that such an experience is only for those whose lives have been notoriously wicked. Not a genuine insight into the variety of religious experiences prevents their calling on all their hearers who have not had this experience to seek for it ; but a superficial assumption that as God is the father of all, all, unless the too manifestly depraved, may be addressed as His children. At the opposite extreme are the preachers who, having themselves had a distinct experience of passing out of darkness into God's marvellous light, address the whole of every congregation as still needing to pass through such an experience. Some with a little more discrimination are careful to divide their hearers into the *saved* and the *unsaved* without sufficiently recognising that God alone can so accurately determine the spiritual condition, and that a man himself, although moving towards the light out of the darkness, may have no assurance that the change is taking place. There are Christians who have not yet gained the assurance of faith even. While it must be maintained that in every congregation there are likely to be those, few or many, who have not yet entered on the Christian life, and that therefore the call of the Gospel to penitence and faith is never unseasonable or out of place in the pulpit; yet he who would do the work of the evangelist must not make dogmatic assumptions such as that all are either saved or unsaved, but must have a psychological understanding of the varied types and the varying phases of the Christian experience, so that he shall so present the Gospel that it will reach each hearer just with the appeal his condition may demand.

3. It will not be out of place at this stage of the discussion to give some fuller notice of what has been done by psychology in recent years to help the Christian preacher both as pastor and as evangelist.[1] While James' *Varieties of Religious Experience* has the defect that it throws into undue prominence abnormal psychical accompaniments of intense religious experiences, it has probably done more than any other single book to show how much this science has to teach the Christian minister. (1) One conclusion from these investigations stands out most distinctly; and it is this, that the religious life, the Christian experience, is far too varied, too much affected by natural temperament, educational and environmental influences, to be forced into one or two moulds. And what Christian preaching, especially what may be called *evangelistic*, has most suffered from is just the failure to recognise this variety and this dependence. A few texts of Scripture, imperfectly understood, such as Jesus' saying about the new birth, have been used as defining what experience must be without the inquiry whether all experience is actually what it is assumed it must be.

(2) Again the difference necessarily made by age has too often been ignored; and childhood and youth have been supposed capable of the same experience as mature years. That children can be, and so ought to be, converted in the same way as grown men, has been a common assumption even in the Sunday school. That there may be a gradual spiritual and moral development without any crisis such as conversion, has been generally ignored by those most zealous to do the work of the evangelist. On the other hand, the value of a definite decision for Christ, in confirmation of the previous life of dependence on Christian influences, when adolescence has been reached, has not been as generally recognised by those

[1] Among recent books may be mentioned James' *Varieties of Religious Experience*; Starbuck's *The Psychology of Religion*; Granger's *The Soul of a Christian*; Cuttin's *The Psychological Phenomena of Christianity*; Steven's *The Psychology of the Christian Soul*; Stalker's *Christian Psychology*; Davenport's *Primitive Traits in Religious Revivals*.

who lay stress on the importance of such gradual development.[1]

(3) That the excitement of a big meeting, when what has been called the "mob consciousness" emerges, is not the best psychical condition to secure a conversion which will be thorough and lasting, is a fact which psychology teaches us, but the professional evangelist habitually ignores. It must be said even that a great deal which is done to secure the success of a special mission, to work up the conditions of a revival, is from the psychological standpoint thoroughly unsound if what is aimed at is not a transitory emotion, but a permanent change of the direction of the life. There are methods used by some evangelists which are immediately effective, but which can be shown to be an illegitimate invasion of the sanctuary of the soul; an insensible and yet not less real coercion of the so-called convert by the evangelist. Such are some of the facts psychology can teach the preacher.

4. It is much to be regretted that the work of the evangelist has been separated from the work of the ministry, and the special evangelistic mission has been set up beside the activities of the Church. It may be admitted that the special mission in the sense of a series of meetings each evening for a week or a fortnight has advantages. There should be a series of subjects carefully selected, leading on from the sense of sin to the hope of immortality through the different stages of the Christian life, setting forth in an orderly succession the steps in the way of salvation.[2] The interval of a week between the services on the Lord's Day allows the impression of one day to fade before the next can deepen it. But when each evening the impression of the preceding is assumed and confirmed, the cumulative effect is great. Not a few young people,

[1] The writer may be excused for referring to his book, *A Course of Bible Study for Adolescents*.

[2] The writer ventures to refer the reader to his little book, *The Joy of Finding*, a series of addresses delivered at such missions, based on the parable of the Prodigal Son, and to *A Guide to Preachers*, p. 223, where the titles of a similar series on Paul's autobiographical references are given.

already influenced by Christian teaching and training, are under such continued argument and appeal brought to more distinct consciousness, and more deliberate volition of their relation to Jesus Christ as Saviour and Lord. If the minister of a church feels that a new voice with a fresh presentation of the truths he himself has been preaching would be more effective than his own, he should get a brother-minister of tested ability in this kind of work to do it for him. It is better not to employ a professional evangelist for two reasons. In *the first place*, the theology of most evangelists is of a very crude type; and it is not desirable that young people accustomed to the more cultured presentation of the Gospel should be subjected to this inferior type of teaching. And in *the second place*, the constant repetition of this kind of work tends to produce in the evangelist a very artificial method, with sometimes even what cannot be otherwise described than as tricks for producing a speedy rather than a lasting impression. The work of the ministry, with its varied experiences, seems to be necessary to keep a man out of this evangelistic rut. For these reasons let the minister himself do the work of the evangelist.

5. It used to be the practice of many ministers to address the "saints" in the morning, and the "sinners" in the evening service. There are congregations which are in the evening of a much more varied character than in the morning, containing fewer of the regular members, and more occasional hearers. And it may be conceded that it would be well to make some variation in the type of the two services. But, on the other hand, there are congregations which in the evening consist of the devoted members who are not content with attending only one service; and their presence should be taken into account. No rigid rules should be laid down in this regard. Again, there are preachers who try to end every sermon with an application *first* to the saved, and *then* to the unsaved. The application is often altogether forced; and the following of any such rule gives an artificiality, even an impression of

insincerity to such a performance. If the sermon can be developed to such a conclusion, the opportunity should certainly not be neglected ; and the man who has a passion for souls, who yearns and prays and works for the salvation of all whom he can reach, will without any artifice so conceive and so present the Gospel that the fervent appeal will often come quite inevitably—and so altogether effectively. To make a routine of what should bear the marks of spontaneity is to discount the value ; for here undoubtedly "familiarity breeds contempt." Not in every sermon can the preacher force himself to be the evangelist, as he must aim at variety, adaptation, progress in his teaching ; but if he himself dwells near the centre of the Christian revelation in the redemption which is in Christ Jesus, whether his sermon leads up to the distinct appeal for decision for Christ or not, he will be bringing to bear upon the minds and hearts of his hearers the tender and yet mighty constraints of the Saviourhood and Lordship of Jesus Christ. He will be led from time to time to set forth explicitly the answer to the question that is often in the heart when it does not rise to the lips—"What shall I do to be saved ? " and yet he will so answer that the saved will find the confirmation of their own faith, and the inspiration of their own consecration, when once more they see their Lord uplifted on His Cross. If his spirit as well as theology be evangelical, even if his method be not what is generally called evangelistic, he will prove himself ever an evangelist.

6. There is a work which may fall to the preacher as evangelist which must be mentioned. It is the work of home and foreign missions. The preacher may find, and if he is earnest in his work he will seek, the opportunity of preaching to those who are altogether outside the Church and its ministries. At home in large cities there are multitudes who never enter a church door; and they ought to be sought. Open-air preaching, the general method of Jesus, is not used by the Christian ministry as it should be, and is often left to the incompetent; and yet

some may be reached in this way who could not be otherwise won. Public halls, theatres, and other buildings, to which the "lapsed masses" are in the habit of going on week days, might be more used than they are for this purpose. Such preaching must command the interest to hold the attention of the hearers. If a preacher in the open air ceases to interest, his audience will leave him ; the people will not come to a meeting unless they are attracted. It is rather a disadvantage that the preacher in the church is not tested in the same way, so that he cannot discover whether his preaching is effective or not ; but often routine brings many hearers to church, and decorum keeps them there even when they are uninterested. To be interesting the preacher must know his audience, and adapt himself to it, not by vulgarity or sensationalism, but by simplicity, variety, directness and intensity of speech, by the use of illustrations which ordinary people can understand, and of arguments and appeals which go home to them. Into further details regarding this special work we cannot now enter.

7. Still more needful will the power of adaptation be to the missionary abroad. Much of his preaching will be in the open air, by the roadside, in the bazaar, wherever he can get the people together around him. Unless he has a regular congregation of converts, he will not attempt to deliver any formal discourse. Whatever the temporary circumstances, or the local customs require, he must be ready to do. To talk, to argue, to answer questions and even invite them, to bear with, and make the best use of interruptions, to be content with an audience of one—all this belongs to missionary preaching. The missionary must know and understand the life and thought of the people, and he must use the language that they not only understand, but by which they are most easily moved and deeply impressed. For him it is in the highest degree needful to recognise that never man spake as Jesus did, so that he may learn all he can from the Master's method. Religious beliefs and rites, moral standards and habits,

however crude, should not be disdained as points of contact. With the learned in the Sacred Scriptures of any ancient faith the missionary must be prepared to show the superiority of his Holy Bible. So varied are the conditions of foreign missionary preaching that no more than a statement of these general principles can be here attempted. The theory of preaching for the foreign field has not yet been developed; and this is a task the urgency of which is now being recognised, but only inadequate efforts have as yet been made to meet the demand.

PART III.

THE PREPARATION AND
THE PRODUCTION OF THE SERMON.

INTRODUCTORY.

IT is on the sermon that the Christian preacher fulfils his callings; in it the δύναμις of which the previous division treated becomes the ἐνέργεια, the faculty functions. In the process we may distinguish two stages, there is *the preparation* (the *invention* and the *disposition* of the ancient rhetoric) and *the production* (the elocution, including both the composition and the delivery of the sermon).

1. The *preparation* of the sermon may be taken in a narrower and a wider sense. All that makes the preacher also makes the sermon. The entire development of the personality as the channel of Truth may be said to belong to the preparation. As apostle, prophet and scribe the preacher is getting the content of his preaching.[1] As scholar, sage, seer and saint he is fitting himself to convey the message he receives.[2] As priest, teacher, pastor and evangelist he is fixing the forms of his preaching by its purposes.[3] It seems necessary to lay stress on the preparation in the wider sense, as on that will depend the facility and the excellence of the preparation in the narrower sense. Each sermon should not in itself be an immense labour and crushing care to the preacher, who has constantly and diligently been making himself fit and

---

[1] See Part II. Chapter I.   [2] *Ibid.*, Chapter II.
[3] *Ibid.*, Chapter III.

ready for the task.[1] It should be a free and happy
exercise of powers that have been fully developed by a
fruitful self-discipline. It should not be necessary for him
to spend hours in trying to find a text; but he should be
so familiar with the Scriptures that a multitude of texts
should be at his command, and that these texts should
suggest their treatment at once because he so thoroughly
knows their contexts. It should not be necessary for him
to search high and low for material for his sermon; but
he should be so much at home in Christian thought and
life that he will have abundance to say worth hearing
about doctrine and practice, principle and application alike.
It should not be necessary for him to go in search of
illustrations, but his reading and his experience alike
should readily offer him the pictures through which the
truth may shine. It should not be necessary for him to
rack his brains to discover divisions or heads, but his logic
should be keen enough, and his psychology subtle enough,
to put him in the way of an arrangement that will be
spontaneous and effective, and not arbitrary and futile.
Many preachers find their preparation so painful and
fruitless a toil, because they forget or neglect the fact
that the stream cannot rise higher than its source; the
poor personality will not produce the rich sermon. Here at
the outset of the discussion all emphasis must be put again
on the definition of preaching as *truth through personality*.

2. The purpose of preaching must also at this stage
be recalled. It is for the eternal life of the hearers, for
it is so easy for other interests, valuable in themselves, to
become unduly dominant. (1) One interest that may
obtrude itself is the personal. The preacher may think
too much of his sermon as a deliverance of himself, as
self-expression. From what has already been said it is
quite evident that the writer does not depreciate the
personality of the preacher, and yet the personality may
become too prominent. It is true that the preacher must
himself be interested if he is to interest; his themes must

[1] See Hoyt, *The Work of Preaching*, pp. 47–84.

appeal to himself if he is by them to appeal to others; but he must always be on his guard against self-absorption in his own ideas, moods, aspirations. The pulpit is not exclusively his confessional or his platform. He speaks as representing Christ and His Church, and it is not himself that he should impress on others, but the common salvation. The books he reads, the persons he meets, the experiences through which he passes, the conclusions about faith, duty or destiny he reaches as the result of his study and meditation, may and must affect his preaching; but it is not that he may candidly, confidently and courageously express himself with respect to any of these that he ascends the pulpit. The subjective egotism of the pulpit is an evil to be guarded against by preaching the objective universality of the Gospel committed to the preacher to be delivered by him.

(2) In the demand that preaching should be more expository and less topical, there lurks an error as well as dwells a truth. In what has already been said about the preacher as scribe the truth has been fully acknowledged. As the literature of the divine revelation and the human redemption in Christ Jesus the Holy Scriptures must have a large place in Christian preaching. How necessary and valuable to the preacher in the preparation of his sermon the study of the Scriptures is, will in a subsequent chapter be still more fully shown. Now the error in the demand must be exposed. It must be said quite boldly that the end of preaching is not to make people familiar with the Bible, still less with what modern scholarship has to say about it; it is to bring God in Christ to men, and men through Christ to God; and the Bible itself must be prized and used only as a means to this end. That in the Bible class or by special courses of lectures the preacher may share with others his scholarly knowledge of the Bible, is not only freely conceded but even warmly commended. But in the sermon as not only part, but even an act of public worship, information about, or explanation of the Holy Scriptures must be subordinate to

imparting through the Gospel the eternal life in God. Historical, literary and even theological exposition must always be secondary, and be kept within the narrowest limits the object allows, so that it may be the substance of revelation which is conveyed to the hearers.

(3) The hearers have a necessary place in the interest of the preacher. He should always have the genuine and intense pastoral solicitude. He should be guided in his preaching by his knowledge of their needs, and they should feel that the man who speaks to them cares for them with individual affection. There may be occasions when it is both legitimate and necessary for the preacher to deal explicitly with the personal and domestic circumstances of some of his hearers. The death of one of the members, workers or officers in the church may warrant a memorial sermon; but this should not be a frequent practice, and even here the personal appreciation should not form the whole sermon, but should be dependent on, and subordinate to, the main function of the pulpit to present Christ, and even His saints only as they reflect rays of His glory. Some preachers delight in personalities and domesticities; every event of importance or interest to their congregation they deem worthy of notice in the pulpit: thus they flatter vanity and foster triviality. To the pastor all that affects his people should be of interest, and he should have the fit words of counsel, cheer or comfort in his private relations; but in his pulpit he is concerned with the permanent and universal interests of men as sinners saved by grace, and saints being made meet for glory, and in his sermon he should regard and treat his hearers in this aspect and relation, and no other.

3. The preacher's interest is in the truth of the Christian Gospel not as abstract theology or ethics, but as the testimony to and interpretation of the divine revelation and human redemption in Christ Jesus the Lord, in his own personality only in so far as he may make it as wide, deep and unimpeded a channel for the current of the truth, and in his hearers as called to and

capable of the eternal life in God. The first interest will demand that he shall present as far as he can apprehend the whole counsel of God. In his choice of subjects he will endeavour to preserve the proportion of faith; he will not magnify minor subjects which interest himself and will not give a subordinate place to themes which God has Himself exalted; he will linger often at the centre, and will not wander much at the circumference of the content of the divine revelation. While bound by sincerity and candour to preach only as he believes, he will not pride himself on, and be content to abide in, the peculiarity of his own beliefs; but will try so to appreciate for himself that he will be constrained to commend to others all that it is in their highest interests to know and hold. Whatever it is profitable for them to hear that they may grow in the knowledge and grace of the Lord Jesus Christ, that he will endeavour adequately and proportionately and harmoniously to offer as the content of his preaching.

4. The purpose of preaching must determine the form. (1) As the first section of this volume has shown, the earliest form was the *homily* and the *sermon* came later.[1] The homily is a familiar informal talk within the Christian brotherhood in explanation of Christian faith and duty. As the *Epistle of James* and the *Epistle to the Hebrews* show, the homily might have less or more formal arrangement of the matter treated. It might be a succession of counsels, or a development of an argument. Unity of structure was not a primary object. Soon the homily attached itself to a passage of Scripture, and became a running commentary on the text, taking up clause by clause or verse by verse. In the sermon, on the contrary, a theme is chosen, and it is attached more or less closely to the text. Both of these forms have survived to the present day. The homily is represented by the *lecture* on a portion of Scripture which was until recently the practice of many Scottish preachers at one service at least each Sabbath. Entire books of the Bible were there dealt with, and the

[1] See pp. 57–58 and p. 89.

exposition of one of the Epistles sometimes extended over several years. This method has fallen into disuse, and the revival need not be desired, as a better use for the ends of preaching can be made of the Holy·Scriptures. The sermon is now generally accepted as the desirable form of preaching. What is now in discussion is whether the sermon should be *topical* or *expository*; should it deal with a subject, or treat a text?

(2) In seeking to answer this question, we must make clear what we mean by our terms. If by *expository preaching* is meant the explanation of the separate clauses of a verse, or the separate sentences of a passage without any attempt at unity of presentation and impression, except such as is implied in the verse or passage itself, we need not say a word in its support, as such unity should be the aim of all effective public speech. If by *topical preaching* is meant the choice of subjects of accidental interest or trivial importance, with little (if any) connection with the Christian Gospel, which can, therefore, be attached to a text of Scripture only by a *tour de force* of exegesis, it can be unreservedly condemned. Between the expository and the topical sermon which can be approved there is no necessary antagonism. A text which can be the basis of a sermon must contain a subject, and a subject may be explained by means of a text; we come to a knowledge and understanding of both together. If a text dealt with a number of subjects it would not be suitable for the basis of a sermon unless the subjects could be so related as to be brought into an intelligible unity; and as all portions of the Bible "make sense," few texts there are (if any) in which such unity cannot be found, even though it may mean some study and meditation to discover the principle of synthesis in each case.

(3) It may be admitted, however, that while these two objects are quite consistent, yet a difference will be made in the structure of the sermon as one or other is primary. Can we determine which should be primary? With some hesitation and diffidence the writer ventures

to give his own definite judgment that the sermon should be the presentation of the subject primarily and the exposition of the text secondarily. For this view a *material* and a *formal* reason may be given. (*a*) As regards the first, we now hold that the Bible is not the Word of God, but contains the Word of God; and what we have to do is to discover the heavenly treasure in the earthen vessel. Unless in exceptional circumstances, the subject of every Christian sermon should be some part of this Word of God; and to subordinate the text to the subject of the sermon is nothing else than exalting the treasure above the vessel. We must present the truth taught in any text in such a form as will make it most intelligible, attractive and authoritative for those who hear; and often the text is not explicitly and directly the truth for men to-day; but they must be shown how to find it there. But what concerns preachers and hearers alike is not the text that contains, but the truth that is contained. Of topical preaching in the objectionable sense, the writer is no advocate when he thus pleads that the text must be subordinated to the truth.

(*b*) As regards the second reason, a sermon should be a unity, and unity is much more likely to be attained in the presentation of a subject than the exposition of a text. For the first purpose it might be necessary to omit a good deal that the second would demand. An exhaustive exposition of the text might carry us far beyond the bounds of an adequate presentation of the subject.

(4) This judgment does not involve, however, as might at first sight appear, that the sermon is not to be expository in the best sense of the word. If, as we believe, the Scriptures contain the Word of God, we go first of all to the Scriptures to discover what the Word is. The preacher will hesitate about dealing with subjects which are not suggested to him by the Scriptures, while recognising that as there is progress in the Kingdom of God there may be aspects of the divine truth important for us to-day which have little (if any) attention given to

them there. He may find implicit in a text a truth he wants to make explicit, and as an honest man when he takes the text, he will frankly state this difference. What is suggested rather than asserted by the text he will deal with only as suggested. Freedom without arbitrariness must be insisted on as necessary for the modern preacher in his choice and treatment of texts. Most themes with which the Christian preacher wants to deal are, however, explicitly presented in texts; and in dealing with them, he will derive his presentation of the truth as fully as he can from the exposition of the text. Understood in this way the demand for expository preaching is entirely justified, and is not at all inconsistent with topical preaching in the proper sense.

5. In answering the question of the form of the sermon in favour of the topical rather than the expository on the formal ground that the unity of the sermon is more likely to be attained, the writer may have appeared to commit himself to an opinion as regards the relation of rhetoric to homiletics. The question has been much discussed by writers on the subject, whether homiletics should be based on rhetoric or not. As a form of public speech the sermon must necessarily be constructed, if it is to be as effective as possible, in accordance with the psychological, logical and literary principles of effective speech; and about this position there should be no dispute. The question to be determined is this: does the theory of public speech, known as rhetoric, which has come down to us from ancient Greece, contain such permanent and universal principles as demand acceptance from the modern preacher, or are these principles, even if contained in it, presented in a form so limited by the conditions of ancient oratory as to be valueless for him? Christlieb [1] very decidedly excludes rhetoric from homiletics. "From this whole higher sphere, *i.e.*, from the contents and spirit of the Gospel corresponding to the nature and aim of the Kingdom of Christ, and in particular, of Christian worship,

[1] *Homiletic*, English translation, p. 22.

homiletic, as a *science peculiar to Christianity*, and therefore *occupying an independent position in relation to rhetoric*, has to develop the idea of preaching, and its execution in matter and form." In Chapter IV. his treatment shows that this cannot be an absolute independence. Bassermann,[1] on the contrary, deals in the first part of his book with Rhetoric generally before in the second part dealing with Worship, and the third with Christian Preaching. His subsequent representation of the sermon as a work of art, however, limits his outlook, and he puts fetters on Christian preaching which should not be imposed on it. He illustrates the peril of allowing theory to dominate practice. Vinet[2] takes the proper middle course. "It is certain that eloquence is one; that a man is not eloquent in the pulpit on other conditions than in the rostrum or the bar; there are no more two rhetorics than there are two logics; but the nature of ecclesiastical discourse brings differences, adds rules, which form a special art, under the name of homiletics. . . . Rhetoric is the genus, homiletics is the species." He divides his treatment into three parts, *Invention*, *Disposition* and *Elocution*. The Christian preacher should be the master, and not the slave of the Ancient Rhetoric.[3] The spirit, purpose and content of Greek or Roman eloquence were so different from those of Christian preaching that the rules of the one cannot simply be transferred to the other. And yet, as Vinet properly says, the principles of eloquence are the same for all time. Learning all he can from homiletics about his art, the preacher must not be brought into subjection to his art, for preaching is more and greater than an artistic dis-

---

[1] *Handbuch der Geistlichen Beredsamkeit*; see § 34, pp. 211–219.

[2] *Homilétique ou Théorie de la Prédication*, p. 5.

[3] Bassermann in his book deals first of all with the nature of **Rhetoric** as a natural power, an art, or a science, and gives an account of the differences of opinion on this question among the ancient writers. Secondly, he shows that among the ancients Rhetoric was not developed scientifically or in such a way as to give it a genuinely æsthetic character, and that it ran counter to our moral ideas inasmuch as it aimed at persuasion not by evidence and argument only, but by an appeal to passion. Thirdly, he sketches the

play, and the preacher must always claim the Spirit's freedom.

6. The writer desires to emphasise his claim for the freedom of the pulpit. Sermons are not to be made according to rule or pattern; imitation of great preachers is a tragic mistake for lesser men; a man must be as fully himself as he can in the pulpit. All that a book on Homiletics can do is to state what have been found to be the principles of effective preaching, to warn against mistakes, into which inexperience may fall, to offer counsels which experience suggests, to show how each preacher with due regard to his own individuality may set about gathering his material and putting it into the best shape. The preparation and production of a sermon is a living process, and should have the spontaneous movement of life; but as health can be promoted and disease averted by a wise and good *regimen*, so the preacher may be guided and guarded. The genius in the pulpit goes by no rules, and does not need them; but as all preachers are not geniuses, they may wisely look for some direction in doing their work. The

influence of the Ancient Rhetoric in the Middle Ages and at the Reformation. To the three kinds of oratory, recognised by the classical orators, *genus judiciale, demonstrativum, deliberativum*, Melanchthon added *didacticum*. Fourthly, he deals with the revival of oratory and rhetoric in the eighteenth century and the discussion of the subject in the nineteenth. The revival was represented in Germany by Gottsched, in France by Fénelon, and in Great Britain by Blair. Fénelon very briefly states the aims of oratory. "Ainsi je crois que toute l'éloquence se reduit à prouver, à peindre et à toucher." (Accordingly I believe that all eloquence is reduced to proving, painting and touching.) Blair in his lectures on *Rhetoric and Belles Lettres* (1783) was influenced by Hume's *Essay of Eloquence*, the first summons to ennoble oratory by following the best examples of antiquity. Blair defines eloquence as "the Art of speaking in such a manner as to attain the end for which we speak"; but he distinguished the eloquence of the pulpit from that before popular assemblies, or at the bar. *Schott* tried to defend Rhetoric against the charge of Kant, that though its end might be good, its means must always be bad, and argued that the orator may make a moral use of all the means of influencing men which psychology reveals to him. *Theremin* insists on the ethical character of rhetoric as purposeful action on others. Lastly, after this historical sketch Bassermann gives his own theory, which need not be here reproduced, as what seems of value in it has been taken due account of by the writer in the subsequent chapters of this volume.

genius cannot always give a disclosure of his secret, and may even, if he attempt it, mislead men who have not his gifts. What follows is not offered to those who do not, but to those who do need help, and is offered as the result of experience, study and meditation.

CHAPTER I.

THE CHARACTER OF THE SERMON.

1. WHAT is lacking in many books on preaching is an adequate recognition of the variety of forms which the public speaking of the Christian minister must to-day assume; and before dealing with the kinds of sermons which the preacher may be called on to prepare and produce, the writer would direct attention to this bewildering variety. The minister may be expected to deliver a lecture, to teach a lesson in Bible class or Sunday school, to offer a few remarks, to give an address, to make a speech.

(1) As regards the first two, *instruction* is the primary object; and here command of the subject to be taught on the one hand and acquaintance with the methods of teaching on the other hand are important. The study of a subject outside of the routine of the pulpit, be it historical, literary or scientific, is a great advantage to the preacher; and, if he have the opportunity of showing his interest in, and offering his assistance to any movement for the diffusion of culture, he should readily and gladly undertake the duty, if he have any competence to discharge it. Accurate and adequate knowledge, clear exposition and orderly arrangement are here the conditions of effectiveness.

(2) The Bible class is to the minister who conducts it himself a valuable discipline, if he takes its claims as seriously as they should be taken. Apart from the practical advantage it offers for close contact with the young men and women of the Church, at an age when they are most sensitive and responsive to influence, it should

give him a stimulus in his own study. He should select a subject which will require of him special reading, so that he will be improving himself as well as others. Much modern scholarship about the Bible, the history of the Christian Church, theology and ethics, of which he cannot make direct use in the pulpit, may here be utilised in preparing the young people for facing the dangers, difficulties and doubts of the world into which they are passing. That this may be presented so as to interest and attract, there must be the art of the teacher. While there is a natural gift for teaching, which all do not possess, study and practice may develop even a very small capacity. And the preacher in the pulpit will be the better of some knowledge of and skill in the art of teaching. In the Sunday school even more than the Bible class this art will be necessary. It seems unreasonable to demand that every minister shall be initiated into the mysteries of the Beginners' and Primary Department; but it is reasonable to expect them to know enough about the method of education, based on psychology, to be able to hold the attention by keeping the interest of boys and girls from nine years to fifteen. The writer cannot here attempt to expound the method, but can only insist on the gain of a knowledge of it.

(3) The request to offer a few remarks should not be regarded as justifying a waste of the time of the hearers by irrelevant and futile talking. The occasion may supply the content, but there should be even in such a case the endeavour to say something worth saying in a form not unworthy of one who fulfils the calling of the preacher. Humour and geniality may be altogether in place, but silliness and familiarity are not.

(4) It would be difficult to state precisely wherein an address is expected to differ from a sermon. It is usually shorter, has no text, and is less definite in form, but the less the time available the more need of making the best use of it possible. A definite purpose there should be, even if no subject is explicitly mentioned, and the rules of

clear exposition and orderly arrangement apply no less than to the sermon. If there is any difference between an address and a speech, it is that the address aims at moral and religious influence, the speech belongs to the realm of civic and political activity.

(5) Without entering on the controversial topic of what share the preacher should take in the public life of the community to which he belongs, one may venture the opinion that the preacher should at least have the capacity to speak intelligently and effectively on subjects that lie beyond the range of his more immediate interests. In such speech it will be well for him to avoid giving the impression that he is transferring to the platform the method and manner of the pulpit. Information, exposition, illustration, argument, and appeal in simple and direct language are what such speaking demands; humour is here of great value, and readiness to take advantage of objections or interruptions.

2. Coming now to the preacher's more immediate concern, it is to be observed that differences of purpose, audience, occasion, etc., demand variety in sermons. The first broad distinction which must be recognised is that between what may be called *edifying* and *evangelising* preaching.[1] (1) As has already been maintained, the sermon is a part, and even act of worship, as the confession by the community of the faith it holds, and the life it seeks for itself; it is gratitude for God's grace, and aspiration for man's goodness. The preacher here represents the congregation before God. (*a*) This confession does not, however, exclude edification. To hear from another explicitly what one believes and aims at is to be confirmed in faith and duty. When ideas and ideals are made more certain and definite by another, specially qualified for such a task, than they have ever been in one's own thought, one is instructed and influenced. What is already possessed is now more fully possessed than it was before. This is the answer to those who object that the pulpit has nothing new

[1] See Hoyt's *The Preacher*, chaps. 13 and 14, pp. 259-304.

to teach Christian people, but only repeats what they have known from youth. There is a repetition which can only weary, and that certainly the pulpit must avoid; but there is a reaffirmation which can come ever with freshness of interest and influence; and the test of the capacity of the preacher is whether he can on behalf of the community reaffirm freshly without wearying repetition. (*b*) This objection leads some preachers to a mistaken search after originality in the content and form of their preaching. It may be said, however, that there is a kind of originality which is infidelity to the common Christian inheritance, and a freshness which is gained at the expense of truth. Many sermons from the Christian pulpit assume, and rightly assume, that those addressed share the common Christian faith and life with the preacher. To enlighten, quicken and strengthen believers is the task the preacher must set himself. So varied is the presentation of the inheritance of the Christian Church in truth and grace in the Holy Scriptures that it cannot be exhausted by him who is *an instructed scribe*. So manifold are the needs of a Christian congregation that no monotony in applying the divine provision to the human necessity should be feared. So progressive may be the development of the Christian preacher, that it is not necessary for him to be repeating himself. It is to be feared, however, that preachers and hearers alike do often grow "stale"; if familiarity does not breed contempt, it at least lessens sensibility, and tradition and convention banish the surprise and wonder with which the Gospel should be received. A religious revival begins when the old truth is freshly presented with a new apprehension, or a fuller conviction. But the preacher should ever make it his aim that he will so far as in him lies, strive ever to present the old truth freshly even to those who already know it, believe it, and live by it.

(2) Even if in the ordinary congregation there should be very few who are still outside of the Kingdom of God, strangers to the grace of Christ, the preacher should not forget and neglect his duty as an evangelist. Even if the

unevangelised be few, they are not to be disregarded (would that there were more of them within the sacred walls !), for the Good Shepherd went after the one sheep that was lost.[1]   Besides, many young people, who cannot be regarded as not Christians, still need to be summoned to a more deliberate and decisive relation to Christ as Saviour and Lord.   Those who know most of the Christian life are the least likely to be displeased with the argument and appeal which would bring others to their Saviour and Lord.   In this kind of preaching there is the danger of a deadening repetition.   To begin with the question, Are you saved ? is not the most effective method of making men concerned about their salvation.   To end the sermon with words specially addressed to the unconverted, if what has gone before has not been fitted to arouse any interest, is to indulge in a foolish futility.   The professional evangelist who has acquired "the tricks of the trade" is the last person from whom the Christian minister should learn how to do "the work of an evangelist."   If he does not see clearly and feel keenly the difference between life without and life in Christ, if he has not the passion to seek and save the lost, he had better not try to address the unconverted; but he should then ask himself if he is at all fit to be a Christian minister.

(3) Recognising the broad distinction between *edifying* and *evangelistic* preaching, and maintaining that the definite purpose of a sermon should be either the one or the other, we should not press the difference unduly, for a text may allow an application both to the saved and the unsaved, and a subject may have an aspect turned to each ; and the preacher would be a foolish theorist who did not use his opportunity to impress and influence the one or the other.   There may be places and times (and would to God that for most preachers there were more of them !) when the godless can be reached, and then the worship and sermon can be more completely concentrated on the one object to win men for Christ.   But even in the ordinary

[1] Lk 15⁴.

conditions amid which most preachers do their work, the desire and purpose to present Christ as Saviour and Lord to those who as yet know Him not should be constant.

3. The preacher must also take into account the difference of age in those whom he addresses, and must try and adapt himself to their varying needs. (1) In recent years, much more attention has been given to the boys and girls, the young men and young women. For the first class it is usual to provide a short address often called the Children's Portion (five to ten minutes) at the ordinary morning service; but it may well be asked, Is that enough?[1] A children's service held in a hall, and conducted by another person than the minister, has the disadvantage that it detaches the religious interests of the children from the public worship of the Church, and the habit of church-going is not begun at the age when it is most easily formed. The writer himself in his last pastorate devoted the ordinary morning service on the first Sunday of each month to the boys and girls; and as this service was confined to an hour, time remained for a special address to the older people at the Communion Service which followed. While a knowledge of the method of teaching is here an essential qualification, the Children's Sermon[2] should not be forced into the mould of the Sunday-school lesson. It is well for the boys and girls to get accustomed to the form of preaching to which on other Sundays, as they sit with their parents, they will be expected to give such attention as they can. A text, an incident, a conversation, a character may be taken as the subject. The language must be simple and clear (but not babyish talk), the arrangement orderly; alliteration and other aids to memory should not be disdained in presenting the main divisions of the sermon; the illustrations should be abundant, but care should be taken that

---

[1] See Hoyt's *Vital Elements of Preaching*, pp. 141–160.

[2] So it is called, but it is really in most cases addressed to those who object to being called and treated as children, the boys and girls above eight or nine years of age.

they do not awaken incredulity, as many stories about extraordinarily good and godly boys and girls do, or provoke ridicule, since the sense of humour is often very quick in youth; the starting-point should be from what is familiar to the boys and girls in their common surroundings, and the goal should be an application of what has been taught to their daily life. There must be familiarity and sympathy with young life so that adult experience and character shall not be demanded, but only such Christian life as belongs properly to the stage of the natural development which has been reached. As the Bible has been written not for children but adults, it is not in all its parts equally suitable for them; and yet as parts were written for adults at an immature stage of moral and religious development, much can be found in it that fits their capacity. The Christian life as the faith, hope and love of the child of God towards the Father in personal discipleship of the Lord Jesus Christ is one which in all its essential features can be lived by boys and girls; and there need be no fear of premature development in seeking to win boys and girls for this relationship to God in Christ. The stories about children, boys or girls, in the Bible, the dealing of Jesus with the young, the graces, virtues and duties which belong even to youth, may be dealt with in the Children's Sermon.[1] As regards the Children's Address at the ordinary service a single story or picture or symbol may be all possible within the time; it may convey its own lesson, but the writer fails to see why the speaker to children should be forbidden, as he is by some theorists, to help them to understand the truth it may contain. If the Children's Address can be related to the subject of the sermon, it may awaken the interest of both old and young for the sermon; but it should not be so subordinated to the sermon that the interests of the boys and girls would be sacrificed in any degree.

(2) Not less urgent is the claim of the young men and

---

[1] See the writer's *The Minister and the Young Life of the Church*, chap. iii.

young women on the solicitude of the preacher. To attract them it may be necessary that the preacher should allow himself a wider range of subject and treatment than is common in the pulpit.[1] Much to the indignation of a few narrow "saints," the writer ventured to give two series of lectures on *Christian Truth in Modern Literature*, using classic works in illustration of lessons of faith and duty necessary for, and profitable to, those entering on manhood or womanhood. The literary interest was subordinate to the religious and moral; and yet it was an added gain that an interest in good literature was promoted among at least some of the hearers. The moral dangers, the intellectual difficulties, the social responsibilities of the class addressed may be dealt with; but what should be put in the forefront is the urgency of conscious and voluntary decision for Christ for those who have not yet taken the step as the essential condition of the fulfilment of the promise and the avoidance of the peril of their life, and the summons to those who are already Christians to make their experience more vitally and their character more vigorously Christian than was possible in adolescence. The writer never found it necessary to address the young men separately; and the larger influence and service of women in modern society makes imperative that they should not be less considered than men have been hitherto.

(3) His pastoral experience has convinced the writer that the middle-aged need the attention of the Christian preacher no less than the young. If the passions of youth with their perils have abated, middle age has its own evils: a lessening enthusiasm, a growing indifference, an increasing absorption in the cares of the world and the pursuit of wealth, an imperceptible decrease of the vitality and vigour of the soul. An occasional sermon of warning and encouragement to the fathers and mothers as well as the sons and daughters is not less necessary.

(4) The comfort that is spoken to the aged meets not these cases alone, but also the needs of the weary,

---

[1] See the book just mentioned, chap. vii.

the burdened, the sick, and the bereaved, represented in every congregation.[1] The Bible is a book of consolation; and the preacher does not do justice either to its wealth or the needs of men if he does not include among the kinds of sermons which give variety to his ministry those in which he applies its wealth to their needs. For the varying circumstances of life the preacher must have a quick eye, and a heart ready to respond to the appeals of human hearts as affected by them. It is often only by a personal experience of bereavement that a preacher learns how deep is the desolation that death brings into the home, and yet also how sustaining the hope that Christ inspires; and then he resolves that he will seek to comfort others as he himself had been comforted; but why does he wait to be taught by his personal experience what sympathy with others should have taught him?

4. The preacher must also ask himself the question: What impression does he intend to bring about? For it surely need not be said that he wants to secure the attention and command the interest in order that he may exercise an influence over his hearers. (1) In order that he may do this, his sermon must have not only a formal but even a material unity. Many preachers divide attention, distract interest, and so destroy influence by having "too many irons in the fire," to use a homely phrase. Not only from the æsthetic point of view is this a mistake, but still more from the practical. As regards the æsthetic point of view, a few sentences from Bassermann[2] may be quoted.

"As the chief law of all artistic production we recognized oneness in manifoldness, an inner harmony of the varied which appears combined into a work of art, produced by an idea ruling the whole and determining from within each single member, an organic combination of a single centre and a multiplicity of parts, which so presents itself to the observer, that it awakens his satisfaction and compels him to judge it beautiful." As regards the practical stand-

---

[1] Cf. Hoyt's *Vital Elements of Preaching*, pp. 117-137.
[2] *Handbuch der Geistlichen Beredsamkeit*, pp. 212-213.

point, Vinet [1] states it fully and clearly. " The oratorical discourse still more imperatively (than the work of art) demands unity. Not being read, but heard, it would more quickly fatigue the attention, if it compelled it to move successively in several directions. Lasting in comparison with other productions only a short time, it is still less allowable for it to occupy the hearer with several subjects. Summoned to act upon the will, it gains in this respect in concentrating itself on one single thought. There is the same difference between a discourse full, but incoherent, uncertain in its direction, or undisciplined, as between a crowd and an army. The strongest thoughts, which have not a common bond, injure one another, and by so much the more as they are stronger. It requires very strong minds to draw profit from what is not one, or does not of itself fall into unity. Assailed in turn by a crowd of impressions which neutralise one another, they are not made captive by any, and are not fixed on any."

(2) These considerations are here presented, although the subject of unity must be considered more fully in a subsequent chapter, as a reason why the preacher should determine at the very outset of his sermon what is the precise object that he is setting before himself. Does he desire to enlighten the reason or conscience, quicken the sentiments, or determine the will of his hearers ? It is true that the human personality is a unity, and that we cannot regard thinking, feeling, willing as separate faculties, the operations of which it is possible to separate from one another; and it is true also that in preaching *cognition* must be subordinated to *conation*, knowledge to action ; and yet we may distinguish sermons as *didactic*, *devotional* or *practical*, according to the emphasis on knowledge, emotion or action. In a previous chapter it was urged that it is a one-sided view to insist that sermons must be always directed towards practice, that each sermon must set a task to be done. Just because of the unity of personality the part may be presented in a sermon, and yet issue in the whole. The object of Christian faith may be presented to the mind of the

[1] *Homilétique*, pp. 48–49.

hearer, and yet if really presented may touch the heart and move the will. Distinct and adequate presentation may be the preacher's object, and he may leave these other effects to follow of themselves. He may also desire to leave as the result of his preaching the mood of devotion, adoration, gratitude. Not by the stimulant of excitement, but by the stimulus of inspiration he must seek this end, and this human inspiration can be only the response to the divine revelation presented in the sermon. The presentation is, however, in this case means and not end. The will cannot be moved to action apart from thought and feeling; but the preacher may distinctly and decisively will that the whole content of his sermon shall be directed towards influencing the will of his hearers. The text chosen will in most cases suggest where the emphasis should fall, or the preacher with a definite intention may seek out the text that will be most appropriate. While the preacher must retain his freedom under the Spirit's guidance, yet definiteness of intention will be gain and not loss.

5. In order to influence his hearers intellectually, morally or practically, the preacher must *interest* them; in order that he may do this he must discover what are their interests: he must pass from the subjective effect to the objective cause. (1) "*Interest*," says Vinet, "a subjective and an objective word, is in the second sense the property which an object has of drawing towards it our thought and our soul, so that a part, more or less considerable, of our happiness depends on it. The etymology (*inter esse*), as usually, defines the word. (In the subjective sense the interest consists in an identification, more or less profound and durable, with an object outside of us.)"[1] Knowledge depends on *selective interest*, as we attend to, and so become familiar with what interests us; the same river is not the same for the angler and the artist, because the one cares for fish the other for scenery.[2] His hearers'

[1] *Op. cit.*, p. 66.
[2] See Ward's *Naturalism and Agnosticism*, ii. p. 131.

interests are the points of contact for the preacher. There are many accidental, trivial, and artificial interests, and the preacher would degrade his office by allowing these to determine his choice of subject; although he might be justified in his introduction to refer even to such an interest to gain attention in order that as quickly as possible he might lead his hearers away from and above it.

(2) There are more permanent and universal interests of man, which, if not primary in the Christian Gospel, are consistent with it; and may serve as leading men to it. (a) As God is the Creator, so nature may lead to God. The scientific, the æsthetic, and the utilitarian interests of men in nature are not to be ignored, or neglected by the preacher, for the divine wisdom, the divine glory, and the divine goodness may all be disclosed in it.[1] For certain audiences it may be necessary to deal with the difficulties of, and the objections to, this *natural theology*. To make faith in God as Maker less difficult is a task the preacher need not disclaim, if he is competent to discharge it. But an ill-formed or ineffective apologetic is worse than useless.

(b) As God is the Ruler, so history may disclose His Providence.[2] As these sentences are being written the war of the Allied with the Central Powers of Europe has raised the problem of God's government in human affairs in a very acute form; but at all times *theodicy* claims a place in Christian preaching, since evil and sin are universal and constant facts for mankind. History claims the interest of men, and for moral and religious instruction no rigid boundary need be drawn between sacred and profane, as such a distinction represents a superseded standpoint of thought. There was a preparation for the Gospel in Greece and Rome no less than in Judæa; there is to-day a preparation for the Gospel in India, China, Japan. Human events have divine significance. The Christian revelation is historical in its character, not by accident, but of its very essence, for it is not so much a

---

[1] Cf. Vinet, *op. cit.*, pp. 93–94.   [2] Cf. *op. cit.*, pp. 90–93.

divine word spoken as a divine deed done; it is not an abstract illumination, but a concrete salvation. The greater part of the Holy Scriptures is historical record, and even prophetic and apostolic discourse can best be understood in its historical setting. Abundant material is thus at the preacher's hands in addressing himself to this common human interest in history. He who can make the past live in the present by vivid description and vigorous narration, may so capture the interest of his hearers as to bring them into the presence of the Living God in history.

(c) But God is not the sole actor in history; and we must recognise that many men are more interested in the activity of their fellow-men in history than in the overruling of God. This interest to-day is not in action and its results alone, but in personality, experience, character, the inner life and growth, the progress or deterioration of individuals.[1] Modern psychology and modern imaginative literature, which is dominated by the psychological interest, are opening up wide stretches of the realm of the soul. By this method the biographical and autobiographical material of the Holy Scriptures can be made more intelligible and attractive than ever before. The great masters of fiction, by their insight into and disclosure of the secrets of the soul, offer abundant illustrations of the teaching of the Gospel regarding man, his peril and his promise, his degradation and his dignity. With all reverence for His uniqueness, we may even venture by this method to make the personality of Our Lord Himself more luminous.

(d) By addressing these interests, in nature, history, man, the Christian preacher greatly widens the range of his preaching; but does he not also lower its authority and weaken his appeal? Is there not in the New Testament an exclusive, almost intolerant urgency regarding the one thing needful, the good part which shall not be taken away?[2] The treatment of such subjects as have

---

[1] See Vinet, *op. cit.*, pp. 95–98.   [2] Lk 10⁴².

been mentioned is not to be a substitute for, but sub-ordinate to, and even only a transition to the supreme interests of the Gospel. In all, through all, over all, Christ is to be preached and can be preached. Jesus Himself used nature, history and human life to illustrate and enforce His teaching. A constant reiteration of a plan of salvation, a theory of the atonement, an appeal for conversion defeats its own purpose: men grow "Gospel-hardened." The method of indirectness in dealing with souls is often more effective. "The man of God is to be thoroughly furnished unto all good works"; and the Church cannot confine itself to breathless evangelisation, but must seek to edify at leisure. These interests are themselves legitimate and belong to the completeness of the Christian personality. Variety and even novelty are conditions of evoking and sustaining the interests of congregations. Men must be sought where they are, and brought by the ways most open to them to where Christ is.[1]

(3) In the Gospel itself there are three interests, which in many hearers may have become dormant, but to which no soul is altogether insensible, and which, therefore, the preacher may by argument and appeal, hope to make active again. Vinet mentions two, the *dogmatic* and the *ethical*,[2] or in God and goodness. It seems to the writer that we should distinguish a third, although it might be included in the first as God's gift, or the second as the fruit of goodness; this may be described as the *personal* interest in immortality. On the one hand, this division corresponds to Kant's three postulates of the practical reason, God, freedom and immortality, and, on the other, to the three Christian graces, faith, love and hope. Surely the questions of interest to every man are: What must I believe? What ought I to do? What may I hope?

(*a*) In dealing with these subjects the preacher must

---

[1] Cf. Vinet, *op. cit.*, pp. 98–101.

[2] *Op. cit.*, pp. 74–90. Cf. Christlieb, *Homiletic*, pp. 193–203, and Hoyt, *The Preacher*, pp. 305–348.

always keep in mind the difference between his interest in these interests, and the interest of his hearers; for he and they are not in the same way affected by the common objects of interest. As a student, a scholar, a thinker, his interest is intellectual, but theirs is practical; he as a man shares their interest, but they do not share his. He seeks for himself the unity of system; that is not their concern at all. They want counsel, comfort, cheer, help, guidance in and for daily life with its trials, struggles, temptations, doubts and fears. Their individual interests may be partial; and it may be his duty to widen their outlook, so that they may discover that aspects of truth, duty. promise which seemed meaningless for them hitherto have a great and an abiding worth. For the sake of formal completeness he must not, however, force upon them considerations altogether unrelated to their needs and aims, while striving ever to lead them out into a wider Christian thought and life. General principles must in preaching receive not so much abstract exposition as concrete application. Many a question intellectually interesting to the preacher may be practically uninteresting to his hearers.

(b) The older method of preaching in which a system of doctrine was presented in the language of the schools is quite out of date. Theology and ethics alike must be presented experimentally and untechnically in the language of, not the *man-in-the-street*, but of common life among cultivated men and women. There must be individual diagnosis alike spiritually and morally, so that both the disease may be exposed, and the remedy proposed. Without encouraging morbid introspection on the one side or casuistic investigation on the other, the preacher must nevertheless deal with human experience and character, at close quarters, with intimate knowledge, so as to bring the Gospel just where and just as it is needed, and can work good.[1]

[1] A great preacher has dealt with this subject. Henry Ward Beecher's *Lectures on Preaching*, third series, contains a most interesting and valuable discussion regarding the treatment of such themes in the pulpit.

6. The occasion may also determine the purpose of a sermon. (1) In the Churches in which there is a lectionary giving due regard to the Christian year, the preacher is provided with the guidance he needs.[1] But even in the Churches in which the Christian year is not recognised, it is customary to observe Christmas, Easter, Whitsuntide ; and the preacher loses an opportunity of which he should make the most if he does not make these festivals the occasion for presenting the great facts of the Christian faith, the Incarnation, the Death and Resurrection of Christ, and the Descent of the Spirit. When Christmas Day itself is not observed the Sunday nearest the date should be marked by the appropriate services ; and when Good Friday is not kept, at one of the services on Easter Sunday, or on the previous Palm Sunday, the sacrifice of our redemption should be proclaimed. In days when the historical basis of the Christian faith is being assailed, it is of urgent importance that these facts should be kept prominent in the mind of the Christian Church. So many-sided are these facts, that no preacher need ever be at a loss for a subject or text suitable for the occasion.

(2) It is customary in many churches on the Sunday nearest Christmas to call attention to the subject of *Peace*. It will be more than ever necessary for the Christian Church to bear its testimony to the Christian ideal of a humanity itself reconciled in its reconciliation with God. Discord and division are not confined to the relations of nations to one another ; in the family, industry and society there are antagonisms to be removed ; and the proclamation of Christ as *Prince of Peace* in all human relations is always appropriate at the Christmas season. With Whitsuntide another interest is often very fitly connected, the unity of the Christian Church. Even if the preacher has no scheme of reunion of Churches to advocate, it is well that the Christian believers should be reminded that they are members of one body in Christ, that amid all outward

[1] In Christlieb's *Homiletic* will be found many suggestions of subjects for the festival seasons, pp. 226–274.

divisions inwardly there is only one Christian community in earth and heaven.

(3) These Christian festivals not only call for the appropriate subjects, but might at least sometimes serve as guides to the preacher in the choice of his themes for the greater part of the year. From October till December he might let the thought of the Lord's Advent guide him, and he might give a series of sermons on the preparation for Christ's coming in the Old Testament. Between Christmas and Easter he might deal with the outstanding features of the ministry of Our Lord. From Easter till Whitsuntide the doctrine of His Person and Work might be expounded. After Whitsuntide the functions and obligations of the Christian Church might be discussed. There can be no doubt that what is needed by most Christians is a more comprehensive and systematic knowledge of the common beliefs of the Church, and the preacher should aim at imparting such knowledge.

(4) While the divisions of the calendar are artificial, yet the last or the first Sunday of the Year, whichever is nearest New Year's Day, offers a suitable occasion for calling attention to the passage of time, the changes in life it brings with it, the use of remembrance and anticipation in the progress of the soul, and the context of eternity in which God has set the life of man. A correspondence with nature is to be noted, as after the shortest day the renewal of nature has already begun, even if the first signs of its resurrection are not at once observed. Easter Sunday may without any detraction from the supreme importance of the event it commemorates receive its reference to nature also; for then the renewal has become manifest. That on one Sunday in summer there should be Flower Services, and on one in Autumn the Harvest Festival, is an arrangement which the preacher may gladly welcome. For God is the God of Nature as well as of Grace; and while in some of its aspects nature may present problems which only the confidence which grace inspires enables us to bear unsolved and yet keep

faith in God, there is also an accord of Nature and Grace, as the greatest of all Teachers made so clear in His sayings. Modern civilisation and culture remove most men from the constant and close contact with nature which man needs for the wholeness of his life, and these two occasions at least should be used to bring home to human self-sufficiency man's complete dependence on God in nature. Piety would be enriched were the religious significance of nature fully recognised in the teaching of the pulpit.

(5) There are certain moral or religious interests which are claiming notice in the pulpit on a fixed occasion. There is a world-wide observance of Temperance Sunday early in November. While the primary intention is to call attention to the vice of drunkenness and to the duty of Total Abstinence, the preacher may sometimes take a wider outlook, and deal rather with general principle than particular instance. Drunkenness is one form of self-indulgence, and total abstinence one form of self-control ; and it is not asking too much of the preacher that once a year at least he should call attention to the peril of the one and the blessing of the other. Although there is more in the Bible about the evils of drunkenness than at first appears, and the preacher might find many texts to serve his purpose, yet it will be well for him generally to take a wider standpoint.

(6) Most denominations also have their Missionary Sunday, when either a missionary occupies the pulpit or the minister himself is asked to deal with the subject of foreign missions. Christianity is by its character universal, and it must be in its method missionary ; and not once a year only will the preacher who prizes its character enforce its method. But once a year at least in more explicit form and with more deliberate intention should its world-wide destiny be proclaimed. The minister who desires himself to understand the Gospel and to present it to others adequately, will not be content to have a missionary as his substitute in the discharge of this duty. If not on Missionary Sunday then on other occasions he

will bear his testimony regarding this primary obligation of the Christian Church. The grounds on which the appeal for sympathy and support, service and even sacrifice, may now be made are different from what they were at the beginning of the modern missionary era, but they are not less solid than they were; and even from the standpoint of modern scholarship and knowledge, the material the Holy Scriptures and the history of the Christian Church offer is more abundant than ever, and its argument even more cogent.[1]

(7) In recent years an appeal has been made in some districts for the observance of a Civic Sunday; and the appeal should not be lightly set aside. Social reform has a place in the thought and life of to-day such as it never had before. The Churches have lost and are losing influence because many ministers have been too indifferent in these matters. The working-classes are in some parts of the country being estranged from the Christian Church because they do not find in the pulpit the interest they themselves feel. It seems imperative that the Christian ideal should be presented in its corporate as well as individual appeal: for modern conditions have proved the inadequacy of philanthropy, and the necessity of what has been called social politics.[2] Many of the worst evils can be removed only by the efforts of the community as a whole. Again it does not seem to be too much to give at least one day in the year to the advocacy of social reform. To this course two objections are often offered, which must be met as briefly as can be. (a) It is said that these social questions cannot be dealt with without political partisanship. If one party has identified its interests with the protection of some monstrous social evil, such as the liquor traffic or the opposition to some imperative social good, such as an improvement of the land system, it is intoler-

---

[1] The writer has attempted in his book on *The Missionary Obligation* to restate the argument and appeal.

[2] See Kirkman Gray's *History of English Philanthropy*, and his *Philanthropy and the State*; also Hoyt's *The Preacher*, pp. 239–256, and Coffin's *In a Day of Social Rebuilding*.

able that those who, though Christian, are pleased to belong to it, should claim to impose silence on the pulpit. The preacher must avoid partisanship; but he must not be charged with it because in his advocacy of social reform, he offends the partisanship of some of his hearers. There are some signs of the times that we may soon reach a larger measure of agreement among all men of good will, so that the common good will not be as much as it has been the sport of party.

(b) Further, it is objected that the preacher is not an expert in economics or politics, and that therefore he abuses his position, if he uses his authority to cover his ignorance and incompetence. It may be admitted that Social Problems cannot be solved without expert knowledge. But the preacher can make himself acquainted with the conclusions of experts, and he can then exercise his judgment, trained in other studies, upon these. The work of the experts has been done, when a Social Reform becomes practical politics, and in giving his support to measures which the knowledge of experts justifies, the preacher does not abuse his authority. Still more, the main function of the pulpit in this connection is not so much to advocate reforms, although it may do this even, as to set forth the Christian ideal of brotherhood as standard and motive of all social reforms. The prophets show in their teaching that social morality and genuine religion are inseparable; and the teaching of Jesus and the life of the Apostolic Church contain abundant material for the preacher who wants to show his hearers how each may love his neighbour as himself.

(8) Most Churches have their Sunday-school Anniversary or Children's Day. There is often a Children's Service at which the preacher addresses himself to the children. But the question arises, what use is to be made of this morning and evening service? Many preachers, to draw a conclusion from such information as the writer has been able to gather, make no attempt to take appropriate subjects, but preach sermons which might be given

on any Sunday in the year.   The interests of the young life are so important, that this seems to be a neglect of duty.   The place of the child in, and the claim of the child on, the Church should in some form or other be presented at these services.   In view of the present conditions which imperil the Christian home, it does seem fitting and useful to address Christian parents on their privileges and obligations at one of the services.   The failure of the Sunday school to retain its older scholars, and to pass them on into the membership of the Church on the one hand, and the progress in Sunday-school methods now possible on the other, suggest themes for the other service.   For a number of years the writer addressed parents in the morning, children in the afternoon, and teachers in the evening, and never found dearth of material; and it is a proceeding which, as practicable, he would venture to recommend to others.

(9) Within the last few years the Student Christian movement has also made an appeal, that on one Sunday in the year reference should be made to the peril and the promise of the youths and maidens in universities and colleges.   The writer does not suggest that the preacher should make a practice of once a year dealing with this subject; but he does say that the subject of education in the widest sense is important enough for occasional treatment in the pulpit.   The advocacy of as accessible, as co-ordinated and as complete a system of public education as possible does not seem to him at all out of place in the Christian Church.

(10) In some churches it is the practice to hold a church anniversary and a pastor's anniversary.   On these occasions many preachers make no attempt to take an appropriate subject, and yet surely the Christian ideal of the Church and of the Ministry is well worth recalling both for reproof and encouragement; and the New Testament deals with this subject so frequently and so variedly that there need never be a want of matter.   The conception both of the Church and the Ministry is among many

Christians so much lowered, that the opportunity should not be lost to correct the error by the teaching of the Bible. A preacher will find his own sense of his calling deepened if he will endeavour to gather together what the New Testament has to say about the Church and the place of the ministry in it; and if he succeeds in his object in conveying to his people that teaching, his relation to them will be cleansed and hallowed. For this reason even if it be not the practice of the Church to hold an anniversary, the pastor will do well to set apart for himself, whether he intimate it to his people or not, a Sunday when he will examine himself and help them to examine themselves regarding his and their high and holy calling in Christ Jesus. The tendency to turn the preacher into the orator, and the Church into the audience, can be arrested only by a recovery of the blessed and fruitful pastoral relationship, and to this end the pulpit can make its contribution in this way. On such an occasion, too, an appeal might be made to the youths and young men to consider seriously the claims of the Christian ministry as a life calling.

(11) A protest is frequently made against the multi-plication of such special occasions, and certainly the appeals are often trivial enough. An Anti-Nicotine Sunday would be an absurdity, although in a sermon on Temperance excessive smoking might be rebuked. While a sermon might be preached very profitably on Kindness to Animals, such a subject can scarcely be made an annual fixture. The occasions which have been mentioned, however, seem to the writer rightfully to claim a place in the Church's calendar. Both services need not be dedicated to the same subject, except on the Christian festivals. If to deal with them it were necessary for the preacher to abandon the preaching of the Gospel, the writer would not have a single word to say in their support. But in dealing with them the preacher should be preaching the Gospel in its manifold applications to the faith and duty of man. For Christ is to the Church wisdom and righteousness, truth and grace, in all the varied relations and all the varying interests of

the life of mankind. The preacher should touch no subject, however much it may be pressed on his notice or appeal to his interest, that he cannot bring into captivity to Christ, and he need refuse no theme, in dealing with which he is able to set forth the length and breadth, the depth and height of the divine revelation and human redemption in Him. As he is Christ's and Christ God's, so all things are his.[1]

(12) Christlieb has a section[2] dealing with " the events and Church needs of the individual Christian life (occasional addresses)," to which church customs in Germany give a prominence that is not generally given to them in Great Britain. At a baptism, or marriage, or a funeral, it is not usual to deliver a long address; when such is given the significance of the ordinance in the first two cases, and the obligations it imposes, should be simply and shortly stated; in the last case an estimate of character, which should never exceed the bounds of truth, and be controlled by delicacy of feeling, should be subordinated to the declaration of the Christian hope with the comfort for the mourners which it can bring. The confirmation address has no place in the Churches which do not observe this ordinance; and yet it would be well, if when a number of young persons are being welcomed to the fellowship of faith, the privileges and duties of this sacred relationship were set forth. When the ordinance of the Lord's Supper is being observed, a preparatory address may be commended. While there must be a call to self-examination and self-dedication, penitence and faith, what man should do must not be as prominent as what God has done in " all our redemption cost—all our redemption won."

[1] 1 Co 3[22, 23].
[2] *Op. cit.*, pp. 291–307; cf. Bassermann, *op. cit.*, pp. 440–452.

CHAPTER II.

THE CHOICE OF SUBJECTS AND TEXTS.

1. SEVERAL references have already been made to the common Christian practice of attaching a sermon to a text, and reasons suggested for the continuance of the practice. Vinet [1] discusses the question more fully than most writers in Homiletics, who usually take the custom for granted. In dealing first with the subject, setting aside the text, the writer has made it clear that he does not regard a text as essential to the sermon, and in fact it is not. What makes a sermon Christian is not the employment of a text, but the spirit of the preacher. (1) A sermon may be Christian without a text, and may under a text conceal its un-Christian character. Subject and text may be forced into an unnatural alliance. Not every text contains a subject for a sermon, and some texts contain several subjects. Sometimes the text does not contain all the subject, and sometimes a great deal more than the subject. Why not abandon the text, and let the preacher fall back on his growing experience as well as the Bible? Thus the preacher would be freed from either bondage to his text in treating his subject or doing violence to his text for the sake of his subject.

(2) While recognising the force of all these considerations, Vinet nevertheless decides in favour of the use of the text for the following reasons: (*a*) the consecration of this method by universal and permanent custom in the Church, and the offence which would be given by its abandonment; (*b*) the indication the text gives that the preacher is the Servant of the Word of God; (*c*) the real

[1] *Homilétique*, pp. 102–114. Cf. Christlieb, pp. 135–160.

advantages it offers; it is a moral benefit to the preacher that he must attach his sermon to a text; it inspires the respect of the hearer to listen to a saying of the Holy Scriptures at the very beginning of the sermon; generally a sermon developed out of a text will be better than one resting on an abstract subject; and for most preachers texts suggest subjects, and so give greater variety to their preaching.

(3) Having reached this conclusion, he shows that the difficulties are in theory greater than in practice. Three cases have to be considered. It often happens that text and subject exactly correspond, and no difficulty is felt. If the preacher has been led to a subject, for which he cannot find a text which quite fits it; yet if it be a subject, Christian in character and intention, it will not be impossible to find a connection between it and a text. The subject may be the genus, of which the text offers the species, or *vice versa*. The text may be the concrete instance and the subject the abstract principle. The text may be a general statement, of which the subject offers a particular application. Peter's refusal to let Jesus wash his feet illustrates *false independence*. The words about love as the fulfilment of law may be applied in commending *total abstinence*. (At a later stage the connection of text and subject will be treated in detail.) If the preacher is familiar with his Bible, texts will suggest subjects, and without any violence the one will as it were grow out of the other.

2. The use of a text, however, imposes an obligation not to handle the Word of God deceitfully.[1] The preacher must see to it that his subject is congruous with his text, and that the text justifies the treatment which he gives to his subject. He must not claim the authority of the Holy Scriptures for his individual opinions and even for his private interpretations. Several rules may be laid down for the preacher's guidance and warning. (1) We cannot now treat the whole Bible as a text-book of theology and

[1] 2 Co 4².

ethics; but within the Bible must recognise differences of inspiration and degrees of authority. We must not deal with an utterance of Job in his sore bewilderment of soul as conveying the mind of God as adequately and directly as a saying of Jesus. The subjective feeling of a psalmist regarding his relation to God does not correspond accurately with the objective fact of God's relation to him. The details of a parable are not the contents of a creed or a code. One link in a chain of argument is not to be made the foundation of a doctrine. It is the Word of God, the Gospel of grace in the Bible, of which the preacher must lay hold for himself and set forth to others.

(2) But even here it would not correspond with the genuinely Christian faith, which knows not the bondage of the letter, but lives in the freedom of the Spirit, to make any attempt to impose even the Word of God and the Gospel of grace by authority merely without commending it to the reason and the conscience. The authority of Christ is a reasonable and righteous authority; it is not outward compulsion but inward constraint; it claims the intelligent assent and the voluntary consent of man. The preacher must not try to cover his incapacity to appeal to reason and conscience by quoting Scripture dogmatically. The reverence for the Holy Scriptures which the Christian congregation cherishes, and which gives speaker and hearers a common ground, must not be abused, but used with respect for the reason and conscience of both. It is the preacher's business so to present his subject in expounding his text that the acceptance of his message will be intelligent and righteous.

(3) In a Church in which the Apocryphal writings are not accepted as canonical, a text from these writings would be out of place, and would not serve the purpose for which a text is chosen. But it would be equally an abuse of the confidence of a congregation for a preacher to take his text from the Authorised Version, if either the reading or the rendering is doubtful. To take a verse out of the passage in Mark's Gospel (16^{9-20}) which is by evidence of the MSS

proved not to be an original part of it, but a later addition
of doubtful origin, in order to preach about the evidence of
the Resurrection or the last charge of the Risen Lord,
would be simply dishonest.   Not less so would be the use
of 1 Jn 5[7] to prove the doctrine of the Trinity, as that
verse is very generally recognised as spurious and is
omitted in the R.V.   To take advantage of the mistranslation in Ac 26[28] "Almost thou persuadest me to be a
Christian" to represent Agrippa as a type of the anxious
inquirer, or to expound the beginnings of the Christian life,
would be no less blameworthy.   A variant reading as in
Ro 12[11] in which the last clause runs either *serving the
Lord* or *serving the opportunity* (R.V.marg.) might quite
legitimately, with due explanation, be used as suggesting
the connection between the service of God and the best
use of our time.   When differences of rendering are
warranted by the original text, the thought of the hearers
may be enriched by calling their attention to the variations
of meaning, and the preacher may find useful material for
his sermon in giving his reasons for preferring the one or
the other rendering.   What must be required is absolute candour ; the preacher must not snatch any advantage from the
ignorance of his hearers regarding readings and renderings.

(4) There are many cases in which the same words
may bear different interpretations apart from or in their
context.   The practice of the apostolic writers in dealing
with the Old Testament cannot here be our guide, as in
their quotations they pay no regard to the context.   Thus
Matthew's quotation from Hos 11[1] in 2[15] "Out of Egypt
have I called my son," applies to Jesus what is written of
the exodus of Israel from Egypt.   "Ephraim is a cake not
turned," [1] dealt with by itself, does suggest a one-sided
development of human character, as it seems to describe a
cake cooked too much on one side and too little on the
other.   But the context shows another meaning, *i.e.*,
Ephraim, because not snatched from the fires of judgment
by God's mercy, will be destroyed, as the cake is burned

[1] Hos 7[8].

which is allowed to remain on the hot oven. The preacher must not ask himself : What meaning can I impose on the text ? but : What meaning did the writer or the speaker intend ?   Whatever excuse there might be for preachers of former times, the preacher of to-day is without excuse if he does not follow the *historical* interpretation of the text ; and this involves a study of the literary character of the writing with which he is dealing (prose or poetry, history or parable, reflective or devotional literature, prophecy or apocalyptic), the purpose, occasion, date, authorship, etc., of the writing, and where that is ascertainable, the personal characteristics of the writer.   Exegesis with literary and historical criticism is a labour which the preacher must be ready to undergo, in order that he may lawfully and not unlawfully use his text in accordance with what it does mean, and not what he thinks it may mean, or wishes it to mean.[1]

3. If the sermon should begin with a text, and should attach itself to the historical interpretation of the text, two questions arise : How shall the preacher find the appropriate text ? and, What connections between the sermon and the text does the historical interpretation afford or permit ?   In the preceding pages it has been assumed that the unity of the sermon is secured rather by the presentation of a subject than the exposition of a text, although in many cases there is so close a correspondence between subject and text that the presentation of the one can be best secured by the exposition of the other.   We must recognise, however, that for the preacher who is more at home in his Bible than in any other realm of knowledge and understanding, the more common experience will be that he finds a text before he thinks of a subject.   Reserving at present the other case where a subject is first thought of and then a text for it desired, we may now confine ourselves to this case.   (1) Is the finding of a text an accident, a providence, an inspiration ?   It has some-

---

[1] The writer has devoted a section of his book, *A Guide to Preachers*, to answer the question—*How to Study the Bible ?* pp. 7–103.

times been assumed that the preacher should wait till God gives him a text. A text, as it were, strikes him suddenly; it lays hold on him; it will not let him go till he preaches on it; and till he has dealt with it no other can claim his attention. Every man who has any belief in the guiding hand of God, and is ever seeking to be guided, must have had such an experience. The writer himself on one or two occasions has been compelled to change text and subject even in the pulpit; he found himself unable to deliver the sermon he had prepared, and compelled to deliver a message which took possession of him to the exclusion of any other. This he must add, that the subject which thus laid hold on him was one on which he had meditated much, for the treatment of which the material was already present in his mind as it were in solution, needing only the insertion of the text for its precipitation. There may be some preachers for whom this waiting upon God for a text appears a necessity, and whose experience justifies this practice, but it is to be feared that many men who are not living on the highest levels of meditation and communion more often get their texts by accident, a chance suggestion, a trivial association, or even have to choose some text out of sheer necessity because they cannot delay the choice any longer.[1]

(2) The writer is convinced that for most men the better and wiser course is to exercise some foresight, even to follow some system. The preacher should be a constant and diligent student of the Bible, studying it with the best aids modern scholarship can offer, and studying it disinterestedly that he may fully know and truly understand it, and not merely that he may find in it texts and material for sermons. But there is no need that as a scholar he should divest himself of his interest as a preacher; and he need not be less accurate as a scholar because the Bible has for him the value not of human literature alone, but of the channel through which God gives him his message to

[1] A passage in which this method is ridiculed may be referred to in Watson's *The Cure of Souls*, pp. 5–7.

deliver to men. In his study a number of texts will be
suggested to him, and suggested for their proper use, as he
comes to them in their context, and so runs no risk of
imposing an artificial sense arbitrarily upon them. It will
be no adventitious quality of strangeness or picturesqueness
or dramatic force that will arrest his attention, but their
inherent value as focusing the truth taught in the whole
context. It will be not the outward appearance, as it were,
but the inward reality of the text that will determine his
choice. If he goes systematically through the Bible,[1]
although, of course, all parts are not equally fruitful for the
preacher, selecting the pregnant texts which can bring to
the birth of his sermon the fairest and noblest offspring of
the Word of God, he will have a selection of texts at his
disposal which will present not fragmentarily and dispro-
portionately, but with some approach to adequacy, the
contents of the Divine Revelation.

(3) But even if he has this store of texts, how shall he
use it ? The purpose or the occasion of his sermon may
limit the range of his choice. His personal preference
may draw him so strongly to one text rather than another
that he may regard this as an indication that his meditation, his disposition, or his aspiration at the time qualify
him to deal with it with clearer understanding, deeper
feeling, or more steadfast purpose than with any other.
The necessities of his congregation must also be present
with him. There may be circumstances important and
urgent enough to have influence on his choice. But allowing for all these special motives, the writer still holds that
there may be system in determining the choice out of this
store of texts. It is to be feared that many congregations
to-day are impatient of continuous instruction ; and it is
not necessary for the preacher to intimate his intentions, if
such an intimation is undesirable. He may have a definite
plan in his own mind, and his hearers, although they know
it not, will get the benefit of a method, against which they

---

[1] This method is recommended by one of the greatest preachers of to-day,
Dr. Jowett, *The Preacher : his Life and Work*, pp. 120–122.

have only a foolish prejudice. To give a few instances, he may take a characteristic utterance from each of the prophets, and may present these oracles in such an order as will reproduce the progress of the divine revelation; he may deal with sayings of Jesus so as to convey the main features of His religious and moral teaching; he may take Paul's autobiographical references in his Epistles so as to exhibit his Christian experience. The sermons in such a series need not be given on successive Sundays, but may be given once a month.[1] The preacher may reserve himself freedom to take up any other topics at any time; and yet such a plan in his own mind will save him a great deal of wasted time and toil in trying to find texts, and will benefit himself as well as his hearers.

4. We may now turn to the other case where the preacher starts with the subject. (1) Here again occasion, purpose or personal preference may lead him to determine on treating a subject. Only in very exceptional cases can the subject be such as not to allow the ready and easy choice of an appropriate text. The more familiar the preacher is with his Bible, the greater his command over such a store of texts as has just been spoken of, the less difficulty he will meet, and the more success he will get in his endeavour to join together fitly subject and text. (a) The connection may be very varied in different cases. Does he wish to deal with the question of theatre-going, card-playing, dancing or any amusement? Paul lays down the principle, "Whatsoever is not of faith is sin,"[2] and the preacher may show the application of the principle in each case. Whatever injures the Christian's personal relation to Christ as Saviour and Lord is unlawful for him; whatever furthers that relation is lawful. Does the preacher desire to deal with the burdens which human relationships and social arrangements impose, which cannot be regarded as personal duty, and yet in the cheerful acceptance of

---

[1] The writer, when pastor of a church, in the summer vacation, planned his work for the following year, and for himself found benefit in the method.

[2] Ro 14²³.

which there comes blessing? May he not turn to the story of Simon of Cyrene, who was compelled to bear the Cross with Jesus, whose name is now remembered for this enforced service wherever the Gospel is preached, and to whose home a blessing seems to have come also, if the sons are mentioned by Mark as fellow-believers?[1] In the one case the reasoning is *deductive* from the general principle to the particular instance; in the other *inductive* or *vice versâ*. For the enforcement of the duty of total abstinence in view of the evils of intemperance, direct appeal may be made to the teaching both of Jesus[2] and of Paul[3] regarding "offence." The mutual toleration of the "conservative" and the "liberal" members of the Christian Church might legitimately be enforced on the ground of Paul's teaching about the "weak" and the "strong" in Romans 14, even although the difference was practical and not doctrinal, as these are co-ordinate particular instances which can easily be brought under the general principles of individual liberty and mutual responsibility as reciprocally defining and limiting each other.

(*b*) Reasoning from analogy is here very helpful. If the preacher desires to warn against the peril of lowering the Christian ideal in a time of war, he may take as the basis of his sermon the 137th Psalm as presenting in the condition of the exiles in Babylon a sufficient resemblance to warrant such an argument. It will be quite legitimate for a preacher, who desired to discuss the steps to be taken to delay and prevent war, to deal with Jesus' instructions regarding the treatment of an offending brother in detail,[4] suggesting the counterparts of diplomatic remonstrance, arbitration and cessation of diplomatic relations with the offending nation by other nations, parties to the agreement.

(*c*) The subject may connect itself with what in the text is subordinate relatively to the context, and yet may be of primary importance as regards the subject. Thus in Jn 12[32] the necessity of the death of Christ is the pro-

---

[1] Mk 15[21].
[2] Mt 18[6-10].
[3] 1 Co 10[32].
[4] Mt 18[15-17].

minent thought relatively to the general principle laid down in the figurative saying of verse [24]. But the preacher may lay hold of the idea of Jesus' *universal attractiveness* in order to preach a missionary sermon, and His sacrificial love may be brought in as a subordinate thought, as one of the reasons for the *universal attractiveness*. But it would be only right in this case that the preacher should state what the primary idea of his text is, and should show reason why he takes the subsidiary idea as his subject. Again, the subject may allow for the treatment of only part of the text, and not of the whole, as in the above instance, where the proof of the necessity of the death of Christ is what the text itself calls for; in such a case the partial treatment of the text is justified only if its incompleteness is frankly stated. If a preacher could not honestly preach the necessity of Christ's death, to the writer at least it seems that he would have no right to use this text without confessing his inability. But we must claim for the preacher freedom to treat his text incompletely in accordance with the limits imposed by his subject, so long as the incompleteness is clearly stated, and in the Introduction the text is briefly explained as a whole.

(*d*) It may not be by any recognised process of reasoning that a text and a subject are related, although it will be well for the preacher as a rule to avoid connecting a subject with a text unless he can show such a process, if not explicitly to his hearers, yet at least to himself. There may be a connection that comes under the more general term of *suggestion*. If a man has a fanciful, wayward mind, if he is imperfectly instructed in the Holy Scriptures and Christian truth, it will be at his peril that he will follow the suggestions of his text, for as a rule they will be " will-o'-the-wisps " leading him into a mental bog. But if a man has adequate knowledge and disciplined judgment, suggestion, even when it cannot be reduced to rigid logical form, may be a helpful guide. The details of the parables of Jesus, for instance, should not be allegorised; and yet they are often very suggestive; and it would be an unnecessary restriction of the liberty of the preacher never to allow him to use what these details suggest. The parable of the *Prodigal Son* (to use the common designation) is not intended to be a complete system of theology, and yet it suggests the answer to a number of important questions regarding God, man, sin, judgment, penitence, pardon, etc., and it would be ridiculous to forbid a preacher's use of it in this way! [1] In this case perhaps the principle of analogy offers some sanction; but even if it did not, suggestion, so long as it is given only as suggestion, may be justified.

(*e*) One text may contain a number of subjects, and the preacher may desire to deal with only one of them; but it is well if in treating that one he is able to subordinate the others to it. We may examine as a concrete instance Jn 3[16]. Here there are four great themes for the Christian preacher, the love of God, the gift of Christ, the sufficiency of faith, the eternal life. Each might be made the subject of a sermon, and the others be worked into the treatment of it. Most preachers would probably lay hold on the first as the predominant theme, but the context rather indicates that it is the last, the eternal life. If we take *the love of God* as subject, the outline of the sermon might be as follows:—(1) the distinctive character, (2) the exhaustive measure, (3) the universal demand, (4) the final result. If we take *the eternal life*, the divisions might be (1) the distinctive character, (2) the ultimate cause, (3) the immediate channel, (4) the essential condition. The *gift of Christ* might be discussed as regards (1) its reason, (2) its riches, (3) its requirement, (4) its result. The *sufficiency of faith* might be proved as follows:—(1) because all men can exercise it; (2) because its exercise secures eternal life; (3) because that eternal life is the purpose of the gift of Christ; (4) because the gift of Christ is the highest expression of the love which is the perfection of God. A preacher will find that he can preach a number of sermons on one text, taking now one subject, then another contained in it.

(*f*) A text may serve to focus a character, an event, a

---

[1] See the writer's *The Joy of Finding.*

period; and it would be unreasonable not to allow the preacher to use the text as the starting-point of the discussion of the whole subject. The verses in which the evangelist records the look of Jesus which brought Peter to repentance[1] may fitly serve as the text for a sermon on Peter's fall and recovery, including necessarily some discussion of his experience and character. With the 137th Psalm as starting-point the preacher might sketch the history of the exiles in Babylon and draw from it the lessons it can convey even to the Christian nations; and the following divisions of his theme might be suggested: (1) the difficulty of singing the Lord's song in the strange land; (2) the danger of forgetting the Lord's song in the strange land; (3) the discovery of the Lord as ruling even in the strange land (Cyrus' decree of return); (4) the disclosure of the truth of the Lord in the experience of the strange land (the Prophet of the Exile, especially the picture of the Suffering Servant). Just as the preacher is not always bound to exhaust the text in his treatment of his subject, so neither should he be limited in his treatment of the subject by the text. So long as he avoids arbitrary and artificial connections, so long as his sermon is an organic development, of which the text is the germ, he is using his lawful liberty and is not guilty of blameworthy caprice.

(2) The choice of subjects for treatment no less than of texts calls for some method and system. Without this the danger is that the congregation will be made the sport or victim of the individual peculiarity of the preacher. His circumstances, his moods, his interests, his studies will too exclusively determine what his subjects will be. A great defect of Christian thought and life to-day for which the pulpit must accept a large share of responsibility is partiality and disproportion, the lack of an all-round knowledge of Christian truth and duty.[2] The pulpit is not a

[1] Lk 22[61-62].

[2] The ignorance of the mass of the people of what Christianity really is is insisted on in the volume, *The Army and Religion.*

lecturer's desk, or the church a class-room ; and the writer would be the last to suggest that the method (or at least the supposed method) of the one should be transferred to the other. Fully recognising that the sermon should be both an act of worship and a work of art, the writer would urge that there might be more continuous and progressive instruction. A preacher might resolve that he would in order take up the great doctrines of the Christian faith, especially those that are falling into neglect or are being assailed (the latter he may treat constructively and not apologetically or polemically). Or he might set forth the great Christian virtues and graces (with special reference to the actual conditions of his time and neighbourhood). There are so many influences adverse to the Christian view of life that it is the duty of the pulpit to expound and enforce it.[1]

5. It is usually taken for granted that the text is a verse or part of a verse, or at most a few verses of Scripture : and this treatment of the Bible in broken fragments has many disadvantages, which can, however, to a considerable extent be removed, if the preacher will not only study, but also present his text always in relation to the context. As will be shown in a subsequent chapter, the introduction of the sermon should aim at replacing the part in the whole. (1) In fixing the limits of the text and the context, the preacher needs to be warned against a false reliance on the chapter and verse divisions in the Authorised Version. If preachers would always use, if not the original texts, at least a modern paragraph Bible, where the verse divisions disappear, and such divisions as are indicated by the paragraphs are based on some intelligible principle, they would escape this " snare and delusion." There is no valid reason, since the division into verses is arbitrary, why a text should not consist of a number of verses, a psalm, a parable, a speech, an oracle, a complete argument, an entire illustration. The only valid limitation

---

[1] See Henry Ward Beecher's *Lectures on Preaching*, third series, and Dale's *Christian Doctrine*.

is that the portion can be treated as a whole, and the unity of the subject of the sermon be preserved.

(2) Such a portion need not be treated as in the homily by a continuous, verse by verse, exposition, but the skill of the preacher in constructing the sermon will be shown as he can present it as an organic unity. The story told in John 9 can be so presented as an orderly whole, the development of the faith of the blind man being the unifying principle. Here a character and experience are presented in one portion of Scripture, which can be taken as text; but very often a career is sketched for us in a number of detached passages. There is no reason why the preacher should not take a life for his subject; but there would be undoubted inconvenience in his asking the congregation to take all the scattered references as his text; in this case it is advisable to take one incident or one saying or one statement of praise or blame as the text, and making that as it were the focus for the manifold rays of allusion to the biography. If what the preacher intends is not to deliver a lecture, but to preach a sermon, he must, however, be careful to subordinate all the details to the one impression that he desires to make.

(3) The preacher needs to be warned also against needlessly dividing a unity. For instance, 1 Co 3^{10-15} presents one picture to the imagination, and should be treated as a whole in any sermon, and not be broken up into verses and clauses: so also 2 Co 2^{14-16}. The phrase in Is 61^3 (R.V.) "a garland for ashes," presents a complete picture, and interpreted by the context can serve as a text for a sermon on *How God turns Sorrow into Joy*. Short or long, if the text has a unity, it is suitable for the use of the preacher.

6. As in this chapter we have been concerned with the use of the Bible by the preacher, it is fitting that it should close with the words of a great preacher on *How to Use the Bible*. "There are," says Beecher, "what may be called, then, the Bible of the closet, the Bible of the classroom, and the Bible of the pulpit. I do not mention these

as being separate from each other, because all of them run more or less into one another. Still less do I speak of them as being antagonistic, because they all have or may have an auxiliary relationship to each other. So that the most perfect use of sacred Scripture will be that which combines the three." [1] The first " is interpreted by personal necessity, and by elective affinity." [2] The second " is the Bible philosophised and interpreted according to some system. It is indispensable that there should be a Bible of the Classroom." [3] The third " is really the combination of the other two." [4] " At last," he says, " you will come to the preacher's Bible itself, with all its vast resources, from which you will take truths that are good for your own soul and for other men's souls, that you may bring them, with all the vigour and unction and emotion which comes from your personal participation in them, home to the salvation of men. When you have the preacher's Bible you have that which is like a living power, and you are a trumpet, and the life of God is behind you, so that the words which come from you are breathed by Him." [5]

[1] *Lectures on Preaching*, p. 21.   [2] P. 27.   [3] P. 28.
[4] P. 42.   [5] P. 43.

CHAPTER III.

THE CONTENTS OF THE SERMON.

1. In the Ancient Rhetoric, the *invention* was dealt with before the *disposition,* and Vinet in his *Homilétique* and Bassermann in his *Geistlichen Beredsamkeit* follow this method. But it may be questioned whether for the Christian preacher for whom the text with its context should indicate the contents, this is the better way than that which the writer himself found more easy and fruitful. When the subject has been selected and the text found, or *vice versâ,* the next step seems to be at once to make the outline of the sermon, or determine its division. As a rule, the text itself combined with the subject will suggest the division, if there is a close enough correspondence between them to make the exposition of the text identical with the treatment of the subject. If, however, the subject and text are more loosely connected, so that the text in its context does not at once suggest the outline of the sermon, it may be necessary to gather the material first of all in explanation, demonstration, and application of the subject, and to determine the divisions only when that has been sifted, tested and set in order.[1] If the preaching is *expository* in the sense already advocated, the first course will usually be followed. If the preaching is *topical* in the sense that the text does not yield the material for the treatment of the subject, the second course will need to be adopted. Although contrary to his own practice as a

[1] It is such a process that Watson has in view in the account he gives of the "Process of Elaboration" (*Cure of Souls,* pp. 21–22). For the writer himself such a mode of *invention* would be simply impossible. The result must surely be an artificial mosaic of thoughts, and not an organic development of thought.

preacher, the writer in accordance with the usual order of treatment in homiletics, will now deal with the contents of the sermon.

2. The primary elements in a sermon are definitions and judgments. (1) As Christianity is a historical religion, the exposition of *facts* will often have a foremost place in it. In this exposition we may distinguish *description* and *narration*.[1] A situation or a personality may be described, an event or a career may be narrated. Apart from the literary qualities, to which we shall return, which the discharge of such a task demands, harmonious unity in description, and progressive movement in narration, accurate knowledge, sound judgment, and keen insight are necessary. Here the significance is to be apprehended and the value is to be appraised. What may be called psychological divination is a very desirable qualification ; the ability to understand the action as an actor (the psychical standpoint) and not merely to view it as a spectator (the psychological) by putting oneself in the place of the actor, is in some degree necessary to make the past live again. The deeper interest we now have in personality, experience, character, should be an encouragement to the preacher to give in his sermons a larger place to history (outer and inner) than to theology and ethics; or rather doctrine and practice can be most effectively taught when presented concretely in belief and life. The inner life of Jesus, described and narrated with reverence and sympathy, will make His divine human personality more real than would the exposition of a Christology.[2] To sketch Paul's experience of salvation with love's insight will make grace more intelligible than to give a plan of salvation, or a theory of atonement. A whole sermon might so present to the imagination and the affections of a congregation, through description or narration the person or work of the Lord, or the life in Him of His

[1] Vinet, *op. cit.*, pp. 179–194, and Christlieb, *op. cit.*, pp. 135–150.

[2] This the writer has attempted to do in his book, *Studies in the Inner Life of Jesus*, into which he has gathered the contents of eighty sermons preached to one congregation.

servant, that little (if anything) would need to be added in commendation of His truth and grace. But even if in a sermon theology or ethics is expounded, in the introduction the exposition of the text will often demand description or narration, so that idea and ideal may be rooted in, and draw nourishment from historical reality. This description and narration must not be overdone, merely as an artistic production to gratify æsthetic taste. Beauty is not out of place in the pulpit; but it is there not in its own right, but as the servant of truth and holiness.

(2) So closely in the Holy Scriptures is human history related to divine revelation, outward events to inward experiences, that the description or narration of facts can only in theory be distinguished from the exposition of *ideas* and *ideals*. These ideas and ideals should not in preaching be presented as abstractions, but as realities, for they are the faith and the duty of living men, to whom God and goodness are real. It is true that often to make these realities intelligible, it is necessary to define them as abstractions. We may apprehend the reality of love as presented in the person and work of Christ; and yet we may come to understand what love is even in Him more clearly and fully if it is defined for us in relation to the manifold activities of the personality which loves, *as the judgment of value of the mind, the feeling of interest of the heart, the purpose of good of the will, the giving of one self to another in order to find itself in another.*[1] However valuable Bergson's doctrine of *intuition* may be as a corrective of an exaggerated or exclusive intellectualism, he has not disproved the advantage and the importance of general ideas. The presentation of *faith*, for instance, in the teaching of Jesus, the doctrine of Paul, the polemic of James, the description of Hebrews, can be brought into harmony by forming a conception, in which the various elements or aspects are brought together, and shown to be

[1] The writer retains the sentence for the reason given above, despite the depreciation of any such attempts to define which recently fell from the lips of a greater preacher.

related to and consistent with one another. *Christian Faith is the belief of the mind, the trust of the heart, the surrender of the will in relation to the invisible and the future as made present and certain in the person of Christ.*

(3) In the definition of ideas and ideals the Christian preacher must avoid the jargon of theological and ethical systems or schools, he must use the language of common (not vulgar) life; but a knowledge of systems and schools will give accuracy to his knowledge, authority to his judgment, and so distinctness to his *definitions*. As all his definitions are intended to make religion and moral life more intelligible, he must be constantly returning like Antæus to his mother earth, with reference and illustration to life. It is because doctrinal and ethical preaching was formerly so abstract and technical that it has fallen into such disrepute. But the reproach may, and ought to be removed. In all realms, men are seeking distinct conceptions based on adequate knowledge. Should the moral and religious life be allowed to remain an exception? To recall Kant's statement, the concept without the percept is empty and the percept without the concept blind; or to put it in more directly applicable language, theology and ethics without experience and character are empty, but experience and character without theology and ethics are blind. The preacher then need not dread definition; it is his task to make ideas and ideals intelligible. Let him not offer his definition formally as such, but let him make sure that, however informally, he is conveying quite distinctly to his hearers the contents of a definition of his subject. A preacher will be greatly helped in his labours, if he does not wait to define a subject till he is trying to deal with it in the pulpit. Let him be constantly thinking on the contents of the theology or ethics he preaches, and let him, when he has reached a distinct conception for himself, labour to give it as accurate and adequate, distinct and memorable a definition as he can command.

(4) The exposition of a subject will not and cannot stop short at a definition. This must be expanded in

instances. Thus humility will be better understood if the preacher recalls Jesus' claim for Himself as the meek and lowly in heart,[1] the washing of the disciples' feet,[2] His entry into Jerusalem, not on the war-horse, but the peaceful ass,[3] Paul's reference to His poverty by which He makes others rich,[4] or to His self-emptying in assuming the form of a man, and becoming obedient unto death.[5] Faith can be illustrated by the Roman centurion,[6] the Syrophœnician mother,[7] the sinful woman[8] and the penitent thief.[9] The better the preacher knows his Bible, the readier will he be in making his definition more intelligible by pictures taken from life itself. The Bible is not the only treasure-house to which the preacher can turn. The history of the Christian Church, the biographies of great and good men, even imaginative literature (poetry and fiction) can afford abundant material to make an idea or ideal more vivid and so more real to the hearer. With the use of illustration in argument we shall deal later in the discussion, at this point what must be insisted on is that, while the intellect has its right to the abstract definition, the imagination has its claim to the concrete instances; and the preacher must observe the due proportion of both.

(5) But thought cannot move in definitions only; if it did, it would be moving in a circle; for a definition is analytic; it only exhibits what is already contained. The first step in argument or reasoning is the judgment in which we relate one idea to another idea, which is not included in it. When we say that faith is itself sufficient for salvation, our thought is moving from the one idea, faith, to the other idea, *sufficient* for *salvation*. The connection between the two ideas may be so familiar, or obvious, that all the preacher needs to do is to state the connection; and, if he wants to give freshness to his presentation, he may add some instances of the connection. But the preacher should be on his guard against filling

---

[1] Mt 11²⁹.   [2] Jn 13¹⁻¹⁷.   [3] Mt 21⁵.
[4] 2 Co 8⁹.   [5] Phil 2⁶⁻⁸.   [6] Mt 8⁵⁻¹⁰.
[7] Mt 15²¹⁻²⁸.   [8] Lk 7⁴⁷⁻⁵⁰.   [9] Lk 23⁴³.

his sermon with truisms or commonplaces. He wants to lead his hearers to "fresh fields and pastures new." He will therefore aim at thinking things together in the sense of connecting religious or moral ideas which are not for common thought connected. In the Beatitudes,[1] Jesus connects with the common thought of blessedness a number of inward conditions which were not generally so connected; so that this statement came as a surprise. The preacher cannot attempt in his judgments to be always offering surprises, to be adding fresh truths to the thought of his hearers; the effort to be constantly original would quickly bring him into the paths of error rather than of truth. The task is mainly to bring things to remembrance, to make explicit connections of ideas already implicit in the minds of his hearers; as a scribe who is a disciple of the Kingdom he should bring out of his treasure things new and old.[2] The old truth may have become so neglected, that the statement of it again may make it appear new; or even if the old truth has not been forgotten it may be stated so freshly that it does come as new. In a later chapter we shall consider whether the subject of the sermon should be stated as a thesis, or judgment. Whatever the form may be, the sermon must move from idea to idea in judgments.

3. It often happens that the connection between the two ideas in a judgment cannot be taken for granted, or be simply imposed by the preacher on his hearers. He must justify the connection; he must so present the connection as to win the assent of his hearers. (1) He must therefore give *reasons*, or links of connection between the two ideas which are not obviously immediately related to one another.[3] In the Beatitudes, Jesus gives a reason for the connection of ideas in each case in the clauses beginning with the conjunction *for*. The writer of the Epistle to the Hebrews[4] recognises that his statement, "without faith, it is impossible to please God," needs proof,

[1] Mt 5³⁻¹⁰.   [2] Mt 13⁵².
[3] Cf. Vinet, *op. cit.*, pp. 195–236.   [4] He 11⁶.

and so he adds, " for he that cometh to God must believe that He is, and that He is a rewarder of them that diligently seek Him." The reason is usually introduced by the conjunction "for" or "because" ("Because thou hast seen Me, thou hast believed"[1]). We cannot ordinarily press the distinction that "for" introduces a *reason* (a subjective ground) and "because" a *cause* (an objective ground), although the thinker will always have present to his mind this real distinction between the *ratio essendi* and the *ratio cognoscendi*. We may, however, in preaching keep in mind that the reason may be a fact, or an idea or ideal (outward or inward reality). A reason may be given for a statement, even when the formal "for" or "because" is absent. In He 12[2], the relative clause "who for the joy that was set before Him endured the Cross, despising shame," is not merely a description of Christ, it is the reason why He is declared to be "the author and finisher of faith"; His willing death in hope of His rising again is the typical instance of faith, which gives Him the supreme place among the heroes of faith. It might not be quite superfluous to point out that the connection of judgments may sometimes be so stated that it may be difficult to distinguish antecedent and consequent. In Lk 7[47] the clause "for she loved much" would appear to give the reason why "her sins, which are many, are forgiven"; but in truth the much love was the sign or token that many sins had been forgiven; it was faith that saved her.[2] The sign or token, as in this case, may be more prominent than the cause, and may thus very easily be mistaken for it. The fruits of faith may take the place of faith as the cause of salvation.

(2) This discussion leads us to a very material consideration for the preacher, the kind of reasons that he is to employ. There was a time when in most congregations to quote a text of Scripture was to clinch an argument, to end a controversy. The preacher should not regret that that time is past. He wants rationally to convince,

<hr>

[1] Jn 20[29].   [2] Lk 7[50].

morally to persuade, spiritually to constrain his hearers; and so he must desire to use no other reasons than can win a free and intelligent assent. Reason, conscience, the soul, however, in men are not uniform, but differ with time and place. As knowledge widens and thought moves on, the reason develops, and what captured its assent at one time does not at another; even in different persons at the same time an identical reason cannot be assumed. Even so standards of right or wrong change and vary; the conscience of one man acquiesces in, if it does not approve, what another man's condemns. The aspirations of the soul are not the same always and everywhere. One man feels most keenly the need of forgiveness; another longs for the promise of immortality; a third hungers and thirsts for the living God Himself. These variations and varieties of inner life the preacher must have present to his thought; when he is seeking the reason he will advance to win the acceptance of his hearers for the judgment which he desires to impart to them. He must find the points of contact intellectually, morally, spiritually, between himself and his hearers, so that he may bring them into closer agreement.[1]

(3) The statement of a reason may not be sufficient to commend a judgment at once; the mind of the preacher and his hearers may not yet be in sufficiently close contact. It may be necessary for him to follow a *line of reasoning* as well as to give a reason. A distinguished man of science, who at times as a by-product of his manifold activities undertakes the task of teaching theologians their business, some years ago declared that the Christian pulpit is mistaken in saying so much about sin and the forgiveness of sin, as the man of to-day does not worry about his sins, and is not to be severely blamed for not worrying. Shall the preacher then cease to deliver the Gospel, which has been light out of darkness, life out of death to an immeasurable multitude, out of deference to this modern

[1] Such adaptation is the theme illustrated and enforced in Jackson's *The Preacher and the Modern Mind.*

peculiarity, if indeed it be so ?   Let him seek for a point
of contact ; for many men he will find it in the growing
interest in social reform.   Reform involves that there are
wrongs which must be removed.   Are these wrongs the
inevitable result of an economic system, or a social order,
which no man produced, no man can alter, and for which,
therefore, no man is responsible ?   Such a conclusion would
make reform, which it is assumed the hearer desires, an
impossibility.   Men are morally responsible for the continuance of wrongs which they can remove.   But if they
can remove them, they are surely not altogether without
responsibility for the existence of them.   A closer scrutiny
will disclose the fact, that social wrongs are in many cases
due to individual sins, not deliberate it may be, or intended
to have these results, but still the cause of them.   Greed,
selfishness, carelessness, idleness, self-indulgence are real
causes of many present evils.   If we want social reform,
there are some sins we must worry about in order to get
social wrongs removed.   In this way it may be the
preacher can move some of his hearers to have that godly
concern, to which his Gospel makes its appeal.   Again, how
many, hitherto indifferent to the evils of drunkenness, have
been aroused to anxiety because intemperance decreases
efficiency in a time of war.   Once more, the claim of
foreign missions may be attached to the growing imperial
sentiment, or it may be shown that as the world is increasingly becoming one in commerce, civilisation, culture,
the conflict of races can be avoided only by the supremacy
of one universal faith.   The age has an aversion to the
belief in miracles or the supernatural ; it appreciates religious experience, moral character, and personal influence.
The Christian preacher who wishes to prove the divinity
of Christ will be wise if he does not begin, although his
convictions may require him to end with the doctrine of
the Logos, the facts of the Virgin-birth, the miracles and
the Resurrection of Christ, the testimony of the Apostles
to the Risen Lord.   He will seek to show that the
perfection of the character, the absoluteness of the

experience, the supremacy of the influence of Christ among
men demand the confession that He is more than, and
above men, and so unique that He can claim to be called
divine.   The rule for any such argument is that the
preacher starts from what he may assume his hearers to
concede, and goes on by such steps as carry their assent
until he brings them to the goal of conviction to which he
desires to bring them.   In these days of doubt, difficulty
and even denial, the preacher must be prepared to follow
a long course of reasoning as well as to give reasons.   It
is not suggested that every sermon, or even many sermons,
should be *apologetic*, still less *polemic* ; but even in a doctrinal,
practical or devotional sermon, which does not assume, or
challenge contradiction, unless the preacher is going over
an oft-told tale, it will be necessary for him to keep in
touch with the mind of his hearers, and to carry their
thoughts along with him.

(4) It is not necessary to discuss technically the forms
of reasoning, as the preacher of wide knowledge and
sound judgment will use them all fitly, without being
aware that he is a logician.   It may, however, be pointed
out that there are some forms of reasoning which are more
effective than others.   The deductive reasoning of the
syllogism is out of place in the pulpit ; and even argument
from general principles is, as a rule, less effective than from
concrete instances, for men want facts rather than ideas,
observation rather than speculation.   (a) There are, of
course, general principles which are almost universally
admitted, and from which the preacher may draw his
inferences with the confidence that these will find general
assent.   Thus the universal Fatherhood of God has become
a common article of the Christian faith.   Men will accept
what is consistent with that truth, and reject what is in
contradiction to it.   Thus man's personal immortality may
be deducted from the relation of God to man as Father to
child.   Most men now reject the doctrine of eternal
punishment, in spite of all the Bible texts which may be
quoted in support of it, and even the facts of life that seem

to point in the same direction, because it contradicts the truth; and few men can now persuade themselves to accept the doctrine of conditional immortality, despite the zeal of its few advocates, because it seems inconsistent with that truth.   In such deductive reasoning, however, the warning is not out of place, that we have not so complete a knowledge, so infallible a judgment in regard to this general principle as to warrant us in drawing too confidently our deductions from it.   The truth is expressed in a metaphor, and our reasoning from it may really be analogical when we assume that it is deductive; we are making the possibility or the necessity of the human fatherhood the measure of the divine.   This consideration is of wider application; for we must remember that the knowledge of the divine, the eternal, the invisible is not yet "face to face," but as in a mirror "in a riddle." [1] Because we recognise the limits of our knowledge on the one hand, and also the limits of the revelation of God on the other, as adapted to our limitations, we cannot in the pulpit use the deductive method as did preachers of a former generation.   We do not attempt to prove by a logical demonstration the necessity of the atonement; we admit that the appeal must be to moral and religious intuitions, which go deeper than logic's plummet can fathom.

(b) Much of our argument must necessarily be *analogical*, as was that of Jesus.   The fact of the Incarnation both warrants and limits *anthropomorphism* in our religious thought.   God is both like and unlike man.   The failure to recognise that Jesus was the Word as flesh, with the consequent tendency to assert the identity without also recognising the difference between the historical reality and the eternal truth, is responsible for a too familiar and not reverent enough handling of the doctrine of God in the pulpit.   If in former times God was spoken of as almost a Shylock who will have his pound of flesh, in the present day He is sometimes talked about as if He were a very

[1] 1 Co 13[12].

foolish and weak parent who let His children have their way, and neither bothered Himself nor them about their disobedience.   Within the limits that the difference between Creator and creature, Sovereign and subject, perfect Father and imperfect child imposes, reasoning from analogy is not only legitimate, but inevitable.   But we must argue not from what man's reason, conscience and affection regard as least, but only from what they acknowledge as most worthy in man; to see God we must not look to the lowest depths to which man can sink, but to the highest heights to which he can soar.   The reality of God corresponds to man's ideal, and not his actual, to what he wants to be in his best moments, not to what he is in his worst.   The personality of the preacher will thus affect, and cannot but affect, his use of this argument, for he will shape God in his own likeness.[1]   The preacher will be wise, however, if he will, as far as he can, make not himself, but the best men and women he knows personally or by reading the human reality from which he argues to the divine; for a man's capacity for admiration rises far above, and goes far beyond the actuality of his imitation.   The value of biography and history is in this connection obvious.   As Christ is God incarnate, it is legitimate to infer from what Jesus was to what God is, to seek the likeness of the Father in the Son; but even here the difference incarnation involved must be recognised.   The statement that " Jesus Christ is the same yesterday and to-day, yea and for ever,"[2] warrants another kind of analogical argument; we may reason that as the Jesus of the yesterday of the earthly life was, so is the Christ of the to-day of Christian experience, and so will be the Lord of glory for ever.   While "eye hath not seen, nor ear heard, neither have entered into the heart of man the things which God hath prepared for them that love Him,"[3] and while "it doth not yet appear what we shall be,"[4] yet

[1] Cf. Browning's poem, "Caliban upon Setebos; or, Natural Theology in the Island."

[2] He 13⁸.   [3] 1 Co 2⁹.   [4] 1 Jn 3².

the assurance that we shall be like Him, who is the same,
when we shall see Him as He is, warrants our working
out the analogy of the present and the future life in
Christ. If any present relationship is so consecrated by
the common life in Christ that it enriches that life, we
are warranted in inferring that it has the promise and
pledge of continuance hereafter. We may use the identity
between the God of nature and the God of revelation, not
as Butler in the *Analogy* did, to bring revelation down to
the level of nature, however necessary and legitimate for
his immediate purpose his procedure was, but rather to
find the solution of the problems of creation and providence
in redemption. If "it became Him, for whom are all things,
and by whom are all things, in bringing many sons unto
glory, to make the captain of their salvation perfect
through suffering," [1] we may better understand why God,
as it were, stays the hand of His omnipotence from removing many physical evils, and by means of these even works
out His moral and spiritual purpose. Suggestions have
already been made of fruitful analogies which can be
worked out between the history of the Hebrew nation and
present experience, whether individual or collective.

(c) If the limits of our knowledge forbid much deductive argument, if the likeness between God and man
permits and even requires much analogical reasoning, the
difference involves that the form of argument known as
a fortiori must have a large place. It has a large place
in the teaching of Jesus. "If ye, then, being evil, know
how to give good gifts to your children, *how much more*
shall your heavenly Father give the Holy Spirit to them
that ask Him." [2] The most elaborate argument of this
kind is found in Ro 5^{12-21}. If the disobedience of Adam
has been efficacious in introducing sin and death into the
world, *how much more* efficacious is the obedience of Christ
in bringing righteousness and life to all men. The argument may be present even when the formula *how much
more* is absent. "Where sin abounded, grace did much

[1] He 2^{10}.   [2] Lk 11^{13}.

more abound," [1] is an implicit *a fortiori* argument. The
wider diffusion of grace may be inferred from its inherent
superiority to sin, as it is the act of Christ who is greater
than Adam. It is implied also in Jesus' counsels to His
disciples in Mt 5[43-48]. The conduct of the disciples is to
be as much better than the conduct of publicans as is
their relation to God more intimate. In all preaching
about God, His works and ways, His transcendence of
man must be emphasised; but this can be done in a
wrong way as well as a right. We may so assert God's
unlikeness to man as to rob men of the help and comfort
of the thought of His likeness, and may thus drive them
from Christian faith to agnosticism. To say that God is
supernatural is to deprive ourselves not only of the
analogical, but even the *a fortiori* argument, for both
assume difference within resemblance. God's truth, goodness, love, are not of another kind than ours, but of a
higher degree; all these terms mean not less, but more
when we apply them to God. God is truer, better and
more loving than we are; and this assertion of difference
enhances and does not exclude the resemblance; God
cannot do less, and He will do more than the wisest, best
and kindest human parent would do. The ideals and
aspirations of man show the direction of the character
and the purpose of God, even if they do not, and cannot
fix the limits of His perfection. The *a fortiori* argument
is a most comforting and encouraging form of reasoning
about God for the preacher to employ. God is not below
the downward limit of man's actuality, but above the
upward limit of his possibility. It is this argument
which is employed with such force and beauty in
Browning's poem of *Saul*. We may even extend the
argument in this way. God's fulfilments transcend His
promises, as the contrast between the Messianic hope and
the reality in Christ shows, for His promises must always
be limited by men's understanding, and by them God
prepares men to receive fulfilments which exceed the

[1] Ro 5[20].

expectations of which they were capable.   If God has promised, *how much more* will He fulfil.   How inspiring a prospect such an argument opens!

(*d*) As the preacher wants to keep as close as he can to life, his reasoning must be largely *inductive*, that is, he will confirm and commend a general principle by individual instances.   This was characteristic of Jesus' teaching, and because it has not been recognised as such, mistakes have arisen.   The individual instances of duty which necessarily were determined by local and temporary conditions have been taken as general principles of permanent and universal validity.   The instance most relevant to the moment is His teaching about non-resistance of evil.[1]   We have often from the individual instances to rise to the general principle, and then we must come down again to individual instances of its application to-day.   What we have to beware of, however, is that we substitute for the *maximum demand*, which Jesus always puts forward, the *minimum demand*, to which our moral weakness inclines.   If our application of the law of equal love to self and neighbour is easier and costs less than Christ's, we should suspect it as inadequate.   In the application of any general principles in individual instances the preacher must always keep in mind for his guidance two considerations, first, that Jesus came to fulfil (fill full or complete) law and prophecy,[2] and that the righteousness of the disciples of Jesus must exceed the righteousness of the Pharisees;[3] in other words, the Christian ideal must in itself always complete the highest moral standards of any land or age, and Christian men and women should always aspire to a morality above and beyond that of the men and women deemed most moral. There is very wide scope for the preacher in taking the individual instances of morality enjoined in the prophets, the Gospels and the Epistles so as to discover the general principles implied, and in then applying these principles to the instances of duty for his hearers.   While Protes-

[1] Mt 5$^{38-42}$.　　　　[2] 5^{17}.　　　　[3] 5^{20}.

tantism shuns the Confessional, and shrinks from casuistry, it often neglects the duty of distinct moral guidance. The reason why the reasoning here should be mainly inductive is that an abstract principle does not make the same appeal as a concrete instance. The widow's mite touches the heart as well as enlightens the conscience more than a definition of generosity or sacrifice would.[1] What gives the Bible its charm and power as the literature of moral and religious life is that it not only gives commands, but offers examples. One illustration of the advantage of inductive reasoning in the pulpit may be given. Conversion, regeneration, new birth are declared necessary to the beginning of the Christian life; and doubtless preachers have talked a great deal in abstract terms about the necessity of the change without making much impression. Now Jesus refers to both in concrete cases. He tells His disciples who have been quarrelling about the highest place in the coming Kingdom, after setting the child in their midst, "Except ye turn (convert) and become as little children, ye shall not enter into the Kingdom of heaven."[2] Conversion is a turning from ambition, rivalry, conflict to dependence, humility, obedience. He brushes aside Nicodemus' patronising compliments by the unexpected demand: "Except a man be born again, he cannot see the Kingdom of God." He meets his incredulity by a more explicit statement: "Except a man be born of water and of the Spirit, he cannot enter into the Kingdom of God."[3] The new birth includes the penitence, or renunciation of the sinful life, of which baptism is sign, and the faith which claims the new life from God in fellowship with God. The more explicit statement includes a personal reminiscence of Jesus' own baptism, an immediate requirement of the Pharisees, of whom Nicodemus was the representative, and a universal demand. Now this universal demand we must interpret in the light both of the personal reminiscence and the immediate requirement. What did His baptism mean to Jesus? What was need-

[1] Lk 21[3, 4].   [2] Mt 18[3].   [3] Jn 3[3-8].

ful for Nicodemus to become a disciple ? We can illustrate it further by the fall and recovery of Peter, the dejection of the Christian community at Jesus' death, and the exultation at Pentecost, the change of conviction (not of character) of Paul at his conversion. A much wider view will thus be obtained; and a due discrimination will be shown in applying the demand to those who have been Christian since childhood, those who have outwardly conformed to, rather than been inwardly transformed by the Christian faith, and those who both outwardly and inwardly have been altogether strangers to grace, and even enemies of goodness. This example must surely enforce the need of the preacher's never losing himself and his hearers in abstractions, theological or ethical, but always keeping close to life itself, personal experience, individual character. The writer has found for himself most advantage in thus presenting doctrine and practice alike in the concrete instances in which the Holy Scriptures abound. The preacher need not confine himself to the Holy Scriptures. Biography and history make rich provision for his need of suitable material.

(e) There are two other forms of reasoning which the preacher will only rarely employ, but he cannot be forbidden their use altogether. For the *argumentum ad hominem* there is Jesus' authority in Mt 22$^{41-46}$. He puts the opponents to silence by confronting them with the difficulty of David's calling the Messiah, if his son, Lord. Paul develops this type of argument in Ro 9—11. Butler's *Analogy* is an instance of it also. It is only in controversy with opponents whom one cannot hope to convince that this argument is useful. The *reductio ad absurdum* is used by Jesus in refuting the charge of His league with Satan in Mt 12$^{25-30}$, and often by Paul in Galatians when he shows the absurd consequences of denying that faith is sufficient for salvation. These weapons of polemics the preacher will seldom, if ever, need to use; they may be passed over with this brief mention.

(f) There is a movement of thought of which the formal logic does not take any account, but which plays the leading part in Hegel's *logic*. It must be recognised as a real mental process. It is the triple movement of *thesis—antithesis—synthesis*. The preacher will find that it is a method which sustains the interest of hearers. To take some instances, religion requires faith, morality demands works; we must have a moral religion and a religious morality, in which faith finds its fruits in works, and works find their roots in faith. Religion emphasises the dependence of man on God, morality his self-sufficiency as capable of obeying the *categorical imperative*; both find fulfilment in the liberty of the sons of God. The conditions of the apostolic age are entirely different from those of the twentieth century. Even the life of Christians outwardly is unlike in both ages. When the thesis and antithesis have been clearly and fully presented, then the synthesis of the essentially similar attitude to God and goodness of all Christians can be asserted. Philanthropy and piety have often in the doctrine and practice of the Church been opposed; Christ unites them in identifying Himself with even the least of all His brethren.[1] Christianity as the religion of reconciliation is the type of this triple movement, and in expounding and applying its teaching the preacher will often be helped by letting his mind work in this way. It will awaken interest to present a problem so as to lead the mind to its solution.

4. The pulpit seeks to reach and move the whole man, to convince the intellect that it may constrain the will; the argument for the mind is meant to be, and if properly presented will prove to be, an appeal to the will. *Reasons* will in this case become *motives*. But the will can be moved otherwise than by the intellect alone; man has emotions, affections, sentiments; and the preacher cannot disregard and disdain this method of approach, by which many can be reached more readily and surely than through the intellect alone.[2] To excite feelings alone without

[1] Mt 25⁴⁵.

[2] Cf. Vinet, *op. cit.*, pp. 236–261, also Niebergall, *Wie predigen wir dem modernen Menschen*.

quickening the conscience and enlightening the reason is unworthy of the pulpit; it should be left to quacks and not physicians of the soul.   Such a treatment effects only apparent and ephemeral cures, as the story of revivals in many painful instances shows.   (1) There are the human affections, however, to which the preacher may make his appeal.   Whatever be the exact explanation of the *baptism for the dead*,[1] any possible explanation involves the recognition of human affection as a legitimate motive for holding fast the Christian faith.   Paul's reference to the faith of Lois the grandmother and Eunice the mother of Timothy,[2] in order to confirm the faith of Timothy himself, is the use of the same motive.   How often does Jesus in His farewell discourse appeal to the love of His disciples as the motive of their obedience, and how often Paul to the affection of his converts for himself !   Paul's confession, " The love of Christ constraineth us," [3] discloses the deepest, most enduring, and strongest motive of the Christian life, and surely sanctions the use by the preacher of even the human affections as motives.   It is true that human affections may be put to base uses ; parents may sin to advance their children's welfare, but these affections are themselves worthy, God-given and God-like, when not so prostituted, and when appealed to as motives of goodness may be placed beside, but always below, the distinctively Christian motive Paul confesses.[4]   Abstractly the question may be raised, although concretely it does not arise, whether the love for Christ which the love of Christ awakens is the highest motive. Kant in his *rigorism* would deny that it is ; for him respect for the moral law itself is the only moral motive.   But we may well ask, Are not law and morality mere abstractions, are they not real only in persons and the relations of persons ?   Is there a higher moral good than the love of persons in a holy fellowship ?   There is no surer path to perfection than the love of the Perfect.   The reason for

---

[1] 1 Co 15[29].   [2] 2 Ti 1[5].   [3] 2 Co 5[14].
[4] Cf. the influence of Pompilia on Giuseppe in Browning's *The Ring and the Book*, and *Silas Marner*.

seeking perfection Jesus gives is the perfection of the
Father, and the desire of the children to share that perfection.[1]　Beside this surely Kant's moral motive is imperfect,
inadequate and ineffective.　The preacher will be wise, then,
if he presents often with reverence, gratitude, adoration,
the love of Christ, most of all in His Cross, to his hearers,
and also, but always in subordination to this, the love of
parent, husband or wife, child, friend as a motive of
godliness and goodness.

(2) Even where there is not what can be properly
called affection, because the knowledge may be inadequate,
and the intimacy not close enough, there may be admiration
for greatness, wisdom, goodness, as embodied in the tale of
achievement, experience, character.　By study of Paul's
letters it is quite conceivable that a man may to-day even
reach a personal affection for the great apostle, for he seems
so close to us, lays his heart so bare.　But the Holy
Scriptures, biography and history, present to us many
personalities who gain admiration rather than win affection.
If this admiration depend on what is from the Christian
standpoint admirable, the preacher need not hesitate about
seeking to awaken it by the way he presents these personalities in his sermons.

(3) There are some persons (if few) who do reverence
truth and holiness in and for themselves, and the preacher
in presenting instances of these qualities should not so
exclusively emphasise the personal embodiment as to miss
the appeal which the presentation of these excellences as
such may make to some minds.　The preacher may, and
should assume, that his hearers have minds that desire
truth, and hearts that aspire to holiness, and not merely
personal affection or admiration for the persons in whom
these are found.　Unless he himself is of too one-sidedly a
sentimental type, he will understand, because he himself
shares these motives.　Worthy in themselves, they may
become tutors which lead to the teacher Christ.[2]

(4) Even so stern and rigid a moralist as Kant recog-

[1] Mt 5$^{45-48}$.　　　　　　　　　[2] Gal 4^2.

nised that man has a desire for happiness, and he tried to assure the satisfaction of that desire for the good by *the postulate of the Practical Reason*, God who hereafter will bring character and condition into accord. Jesus Himself spoke of the blessedness of His followers, but He did not urge that this blessedness should be sought as an end. It is one of the surest results of experience, that pleasure, if sought for its own sake, is not found. The Bible, however, promises rewards of goodness, and threatens punishment of wickedness; the Old Testament generally makes the present life the scene of this divine judgment of human conduct, the New Testament for the most part the next. May the preacher appeal to this motive, the desire for happiness, the fear of pain and the hope of pleasure? It may at once be said that the transference of the object of choice from the present to the next life, if it remain the same in quality, does not cleanse or hallow the motive. Selfishness for eternity is no better than selfishness for time. It is to be feared, however, that many preachers, who would have hesitated about recommending honesty as the best policy, have made a practice of appealing to the fear of hell or the hope of heaven. Regarding this three considerations may be offered. (*a*) The preacher is within his right and duty in presenting plainly and fully the consequences of actions —good or bad. Men should not be left in ignorance of the results, here and hereafter, of the deeds they do; they should be made aware that in forming character they are fixing destiny. Warning and encouragement are necessary elements in the appeal of the pulpit. (*b*) The preacher who desires to maintain the Christian standpoint will emphasise inward rather than outward consequences; if he does mention, and it may be necessary that he should mention, physical pains or economic losses as penalties of vice, he will always lay more stress on the moral deterioration and the spiritual departure from God, which result from sin. When he does dwell on the blessedness of the saints, he will so present it that it cannot be a bribe to virtue, but a good which only the good can appreciate.

(c) There are hearers who can be stopped in the path of sin only by being made to acknowledge that it is also the way of folly. There are men who will not confess, *I am a sinner*, until they have been forced to admit to themselves, *I am a fool*. The preacher must not think only of the respectable; he must also regard the disreputable.[1] He must have a message which reaches them. To invent terrors in order to impress is dishonest; to state that the wages of sin is death, is to utter a truth which some hearers may need. This motive will be so repugnant to his own feeling that he will not urge it oftener or farther than his responsibility and solicitude for souls may demand. As often and as quickly as he can he will present the higher motives which have been mentioned.

(5) There are men to whom beauty appeals more strongly than does truth or goodness or even happiness. Has the preacher to disregard their peculiarity? Or must he not seek the point of contact with them in their æsthetic sense? To the beauty of form in a sermon we shall return in a later chapter. What we are now concerned with is the question whether goodness and godliness may be presented as beautiful in order to be commended to such natures. As to the fact that Christian saintliness may be lovely as well as of good report, there can be no doubt.[2] The aspiration of a saint or the achievement of a hero do often gratify our sense of beauty. What God hath joined together, why should the preacher put asunder? He must, however, beware lest he give only æsthetic satisfaction without awakening through it ethical admiration or spiritual appreciation. The appeal to good taste alone does not afford a foundation solid enough for the building of a Christian life.[3]

---

[1] This distinction must not be taken as determined by social class or economic circumstances, but by moral character.

[2] Phil 4⁸. Cf. the phrase in Ps 110³ *the beauties of holiness* (probably a mistranslation), see Ruskin's *Modern Painters*, ii., for an analysis of the source of Beauty.

[3] Sermons have been preached which have commended Christianity as genteel, as suitable for a lady or a gentleman!

(6) Closely akin to the conscience is the sense of
honour, although that sense may sometimes become very
artificial. Christianity emphasises humility, man's sense of
dependence on God ; this sense of honour emphasises rather
man's dignity, the debt he owes to his own personality ;
and yet they are not necessarily opposed. For Christianity
does not depreciate nor degrade manhood in humbling man.
If the sense of honour in its requirements is consistent
with the dictates of conscience the preacher may claim it
as an ally, while careful to assert the ultimate moral
authority, the will of God, and not what man thinks of
himself, and wants to make of himself.[1] To young people
at a certain stage of development, it is quite legitimate to
point out that a certain course of conduct is not " cricket,"
that it is not " playing the game." That a man should
respect himself may be urged as an encouragement to the
right course ; that he should shrink from being ashamed of
himself as a warning from the wrong course. Care, however, must be taken to point out that the sense of honour
is not always a sure guide, and the feeling of shame an
adequate defence ; for the artificial standard of a society
may exalt what should be abased—*e.g.*, duelling and " debts
of honour "—and abase what should be exalted. It may
be a very important function of the preacher to correct the
moral fashions of an age or a society. Only in so far then
as the sense of honour and the Christian ideal point the
same way, can the preacher use it as a motive, and that
even only that he may as soon as he can bring higher
motives into play.

(7) To chastise folly and vice the satirists have used
ridicule. The Christian preacher will make a very limited
use (if at all) of this dangerous motive. It does not
accord with the Christian spirit, and its effects, if there
are any, fall short of what the Christian preacher desires.
The cross of Jesus Christ does not make sin look absurd,

---

[1] The preacher should not, however, imitate the mother who rebuked
her boy for swearing in the words, "It's wicked ; and what's worse, it's
vulgar."

it makes it appear tragic beyond all telling. Ridicule may restrain from the evil way; it cannot constrain to the path of life.[1]

(8) While ridicule is usually out of place in the pulpit, the writer cannot persuade himself that humour is, for humour seems to him to be too good a gift of God in lightening the burdens and easing the yoke of life. Without entering on the interminable debate of what humour is, it seems to him that the contrasts, contradictions and incongruities of life would often be too grievous to be borne did not humour relieve the strain. The preacher should not go in search of funniness; but if he is so constituted, it will often be impossible for him to escape humour. He will not indulge himself in it, but will use it only in so far as he can by it more effectively reach others. As the attempt to be humorous must end in disastrous failure; and as a man may use his humour only if he cannot help himself, further counsel on this matter would be of no advantage.

(9) In religious revivals especially, but in some degree in all assemblies for worship, a motive comes into play, which may be distinguished from personal affection on the one hand or moral obligation on the other; it is what may be called *social feeling*. Men will be moved to joy or sorrow, or penitence or faith in the crowd by means which would not have touched them alone. There is always the danger of reaction when this stimulus has been removed; and yet the preacher in measure of his emotional intensity, his personal magnetism, will, as it were, fuse a multitude into one mass of emotion, aspiration, resolve. The danger he must himself remove by his insistence on the necessity of deliberate and voluntary individual decision; and he will never snatch a forced, hasty resolve from this excitement of the crowd.[2]

[1] The writer has twice heard sermons in which satire was the dominating feature, and the effect on himself was irritation at the preachers despite the amazing cleverness of the performances.

[2] The psychology of the crowd has in recent years received special attention; see Davenport's *Primitive Traits in Religious Revivals*;

5. The preacher does not preach himself; and yet he cannot keep himself out of the preaching.[1]   Sometimes it is quite lawful and needful that he should enforce his appeal by the testimony of his own experience of the truth and grace of Christ.   A man of fine feeling shrinks from carrying his "heart on his sleeve," but it may be his debt to his hearers that he enrich them by that wherewith God has enriched him.   But his aim must be not to magnify himself, but his Lord.   To his own character a man will not point, although his character is adding to or deducting from his preaching constantly.   He may enforce an appeal for total abstinence by giving the reasons why he has taken that course, and the advantage he has gained in following it.[2]   (1) His personality will give *unction* to his reaching, or withhold it.

" This word," says Vinet, " taken in its etymology and in its original acceptation, does not designate any special quality of the sermon, but rather the grace and the efficacy which are attached to it by the Spirit of God, a kind of seal and sanction which shews itself less by external signs than by the impression which souls receive.   But when, in going back to the cause of this effect, one distinguishes particularly certain characteristics, it is to the reunion of these characteristics that one has given the name of unction.   Unction seems to me the total characteristic of the Gospel, doubtless recognisable in each of its parts, but perceived especially in the whole ; it is the general savour of Christianity ; it is a seriousness accompanied by tenderness, a severity tempered by sweetness, dignity united to intimacy : the true temperament of the Christian disposition, in which, according to the expression of the psalmist, ' goodness and truth have met each other ; righteousness and peace have kissed each other.' "[3]

A mass of metal needs a certain temperature to fuse together, and to be moulded into a thing of beauty or use ;

McDougall's *An Introduction to Social Psychology* ; Giddings' *Inductive Sociology* and *Elements of Sociology.*

[1] Cf. Vinet, *op. cit.,* pp. 261–295.   Christlieb, *op. cit.,* pp. 307–311.
[2] It may sometimes be his duty to state an unpopular opinion as his own, or to dissociate himself from the popular sentiments of the times.
[3] *Op. cit.,* pp. 261–262.

and in the same way the contents of a sermon need a certain spiritual temperature to become truly and fully Christian. There is emotion, and it should be deep and strong, but it is emotion purified and vivified by the Spirit of God; and a sermon may be emotional, and yet lack unction. It cannot be forced at will; it comes only as Christian experience advances and Christian character develops; and the human personality thus becomes the habitation of God by His Spirit.

(2) It is this unction that will give the preacher *authority*, and the only authority it should be his desire to possess.[1] The place, the time, the object of the gathering, the Scriptures from which he takes his text, the Church of which he is a recognised minister do invest his utterance with authority for many hearers. In the chapter dealing with the preacher's credentials the source of his authority was indicated. He uses, and does not abuse any authority that comes to him in these ways only as it is the truth he preaches, and only as the personality through which the truth comes is fit and worthy of the high and holy calling.

6. It is necessary to answer a question regarding the contents of the sermon which it may be some of the readers will have already been impatiently asking, How can we gather the material which has been described in this general statement? The preacher should not live from hand to mouth; he should have a well-furnished storehouse. It has already been urged that he should keep two lists going, one of texts, and one of subjects; and to each text he

---

[1] See Vinet, *op. cit.*, pp. 266-282. If the preacher has authority over his congregation, it may be needful for him sometimes to use it in the way of *rebuke*; but the relation must be so intimate that this tone will not offend, but improve, and the occasion must be adequate to justify its assumption. Character, experience and age add weight to any such utterance. Irony should be very sparingly used, but cannot altogether be forbidden, when the offence calls for such chastisement, as in Jn 10³². While anger as personal resentment is out of place in the pulpit, yet indignation as the inevitable emotional reaction of the good man against evil need not be repressed, although for full effect it must be restrained in the language in which it is expressed. The preacher may have "the scorn of scorn, the hate of hate, the love of love."

should attach the subject or subjects which it suggests to him, and to each subject the texts which would be suitable. What more should he do in addition to the general preparation already spoken of ?   (1) One noted evangelist, D. L. Moody, wrote the texts that laid hold on him on envelopes. When in his reading or his meditation or his contact with men anything came to him bearing on one of these texts, he wrote it on a slip of paper and put it into the envelope. When he had gathered enough material in that way he worked it up into a sermon.[1]   A sermon so produced is likely to be a cunningly-fashioned mosaic, rather than a developing organism, unless the vital and vigorous personality, such as was Moody's, fuse all the elements together. But the writer has heard sermons so prepared where no such fusion had taken place; they were like Joseph's "coat of many colours,"[2] not like Christ's undergarment that was "without seam from the top woven throughout."[3]   They were made and had not grown in the mind and life of the preacher.

(2) There are preachers who make most diligent use of notebooks carefully indexed, in which they collect quotations, illustrations, arguments; in preparing a sermon they draw on the treasures they have there gathered.   If they can remain masters of their material, the sermon may be a living growth; but the danger here is that material may be used because it is there to be used, rather than because it is the most appropriate for the subject.[4]   They may, as was said by a French girl of the first English preacher she heard, "say too many things."   There may be variety, even superabundant, but not the necessary unity.   The writer has never been able to keep such notebooks, or to prepare

---

[1] *The Life of D. L. Moody*, by his Son, pp. 381–383.

[2] Gn 37³.   In the figurative use of the words of Scripture disregard of the exact translation may be excused.

[3] Jn 19²³.

[4] It is this peril that Watson in his book, *The Cure of Souls* (pp. 12–14), has in view in the process he describes as *Separation*; although he applies it specially to the ideas, it no less holds good of all the other material of the sermon.

sermons in such a way, but he would not impose his inability as a limitation on preachers who can so discharge their task.

(3) The method he has found best is to keep text and subject in his mind for as long a time as possible, so as to let his thoughts gather around this centre by what might be called *the inevitable attraction of a natural affinity*, so that the results of his study and experience come not as an addition to, but as a development of the text and subject.[1] The disadvantage of this method (if it be so) is that there will be very little ornamentation about the sermon, only the quotations and illustrations which spring of themselves out of meditation, and that the preaching will not please the hearers who want the latest novel or review article mentioned to assure them that the preacher is up to date. One advantage may be claimed for it, that the sermon will be a developing organism, the living product of a living soul.

---

[1] Quotations and illustrations will then be relevant and consequently illuminative. They will deepen interest and quicken intelligence, and not distract attention. A parade of learning in the abundance of the quotations and illustrations shows not only a lack of judgment regarding the effectiveness of a sermon, but is an offence against good taste, as the preacher is obtruding himself instead of getting the congregation absorbed in his subject. Quotations which cannot at once be understood or illustrations that need to be explained are altogether out of place in the pulpit, where the object is to carry the message as simply and directly as possible. A few sentences from Jowett's *The Preacher*, p. 143, may be added : "An illustration that requires explanation is worthless. A lamp should do its own work. I have seen illustrations that were like pretty drawing-room lamps, calling attention to themselves. A real preacher's illustrations are like street lamps, scarcely noticed, but throwing floods of light upon the road. Ornamental lamps will be of little or no use to you ; honest street lamps will serve your purpose at every turning." For a further discussion of the subject, the writer may refer to his book, *A Guide to Preachers*, pp. 224–244.

CHAPTER IV.

THE ARRANGEMENT OF THE SERMON.

1. WE now pass to the second part of Rhetoric, which deals with the *disposition*, or arrangement of the matter which by the *invention* has been gathered.[1] There are

[1] Regarding the need of order in a sermon, Vinet quotes Quintilian (Book VII. Preface). " It is not without reason that to the rules of invention we add those of disposition, since without the second of these sections, the first is nothing. Remove from one place to another any part whatever of the human body, or of that of an animal, even if none is lacking, you have produced a monster. However little you displace a member, you rob it of its power with its use ; an army in disorder becomes a hindrance to itself. Those do not appear to me to deceive themselves, who maintain that the disposition of the parts of an object constitutes the very nature of that object ; that disposition changed, all is about to perish. A discourse deprived of this virtue is stormily tossed about ; bubbling without overflowing, it has no consistency. Like a man who goes astray in the night in unknown places, it repeats a good many things, it omits a good many others ; and not having determined either the starting-point or the goal, it does not obey any purpose but chance " (*op. cit.*, pp. 315–316). The difference that a plan makes to the ease and worth of the preacher's own thinking out of his subject he shows by a quotation from Buffon (*Discours sur le style*). " It is for lack of a plan, it is because he has not reflected enough on his subject, that a man of ability finds himself perplexed, and does not know where to begin to write ; he perceives at one time a great number of ideas, and as he has neither compared them, nor subordinated them, nothing determines him to prefer some to others. He remains then in perplexity ; but when once he will have made a plan for himself, when once he will have gathered together and put in order all the thoughts essential to his subject, he will easily perceive the moment at which he should take the pen, he will feel the point of maturity in the work of the mind, he will be urged to make it unfold, he will even have pleasure only in writing ; the ideas will follow one another readily, and the style will be natural and easy ; warmth will be born from this pleasure, will spread everywhere, and will give life to each expression ; all will become more and more alive, the tone will rise, the objects will take colour, and feeling, joining itself to the light, will increase it, will carry it further, will make it pass from what one says to what one is going to say, and the style will become interesting and luminous " (*op. cit.*,

sermons, in which the preacher starts with a text, or
subject, and then wanders on at his own sweet will, as
thoughts about the subject come to him, and in which it
would be very difficult to discover the laws of the association of ideas which have guided (if indeed they have) his
erratic steps. A genius might make even such a sermon
interesting; but such a method is not for ordinary men,
and a preacher is wiser to assume that he belongs to the
second and not the first class. The literary essay without
plan is responsible for a good deal of the loss of influence
of the pulpit. The sermon is not to be read, but to be
heard; and it must be, therefore, cast in such a mould as
will secure the unity of purpose and continuity of development which speech to be remembered and to produce a
definite result must possess. One disadvantage of the read
sermon, or the written sermon which is committed to
memory almost *verbatim*, is that the preacher is prone to
forget that his hearers want to carry away his sermon as a
whole, and that he should make it as easy for them to
remember a great deal of it as he can. The man who has
to remember his sermon not by mechanical repetition
merely, has to cast it into a form in which he can remember
it; and if he does, it will be easier for his hearers also.

2. We may then take it for granted that the sermon
must be arranged according to some definite plan, and that
it is desirable to have such a plan as the preacher will
easily remember himself, and as his hearers will find it
possible to recall. Should the preacher then have definite
divisions, and should he take his hearers into his confidence,
and intimate them?[1]   (1) The elaborate structures of a

pp. 319-320). Thus skilful disposition brings with it easy invention and
fine expression. Order is not only heaven's first law, but the first law of all
rational and æsthetic production as well as moral conduct for men. Vinet's
discussion of the importance of the disposition deserves study (pp. 308-324).
Cf. Christlieb, *Homiletic*, pp. 312-366; Watson's *The Cure of Souls*, pp.
29-51; Hoyt, *The Work of Preaching*, pp. 157-207.

[1] The writer has discussed the various modes of treating a text in his
book, *A Guide to Preachers*, pp. 211-215. The *expository* and the *topical*
have already been discussed in this volume. The first lends itself most
readily to the *analytic*, the treatment of the thought in each part of the text

former time with a third or fourth subdivision of a sixth
or seventh division would only excite irritation or ridicule
to-day. Specimens have been given in the first section of
this volume of the length to which some preachers were
wont to go. Some preachers, innocent of Hegel's philosophy, have had a fondness for a triple movement, a
firstly, secondly, thirdly in addition to an introduction and
a conclusion. But there is no necessity for any particular
number of heads. If there are to be divisions, it is evident
that two must be the minimum, and within the limits of
time allowed for a sermon in these days, it is not likely
that more than four or at most five could be properly dealt
with. The purpose of the sermon, its text or subject, must
determine what the divisions are to be. Just as it is good
for the preacher's clearness of mind that he should take
the trouble to get a title for his sermon that will express its
intention, so it is good for him to take trouble with his
divisions, so that they do not overlap, involving repetition,
and yet cover the subject, or at least as much of it as he
intends to deal with in his sermon, so as to secure adequacy
of treatment. If he has skill in putting his heads in
memorable form by alliteration, assonance, or any verbal
resemblance, he should not scorn his gift. But here artificiality and ingenuity must be avoided; the treatment of
the subject must not be sacrificed in any way for the sake
of smart or "catchy" heads. Only what assists memory
and promotes intelligence is here admissible. The danger
just mentioned arises only when the preacher has his
hearers in view; and we are thus led to answer the second
question: Should the plan be communicated to the
congregation?

(2) In order that the hearers may be taken into
confidence, it is not necessary for the preacher to break up
his sermon into a series of addresses, to stop with his

separately, the second to the *synthetic*, the presentation of each of these
thoughts as interpreting one subject. In the *interrogative* mode we seek to
answer the questions the text starts in our minds; in the *corrective*, to
expose the errors of thought and life by its truth; in the *illustrative*, to give
concrete instances of the general principle it contains; and so on.

firstly, and make a fresh start with his *secondly* ; such a method prevents the cumulative effect of the sermon. The joints should not be heard cracking as the body moves. The transitions should be effected more skilfully than in that way. A sentence may sum up the first division and give the start to the second, and so on. The hearers, however, should be able to pass with the preacher from one division of his subject to another.[1] The writer, at least, when he is hearing a sermon, wishes and tries to discover the plan, even when the preacher has not formally disclosed it. But after the preacher has introduced and stated his subject, should he or should he not indicate the way he intends to treat it ? However informally, he may show his hearers the goal to which, and the course by which, they are going to be led. *Firstly, secondly*, etc., may be avoided, if it is thought necessary, and yet the structure of the sermon may be given in a few sentences. The objection to any such disclosure is often made, that it robs the sermon of the element of surprise, which keeps the attention, and holds the interest of the hearers. He must be indeed a poor preacher who gives the impression when he has stated his subject and divisions that his hearers already know all that he can say to them. Should not the statement of the subject and divisions rather awaken interest, excite curiosity ? Should not the hearers be asking themselves : How is he going to work out the subject according to that plan ? The statement should, as it were, lay before the hearers the problem of which the sermon is the solution, and so arouse their desire to share in the process of solution. As far as the writer has been able to gather from his intercourse with hearers, there is a general preference for a knowledge both of subject and divisions, as the pew likes to be taken into confidence by the pulpit, and not to be mystified by it ; and further, there is no general objection to having the heads of the sermon distinctly indicated even in the formal *firstly, secondly, lastly*, and in as easily remembered words or phrases as possible.

[1] See Watson's *The Cure of Souls*, pp. 32–33.

3. It may be objected, however, that such a division is a hindrance to the unity which should mark every sermon. Dr. Jowett insists that every sermon should contain only one thought, and that that thought should be presented in one sentence, in which it is made quite clear to the hearers. This one thought he himself presents in a great variety of ways; in this he is following the method of Dr. Chalmers.[1] The danger of the method is, as has been shown in a quotation on a previous page [2] regarding Dr. Chalmers' preaching, repetition, an absence of progress. In the hands of a great preacher as Dr. Jowett is, it may amply justify itself. For ordinary men it is not to be urged. In short, there must be freedom in the pulpit. There must be unity; but unity may be secured in various ways. There can be unity in variety, so long as all the thoughts in a sermon combine, and do not conflict. To deal with a series of subjects suggested by the successive clauses of a text is certainly not the way to preach effectively. To determine what the subject will be, and then to use the different clauses of the text to present different yet complementary aspects of the subject, is the method by which most preachers are likely to do their best. Care is necessary to keep the parts duly subordinate to the whole; their interest should lie not in themselves, but only as parts of the whole. Attention must not be distracted from, but interest concentrated on the whole, so that the logical as well as the æsthetic demand on the sermon should be met.

4. We may now look at the parts of which a sermon will usually consist. In doing this nothing should be further from our thoughts than the attempt to provide a Procrustes bed into which each sermon must be forced. The art of the preacher does not lie in any prescribed form, but in his best use for his purpose of any form. It is usual for the sermon to begin with the announcement of the text; and in a congregation of Christian worshippers no better course can be followed, as the Holy Scriptures

---

[1] See *The Preacher: his Life and Work*, pp. 134–135.
[2] See p. 225.

are the common ground on which preacher and hearers meet. He desires to preach only what is in accord with the Word of God as therein contained, and they are ready to hear whatever within this limit he desires to say to them. If, however, a preacher found himself addressing an audience for the most of whom this assumption did not hold, he would be in no way unfaithful to his calling, but only exercising the wisdom which it demands, if he were to begin with some common interest in order to lead his hearers to desire the Word of God, and if when that desire was awakened, he only then intimated his text. It was Jesus' method to attach himself to the circumstances of the moment. With the woman of Samaria He begins with a request for water.[1] Paul followed in his Master's steps. At Athens he started from the altar to *An Unknown God*.[2] It would be well if Christian preachers always claimed a like freedom, when the circumstances demanded a break with hallowed custom.[3]

5. The announcement of the text is usually followed by an *Introduction*. As we have already noted, some of the Pietists of Germany used the introduction to deal with some passage of scripture which was not included in the pericopes prescribed for the worship of the Church. While the modern preacher is not likely to err in this way, he still runs the peril of making his introduction too long by admitting into it much that is not strictly relevant to his subject. It must be insisted that the sole end of the

---

[1] Jn 4[7, 8].   [2] Ac 17[23].

[3] We do well to learn what the pew thinks: "I venture to think it is unfortunate," says Mr. G. W. Pepper, "that an unbending formula should control the beginning of the sermon. We who are accustomed to the argument of cases in court are aware that much of the effectiveness of the oral argument depends upon its opening. The method of opening should differ according to the nature of the case. As one of the lawyers in the crowd, I suggest that the preacher should allow himself a similar liberty. . . . My suggestion is that the sermon should be begun in the way most appropriate to the particular occasion, and that, more often than not, this will require some other opening than the announcement of a text from Scripture" (*A Voice from the Crowd*, pp. 18–19). Be it observed, this is not a reason against having a text, only against always beginning the sermon with a text.

introduction is to *introduce* the subject to the congregation, to prepare them to receive in the best way what the preacher has prepared for them.[1] It is possible, accordingly, that an audience might be so ready for a preacher's theme that no introduction might be necessary, and he could at once enter on its discussion.

(1) In some cases, when the text needs little exposition, a few sentences giving the reason why the text has been chosen, connecting the subject of the sermon with the text, or, if the sermon is one of a series, connecting its contents with what has already gone before, may be all that is necessary, and the preacher should never put into his introduction more than is necessary to win interest, and to fix attention. The circumstances under which the text has come to him may serve as an introduction, if the statement will for the hearers enhance the value of the subject to be dealt with. A passage or a sentence in a book which is just being widely read may have suggested text and subject, and the preacher would not be wise if he altogether neglected such a point of contact with his hearers. While trivial occurrences or sensational happenings should not be exploited by the pulpit, yet an event may be important enough for the notice of the preacher who as prophet is to discern the signs of the times. He may begin with a brief reference to it as the reason why he is dealing with the subject. A correspondence in the daily press may be so concerned with interests of the Kingdom of God that the preacher may connect his subject, if there be a real and not a forced connection, with this discussion. An opinion may have been expressed by a prominent man and may have attracted much notice; in the interests of the application of the Christian ideal, the preacher may introduce his subject as a direct challenge. It was with such a challenge Jesus met Nicodemus.[2] By the opening sentence to excite surprise is not illegitimate, if the content of the sermon

---

[1] See Vinet, pp. 352-366; Christlieb, pp. 352-356; Hoyt, *op. cit.*, pp. 157-170.

[2] Jn 3³.

justify such a beginning. The preacher must be a man alive among men, reading the newspaper as well as studying the Bible, so that he may bring the eternal truth home to the temporary situation, outward or inward, of his hearers, as freshly and forcefully as he can.[1]

(2) Often the text chosen will need some exposition, and while exegesis is not the main function of the pulpit, the preacher will make his sermons all the more useful and fruitful to his hearers, if, when his text requires it, he states all that is needful for intelligence and interest. If the text be a sentence in a continuous argument, the purpose of the argument and its course may be briefly stated. If the text be an utterance of prophet, apostle or the Lord Himself, the historical situation may need to be briefly sketched. If the text be a quotation in the New Testament from the Old Testament, the context in each case should be compared, and the contrast of meaning in each place indicated. The resemblance between the circumstances of the speaker or the writer, whose words form the text, and of the hearers of the sermon, if that be the reason for the choice of the text, should be made plain. A contrast may be effectively used to emphasise the adaptability of the revelation of God to the variety of human need. If a text mark a distinct stage in the development of the divine revelation, its significance and value in that respect should be shown by reference to the thought it supersedes or corrects. The introduction in all these instances should seek to connect the immediate interest of the text with the more general interest which the Bible has, or should have, for Christian people as the literature of the divine revelation. A few sentences in an introduction may demand on the part of the preacher a wide and true scholarship, and may either expose his ignorance or prove his competence. The use of the imagination to produce a vivid picture of the past must be restrained by accurate knowledge, and should not be indulged for

[1] He may serve the Lord ($\tau\hat{\omega}$ $\kappa\nu\rho\acute{\iota}\omega$) as well as the opportunity ($\kappa\alpha\iota\rho\hat{\omega}$), Ro 12[11]; these are variant readings.

æsthetic effect merely, but only to secure attention to the subject.

6. The introduction should lead to the statement of the subject. It is in the interests of the preacher that he should himself know distinctly so that he can state in definite terms what his subject is. A preacher may take a text, and say a great deal about the words, phrases, and clauses of the text without fixing his own mind or the mind of his hearers on any one subject. There are sermons which are like a ruderless ship on a wide sea, driven hither and thither, and making for no haven. If the preacher states a subject, he puts himself under a pledge to his hearers to steer a straight course for some harbour.[1]

(1) How should the subject be stated, as a theme or as a thesis, in a phrase or in a sentence ? Should a preacher on Jn 12[32] intimate that he is going to treat of *the Attraction of Christ*, or that he is going to prove *that the Attraction of Christ is universal* ? In result there need not be any difference ; but in method there may be. A discussion of a theme will not assume quite the same form as a demonstration of a thesis, but it leaves wider scope. The one will be expository, the other argumentative. Some subjects will lend themselves more readily to one form than another ; some may be equally fitted for either treatment. What alone must be insisted on is that whatever form may be adopted should be consistently maintained. A sermon should not be made up of themes discussed and theses demonstrated.[2]

(2) If the preacher limits himself strictly to one thesis about his subject, he will initially exclude all other aspects of his subject. The one predicate bars out all other possible predicates ; he will, if he states as his subject that *the attraction of Christ is universal*, shut himself off from discussing such a thesis as that it is personal, it is sacrificial, it is certain, unless he can bring in these propositions as reasons for this thesis. The same limitation, however, he

[1] Vinet, pp. 367-375.   [2] Christlieb, pp. 321-352.

may impose upon himself by putting only one aspect of his subject into the statement of it, as in such a title as *The Universal Attraction of Christ*, which is implicitly a thesis, as it contains subject and predicate.

(3) This may all seem a mere nicety of form, but it involves an important question of substance. Is it desirable that a preacher should usually limit his subject by a predicate, discussing only one aspect of it, or as many aspects as the text suggests? The two extreme cases may be excluded. A subject may be so great, a text so full, that it may be quite impossible to treat it adequately in the limits of a sermon in all its aspects. An aspect of even a great subject might be of comparatively so subordinate interest that it would be difficult to sustain the interest if it were made the sole subject of a sermon. Some preachers can make so little out of any theme they treat, that they may attempt to deal with all the aspects of a subject without running any risk of overburdening the minds of their hearers. An inexperienced preacher had better leave himself plenty of room to move about in. There are preachers of so wealthy a mind that they can bring abundance where another would find only penury. The preacher who limits himself to one idea, one subject and one predicate, must be pretty sure of himself, that he can say enough about it to instruct and interest adequately and not to send away his hearers disappointed. If a preacher feels it is his wiser course to deal with all the aspects of his subject which the text presents, he is yet under obligation to relate the aspects to one another as well as to the subject, so that his sermon will have an organic unity and development, and not be merely a succession of separate discussions with only the common subject as a very thin thread of connection. Let us take an instance, and let it be the familiar text Jn 3¹⁶. If the love of God be the subject of the sermon, and all other subjects suggested by the verse be treated as aspects of it, yet all of these aspects should be linked together. The nature of God's love is shown in its object, the world; the need

of the world fixes the measure of that love in the gift of Christ; Christ must be represented as in His person and work calling forth the faith, which is the condition of receiving that love; and the result of faith—the eternal life which is the purpose of God's love in giving Christ—must be shown to be congruous both with its human condition and divine reason.

(4) There are in the Bible itself a number of theses, which can at once be made the subjects of sermons. The Beatitudes [1] are a series of theses each with a reason annexed; the treatment of one of them will consist of a discussion of the reason in order to show how it justifies the connection of subject and predicate, the inward condition described and the blessedness promised. Such statements as that God is Spirit,[2] or God is Light,[3] or God is Love,[4] may form the thesis of a sermon; and the treatment of the thesis will consist in showing what the epithet as applied to God means, and it may be if the preacher is greatly daring, in proving why it applies to God, and in the strict sense to God alone.[5] Whenever a text is given as a thesis, or readily lends itself to be put in the form of a thesis, it ought to be treated as such. But with all deference to the judgment of so great a preacher as Dr. Jowett undoubtedly is, the writer cannot persuade himself that necessity is laid on every preacher to force his subject into such a form, or only to take subjects that can be put into it. The statement of a thesis to be demonstrated rather than of a subject to be discussed is less in accord with general pulpit habit, and does not so easily and fitly attach itself to the exposition of a text. So long as the essential condition of unity is secured, the preacher should claim and use the largest liberty in the form in which he conceives his purpose for himself or states it to his hearers.

[1] Mt 5³⁻¹⁰. [2] Jn 4²⁴.
[3] 1 Jn 1⁵· [4] 4⁸
[5] The three texts might also be combined to show how as spirit God must be both light and love, and as perfect spirit cannot but be both.

7. After the statement of the subject there naturally comes the indication, more or less formal, of the divisions. How are these divisions to be got? In many cases the text, when studied in its context, will suggest the divisions. In other cases the material which has been collected for the treatment of a subject will fall into divisions. Where a thesis is to be proved, the reasons suggested by the Scriptures, the study of theology or ethics, etc., will give the divisions. (1) The preacher will be wise not to impose his divisions from without on his subject, but to allow them to develop from within it. Many preachers exercise their ingenuity to discover an artificial arrangement of their sermon, when the text itself, studied as it must always be in its context, would yield them the natural development. The text should suggest not only the subject, but its treatment also; and, unless the preacher has such resources in himself as not to need the aid, he had better choose texts which yield him this guidance. The context of a very short text, which may itself suggest only the subject, may present a historical situation, which by the argument from analogy can be made to yield a very fruitful treatment of the subject. Thus the phrase " a garland for ashes "[1] may, when put in its historical setting of the summons to return from exile in Babylon, present the subject of God's Providence as changing the sorrow for sin into the joy of God's forgiveness. It cannot be too much insisted on that the Bible proves itself inspired by its inexhaustible suggestiveness to him who studies it constantly, accurately and minutely; and it should be used as much as possible to suggest not only the contents, but even the form of sermons, for it must be remembered that contents and form are not external to one another, but the one should determine the other.

(2) The clauses of a text may suggest the parts of the sermon and yet the preacher may lack skill in finding the proper terms for his divisions, so as to relate them to the

[1] Is 61[3].

subject as a whole.   Can the general categories of thought
be of any assistance to him ?   It is generally assumed that
they cannot and will not; but this seems to the writer
too hasty an assumption.   If they are useful in thinking
generally, why should they not be useful in the thought
of the pulpit ?   In the treatment of a subject under
various aspects, we are using, although we may not think
of it, the category of substance and attribute.   Is there no
value in the distinction between the essential and the
accidental attributes of a subject ?   The new birth is an
essential attribute of the Christian life; but a sudden
conversion is only accidental, although some preachers
confuse the one with the other, and think they can assert
the one only by insisting on the other.   A preacher may
apply to his text the question: Is this epithet of the
subject here a necessary or an accidental attribute ?
Such a question would prevent much hasty generalisation
on insufficient data.   Again a great deal of the matter
of preaching can be arranged in the relation of *genus* and
species, as, for instance, love with charity of judgment,
generosity of gift, beneficence in service as subordinate
forms of it.   A general moral principle may include
principles of lesser generality; thus justice will include
honesty in dealing, fidelity to promises, veracity in speech.
An abstract idea may be illustrated by concrete instances,
Scriptural, historical, biographical, literary.   A personality
may be sketched as regards heredity, environment,
development, capacity, character, career, reputation.   An
event may be examined as regards time, place, antecedents,
consequents, human conduct or divine providence.   A
nation's history falls into periods separated by crises.
The moral quality of an action may be judged as regards
motive, method, manner, intention, result; its religious
significance may be determined in its conditions and
issues as regards the relation of God and Man.   A vice,
virtue, or grace may be analysed psychologically as regards
thought, feeling, will.   A statement may be broken up
into its parts, *e.g.*, Evil company doth corrupt good

manners.[1] (1) What is evil company? (2) Wherein
do good manners consist?   (3) How does the first
corrupt the second?   The inquiry might be extended
thus. (4) Why does it corrupt?   The expansiveness
and pervasiveness of personal influence would be the
answer. (5) How is this corruption to be prevented?
A subject can be dealt with in its various relations, as
love in relation to God, self, neighbour. The various
reasons for a thesis may be stated in order, as for the
statement that Christ is divine: (1) His sinless and
perfect moral character, (2) His unique and absolute
consciousness of divine sonship, (3) The constancy and
efficacy of His mediatorial function. These are the sort
of questions that the preacher in thinking over a subject
may, as it were, address to himself. The same subject
may be examined in different ways in accordance with
the purpose for which it is being dealt with. One text
might serve for several sermons. It is not suggested
that the preacher in thinking should take up one set of
categories after another, and try to apply them to his
subject. Thinking of any value is not a mechanical
process of that sort. A man's genius consists in his
doing spontaneously, without troubling about the process,
what another man must discipline himself to do. If a
preacher finds himself lacking in fertility and facility of
thought, he may develop his powers by deliberate practice
in the formal application of the categories of thought; and
in due time he may discover himself thinking freely and
quickly.

(3) There are certain logical rules that the thinker if
he would think correctly must observe. Vinet [2] mentions
four, which may be briefly summarised. (a) *The species
which is subordinate to the genus must not be co-ordinated with
it.* Sympathy, service, sacrifice are all forms of love, its
exercise, and should not be placed alongside of it.

(b) *What does not differ should not be distinguished.*
To warn against an action because it is contrary to

[1] 1 Co 15³³.   [2] *Op. cit.*, pp. 333–336.

common sense and to self-interest is giving motives that
overlap, as common sense takes account of self-interest.
To say that a course of action will promote peace and
tranquillity is repetitious, unless peace be used in the
restricted sense of outward condition and tranquillity of
inward, and such a restriction is not usually accepted.

(c) *The association of ideas must not be allowed to draw
an idea from one part of the discussion, to which it logically
belongs, to another part, where it is only a repetition of what
has already been said, or an anticipation of what will be said.*
In a sermon on Christ's divinity His filial consciousness
must not be brought in as one aspect of His moral
character, if it is afterwards to be dealt with as an independent reason for the belief.

(d) *An idea must not be treated before its proof, the
discussion which is to prepare for it and explain it.* If, for
instance, the love of God is to be proved by the grace of
Christ, it must not be first dealt with in the sermon.   An
arrangement of a sermon, however ingenious, which does
not conform to these rules of logical thinking, will confuse.
The structure of a sermon should correspond to the
development of the thought which it contains, and should
not be imposed upon it from without.   Here lies the
danger for a preacher who borrows an outline from even
the best preacher; the progress of the sermon is not in
accord with the movement of his own mind.

(4) The rules for the general arrangement of the
sermon apply to the special arrangement of each part of
the whole.   Vinet [1] thinks it necessary to add three
counsels regarding the treatment of the parts.   (a) In the
first place, he urges that each part should not be treated as
a whole in itself according to its own plan regardless of the
plan of the whole, but only in relation to the whole, so that
there should be a continuous movement.   Accordingly he
deprecates the writing of portions of the sermon beforehand,
and then putting them into the sermon; either the portions
will need to be modified so as to fit into their place, or the

[1] *Op. cit.*, 336–340.

progress of the thought will be interfered with. (b) In the second place, he maintains that, while in the parts there must necessarily be the treatment of the subject in the details, and not in generalities, yet the unity of the subject must not be lost in details; the details must not be an accumulation, but an organic development. The man who in preaching can indulge only in generalities shows the poverty of his own mind in not being able to think out the details, and will soon exhaust his material, and begin to repeat himself. (c) The second rule, according to Vinet, leads to a third, and it is already suggested in the second. The details must result from the analysis of the general statements about the subject. While an over-subtlety must be avoided as that wearies and irritates, so long as interest can be maintained the analysis must be made as complete as possible.

8. So far we have been dealing with the *disposition* of a sermon from the logical standpoint, the appeal to the intellect, but the sermon is intended not only to enlighten the mind, but also to stir the heart and move the will; and the preacher must through his whole personality address himself to the whole personality of his hearers.[1] The *oratorical* standpoint is complementary to the *logical* for the preacher who desires to be in all respects effective. Between the two arrangements there is not, and cannot be, any contradiction, as there is no schism in man's nature. An illogical arrangement cannot be oratorical, and the logical arrangement is not only the basis of the oratorical, but is already in some measure oratorical, as it appeals to the intelligence, part of the personality oratory seeks to make captive. And not to the intelligence alone, for the truth which is being thus logically presented by its very nature affects the heart as well. There is, however, a logic of the soul as well as of the mind; and the preacher must recognise that to secure the full effect of his appeal. This

---

[1] Cf. Vinet, pp. 340–352. There must be, as a well-known preacher said to the writer, "*a release of the personality*"; while exercising due self-restraint, *the preacher must sometimes let himself go.*

logic of the soul may be summed up in Cicero's saying, *Eloquentia nihil est nisi motus animæ continuus.*[1] Movement towards a definite goal is what the soul demands, from indifference to interest, from indecision to decision, from separation or even opposition to the truth to an ever closer self-identification with it.

(1) This movement must be continuous. A speaker might by violence of thought, voice or gesture give his hearers a momentary shock, or even a succession of such shocks; but this is not eloquence; for eloquence aims at gradual and yet permanent effect. The orator is seeking to capture for the truth the whole personality of those whom he addresses. The means must be consistent with the end. To ensnare the unwary hearer by pandering to prejudice, or by provoking passion, or even by stirring the emotions without any enlightenment of the intellect, is unworthy of the object which the preacher sets before himself. Light and heat must go together where eloquence is concerned with the truth. As he does not seek to catch unawares, or by surprise, but to win his hearer surely because slowly in accordance with the movement of thought and feeling, he must not let go as he tightens his grip. All irrelevancies, digressions, repetitions, returns on his own path, turning aside even for a moment from the way that leads straight to his destination, must be avoided. He must not himself obliterate the impression he has made by competing or even conflicting considerations or motives. The divisions of the sermon must not be so announced, or treated as to break up the one continuous movement into a succession of lesser movements. There must not be a peroration at the end of one division, and an introduction to the next, like the flood and the ebb of the tide. This is not, however, an argument against divisions, or even the announcement which makes the hearers aware of them, although the preacher with the orator's instincts will know if a *firstly* or *secondly* would or would not be like a stone of stumbling in his path, and will or will not indicate his heads accordingly.

[1] Quoted by Vinet, p. 342.

But it is an argument against any artificial division that hinders and does not help the advance of thought, or any excessive division or subdivision, which unseasonably interrupts the movement.

(2) This movement is not only continuous, but also progressive; it is towards a goal. It is not a Bergsonian *élan vital* without a teleology. The preacher has not only an impulse to speak, but also a purpose in speaking. Here dramatic art is significant for the orator. Modern psychology places conation above cognition; life is the end of thought; volition completes intellection. (*a*) Accordingly progress in the sermon involves movement from doctrine to practice, from idea to action. When the nature of a duty has been explained, the motives for doing it must be urged. (*b*) Even where considerations are presented to the mind alone, progress depends on movement from the abstract to the concrete, from the general principle to the individual instance, as the latter stirs the sentiments, which move the will more readily and deeply than the former. (*c*) Where reasons and motives are being presented, progress is secured by passing from the weaker to the stronger. But it may be objected: Are not these only relative terms, as regards motives, even more than as regards reasons, for we can assume a common reason with better right than rely on a common conscience? As a rule, however, the simpler the reason, that is, the more self-evident, the stronger it is. As regards motives, while there may be hearers, in whom self-interest is stronger than regard for man or reverence for God, yet the preacher should advance from the lower to the higher, *e.g.*, from the fear to the love of God, from God's law to His grace. It may be asked, however, why should there be this advance at all, why not present the highest reason or motive at once? In answer several considerations may be offered. A preacher while aiming at practical result, desires also, and rightly, to present his subject as completely as he can, to place the motives in their proper relation to one another. Again the moral and religious condition of any congregation is so varied, that what

reaches one mind or heart may not reach another, and the preacher wishes to reach all, and each in the most effective method.   Further, while a man giving account to himself of his reason or motive of action will probably think only of one, yet the process of decision is far more complex. He has been affected by other reasons and motives, and if he had not been so affected, what he reckons as the all-decisive reason or motive would not have had its full effect. The argument or the appeal must be a cumulative one. While the preacher cannot be restricted to the highest reason or motive only, but must lead up to it from lower levels of thought or feeling, he does not strengthen but weakens his argument or appeal by a multitude of weak considerations, as quantity cannot make up for quality. There must be selection of only what is worthy of the occasion and purpose, although there may be degrees of value in what is so selected.   The more deeply moving an appeal is the more carefully should it be prepared for, as the preacher does not want to catch his hearer unawares, or to rush him into a hasty decision ; the issue, moral or religious, is too serious for stratagem of any kind.   (d) To the question whether doubts and difficulties should be met before the arguments are set forth, or after them, no one answer can be given.   There are misconceptions or misrepresentations which can at the beginning be brushed aside in order to clear the ground for the proof proper.   Objections may be so serious that it would be a mistake to present them before the evidence has made its due impression.   If, however, they are dealt with after the proof, they must be so handled that their refutation will be a confirmation of the argument, and so the last impression on the mind will be not a challenge by error but a conquest by truth.   The sermon should thus move forward, not always at the same pace, for that would cause strain and bring weariness, but more swiftly towards the close ; the conclusion should have the momentum of the whole previous movement.

(3) That the continuous and progressive movement may be maintained, the utmost importance attaches to the

transitions.[1] The parts of a sermon should not be placed
in juxtaposition, with the separation offensively visible.
What logic would not condemn, rhetoric disapproves.   It
is not the statement that a new division is being begun
that is the offence; but the ending of one division and the
beginning of another without any dove-tailing.   A particular instance will be more convincing than a general
statement.   In dealing with the divinity of Christ the
transition from the first proof, the sinless and perfect
moral character, to the second, the absolute and unique
religious consciousness, might be made as follows: How
can this character be explained?   Not by heredity,
environment, genius (each of these parts might be briefly
treated).   The explanation lies where Jesus Himself put
it, in His relation as Son to God as His Father.   Accordingly we pass (or thus we are led) to the second proof.
Once more the transition to the third proof from the
second might be made as follows: Both as regards moral
character and religious consciousness Jesus stands alone,
above all men; and yet He does not will to remain alone,
but to gather around Him those in whom He reproduces
His goodness and His fellowship as Son with God as
Father.   He brings God to men in grace, and men to
God in faith.   The third proof of His divinity, therefore,
is the constancy and efficacy of His mediatorial function,
for the Sinless Son of Man and the only-begotten Son of
God is the Saviour and Lord of men, the firstborn among
many brethren.   If care were taken about the transitions,
the common objection to divisions in a sermon as breaking
it up into fragments would be deprived of any good reason.

9. The last part of the sermon is the *conclusion*, or,
if the sermon has any claims to eloquence, the *peroration.*[2]
(1) Not every sermon, it must be insisted, needs, or lends
itself to such an addition.   If there has been the progressive continuous movement in the sermon which has

[1] Cf. Vinet, pp. 376–380.
[2] See Vinet, pp. 381–393; Christlieb, pp. 363–366; Hoyt, *The Work of Preaching*, pp. 195–207.

been described as its ideal, although the reality often falls short of it, and the cumulative effect of the whole has reached its limit at the close of the last division, nothing more is needed, or should be attempted. Many a conclusion is a fresh start from lower ground; and many a peroration changes the upward to a downward flight. Often the preacher fails to stop when he has done his best.

(2) If, however, the truth explained or the duty enforced has not been brought quite home to the reason or the conscience of the hearers, an application at the end may be both necessary and legitimate. This does not, however, justify the assumption often made that every sermon should end with an appeal first to the saints or saved, and then to the sinners or unsaved. Such an arbitrary addition is not only illogical and inartistic, but it savours even of insincerity. If the sermon has not shown reasons or motives for the continuance or the commencement of the life in God, such an application would be a lifeless formality. It may be objected that a sermon should be practical throughout, that the truth should be so presented as to be applied from the beginning to the end. And yet, even if this be the case, a more direct application may be necessary. There may be different classes of hearers, the old, the middle-aged, or the young, the anxious, the sorrowing, or the bereaved, the "strong" or the "weak" in faith, the defeated or the victorious in life, and to each may be made the appropriate application.

(3) Again the conclusion may focus the argument or appeal of the sermon. It may weave into a few sentences the explanations, reasons, motives of the sermon. Having stated the teaching of the sermon, it may summon to belief, trust in, and surrender to the truth that has been taught. Its aim may be to produce a devout mood, and not only the acceptance of a doctrine, or the practice of a duty. If the unity of impression desired has not been attained, the conclusion must secure this result.

(4) As the introduction aims at introducing the

sermon by bringing the preacher into contact with his hearers, so that he may not begin abruptly, the conclusion seeks to leave the hearers in contact with the preacher, so that he may not end abruptly, but that the truth he has taught may go with them to their homes because of its lodgment in their hearts.

(5) The preacher will desire to leave his hearers on the loftiest height of faith, reverence, aspiration and purpose to which he is capable of raising them. The argument should be most convincing, the appeal most persuasive at the close. Imagination will be most vivid, feeling most intense, language most elevated and passionate in the peroration. It is true that the orator may fitly desire to leave his hearers not so much in the temporary emotion he has produced, as in the permanent mood, which will perpetuate it, and so carry the impressions and influences of the sanctuary out into the world. He may end in a tranquil minor chord after the triumphant major. Browning's poem *Saul* may be studied for such an effect. This is not anti-climax, but rather a resting on the height which has been scaled.

(6) It is proper and desirable that the sermon should, as an act of worship, end with the laying of the sacrifice on God's altar in an ascription of praise in the fitting language of Scripture, or an aspiration that God may by His grace enable hearers and preacher alike to live as they have learned, or in an intercession that everywhere the Word preached may have free course, and so by it God may be glorified. If a sermon cannot spontaneously pass into praise or prayer, it has not been what it should have been. To end badly is to undo much that may have been done well; to feel unable to end well shows that what has been done has been badly done.

CHAPTER V.

THE COMPOSITION OF THE SERMON.

1. THE third part of Rhetoric deals with *elocution,* including both the writing of the sermon, if it is written, and the speaking of it. The delivery of a sermon may assume several forms. It may be read from a manuscript; it may be fully written out, and then committed *verbatim* to memory; it may be written out fully, and then without any attempt at memorising be freely reproduced; it may be expounded in free speech in the pulpit from an outline or notes which the preacher has before him; in whatever way it may be prepared beforehand, it may be spoken without any aid to the memory in outline or notes before the preacher. The defects or merits of these different ways will be discussed in the next chapter. Meanwhile we are concerned with the sermon as a literary composition. For it may be urged that even the preacher who does not write fully (or at all) should write a good deal in other ways, and discipline his mind by writing. The speaker who does not also write is in danger of getting very slipshod in his style, very limited in his vocabulary, very stereotyped in his phrases, and often very superficial in his thought. Writing gives time for subsidiary thinking around the primary thought, accuracy in expression, variety in language. It is an almost indispensable discipline for the speaker, the more necessary the more fluent he is, as there is " a fatal facility " which is by no means identical with " a certain felicity " in speech.

2. The complaint is sometimes made that so few sermons are *literature.* Now that may be a reproach, or it may be a commendation. Sermons ought not to be

literature in the sense that the expression is as much as, or even more the concern of the preacher than the content; or that his main purpose is to gratify æsthetic taste by the beauty of his language, or the felicity of his illustrations, or the balance of his periods. He is engaged in too serious a business for such trifling. He wants to enlighten the reason, quicken the conscience, constrain the affections, and move the will for God and goodness as directly, variedly, potently, and effectively as he can; and he must not allow even his own literary feeling to hamper or hinder his carrying out that object. If a preacher is admired for his abilities instead of being respected and obeyed for the truth he declares, he has fallen short of his holy calling. If anything in the form so absorbs interest as to distract attention from the substance of the sermon, it has missed its aim. A man who is so mastered by his message that he can think of nothing but how he may most simply and forcefully convey it to his hearers, and who speaks out of the fulness of his mind and heart, is a better and a worthier preacher than the man who, having literary tastes, desires his sermon to be literary in quality, and labours most for that end. While the second may win man's applause, the first has Christ's approval.

3. But beauty is not the enemy, but the ally of truth. How beautiful in form as well as true in substance was the teaching of Jesus! Seriousness and earnestness need not be shown in ugliness. As Ruskin has taught us, the organ in the measure of its proper fulfilment of function is beautiful![1] The most appropriate and effective language

[1] See *Modern Painters*, Part III. section 1: chap. xiii. 1: "Taking it for granted that every creature of God is in some way good, and has a duty and specific operation providentially accessary to the well-being of all, we are to look, in this faith, to that employment and nature of each, and to derive pleasure from their entire perfection and fitness for the duty they have to do, and in their entire fulfilment of it; and so we are to take pleasure and find beauty in the magnificent binding together of the jaws of the ichthyosaurus for catching and holding, and in the adaptation of the lion for springing, and of the locust for destroying, and of the lark for singing, and in every creature for the doing of that which God has made it to do." An evangelist whose noisy methods were displeasing to a clergyman was

for the purpose of the sermon will be language which will give it the title to be called literature : for let us remember that the themes of the pulpit are of such quality, that the fitting expression of them may claim to be literary, not in the fashion of the hour it may be, but in the enduring appreciation of men who can judge of the true values in the things of the soul. The preacher then must not apply any external standard to his sermon ; but he must, clearly grasping the end before him, seek also the most fitting means to reach it. An effective sermon will attract, and not repel; it will interest, and not distract ; it will address itself no less to the imagination than the intellect ; it will avoid abstract conceptions, and present concrete images ; it will not utter the jargon of scientific, philosophical, theological schools, but the common speech of the human heart, not in its commonplace, but in its exalted moods. Elevated meditation, intense unction, noble aspiration seek and find beautiful expression, unless the speaker's defective development offers an insuperable obstacle to his full and free self-expression. Sermons may be literature.

4. It must not be forgotten, however, that sermons are a particular kind of literature. They must not be written as essays to be read at any time, but as speeches to be delivered on a particular occasion. A legitimate objection of many hearers to the read sermon is due to the fact that it was written to be read, and so has not the qualities of spoken utterance. To be understood and appreciated it would need to be read, and not heard by the congregation. Its niceties of expression, its balance of sentences, its subtle allusions cannot be seized by the hearer ; and he feels as he listens that not only can not he see the wood for the trees, but that the trees even catch his eye only for a moment and are not seen long enough

reminded that the temple of Solomon was built without the sound of any hammer (1 K 6⁷); but promptly replied : "We're not building, but blasting." Whether results justified the methods or not it is unnecessary to inquire, but the retort was an application of the principle that the organ must be judged as it does or does not fulfil its function.

to be fully seen. Phrases distract the attention from sentences, and sentences from paragraphs; the parts take away from the whole. Even if a sermon is written to be read by the preacher, it must be so written as to give the hearers the impression and so produce the effect of free speech. What is composed in the quiet leisure of the study can be appreciated only in quiet leisure. The mood of the study and the mood of the pulpit are not the same; and the sermon even if written in the study should be written as if spoken in the pulpit. The writer should have before him not a solitary reader quietly receiving his message, but an audience which must at once grasp, if it is not altogether to lose the words which fall from his lips. The feeling against read sermons is not in many cases a mere prejudice, but a proof that the sermon has lost its true character as speech, and has become an essay.[1]

5. If the preacher is a student who is widely read in science, philosophy, history, theology, there is a danger as regards his language, which he must carefully guard against: he must not take the technical terms of any of these mental disciplines into the pulpit. There are technical terms which have passed into common use; and so may be employed in the pulpit. But all terms which to be generally understood would need to be defined, must be carefully avoided. The preachers of old revelled in the technical terms of theology. Language of Latin or Greek origin alone befitted the dignity of their message. To-day the danger comes from another direction. Philosophy and psychology so cast their spell over some preachers (especially young men) that they cannot talk in any other language. A man may repeat these terms without thoroughly understanding their meaning; let him, however, try to translate them into the language understood by the people, and he will probably discover that he himself does not completely understand them. If the phrase may be forgiven, the preacher should not "talk

[1] How to avoid this peril Dr. Jowett indicates in a passage in his book, *The Preacher*, pp. 137-139.

shop" in the pulpit; his sermon should present "the finished article" and not "the tools employed in the making of it." The great Hebrew scholar Dr. Davidson maintained that "the language which 'wives and wabsters' speak is capable of expressing everything which any reasonable man can desire to say to his fellows."[1] Let the thought be profound enough for the most thoughtful, the language must be simple enough for the least cultured and intelligent.[2]

6. The opposite danger must, however, be avoided. "The man-in-the-street" with his limited vocabulary, with his commonplace phrases, and his vulgar slang is not the model of language for the preacher. A speaker does not really capture the interest of his hearers by "talking down" to them; they rather even resent his condescension; and the least educated prefer an educated man to speak to them as he would speak to men of the same culture. It is possible to be homely without being vulgar, and simplicity need not be commonness. Here Jesus again is our model; He spoke so that the common people heard him gladly,[3] and while His thought was too deep for them, His words were not beyond their understanding. There is a type of language which is rather more ambitious than that of the man-of-the-street, which is, however, not the speech of educated men; it is practised by a good many journalists, some of whom are often required to do work for which they have inadequate educational resources.[4]

[1] See Rheim, *Messianic Prophecy XVIII.*

[2] See Hoyt, *Vital Elements of Preaching*, pp. 223–240.

[3] Mk 12^{37}.

[4] From this Journalese Quiller-Couch distinguishes what he calls Jargon. "You must not confuse this Jargon," he says, "with what is called Journalese. The two overlap, indeed, and have a knack of assimilating each other's vices. But Jargon finds, maybe, the most of its votaries among good douce people who have never written to or for a newspaper in their life, who would never talk of 'adverse climatic conditions' when they mean 'bad weather'; who have never trifled with verbs such as 'obsess,' 'recrudesce,' 'envisage,' 'adumbrate,' or with phrases such as the 'psychological moment,' 'the true inwardness,' 'it gives furiously to think.' It dallies with Latinity, 'sub silentio,' 'de die in dem,' 'Cui bono' (always in the sense, unsuspected of Cicero, of 'What is the profit?') but not for the sake of style. Your

The preacher who uses this language will not worthily fulfil his calling, for the language of the half-educated is very much more objectionable than the language of those who lay no claim to education. The problem which the preacher has to solve is this : he must so speak that he can be understood by all and yet he must not speak as many of his hearers are in the habit in their daily life of speaking ; and his speech must not offend the taste of any hearers who know good literature.

7. Some noted preachers have practised and commended as a means of forming a good style the imitation of some of the great writers of literature. One eminent theological writer has confessed that he deliberately formed his style after George Eliot ; a famed preacher is reported to have

journalist at his worst is an artist in his way ; he daubs paint of this kind upon a lily with a professional zeal ; the more flagrant (or, to use his own word, arresting) the pigment, the happier is his soul. Like the Babu, he is trying all the while to embellish our poor language, to make it more floriferous, more poetical—like the Babu, for example, who, reporting his mother's death, wrote, 'Regret to inform you, the hand that rocked the cradle has kicked the bucket.' *There* is metaphor ! *there* is ornament ; *there* is a sense of poetry, though as yet groping in a world unrealized. No such gusto marks—no such zeal, artistic or professional, animates— the practitioners of Jargon, who are, most of them (I repeat), douce, respectable persons. Caution is its father ; the instinct to save everything, and especially trouble, its mother, Indolence. It looks precise, but it is not. It is, in these times, *safe* ; a thousand men have said it before and not one to your knowledge had been prosecuted for it. And so, like respectability in Chicago, Jargon stalks unchecked in our midst. It is becoming the language of Parliament ; it has become the medium through which Boards of Government, County Councils, Syndicates, Committees, Commercial Firms, express the processes as well as the conclusions of their thought and so voice the reason of their being" (pp. 84–85). "Have you begun to detect the two main vices of jargon ? The first is that it uses circumlocu- tion rather than short straight speech. . . . The second vice is that it habitually chooses vague, woolly, abstract nouns rather than concrete ones." Some rules are then given : "(1) The words, *case, instance, character, nature, condition, persuasion, degree*, are to be avoided (p. 87). (2) Even abstract terms are to be suspected (p. 90). (3) The trick of Elegant Variation, due to timidity, the fear of repeating the same name, is also to be shunned as jargon (p. 93). (4) Whoever would write well must be on his guard against the phrases 'as regards,' 'with regard to,' 'in respect of,' 'in connection with,' 'according as to whether' (p. 94). (5) The particular should always be preferred to the general, the concrete to the abstract, the definite to the vague (p. 100)."

made a minute study of Ruskin's use of adjectives in order to follow in his steps. The writer cannot believe that this is a desirable practice. The style is the man, and any imitation savours of unreality. As has been already insisted on, the sermon is not an essay, but a speech; and imitation of another kind of literature is not likely to produce the most appropriate or effective style. Each man has his own individuality, and, while he should rigidly discipline it, so as to correct its defects, he should not attempt to suppress any excellences it may possess.

(1) Without conscious imitation there may be insensible assimilation. If birds of a feather flock together, we may reverse the proverb; and if not literally, it is figuratively true, the birds that flock together tend to become of one feather. A man is rightly judged by the company he keeps, because he becomes like his companions.[1] If a man keeps good company in literature, if his chosen companions are the masters of the craft, if he reads carefully, receptively and responsively, he will gain their good manners. There seems no better way of acquiring a good style than a wide knowledge of good literature, which will develop judgment and taste, and so afford a standard of style.

(2) Poetry seems of greater value than prose for the making of the preacher's style. Browning and Meredith, whose meaning it is difficult to discover, are not to be commended for imitation, however interesting and valuable their thought may be. Tennyson is well worth study, for he has most of the qualities to be desired except strength. The translation into English verse of poetry in a foreign tongue, although it may not result in poetry, may yet improve the style. The care which has to be exercised in the choice of not only the word which reproduces the sense but also falls into the rhythm, forms a habit of selection of the best word instead of acceptance of the first word. While any attempt to preserve what is archaic in the Authorised Version of the Bible is an affectation; and any endeavour to find " a language of Canaan " for use in

[1] The highest instance of this principle is described in 2 Co 3¹⁸.

the pulpit alone would be absurd; yet surely very much can be gained from familiarity with the Bible. Valuable as Dr. Moffatt's *Translation* is for purposes of study, its language is not so appropriate for the pulpit as the language of the Authorised Version; and it is devoutly to be wished that the preachers of the *Twentieth Century* may not imitate the language of the version of the New Testament which bears that name. Lastly, substance cannot be divorced from form. Clear thought and deep feeling will clarify and vivify the style. The language which rises out of the depths of the soul will command beauty and strength, colour and movement.[1]

8. We may distinguish the qualities of style which are necessary if the thought is to be conveyed fully and fitly by the words, and those qualities which give it beauty and strength. The essential requirements are that the thought be expressed with *purity* and *lucidity*.[2] (1) The first quality demands not only grammatical correctness as regards both accidence and syntax, excluding all *solecisms*, but also that the words used are recognised as classic or good English words, so that all *barbarisms* shall be avoided.

---

[1] Nichol's *Primer of English Composition* and Foster's *Literary Companion* may be of use to those who have not had a good literary training.

[2] Vinet, pp. 439–464. A short quotation in regard to the qualities to be aimed at may be given from Quiller-Couch's *Lectures on the Art of Writing*. "Let me revert to our list of the qualities necessary to good writing, and come to the last—*Persuasiveness*; of which you may say, indeed, that it embraces the whole—not only the qualities of propriety, perspicuity, accuracy, we have been considering, but many another, such as harmony, order, sublimity, beauty of diction; all, in short, that—writing being an art, not a science, and therefore so personal a thing—may be summed up under the word *Charm*. Who, at any rate, does not seek after Persuasion? It is the aim of all the arts and, I suppose, of all exposition of the sciences; nay, of all useful exchange of converse in our daily life. It is what Velasquez attempts in a picture, Euclid in a proposition, the Prime Minister at the Treasury box, the journalist in a leading article, our Vicar in his sermon. Persuasion, as Matthew Arnold once said, is the only true intellectual process. The mere cult of it occupied many of the best intellects of the ancients, such as Longinus and Quintilian, whose writings have been preserved to us just because they were prized. Nor can I imagine an earthly gift more covetable by you, Gentlemen, than that of persuading your fellows to listen to your views and attend to what you have at heart" (pp. 85–36).

Not only so, but as the pulpit is not the market or the street, the words must be suitable for the time and place, occasion and purpose of the sermon : there must be no *improprieties*, such as slang. To condescend to men of low degree in speech is not a virtue for the pulpit. Stilted language is ridiculous, grovelling language offensive. The rush of eloquence may sometimes strain the syntax to breaking point ; but bad grammar is not good oratory ; while it may not hinder, where unavoidable owing to the speaker's lack of previous education, it does not further the working of the Spirit of God. It is to be regretted that many who speak correctly according to current usage do not show a keener sense for the niceties and subtleties of speech, which the language still retains, as, for instance, in the use of the subjunctive, when not actuality, but possibility is intended, the use of the singular verb after two abstract nouns which as complementary express one idea, the conjunctive omission and the disjunctive insertion of the article before a number of nouns, etc. (*e.g.*, there is a different meaning between the joy, the hope, the strength of life, and the joy, hope, strength of life).

(2) If the first demand is purity the second is *lucidity* (or perspicuity), for the main object of writing must be to be understood, and to be understood without difficulty. If this is a requirement which may be made of all writers it must even more be made of the preacher, whose sermon is to be heard, and not read, and whose meaning must, therefore, be grasped at once, or lost altogether. Lucidity first of all demands simplicity of language, the use of words which are at once understood, and do not need explanation. If for the purpose of the sermon, in theological or ethical exposition, an unfamiliar word must be used, it should be explained. Enough should be said to make the meaning clear, but not more ; for brevity is also necessary for lucidity. To indulge in vain repetitions, or to express one's meaning in a roundabout instead of the straightest way, is also to cause confusion of mind. Diffuseness of language, no less than irrelevancy of matter, must be

avoided, so that the highway of thought in the sermon may be easily followed, and the hearer may not lose himself in bypaths. Pregnant words and compact sentences are desirable, so long as the meaning is always quite plain. There must be *precision* as regards the meaning, both of words and sentences. There should be no ambiguity as to the thought any word conveys; and the clauses, sentences, and paragraphs should follow one another in such an *order* that the hearer will have no difficulty in following the sense.[1]

(3) Order is the demand of the reason on style, as the mind works not at random, but by method. "Without order," says Vinet, "no lucidity, and without lucidity no force. Besides, apart from lucidity, a style in which order reigns is like a wall of which the stones are well joined; it is very much more solid and stronger." [2] The thought should move from the more general to the more

---

[1] A short statement of the necessary qualities of writing may be quoted from Nichol's *Primer of English Composition* (pp. 16–17). "The laws of style fall under one or other of two classes.—Those regarding *Accuracy* and *Clearness* are requisite in all kinds of writing to ensure the faithful presentation of thought. Those regarding *Strength* and *Grace* are more especially applicable to the higher branches of Prose composition and to Poetry.

			Corresponding Violations of the Rules.
Rules relating to Accuracy and Clearness in Style	PURITY prescribes the use of	Correct forms and Concords	Wrong Forms. Solecisms.
		Classic or good English words	Barbarisms.
		Proper words, *i.e.* words fit for the occasion	Improprieties.
	PERSPICUITY prescribes	Simplicity	Roundabout, inflated or pedantic words or phrases.
		Brevity	Tautology. Pleonasm. Verbosity.
		Precision	Ambiguity or Obscurity— *a.* In words. *b.* In sentences from bad arrangement."

[2] *Op. cit.*, p. 465. Besides Order, Vinet mentions several other necessary qualities of style for the preacher. The first of these is *naturalness*. "The natural style   that in which the art does not let itself be perceived,

particular, from the less to the more definite, from the less to the more striking. There should be an ascending and not a descending interest (climax and not anti-climax). We may regard the quality of order as the link between the necessary qualities of style and those which invest it with the higher excellences.

9. The preacher's object is not only to *instruct*, but to *interest*. That he may convey *instruction*, he must arrest *interest*. Not only his ideas, but even the expression of them, must attract attention. It must not be commonplace, hackneyed, just what may be expected. If there is an element of surprise in the vocabulary or structure, so long as there is no bewilderment, the attention will be sustained. Variety both in the choice of words and the make of the sentences keeps the mind alert. The danger of the ready speaker is the construction of the complex sentences, in which it becomes difficult, if not impossible, to follow the meaning. It would be ridiculous to demand, however, that all sentences shall be short and simple. A thought may need to be stated with such limitations and qualifications, as to demand a complex sentence, and

whether art has not been mingled with it, or by the power of art. For the triumph of art is to make itself forgotten or to make itself perceptible only to reflexion" (p. 470). By "convenance" he means appropriateness of the style to the ideas expressed, the kind of composition, the subject treated, and the purpose sought (pp. 474–475). This involves *simplicity*, which for the pulpit means popularity, not in the depreciatory sense now common, but in the proper sense, of that which the people can understand, the common thought and common speech of all classes. But popularity even does not adequately express the simplicity of the pulpit. The people in the church are a family, and so popularity should be *familiarity* (or *intimacy*). The preacher should be at home with his hearers, and they with him. "In the daily contacts of life, of individual with individual, familiarity brings with it the habit of naming things by their name; it prefers the individual to the general designation, the direct affirmations to reticences and allusions, precise to vague indications" (p. 485). On this condition, too, the pulpit "will give to the things it deals with a vivid impress of reality." Familiarity should not lead the preacher, however, to put himself forward; modesty does not forbid the use of "I" when the preacher as it were individualises his congregation. While simple, popular, familiar, the style of the pulpit can, and should remain *noble* as are its themes. It will possess all these excellences in the measure in which it is scriptural (*op. cit.*, pp. 470–506).

so long as the meaning is kept clear, the longer sentences will maintain the variety of structure. A succession of sentences, all made alike, becomes tiresome. A speaker whose sentences are all equally short gives his hearers a succession of shocks, or jolts. Variety may also be secured by the use of the imperative or interrogative as well as the indicative mood. It is not enough to catch the attention at first; it must be kept all through, and the interest should get keener as the theme is developed. This may seem a demand regarding the contents rather than the style of the sermon, but thought and speech can no more be separated than body and soul, and thus interest may be emphasised as an excellence which the writer even in expressing his thought should keep in view. This he will command if his style has *beauty* and *strength*.

10. "Strength and grace of style are," says Nichol, "in great measure the result of strength and grace of thought which cannot be imparted by rules; but there are some rules which have been found useful in the higher branches of Prose and even in Poetry."[1] (1) That the language of the sermon should aim at beauty (or grace) is only fitting, for, whether the translation be correct or not, there is a "beauty of holiness."[2] There is a beauty of sentiment, affection, aspiration and accomplishment; and the inward beauty of the soul should be the source of the outward beauty of the speech.[3] Mean thoughts richly clothed in language cut a sorry figure, like a dwarf strutting in a

[1] *English Composition*, p. 72. [2] Ps 110³.

[3] What Ruskin says of the relation of the mind to the body in respect of its beauty may be applied *mutatis mutandis* to the relation of the thought and feeling to speech. "There is not any virtue, the exercise of which even momentarily, will not impress a new fairness upon the features; neither on them only, but on the whole body, both the intelligence and the moral faculties have operation, for even all the movements and gestures, however slight, are different in their modes according to the mind that governs them; and on the gentleness and decision of just feeling there follows a grace of action, and, through continuance of this, a grace of form, which by no discipline may be taught or attained" (*op. cit.*, xiv. 6). This statement seems to require qualification, as the heavenly treasure does not always so fully change the earthen vessel; but it is generally true of mind and body, and so also thought and s eech.

giant's robe. The demand for beauty should be met not in purple passages here and there like oases in a desert; but the sermon should be as a whole a unity, not only logical, but æsthetic. There must be variety in unity; it must be an organism. As we have already seen, the arrangement must be regarded from the oratorical as well as the logical standpoint. But coming to the language itself, while there must be passages of exposition, demonstration, application, in which lucidity is the paramount consideration, yet the sermon will not be complete unless the imagination is satisfied and the emotions are stimulated; and the way of the imagination leads more quickly to the emotions than the way of the intellect.

(2) Accordingly, as far as possible in the language used the concrete phrase, which suggests a picture, should be preferred to the abstract term, which proposes a problem. If the preacher be a seer, who has the inner vision of eternal spiritual reality, figurative language will come easily and fitly to him. It is not a defect of the Bible, due to the insufficient philosophical and theological education of its writers, that it so abounds in imagery, and the figures of speech which the rhetoricians have recognised; [1] it is its excellence, for religion must so body forth its realities, or else be silent. What is most profound in thought, and most sublime in feeling, cannot be forced into the rigid mould of prose, but must assume the free shape of poetry. How liberally Jesus even lavished His imagery, so that the truth might be seen in many pictures. The informed preacher will know that most common words are pictures —faded beyond recognition for the common mind, and he will try to visualise his language, so that even abstract terms will recover their appeal to his imagination. There may be a "mixed metaphor," when two words brought close together present, thus visualised, incongruous pictures; and such combinations he who values and respects words will avoid.

[1] The writer's *A Guide to Preachers* has given instances of this varied use of figures of speech (pp. 253-255).

(3) Two cautions must be added. Numerous quotations from the poets, however beautiful they may be in themselves, will not make the style of a sermon beautiful, if they are irrelevant, not illustrative, but ornamental, if they do not grow out of, but are stuck on to the thought. Abundant and elaborate scene-painting, which appears only as ornate decoration, may be a blemish in a sermon. Descriptions of sunsets and waterfalls, rolling oceans and beetling crags, which are introduced because the preacher delights in fine writing, and not because his thought must find its inevitable pictorial expression in them, are vulgar offences against the dignity and solemnity of his task.[1] The imagery of a sermon should be, not elaborate, but suggestive, not like the brilliant picture on which the imagination rests satisfied, but like the coloured window through which the sunshine falls, and which leads the mind to the great world beyond. The figurative language should be *coloured truth*.

11. With beauty there must be allied *strength*, and in the pulpit strength is even more necessary than beauty, although there is no reason why on the pillars of strength there should not be the lily work of beauty.[2] The sermon is a deed, and must show force. If it is not only to teach and please, but to move, it must command the will. As regards the choice of words, "the simplest is the most expressive word"; and yet "the plainest language is not always the most forcible," as the emotions may be most deeply stirred, and through them the will be most strongly

---

[1] "Style," says Quiller-Couch, "for example, is not—can never be—extraneous Ornament. You remember, maybe, the Persian Lover whom I quoted to you out of Newman: how to convey his passion he sought a professional letter-writer and purchased a vocabulary charged with ornament wherewith to attract the fair one as with a basket of jewels. Well, in this extraneous, professional, purchased ornamentation, you have something which style *is not*—and if you here require a practical rule of me, I will present you with this: 'Whenever you feel an impulse to perpetrate a piece of exceptionally fine writing, obey it—wholeheartedly—and delete it before sending your manuscript to press. *Murder your darlings*" (*On the Art of Writing*, pp. 234-235).

[2] 1 K 7^{22}.

moved, by words addressed to the imagination rather than the intellect. "In animated discourse or composition, vivacity is often promoted by the use of *Figures of Speech* in which words or phrases are used in a sense different from that generally assigned them." As regards the number of words, "concentration of phrase is like a burning glass which adds to the brightness and the heat of the rays it gathers into a focus." A strong writer will have a terse, concise style. A rapid succession of short sentences, questions, warnings, or appeals, not disdaining repetition of words or phrases, may have a cumulative effect like the swift, sharp blows of the hammer. The interrogative form of sentence summons the intellect to think; the imperative challenges the will to choose. Language may sometimes crash like the thunder as well as rustle as the breeze; it may recall the lofty barren mountain as well as the lowly fruitful plain. As regards the order of words, "rhetorical considerations frequently permit and sometimes enjoin a departure from the ordinary rules of sequence in prose. The disposition of words in a sentence should be like those of figures in a picture, the most important should occupy the chief places." Emphasis is gained by inversion.[1]

[1] Nichol's *English Composition*, pp. 72, 76, 93, 98. He gives the following list of Figures of Speech or generally recognised in rhetoric :

Chief Rhetorical Figures and Forms of Speech.

Resemblance.	Contiguity.	Contrast or Surprise.	Arrangement.

a. Comparison or Simile
b. Metaphor
  1. Identification of like qualities
  2. Identification of like things
c. Personification
d. Allegory
	a. Autonomasia, Individual for Class
	b. Synecdoche, Part for Whole
	c. Metonymy, Cause for Effect, badge for Class, etc.
		a. Antithesis and Epigram
		b. Hyperbole
		c. Irony and Euphemism
			a. Climax.
			b. Anti-Climax.
			c. Inversion.

Miscellaneous figures, "less generally used and not reducible to a distinct head "—

1. Interrogation.   2. Exclamation.   3. Vision.   4. Prolepsis or Anticipation.   5. Metalepsis (punning).   6. Asyndeton (a series of assertions

12. These two qualities of style Vinet treats under other names, and his exposition as that of a master is worth reproduction. *Colour* is what he calls the first of the higher excellences of style, while *movement* is the second.

(1) "What is it," he asks, "to paint one's thoughts, if not to add to lucidity a vivacity which it has not usually, a force which it ignores? We are not concerned then about painting for the sake of painting: it is the means and not the end. This sets the bounds, excludes tediousness and minuteness. In general, the object is to paint and not to describe, to suggest everything and not to present everything. All is subordinate to instruction and to emotion. I scarcely love better the flash of images in the sermon than the gold in the garments of the priest or luxury in the sanctuary. Nevertheless we must make the objects perceptible." [1] "Sometimes it is the character, the idea of the object, sometimes the outward signs that the image makes stand out. One of the methods is rather like sculpture, the other like painting. In their perfection they have an equal value. . . . One can then seize the idea either by some special characteristic circumstance, or by varied details. It is painting which without doubt should be employed the oftener, because it is within the reach of the greater number. Nevertheless the other method, which consists in putting the object itself before the eyes, has a great effect fitly employed." [2] The method is either direct or indirect. The object may be presented in a description or an indication. A great writer can in a few words give a whole picture. This is ever found in the Bible. "A potent and yet dangerous method is the *epithet*, and it is often to this that the image is reduced." [3] The danger of the weak writer is the number of his empty adjectives. Yet, if it be desired to emphasize a particular characteristic, a number of adjectives may be used with force, and attention may be arrested by an unexpected adjective. [4] The object may also be more indirectly approached by figures of speech, such as anti-

without any conjunction). 7. Aposiopesis (a sudden breaking off) and Correction. 8. Catachresis (use of words in unnatural sense, a rarely justifiable metaphor). The terms in the above which are not explained explain themselves. Some of these figures are means of giving the style beauty and others strength (pp. 91-93).

[1] *Op. cit.*, p. 523.   [2] P. 524.
[3] P. 526.   [4] See pp. 524-529.

thesis, metaphor, allegory, simile. The style of the pulpit would gain, if it were less abstract, and more concrete. But those who have a fertile imagination, need to be warned against too abundant use of imagery, for (*a*) this habit may become a mental indolence, and prevent a real understanding; (*b*) it may hide under a flashy outside of form a very empty inside of substance; (*c*) it may even, uncorrected by vigilant thought, introduce and give currency to false ideas; (*d*) it tends to a frivolity which is inconsistent with the gravity that is becoming in the pulpit.[1]

(2) "Movement in style will consist in removing the hearer from one moral position, from one moral situation to another. This movement is not life, but it is the effect and the sign of it. We do not conceive life without movement, and in the long run immobility appears to us death. These two ideas of movement and of life unite so naturally in our mind that wherever we see movement, we suppose or we imagine life."[2] This excellence of style should belong to the sermon as an action, due to an emotion. "If the orator does not unite himself entirely to his subject, if the sermon is not the action of man on man, if it is not a drama with its problem, its sudden turns of fortune, and its catastrophe, it lacks that communicative life, and, one can even say, that truth without which the oratorical discourse fails of its object for the majority of the hearers, who have need of feeling the truth as identified with him who expounds it and seeks to diffuse it."[3] As the orator is moved by his subject and his audience, his emotion must pass into the movement of his style. This movement must not in the pulpit be as violent as it might be in the assembly or the court. Intense as may be the preacher's love of the Word of God, it cannot be described as a passion, and reverence imposes restraint. The characteristic of the expository style is repose, even although there may be movement in the quick succession of the ideas and the liveliness of their connections. But we pass beyond the expository style in the movement, in which the emotion of the speaker and of the hearers is stimulated. The preacher may seek to communicate his feeling to his congregation directly by the freedom and candour of his address. Even if he writes, he will in thought gather his congregation about him, and speak to them. Within

---

[1] See pp. 529–538.   [2] P. 539.

[3] *Op. cit.*, p. 540. These words recall Phillips Brooks' **definition of** preaching.

the expository style there may be movement by repetition, gradation, accumulation, reticence, correction, omission, irony, hyperbole, paradox, vision.[1] Beyond the expository style, movement may be secured by interrogation, exclamation, apostrophe, personification, dramatisation, dialogue, even prayer.[2]

(3) Vinet mentions several qualities of style which belong both to colour and movement, such as *variety* and *elegance* (the avoidance of the vulgar and the trivial). (*a*) Variety is not only necessary to secure interest and maintain attention, but it is closely related to truth, correctness, precision. "A style possessing these three qualities will for the same reason be varied; no one thing being exactly alike to another, to speak of each thing just as it is, whether in respect of words or in respect of form, is to speak of it differently: variety springs from the root of things, as things themselves are different"[3] Repetition shows not only poverty of words but even of thought, of knowledge, of reality. (*b*) Since *elegance* has in it something conventional and artificial, it is in some respects not consistent with the seriousness of the pulpit; and yet a chaste elegance which does not display itself, which is hardly noticeable, which is very near the natural, is not unsuitable for the pulpit.[4] In this commendation of elegance Vinet will appear to many to betray his French culture and taste. Whether the word be the best to employ in this connection, it is well for the preacher to show himself always the Christian gentleman in language as in manner, and the Christian gentleman is one who himself good, seeks also the company of the good.

13. This chapter may fitly be closed with Quiller-Couch's exposition of the two paradoxes of style:

(1) "Although Style is so curiously personal and individual . . . there is always a norm somewhere; in literature and art as in morality." (2) "Though personality pervades Style and cannot be escaped, the first sin against Style as against good manners is to obtrude or exploit personality." He then insists that "essentially it resembles good manners. It comes of endeavouring to understand others, of thinking of them rather than for yourself—of thinking, that is, with the heart as well as the head. It

---

[1] See *op. cit.*, pp. 537–554.   [2] See *op. cit.*, pp. 554–562.
[3] P. 562.   [4] See pp. 562–568.

gives rather than receives; it is nobly careless of thanks or applause, not being fed by these but rather sustained and continually refreshed by an inward loyalty to the best. Yet, like 'character' it has its altar within; to that retires for counsel, from that fetches its illumination, to ray outwards. Cultivate, Gentlemen, that habit of withdrawing to be advised by the best. So, says Fénelon, 'you will find yourself infinitely quieter, your words will be fewer and more effectual: and while you make less ado, what you do will be more profitable.'" [1]

---

[1] Pp. 246–248.

CHAPTER VI.

THE DELIVERY OF THE SERMON.

1. ALL that has been said about the composition of the sermon must be carried on into the discussion of the delivery of the sermon; for what has been assumed throughout is that the preacher is writing what, if he reads, will be read as if spoken, or is writing, in order that when he speaks, he may speak the better.[1] But the question arises: Should the preacher read or speak without manuscript?

(1) There is one method of delivery, which the writer cannot approve for most men, even although some great preachers have followed it: it is the committing the sermon to memory *verbatim* and then reciting it. To this way there seem to be two objections: On the one hand, what a slavish task this learning by heart must be, what a strain on the mind and waste of time it must involve! On the other hand, how stiff and lifeless the delivery in most cases must be! For the effort to remember must hinder the freedom of utterance. The writer has heard some preachers, who follow this method, speak as if they were with difficulty reading their sermon from the back wall of the church. If a man can after reading his MS only half a dozen times recall its contents without strain, and so can deliver with freshness and force, the objection falls to the ground; but these are only a happy few; for most men this method must be a grievous burden.

(2) The advantage of reading is that most men will

---

[1] A passage in Bishop Boyd Carpenter's *Lectures on Preaching*, pp. 156–159, deals with this question.

deliver their message in the best form as regards both contents and style; and they will avoid more easily diffuseness, irrelevance and lack of polish. Unless, however, the preacher is a master of the art of reading, so that it appears and makes the impression on the hearers of free speech, the delivery will not be so direct and forceful; he will not come into as close, living touch, through his whole personality, with his hearers. If he needs to read closely, the hearers will miss the spell of kindling and flashing eye, of the full expression of feeling in the features and by gestures. The voice, too, unless the preacher is a consummate artist, will not rise and fall with the thought, or change with all the varieties of emotion through which he himself is passing. Can the read sermon have for himself all the freshness of free speech, and can he make fresh for others what he does not himself feel freshly? There are so many eminent preachers who read their sermons so admirably, that it is only with great diffidence that these objections are offered: but they apply to the average men who read, and are offered for their consideration.

(3) The preacher who does not recite from memory, or read from MS but speaks freely, may follow several courses in his preparation. (a) He may write out his sermon fully, read it over carefully, but not attempt to commit it to memory. His thought will be more orderly, and his style probably more literary than if he had not written at all. There is always the danger, however, that this method will slip back into the method of memorising; and that without intending, the preacher will be trying to recall what he has written, although he has not tried to commit it to memory. His delivery will inevitably suffer. If the preacher has not other literary work to do, he should certainly write one sermon at least each week for the reasons given in the previous chapter; but if he can keep his style literary by other means, the writing out of the sermon in full may be a hindrance rather than a help to effective delivery.

(b) At the opposite extreme from the preacher who

writes out his sermon fully, is he who puts down only the main thoughts in notes, and with or without the aid of them, develops his theme in the pulpit. The great peril of this method, unless he is a genius, is vagueness of thought, diffuseness of language, and a lack of continuity. The transitions, the importance of which was emphasised in a previous chapter, will be absent altogether, or be awkwardly managed.

(c) Between the two extremes is the preacher who writes an outline of his sermon, in which the leading thoughts are carefully expressed, and the continuity of thought is strictly maintained, so that the sermon as a whole is given in a condensed form, and needs only to be expanded in free speech. He knows his starting-point, his course, and his goal; but his steps by the way are not fixed. This is the method the writer has been led to adopt after trial of other methods; but whether it would suit others as it suits himself he will not venture to say.

(4) He would urge, however, the advantage of the spoken over the read sermon. An audience can kindle the speaker by its enthusiasm, or responsiveness; it can even put him on his mettle by its indifference or opposition. Some men can think more clearly, and express their thought more freely and fitly, face to face with hearers than in the quiet of the study; and they will give their best in free speech rather than in a read manuscript. That the read sermon involves more careful preparation than the spoken is one of the delusions of those who read their sermons, and cannot do otherwise, and thus must make a merit out of their defect. It may be that the one sermon may, if written, require longer special preparation than if spoken; but the general preparation, to which the writer inclines to attach even more importance, of thorough discipline of all the powers must be more exacting for the man who aims at speaking as well as another writes. A man must be fuller of his subject, more possessed by it, who is to speak freely of it without having what he has written before him. The danger of free

speech without writing has already been recognised in the previous chapter; but these dangers can be avoided. If the spoken sermon may lack some of the literary finish of the written, it is likely to have more living force. Unless by persons who affect a superior culture, the spoken sermon is generally preferred to the read. The speaker comes into closer contact with his hearers; he can receive from and respond to them more fully and freely, and they receive from and respond to him more readily; the living bond is more tightly knit. The writer believes most heartily in thorough preparation, and yet he ventures to ask whether he who speaks freely is not quicker to gain and fitter to use any illumination and influence of the Spirit of God which the time and place, the occasion and the environment may be the necessary condition of conveying, and which could not have come to him in his own study?

2. Whatever be the view taken of the best way of delivery—and the writer does not desire to press his own decided preference—it will surely be admitted that even the preacher who thinks it best to read his sermons should endeavour as far as he can to acquire the art of free speech. A minister's usefulness is hindered if he cannot speak the word in season without elaborate preparation. If this be so, then it is worth while considering how this facility can be acquired.[1]

(1) In *the first place*, there must be *fulness of knowledge*; if a man is full of his subject, he will speak more readily and easily, other things being equal, than the man who knows little about it. And surely it is not an unreasonable demand to make of the preacher that he should be full of his subject. He should know his Bible and his Gospel in so abounding measure that it should not be difficult for him, if necessity be laid upon him, or even opportunity offer, to deal with a familiar text or a familiar truth without special preparation. It is not suggested that the preacher should make a practice of going into

[1] See *The Art of Extempore Speaking*, by Ford; *Extempore Speaking*, by Foster; *The Art of Public Speaking*, by S. L. Hughes.

the pulpit unprepared, and of relying on the Spirit for utterance (indolence masquerading as piety). For only he who is constant and diligent in preparation will possess the fulness of knowledge which will enable him to meet with credit and success such an emergency. The general preparation must be very thorough to allow a man to do, when necessary, without the special preparation.

(2) *Secondly, clearness of thought* is essential. The man who is still fumbling about in his theology, who has not thought out definitely the solution of its problems, should not run the risk of speech. Not only will he himself be confused, but in his hearers " confusion will be worse confounded." Is it unreasonable, however, to expect a preacher to have thought out his message before he attempts to deliver it ? There need be no closed mind, no arrest of thinking, no premature conclusion of inquiry, but there may nevertheless be distinctness and certainty about the truths to be preached. A man has not really grasped a truth for himself until it has for his mind assumed so definite an expression that he can convey his meaning to others. In conversation with others thought does often become more distinct and certain ; but distinctness and certainty there must be before public speech.

(3) *Thirdly*, not only must the single ideas be clear, but there must be *an orderly arrangement* of them in the mind. The minds of some men are like a lumber-room, in which many valuable articles are stored, but which offers no comfort or pleasure as a human habitation. There are associations of ideas, there are logical connections of thought, there is a unity of the mind amid all the variety of its contents : and he who would speak well must have an intellectual organism, with the parts properly disposed in the whole. Even a few minutes to set the thoughts in order is what every speaker must have if he is not to talk at random. The habit of preparing an outline which will not be a series of detached notes (a method leading to a series of speeches, rather than one speech), but a development, in however condensed a form, of the contents

of the sermon, should be formed even by the preacher who reads his sermon, as it will develop in him the faculty of orderly arrangement. If his written sermon does not and cannot yield him such an outline, he will have learned a lesson as to the necessity of structure in an utterance which he desires to be both understood and remembered. There are various aids to memory offered to public speakers; but none can compare in value with the faculty of thinking in so orderly a way that in speech the ideas will follow one another, not by an effort of memory, but rather by the inevitable progress of the thought.[1]

(4) *Fourthly*, the speaker should aim at possessing as *abundant and varied a vocabulary* as possible, not that he may be repetitious and diffuse, but that he may be able to choose out of the number of words which present themselves to his mind the "inevitable" word. It is painful to listen to a man who is aware that he has not succeeded in saying just what he wanted to say, and so tries and tries again, and perhaps never gets what he wants. There are slight shades of difference in the meaning of words for the cultured which for the uncultured bear the same sense; and the speaker should in his reading and thinking accustom himself quickly to detect, and instantly to observe these differences. While repetition may be used as a

---

[1] A knowledge of *Logic* will not necessarily make an orderly thinker, although such knowledge is not to be depreciated. While a sermon must not be thrown into the forms which Logic provides, yet familiarity with the main modes of reasoning, induction and deduction, the argument from analogy, from like to like, or *a fortiori*, from less to greater, the *argumentum ad hominem*, or the *reductio ad absurdum* may sharpen the intellectual tool or weapon of the speaker. An acquaintance with the *logical fallacies* may save him from mistake. Going beyond the bounds of formal logic to what Hegel understood by that term, the discussion of the categories of human thought, the preacher may here learn much as regards the thinking of things together. The appropriate categories may give him the question he shall ask about the reality with which he wishes to deal ; and while all this apparatus of the laboratory of thought must be kept out of the pulpit, yet he will not be less effective in the pulpit who knows how to use it in his own thinking. But as the companionship of good writers improves the style, so will a knowledge of the great thinkers, scientific, philosophical, theological, improve the thought. It seems quite unnecessary to mention or recommend any special books for this purpose.

rhetorical device to increase an impression, yet the use of the same word again and again because the speaker can command no other is wearisome. What might be called a sensitive verbal conscience, which does not blur distinctions, is a quality which the speaker should take great pains to cultivate. The reading which makes the full man must be combined with the writing which makes the exact man, if the speaker is to be indeed the ready man, not only able to keep on talking with "the fatal fluency" with which some are endowed, but so the master of speech that he can speak both with fulness and accuracy not only of word, but also of thought. Only such a gift of speech is worth coveting.

(5) While the advantage of developing the gift of ready speech even when there is not much time for special preparation has been insisted on, it should now be added that a man will speak best on a subject on which he has just before speaking been meditating, passing through his mind not necessarily the terms and phrases he will use, but certainly the thoughts in their proper order. By so doing his mind has, as it were, made a beaten track along which his thoughts will travel easily and quickly. This previous absorption in the subject has also an emotional value. The themes with which the preacher deals are such that if he lets his mind dwell upon them, his heart also will be stirred in its depths. As he muses, the fire of adoration, gratitude, devotion, aspiration, will burn. In speaking, this emotion must at first be restrained, because the speaker must try to put himself in touch with his hearers by sharing their mood in order that by his speech he may bring them over to share his. This restraint of emotion will, however, not weaken, but strengthen the effectiveness of his speech. It will make his intellect keener, his imagination more vivid, his language more copious. By letting himself go only gradually his passion kindles a corresponding passion in his hearers, and the flow of emotion should not be reached at the beginning, but at the end of a speech. If the speaker's own emotion begins to ebb before he reaches the

end of his speech he will lose his hold of his hearers. Many speakers go on after the high tide is passed, and end at the low.

3. The voice of the speaker is of very great importance. Here nature does more than art can do. It is true that speakers whom nature had very poorly endowed have by discipline greatly improved the effectiveness of their voice. But undoubtedly the man who has to begin with a clear, full, carrying voice has a very marked advantage; if his voice is also an instrument of wide range so that he can express many emotions with it, he has one of the best gifts a preacher could desire.[1] Apart from physical defects so serious as to prevent distinct speech, nature can be corrected and improved by discipline. Many men speak badly because they have not taught themselves to speak well. For expressive speech it should be possible to raise and drop the voice through a wide range of pitch; but unfortunately the architects of many churches seem to have thought of everything except the acoustics, and in order to be heard the preacher must maintain an almost uniform tone. It is possible, however, even when lowering the voice, to project it by the proper muscular effort, so that it will, as it were, be sent out even to the remote parts of the building. If the preacher is so moved by his theme, however, he is likely to forget this necessity; and some of his most impressive words and phrases may be most indistinctly heard. What has to be remembered is that it is not only distinctness of utterance which is necessary, but

---

[1] How wonderful a gift the voice is may be shown by a quotation. "The 'human voice divine' is perhaps man's most godlike gift. Its capabilities of sound-production, in every variety of intensity and modulation, is practically illimitable. From the shriek of horror down to the gasping whisper of despair, it runs through the gamut of expression of every human feeling and passion—now pouring forth, trumpet-like, fiery denunciation, now calmly enunciating everyday thoughts and desires, and anon, in flute-like sweetness, giving utterance to the tender accents of love. The magic of a rich and powerful voice thrills every human being within its range; its vibrations set in motion the common ties of race and humanity; it stirs into unison, or perhaps throws into discord, the thoughts and feelings of all whom it reaches" (*Voice, Speech and Gesture*, p. 72).

also this projection of the voice to the remotest part of the building.

4. The writer has consulted a number of teachers of elocution, and has discovered that each has his own system, and that there is no book on the subject which all could or would unreservedly recommend; and the subject, it must be admitted, lends itself much more to personal instruction than to general treatment in a text-book.[1] There are also physical and physiological technicalities involved which could not be properly treated here. The preacher should seek a training from a competent teacher. A few notes on the objects of such training may be offered. (1) First in importance assuredly is *voice production*. The raw material of the voice is the breath, and that there should be an abundance of that raw material is essential. Many children have never learned to breathe properly; and there are many speakers who have not repented of the sins of their youth in this respect. *Abdominal* breathing by lowering the diaphragm and not *thoracic* by raising the ribs, is what is recommended, so that the lungs may be well filled with air, and the voice may be sustained. The breath, even if abundant, has to be properly directed by the organs of speech. Some speakers begin the process of making breath into voice too soon, and use the throat too much instead of the mouth. By violent unnatural contractions of the throat they force the voice. Not only by this abuse do they soon tire, but they often bring on disease, such as "the minister's throat." Speaking, if properly done, should not tire nor injure any of the organs of speech.

(2) Next in order comes *enunciation or articulation*; the distinct expression of any sound. There are some letters which are found more difficult to give distinctly than others; and speakers vary as regards their difficulties.

---

[1] A few books may, however, be mentioned. Newlands, *Voice Production and the Phonetics of Declamation*; Rice, *Voice Production with the aid of Phonetics*; Foster's *Voice Production; Voice, Speech and Gesture*, edited by Blackman. In the last volume a statement is made by Dr. Campbell, well worth repeating: "I have often observed marked improvement in health result from the proper use of the vocal organs" (p. 42).

Each of the consonants should be practised by frequent and rapid repetition until it is produced easily and clearly. As different letters are enunciated with different parts of the organ of speech, all these parts should be exercised. " Elasticity of movement in the lower jaw, and mobility of the lips, tongue, soft palate, and pharynx are necessary for good articulation."[1] The lips are used in enunciating *p* and *b* (the labials), the teeth *t* and *d* (the dentals), the upper part of the throat *k* and *g* (the gutterals), and corresponding to these are the spirants *f* and *v*, *th*, etc. If a speaker finds any difficulty with any letter, he should exercise the proper organ until it has gained the necessary flexibility. There are a few letters which present exceptional difficulty to some speakers, thus *l* and *r* (liquids) are often interchanged, with sometimes ludicrous results; *m* and *n* are also dangerously alike. The sounds *s*, *sh*, *z* (the sibilants) and also *th*, *st* are hard to produce, especially when a number come together. " Where neither moth nor rust doth corrupt, and where thieves do not break through nor steal,"[2] is a text which affords good practice in overcoming this difficulty. If Scotsmen can be reproached for their rolling *r*'s (*wourrld*), Englishmen must bear the blame of extinguishing the life of this letter altogether (*wold* for *world*). Every letter has a right to the preservation of its existence; and the tendency to kill letters should be resisted.

(3) After articulation comes *accent*, " the stress of the voice on a particular syllable of a word. All words of more than one syllable have a *primary* accent, and many polysyllables have a *secondary* accent, less clearly marked, in addition to the primary one: thus *gráteful*, *ingrátitude*, *incompréssibility*. Accent is generally, but not always, upon the most important or root syllable of a word. . . . Accent is moved from one syllable to another when a word is compounded: thus, *áccident*, *accidéntal; hármony*, *harmóni-ous*. It is used also to distinguish the same word when employed as different parts of speech; e.g. *cóncert*, *concért*;

[1] Newlands, *Voice Production*, p. 94.   [2] Mt 6[20].

Aúgust, augúst; rébel, rebél. Without accent speech would be monotonous both as regards tone and time, for the stress of the voice intensifies the one, like the beat in music, and varies the other, like the distinction between crotchets and quavers." [1] As the above examples show, the tendency in English is to throw the accent to the beginning of the word, unless there be some reason to the contrary. Many variations of pronunciation are due to the shifting of the accent, e.g., *vágary* for *vagáry*, *ácceptable* for *accéptable*, *sójourn* for *sojóurn*. One hears from the pulpit *Deúterónomy* and *Déuteronomy*, and at one meeting the writer heard *centéenary*, *céntenary* and *céntennary*. In verse the accent may be shifted for the sake of melody : may not impassioned speech also claim this right ?

(4) Native accent should be distinguished from vulgarisms of pronunciation. A speaker often spoils his speech by trying to acquire another than his native accent, as when a Scotsman " eats London bun " (to use a phrase the writer once heard), and tries to speak " high English." Is there any district of England which can claim to have the correct accent, and finds its claim generally admitted ? Do even all men educated at Oxford and Cambridge speak with the same accent, excluding Scotsmen from the question ? It may be suggested even that language does not lose but gain by differences of accent, as unity-in-difference is preferable to uniformity.

(5) For certain vulgarisms, however, no defence can be found ; *e.g.* the omission or insertion of *h*, the furtive *r* after a final *a*, the impure sound of many vowels, *ai* for *a*, *i* for *a*, *ou* for *o*, the elision of the aspirate in *wh*, and the dropping of *g* at the end of the present participle. While regarding the greater part of the English language there is no doubt about the correct *pronunciation*, yet fashion to a small extent rules even here, and within narrow limits some variations are tolerable, e.g. *tēnure* or *tĕnure*, *ĭsolate* or *īsolate*. "The best advice that can be given to the student upon this subject is to exercise a keen ear to the

[1] R. P. Brewer in *Voice, Speech and Gesture*, pp. 67–68.

speech of highly educated men and women, and to consult a good dictionary in cases of doubt." [1]

(6) The words distinctly enunciated, properly accented, and correctly pronounced must then be *projected* as has already been mentioned. The words should not be allowed, as it were, to roll to the lips and then fall over; they should be shot out as at a target to the farthest part of the building. "In public speaking an additional force is added by a propelling movement from the lower part of the chest; in ordinary conversation the breath is propelled out of the mouth by the pharynx. Not only do the chest movements add to the articulation and make the sound-wave travel, but they indicate whether a speaker is animate or inanimate." [2] If a speaker has his eye fixed on the hearer in the back gallery, and thinks himself speaking to him, he will with little consciousness of effort make the necessary movement.

(7) The last words of the preceding quotation "animate or inanimate" carry us over to the next requirement in speaking, *expression*. (*a*) This was the subject to which the older teachers of elocution gave special attention; but their instruction was often far too artificial. Expression cannot be reduced to rules, it cannot even be taught; at least not the kind of expression which is suitable for the pulpit. An elocutionary display, a dramatic recital is out of place in the pulpit. The exaggeration of expression which usually characterises these performances must be most carefully avoided. Restraint rather than excess of expression is to be commended. When a sermon is read, more deliberate art is necessary to secure appropriate and effective expression. In free speech, expression comes more easily. The activity of the mind, the movement of the feelings, and even the resolve of the will to impress and influence combine to make speech expressive. The more vivid the imagination, the more intense the emotions, the better will the expression be. As a man realises in his whole personality

[1] *Op. cit.*, p. 68.   [2] Newlands, *Voice Production*, p. 105.

what his lips are uttering, his varying tones will convey his meaning and his aim to his hearers. Inwardly see and feel what you outwardly utter, and you will so speak that others will see and feel with you. The purpose of expression is to transfer the personality of the preacher to his hearers, so that his words shall live and work in them even as in him. Expression by rule seems to the writer too artificial for the sincerity and intensity which the pulpit demands. Nevertheless a knowledge of the means of expression given in the voice may guide the preacher in making the best and the most of his personality.

(b) Some of the means by which the voice becomes expressive may be mentioned. Just as *accent* is the stress of the voice on a syllable, so *emphasis* is on a word. The important, significant word is emphasised by a pause before and after it; and by change of the pitch of the voice. A wrong emphasis may change the meaning of a sentence, as in the familiar instance, " Saddle *me* the ass. So they saddled *him* the ass." [1] If a whole sentence is to be thrown into prominence, each word may be emphasised. The rapidity with which words are uttered (or the *time* of speech) also gives variety and so expressiveness. Strong feeling may pour itself out in a rush of words. Description, narration, or explanation demand a slow, steady tramp. An aside will be given at a quicker pace. While a speaker must, to be intelligible, give heed to the logical pause represented in writing by the punctuation, effect may be added to sense by the rhetorical pause. Attention to what follows may be arrested by the pause; a sudden unexpected pause challenges notice for the word next uttered. A pause at the wrong place may, however, distort the sense, as in the well-known tale of the petition for prayer: " A sailor who has gone to sea, his wife requests the prayers of the congregation," which was read without the pause indicated by the comma and with a pause after *wife*. The pause may also be used in public speech, but hardly in the pulpit, to " take in " an audience,

[1] 1 K 13^{13}.

to "score off" an interrupter. This has the element of surprise, which appeals to the sense of humour, and so may offer a way of escape from " a tight place." While, as has just been mentioned, rapidity of utterance is sometimes natural, yet usually the meaning is made plain by attention to proper pauses. An explanatory clause or sentence should be preceded by a pause, so should the emphatic word in a sentence; and especially should a change of subject be so indicated, as in writing by beginning a new paragraph.

(c) A very important means of effect in speech is the *pitch* of the voice, the raising or the lowering of its tone. This must to a very large extent be instinctive, corresponding to the emotions. A sudden raising of the voice in the shout or shriek, which some preachers practise, is not only ineffective, but even offensive. The skilful change of voice from high to low, or low to high, gradually, is usually spoken of as *inflection*; it does not involve a change of pitch, but only a rise and fall of the voice. It is natural, and accords with the thought and the feeling. A climax demands the gradual ascent of the voice. A more complex process of the voice is *modulation*.

"What is meant by modulation, as applied to speech, embraces several of the rhetorical incidents already considered, and yet is distinct from each of them. It is partly made up of pitch, tone, and inflection, and at the same time it is something above and beyond them. . . . What light and shade are to a picture, and changes of key to a piece of music, modulation is to speech. What accent is to the syllables of a word, and emphasis to the words of a sentence, modulation is to a composition as a whole. It is like a skilful arrangement of variegated lamps as compared with pure and simple illumination. By modulation is meant the exercise of all those finer and more delicate capabilities of tone-production, which depend more upon the natural quality of the organ than upon cultivation. It requires a perfect flexibility and command over all the gradations of intonation as well as an indefinable *timbre*, which has the power of establishing a sympathy between the speaker and his audience. . . . Like all other rhetorical observances, it may be improved by cultivation, but its essential basis, viz., an organ of exceptional quality, can be no more obtained by human effort than can heroic proportions by a man of meagre frame." [1]

How much *force* and energy a speaker puts into his delivery will depend largely on his temperament, and the degree in which his subject possesses him. A man may be very much in earnest, and yet fail to show it; and an emotional man may throw a passion into his speech which goes beyond his real interest. Noise is not force; shouting wastes energy. Enthusiasm must be restrained and controlled for its full effect.

5. To full expression belongs *gesture* as well as utterance, for the whole body may be used, and not the lips alone. While violence of movement and vehemence of tone must generally be avoided; and the gestures must be graceful movements, and the tones pleasant sounds, unless, as sometimes may be, the desired effect may demand the contrary, as in the expression of loathing, scorn, anger, the speaker should claim liberty, and should not bind himself by rules, still less by imitation of others. Gesture should be appropriate to the emotion expressed: a doubled fist does not enforce a tender appeal, nor a blow on the pulpit clinch a theological argument. The awkward and ludicrous must be carefully avoided; but the characteristic gesture of any speaker is not to be condemned. In this respect as in others, spontaneity controlled, and not artificiality forced, is what the preacher should desire. After dealing very fully with gesture in elocutionary or dramatic display, Henry Neville, an actor and dramatist, very sanely adds this caution: " Clergymen, barristers, lecturers, and public speakers generally must be governed by the different circumstances in which they are placed, and employ ' discriminating ' gestures with simplicity and precision, avoiding the character and parade of graces and transitions which belong to the theatrical. They should be semi-colloquial in style, and emphatic only when suited

---

[1] *Voice, Speech and Gesture,* pp. 83–84.

to the manner and matter.   Even then gesture should not
be too strongly significant and emphatic, or surprising in
attitudes, but employed with manly decorum." [1]

6. It may appear to some readers that there is a
steep descent in this volume from the discussion of the
preacher as an apostle related to Christ, to the treatment
of him as a speaker in regard to voice, gestures, etc.   But
as the apostle of Christ even fails in his mission, if he is
not heard nor understood, he owes it to Christ His Lord to
speak as distinctly and intelligibly as he can ; and all that
has been discussed in this chapter has this as its sole
object, that the truth and grace of Christ may be conveyed
as thoroughly as can be from the personality of the
preacher to the personality of the hearer.   Two extremes
must be avoided.   There are preachers who are more
concerned about how they speak than what they say ;
theirs is but rhetoric, which may deceive some hearers.
There are preachers also who are so absorbed in what they
say that they are careless how they speak ; their imperfect
utterance narrows the range and the force of their influence.   The preacher who is careful both of matter and
manner may hope, if he has the natural gifts, and submits
to the necessary discipline, to attain the eloquence in
which the heavenly treasure is found in a fitting and
worthy earthen vessel.   As of old God's sacrifice had to
be without blemish, so should the preacher seek, as far as
he can, to make his offering faultless in every part. [2]   In
the use of his body to make his delivery of his message as
effective as possible, he can truly present that body as " a
living sacrifice, holy, acceptable to God, *his* reasonable
service." [3]

[1] *Op. cit.*, p. 156.   [2] Ex 12⁵.   [3] Ro 12¹.

BIBLIOGRAPHY.

ALTHOUGH most of the following works have been referred to or quoted in the preceding pages, it will be a convenience for the reader to have them brought together with particulars as to publication: the bibliographies on special subjects given in foot-notes, however, have not been repeated, nor have the books referred to under particular subjects; the books here mentioned are of a general character.

PART I.

Der Lehre von der Predigt: Homiletik, von D. Hermann Hering. I. Hälfte. "Geschichte der Predigt." II. Hälfte. "Theorie der Predigt." Berlin, 1894.

Die Geschichte der Predigt in Deutschland bis Luther, von Lic. Dr. F. R. Albert. Gütersloh, 1892.

A History of Preaching, by Edwin Charles Dargan, D.D., LL.D. Vol. I. "From the Apostolic Fathers to the Great Reformers, A.D. 70–1572." 1905. Vol. II. "From the Close of the Reformation Period to the End of the Nineteenth Century, 1572–1900." Hodder & Stoughton, 1911.

Lectures on the History of Preaching, by Rev. John Ker, D.D. Hodder & Stoughton, 1888.

Crowned Masterpieces of Eloquence. The International University Society. 10 vols. London, 1914.

The World's Great Sermons, compiled by Grenville Kleiser. 10 vols. Funk & Wagnalls Co., 1909.

Library of English Literature, edited by Henry Morley: "Illustrations of English Religion." Cassell & Co.

Great French Sermons from Bossuet, Bourdaloue, and Massillon, ed. by Rev. D. O'Mahony. Sands & Co., 1917.

Puritan Preaching in England, by John Brown, B.A., D.D. Hodder & Stoughton, 1900.

The Romance of Preaching, by C. Silvester Horne, M.A. Jas. Clarke & Co., 1914.

The Teaching Office of the Church, being the Report of the Archbishop's First Committee of Inquiry. S.P.C.K., 1918.

Voices of To-day, by Hugh Sinclair. Jas. Clarke & Co., 1912.

Nineteenth Century Preachers and their Methods, by John Edwards. Kelly, 1902.

The Man in the Pulpit, by Jas. Douglas. Methuen, 1905.

London at Prayer, by Charles Morley. Smith, Elder & Co., 1909.

Short History of Christian Missions, by George Smith, LL.D., F.R.G.S. T. & T. Clark, 1884.

History of Christian Missions, by C. H. Robinson, D.D. T. & T. Clark, 1915.

The Conversion of Europe, by C. H. Robinson, D.D. Longmans, Green & Co., London, 1917.

The Story of the L.M.S., by C. Silvester Horne, M.A. London Missionary Society, 1894.

History of the London Missionary Society, by Richard Lovett, M.A. 2 vols. Henry Frowde, 1899.

For Writings of the Fathers, reference may be made to

The Ante-Nicene Christian Library. T. & T. Clark, 1868 ff.

The Library of the Fathers. Parker, Oxford, 1838–1861.

Nicene and Post-Nicene Fathers. Oxford, 1890 ff.

Special Bibliographies are given in Notes at the end of Chapters I. p. 43, II. p. 58.

PART II.

Handbuch der Geistlichen Beredsamkeit, von D. Heinrich Bassermann. Stuttgart, 1885.

Predigt Probleme, von Prof. D. Otto Baumgarten. Tübingen, 1904.

Wie predigen wir dem Modernen Menschen, von Lic. theol. F. Niebergall. I. Teil. "Eine Untersuchung über Motive und Quietive." Tübingen, 1905. II. Teil. "Eine Untersuchung über den Weg zum Willen." 1906.

Die Predigt, von Liz. Dr. M. Schian. Göttingen, 1906.

Homilétique ou Theorie de la Prédication, by A. Vinet. Paris, 1853.

Homiletic: Lectures on Preaching, by Theodor Christlieb, D.D. T. & T. Clark, Edinburgh, 1897.

Practical Theology, by J. J. Van Oosterzee, D.D. Hodder & Stoughton, 1889.

The Christian Minister and his Duties, by J. Oswald Dykes, M.A., D.D. T. & T. Clark, 1909.

The Ministry of Reconciliation, by J. R. Gillies, M.A., D.D. A. & C. Black, 1919.

Preparation and Delivery of Sermons, by John A. Broadus, D.D., LL.D. New York, 1907.

Lectures to my Students, by C. H. Spurgeon. Passmore & Alabaster. First Series, 1877.

Lectures on Preaching, by W. Boyd Carpenter, D.D., Bishop of Ripon. Macmillan & Co., 1895.

Preachers and Teachers, by J. G. Simpson, D.D. Arnold, 1910.

The Preacher and the Modern Mind, by George Jackson, B.A. Charles H. Kelly, 1912.

The Work of Preaching, by Arthur S. Hoyt, D.D. Macmillan Co., 1909.

The Preacher: his Person, Message and Method. Macmillan Co., 1909.

Vital Elements of Preaching. Macmillan Co., 1914.

The Student's Guide, by John Adams, M.A., B.Sc., LL.D. The University of London Press, 1917.

PART III.

On the Art of Writing, by Sir Arthur Quiller-Couch, M.A. Cambridge University Press, 1916.

The Art of Extempore Speaking, by Harold Ford, M.A., LL.B. Elliot Stock, 1896.

The Art of Public Speaking, by Spencer Leigh Hughes ("Sub Rosa"). Daily News & Leader, 1913.

Voice Production and the Phonetics of Declamation, by J. O. Newlands. Oliphant, Anderson & Ferrier, 1906.

Voice Production with the Aid of Phonetics, by C. M. Rice, M.A., A.R.C.M. Heffer & Sons, 1912.

Voice Production, Extempore Speaking, and Literary Composition, by J. E. Foster. Alfred Watson, Washington, R.S.O., Co. Durham.

Voice, Speech and Gesture: Elocutionary Art, edited by Black-Man. Grant, Edinburgh, 1912.

Famous Speeches, edited by Herbert Paul. Pitman, 1910.

Special Bibliographies are given in Notes at pp. 301, 303, 306, 309, 314, 327, 338.

"Lyman Beecher Lectures on Preaching at Yale University." A complete list will be found in Pepper's volume, but the following may be mentioned specially:

Henry Ward Beecher: *Yale Lectures on Preaching.* J. Clarke & Co. First Series, 1872. Second, 1873. Third, 1874.

Phillips Brooks: *Lectures on Preaching* (1876–77). Allenson's Handy Theological Library, 1903.

R. W. Dale: *Nine Lectures on Preaching* (1877–78). 11th edition. Hodder & Stoughton, 1900.

James Stalker: *The Preacher and his Models.* Hodder & Stoughton, 1892.

Robert F. Horton: *Verbum Dei.* T. Fisher Unwin, 1893.

John Watson: *The Cure of Souls.* Hodder & Stoughton, 1896.

George Adam Smith: *Modern Criticism and the Preaching of the Old Testament.* Hodder & Stoughton, 1901.

John Brown: *Puritan Preaching in England.* Hodder & Stoughton, 1901.

P. T. Forsyth: *Positive Preaching and Modern Mind.* Hodder & Stoughton, 1907.

J. H. Jowett: *The Preacher: His Life and Work.* Hodder & Stoughton, 1913.

C. Silvester Horne: *The Romance of Preaching.* Jas. Clarke & Co., 1914.

George Wharton Pepper: *A Voice from the Crowd.* Oxford University Press, 1915.

Henry Sloane Coffin: *In a Day of Social Rebuilding.* Yale University Press, 1919.

John Kelman: *War and Preaching.* Hodder & Stoughton, 1919.

INDEX.

N.B.—The repeated references in the footnotes to such books as Hering, etc., have not been indexed, but only the references in the text itself.

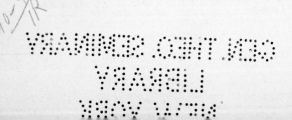